American Historical Press
Sun Valley, California

WISCONSIN
LAND OF CHANGE

AN ILLUSTRATED HISTORY

SHIELA REAVES

Photos attributed to Wisconsin Division of Tourism, Courtesy Wisconsin
Department of Tourism

© 2004 American Historical Press
All Rights Reserved
Published 2004
Printed in Hong Kong

Library of Congress Catalogue Card Number: 2004109457

ISBN: 1-892724-42-1

Bibliography: page 338
Includes Index

CONTENTS

For my parents,
Ben and Dolores Reaves

and my son,
Tom Reaves Capp

*The first permanent streetcar
lines in the United States were installed in Appleton, Wisconsin,
in 1886 and also in Mobile, Alabama. Courtesy, State Historical
Society of Wisconsin*

ACKNOWLEDGMENTS

If the reader finds this history has a ring of authority to it, then it is because I am standing on the shoulders of Wisconsin's scholars and journalists. This book draws together voices and images that I love and deeply appreciate: Indian and immigrant voices, political and environmental views, and the stream of new ideas that protect the beauty of Wisconsin.

I am indebted to the patience and vision of Amber Avines, associate publisher of American Historical Press. When they decided to update the 1988 edition, I discovered I had changed as much as Wisconsin had. So I integrated these new voices because I've learned that a vibrant society is about diversity, innovation, and creativity. You can find this spirit anywhere, perhaps, but I believe it's especially abundant in Wisconsin.

For this second version, I'd like to thank the following people for their advice and insights:

My colleagues and scholars at the University of Wisconsin-Madison gave me generous support such as Ada Deer, Theresa Schenck, Larry Nesper, Patty Loew, and Jacquie Bush Hitchon. I am especially indebted to Tom Still who shared the stories of Wisconsin's new technology. Thanks to the journalists who read evolving versions of the new chapter: Paul DeMain, Karen Lincoln Michel, Nick VanDer Puy, and Ron Seely. I am grateful to my student Jaclyn Potter for fact checking on a tight deadline. I am indebted to the professionalism of Scott Thom at Wisconsin's Department of Tourism in helping me find beautiful photographs and also to Lisa Hinzman and the dedicated staff in the photography archives of the Wisconsin Historical Society. Also, a heartfelt thanks to my new writing partners in crime, Laurel Yourke and Rob Rohde-Szudy.

Thanks especially to my son, Tom Reaves Capp, for his patience when I was researching and writing. And thanks to Mark Anthony Rolo for reminding me, always, that words are magic and that listening for stories is one of life's great joys.

Shiela Reaves

INDIAN LAND, EUROPEAN BOUNTY

In the seventeenth century Indians throughout the fur-trading region of the western Great Lakes supplied beaver pelts to the French fur traders. As the beaver was hunted to extinction in the East, the fur trade moved west into Wisconsin. By 1616 Ottawa and Huron Indians had established fur-trading centers in Chequamegon Bay in northern Wisconsin. Courtesy, State Historical Society of Wisconsin

*The ancestors of Wisconsin's
Indians gathered wild rice in
the Fox and Wisconsin river valleys. These wild rice beds still
exist today. Courtesy, Milwaukee County Historical Society*

The river banks were obscured by stalks of wild rice, and the river itself was broken by many swamps and small lakes. It was easy to get lost, but the two Indian guides led the seven French explorers safely to the portage. From there supplies and two birch canoes were carried 2,700 paces to a new river. And then the Indians turned back, "leaving us alone," wrote Father Jacques Marquette in 1673, "in this unknown country, in the hands of Providence."

During the portage of less than two miles, Father Marquette may have reflected on the advice the Menominee Indians gave before he and Louis Joliet began their journey. The river was dangerous, the Indians said. It was full of horrible monsters and even a demon. The river was watched by warrior Indians, the Menominees warned, and the heat was

Marquette and Joliet to the Mississippi, there had been only rumors of a great river in the western wilderness. Other explorers had surely crossed the Mississippi, but no one had recorded it. Marquette, a Jesuit priest, and Joliet, a fur trader, traveled down the river until they reached an Arkansas village and discerned that the Indians were trading with Europeans. The Mississippi, they decided, emptied into the Gulf of Mexico. Rather than risk being captured by the Spaniards, who claimed the Gulf of Mexico, they returned by way of the Illinois River.

The charting of the Wisconsin River opened a trade route to the Mississippi and helped map Indian lands unknown to Europeans. Wisconsin took its name after the river Marquette first described, but the origin of the word may never be known. Instead of

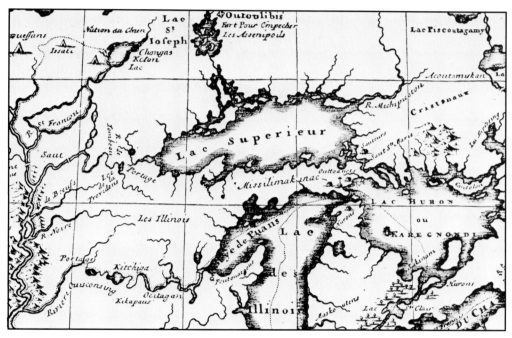

By 1697 Jesuit priest-explorers such as Louis Hennepin had helped map the Upper Great Lakes. In 1673 Father Jacques Marquette and fur trader Louis Joliet had journeyed down the Fox and Wisconsin rivers and discovered the Mississippi River. Courtesy, State Historical Society of Wisconsin

so excessive that it could cause their deaths. In his journal Marquette wrote he had scoffed about the demon and the marine monsters. And then he had said a prayer.

Marquette called this unknown river the Meskousing, later known as the Wisconsin River. He and Joliet did not meet hostile Indians on their journey. Instead they saw deer and buffalo on banks that changed from woods to prairies and hills. And then on June 17, 1673, Joliet and Marquette floated in their canoes into the fabled Mississippi River, "with a joy that I cannot express," wrote Marquette.

Until the uncharted Wisconsin River led

referring to Joliet and Marquette's river as the Meskousing, French and English explorers later called Marquette's river "Ouisconsing" or "Ouisconsin." In 1822 the name "Wisconsin" was applied to the entire land, but scholars cannot explain the origin or meaning of the Indian word. Apparently the original ending, "ing," signified "place." However, that is where agreement ends. Speculation has offered "wild, rushing channel" or "gathering of the waters," but students of Indian languages have not been able to confirm these explanations.

Rivers had shaped European discovery of the

Landfall of Nicolet by E.W. Deming depicts French explorer Jean Nicolet's 1634 landing at Green Bay, where he was met by Winnebago (now known as Ho-Chunk) Indians. Courtesy, State Historical Society of Wisconsin.

Above
The first house was built by Europeans
in the Wisconsin area sometime
between 1650 and 1660. Pierre-Esprit
Radisson explored Wisconsin and
settled for a brief period on
Chequamegon Bay, which was
Chippewa territory. Courtesy, State
Historical Society of Wisconsin.

Above right
This map of North America from 1635
shows the land known to Europeans at
the time of Jean Nicolet's voyages to
Wisconsin. The Great Lakes were
unknown, as was the Mississippi River.
However, in 1635 Jean Nicolet
returned from Green Bay to Montreal
with news that the Great Lakes were
not a pathway to the Orient. Courtesy,
State Historical Society of Wisconsin.

Indian lands in the Northwest. Finding a trade route to China had been the first impetus for French exploration of the New World. In 1534 Jacques Cartier explored the St. Lawrence River looking for the Northwest Passage to the Far East but found only Woodland Indians. Envious of the Spanish bounty in Mexico, the French monarch Francis I originally was interested only in Indians who possessed gold, but fur proved to be an equally valuable source of riches. Trading developed between Indians, who wanted metal knives and hatchets, and Europeans, who prized beaver skins for making felt for fashionable hats.

As the trade in furs grew, the governor of New France, Samuel de Champlain, continued to dream of finding the Orient. The founder of Quebec, explorer-geographer Champlain wrote in 1618 that New France was the route to "the Kingdom of China and the East Indies, whence great riches could be drawn." In 1634 Champlain sent Jean Nicolet to find the route to the South Seas and to arrange peace among western tribes for future trading. In particular he wanted to make contact with the nation called the "People of the Sea," whom Champlain hoped could lead Nicolet to the Orient.

In the service of a French trading company, Nicolet had lived among Huron and Algonkian Indian tribes for eleven years along the Ottawa River. Nicolet spoke their language and knew their customs. Accompanied by seven Huron, Nicolet traveled along the northern shore of Lake Michigan, becoming the first European to explore the great lake.

The People of the Sea, the Winnebago (now known as Ho-Chunk), beheld a sight when Jean Nicolet stepped ashore in Green Bay in 1634. From a narrative written during Nicolet's lifetime, we have a vivid description. Brandishing two pistols, Nicolet "wore a grand robe of China damask, all strewn with flowers and birds of many colors." The Indians were impressed with the guns, the women and children fleeing "at the sight of a man who carried thunder in both hands." The Indians held feasts for Nicolet, but the only seas they could point to were the Great Lakes. Satisfied with his mission, Nicolet returned to Quebec in 1635, a few months before Champlain died.

The People of the Sea did not encounter another European for 20 years. When explorer Pierre-Esprit Radisson visited the land around Lake Michigan in about 1659 he wrote of its natural beauty. "The country was so pleasant, so beautifull & fruitfull," Radisson said, "that it grieved me to see that the world could not discover such inticing countrys to live in. This I say because the Europeans' fight for a rock in sea against one another."

GLACIERS AND THE ICE AGE

The land Radisson found so beautiful was carved by glaciers, whose melting wake left the extensive waterways and wetlands through which he canoed. Wisconsin is world renowned for its well-preserved glacial features, which cover approximately three-fourths of the state. The Ice Age formed the Great

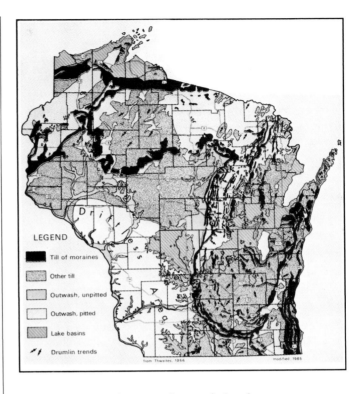

LEGEND

◼ Till of moraines

▨ Other till

▩ Outwash, unpitted

☐ Outwash, pitted

▨ Lake basins

⤢ Drumlin trends

from Thwaites, 1956   modified 1985

The accumulation of glacial drift formed hills and ridges called moraines, which show the advance of the glaciers into Wisconsin. The Ice Age began approximately one million years ago and ended about 10,000 years ago. Wisconsin's Ice Age formations are world renowned. Courtesy, Wisconsin Geological and Natural History Survey

The glacier's last visit to Wisconsin ended approximately 10,000 years ago, and as the environment warmed, animals such as woolly mammoths followed the blossoming vegetation. Painter George Peter portrayed the Paleo-Indians hunting these massive animals in this 1930s painting. Courtesy, Milwaukee Public Museum

Lakes and bequeathed to Wisconsin more than 14,000 lakes—9,000 of which are larger than 20 acres. Glaciers flattened hills and filled valleys, changed the course of rivers, and created gently rolling land.

But the glacial ice sheets missed southwestern Wisconsin, creating a dramatic contrast in landscape. Called the Driftless Area, the land is naturally lakeless and steeper with mounds, valleys, bluffs, and cliffs. The Driftless Area offers a glimpse back through time, and perhaps shows what Wisconsin looked like before the Ice Age.

The Ice Age began approximately one million years ago in eastern Canada around Hudson Bay. Snow accumulated faster than it melted. The snow turned to ice and, by the pressure of its own weight, could move. Great ice sheets formed—in some places as deep as two miles—and slowly the ice advanced. Glaciers also retreated. This glacial waxing and waning falls into four major stages; the last stage is called the Wisconsin Age, which began 70,000 years ago.

The glacier's last visit to Wisconsin, which ended 10,000 years ago, is still etched on the land. Although glaciers evoke an image of crystalline whiteness, underneath they are dirty, vacuuming up the topsoil and carrying this debris along. At the edges of the crushing sheets of ice, this unsorted pile of rock, sand, and gravel bulges outward into what geologists call moraines. During the last advance of the ice, these moraines formed a string of hills, which since have eroded to mounds and ridges. Moraines clearly outline the farthest advances of the ice sheet into northern and central Wisconsin.

The fertility and variability of Wisconsin soils is due to the glaciers that chewed and spread the earth. The glacier, which could grind rock into dust, spread top soil called glacial drift. Ranging from boulders to powder, glacial drift enriched Wisconsin's soil with a variety of rocks, which continuously broke down and released fresh nutrients into the soil.

As the glacier began its retreat, tundra-like plants began to grow on the exposed, damp land. According to geography professor Gwen Schultz, the first trees to appear in Wisconsin were spruces, willows, and tamarack, which were tolerant of moisture. Animals followed the vegetation, and soon caribou and musk-ox appeared along with the woolly mammoth—that shaggy, elephant-like behemoth who probably used its long curved tusks to find hardy plants in the snow.

The mastodons lived in the slowly returning forests. The giant beaver, seven-feet high and weighing up to 500 pounds, lived in the wetlands.

The first people appeared in Wisconsin during the late Ice Age. According to anthropologists, their ancestors had been part of the migration of people who trekked across the thin strip of land that would later submerge into the Bering Strait. From Asia and Siberia people migrated to Alaska, becoming the first explorers of North America as far back as 11,000 years ago.

The Paleo-Indians (paleo comes from Greek for "ancient") who lived in Wisconsin from about 8500 B.C. were nomadic. They hunted deer, moose, caribou, beaver, and hare, supplementing their diet with vegetation as the environment began to blossom.

As historian Louise Kellogg declared, the first miners in Wisconsin were the Indians. From 3000 to 1000 B.C. people living in the northern part of the state began to mine copper from the Lake Superior area. They hammered raw copper into ornaments and jewelry, fish hooks, spear points, and knives. These copper artifacts were an important part of burials and attending ceremonialism of what archeologists call the "Old Copper" culture. Archeologists have suggested that these graves may have been forerunners of the elaborate mound building of the later Woodland Indians. Much later, Indians mined lead for making body paint.

The first gardeners in Wisconsin may have lived as early as 300 B.C. While there is no evidence of large-scale farming, early Indian cultures did store seeds and plant food. The Woodland Indians, who lived from about 1000 B.C. to 1100 A.D., distinguished themselves from the earlier forest-dwellers by making pottery, which provides archeologists with a glimpse of their daily routine. In northern Wisconsin people settled next to lakes and used nets for spring and summer fishing. As winter approached the villages dispersed to follow the winter game of moose, bear, and caribou.

From 300 B.C. to 400 A.D. Wisconsin was part of a commercial and artistic phenomenon known as Hopewell. A commercial trade network developed among Indians from New York to Florida to the Midwest. Commerce thrived on exotic tastes in mica, freshwater pearls, Gulf conch shells, obsidian from Yellowstone, sharks teeth and alligator from Florida, and copper from Lake Superior. Artists took these raw materials and made ornaments, headdresses, and superb carvings. The Hopewell florescence, which created one of the earliest trade networks, was centered in Ohio and the Illinois River Valley, producing some of the finest prehistoric art in North America. The Indians living along the Mississippi in Wisconsin, who were part of Hopewell, were the only prehistoric people to use silver in their jewelry.

The Hopewell traditions provide the first evidence of wealth and power among different ranks of people. In Hopewell an elite arose who wore finely crafted jewelry, furs, robes, and woven cloth. This wealth, ostentatious and reserved only for the few, was buried alongside the elite in mounds that were often built into geometric earthworks.

Southern Wisconsin was the primary setting for effigy mound builders who designed birds and animals in the earth. These three-foot high mounds were shaped into panthers, turtles, birds, and bears. Buried treasure was not a part of mound-building among the Indians who came after Hopewell. Some archeologists believe these mounds may have served as territorial boundary markers. The effigy mound builders, who began building the unique mounds as early as 300 A.D. and as late as 1642, usually chose lakes, rivers, and wetlands as their setting. In the

Madison area, which has the highest concentration of effigy mounds, one scholar counted more than 1,000 mounds near and around the four lakes in 1937.

Using the river for trading, a group of Mississippian Indians migrated from Southern Illinois to present-day Jefferson County in southern Wisconsin, where they built a fortified village. The people were vigilent and defensive. Their village was rectangular and surrounded on three sides by a high fence of stakes, with watchtowers every 80 feet. The fourth side was protected by the Crawfish River. Inside the people built three pyramid-shaped, flat-topped mounds for religious ceremonies. They grew corn and made pottery that included bottles,

Painter George Peter depicted the 1673 French discovery of the Mississippi River by Jesuit Priest Jacques Marquette and fur trader Louis Joliet, an event that opened the Upper Great Lakes region to the fur trading industry. Courtesy, Milwaukee Public Museum

beakers, bowls, and jars. The Wisconsin pioneer who first described the site, Nathaniel Hyer, called it Aztalan which evoked images of an Aztec legend about a northern colony. However the only southern connection to Aztalan is Cahokia, Illinois. The people of Aztalan lived within their barricaded walls from about 1100 to 1300, and like so many Indian cultures, vanished without a clue for archeologists.

Until contact with the Europeans created the fur trade, the Woodland Indians of Wisconsin—including the Winnebago, Chippewa (now known as Ojibwe), and the Menominee—continued their rhythmic responses to the seasons. In the spring and summer they formed semi-permanent villages by lakes and rivers where they fished and hunted. They tapped the maple trees for maple sugar, gathered wild berries and nuts, and grew small gardens of corn, squash, and beans. In the late summer they harvested wild rice in the wetlands. By winter they had broken into smaller groups, following deer and moose. Birch bark canoes connected tribes and trading partners along glacial rivers and lakes.

TRADE AND COLONIZATION

The fur trade began to irrevocably change Indian life as it built an empire for France. Farming became less important to the Indian economy compared to hunting lucrative furs. "In truth," said one Indian chief, "my brother the beaver does everything to perfection. He makes for us kettles, axes, swords, knives and gives us drink and food without the trouble of cultivating the ground." The Indians traded for items that improved their own customs. Metal tools replaced stone tools, and metal cooking utensils were preferred to pottery. The Indians acquired guns and rifles and gradually abandoned the bow and arrow.

As the beaver was hunted to extinction in the eastern Great Lakes, the fur trade moved west into Wisconsin. By 1660 the Ottawa and Huron Indians, the middlemen for the French, had established permanent trading centers at Chequamegon Bay in northern Wisconsin that served the upper Mississippi Valley and western Great Lakes.

Competition for furs erupted into warfare among the tribes of the region. The Winnebago of Wisconsin were attacked in the 1630s in a trade dispute with the eastern Ottawa and Huron. From 1640 to 1660 the French and their Ottawa and Huron allies were thwarted by the powerful Iroquois from upper New York. Armed by Dutch traders, the Iroquois fought for possession of trading routes throughout the St. Lawrence River. The Iroquois wars drove the Algonkian-speaking Fox (now known as Mesquakie), Sauk, and Potawatomi into Wisconsin. Other refugees from the eastern Great Lakes region were the Miami, Kickapoo, and Mascouten.

The French built forts at strategic sites to control vital waterways and subdue hostile tribes. The central fort of the Northwest wilderness was at Mackinac, which housed a missionary and a royal notary. For French traders, a trip to Mackinac was a visit to one of the farthest outreaches of the French regime.

The French were not interested in forming colonies but in hunting and trading for furs to take back to New France. The largest French settlement in Wisconsin was around Fort La Baye, which was built in 1717 in present-day Green Bay. There may have been a few permanent French dwellers in Prairie du Chien along the Mississippi River, but not many before 1761.

In order to survive in the Wisconsin wilderness the French fur traders adopted Indian ways. They traveled by canoe, snowshoe, and toboggan; they learned Indian languages and ate native food. Their knowledge of Indian ways ensured their survival and also improved business. Some married into tribes. The official traders were licensed by the crown and called voyageurs. They gathered furs or arranged for the Indians to bring the furs to the annual fairs at Montreal and Quebec. The interlopers were unlicensed and called coureurs de bois, or "wood rangers." Because wood rangers were unlicensed they sold furs to either licensed traders who did not want to travel deep into the woods, or else to the English.

One of the most influential traders in New France and Wisconsin was Nicolas Perrot, who visited Chequamegon Bay and Green Bay around 1667 to form alliances between the French crown and the Indians. Perrot established posts along the Mississippi and served as interpreter at peace negotiations with the Wisconsin Indians, building a reputation for diplomacy. "The savages could not understand why these men came so far to search for their worn-out beaver robes," he wrote. "Meanwhile they admired all the wares brought to them by the French, which they regarded as extremely precious." The French traders preferred worn beaver robes, which were supple and brought better prices at the market than the stiff new robes.

French traders mingled easily with the Indians, but the black-robed Jesuit missionaries mystified the Indians. Father Rene Menard, the first Jesuit sent to Wisconsin, died in the dense forests of northern Wisconsin in 1661 while searching for a Huron village near Lac Court Orielles. Father Claude Allouez opened a mission on Chequamegon Bay in 1665, which would later be run by Father Jacques Marquette, and another at Green Bay. Despite the missionaries' zeal, the Indians remained content with their indigenous religions. "I spoke their language," Father Claude Allouez said about his parish at Green Bay. "But alas, what difficulty they have in apprehending a law that is so opposed to all their customs!" Except for a token crucifix, it was often difficult to distinguish between a Christian Indian and a traditional.

While at Chequamegon, Father Allouez reported the vast copper mines around Lake Superior, prompting a search by, among others, Louis Joliet. The Indians were unwilling to reveal the exact locations of mines, and tribal warfare prevented exploration of mines and transportation routes.

Whether the Indians became Christian or not, their lands became France's on June 14, 1671, at Sault Ste. Marie, the post between lakes Superior and Huron. The French proclaimed Louis XIV king of the Great Lakes region and ruler of the lands "to be discovered." With Nicolas Perrot as translator, 14 Indian tribes politely witnessed the ceremony, new subjects of the French Sun King. Eighteen years later Nicholas Perrot proclaimed Louis XIV king of the Wisconsin area at Lake Pepin. The English would contest the Sun King's claims to Indian land.

Competition in the fur trade intensified. The English had allied themselves with New France's old enemies, the Iroquois, and this alliance interrupted New France's near monopoly in furs. The English consistently undercut French prices and exchanged guns and supplies for fewer pelts. In Montreal one gun cost five pelts, but in Albany a gun cost only two pelts. With prices so good, even French wood rangers traded with the English.

This rivalry was not limited to the New World. In Europe, France and England began the first of four wars they would fight between 1689 and 1763. After King William's War ended in 1697, the French realized the need to protect their trade in the western Great Lakes. The sites they chose to build forts grew to become Chicago and Detroit. In 1701 they built Fort Detroit to serve as a primary trade center and also to guard against British incursions. But peace was not in sight.

The Fox Indians, who dominated the lower Fox River in Wisconsin, resented the French for trading directly with the Sioux on the Mississippi. The Fox, who wanted to serve as middlemen, exacted tolls along the Fox and Wisconsin rivers and jealously controlled access to the Mississippi. About 1,000 reluctant Fox were persuaded to settle in Detroit, built by the French as a trade center and fort to guard against British incursions.

During the winter of 1711-1712, however, a fight erupted between the Fox and Ottawa that escalated into a 19-day siege. The French supported the Ottawa and eventually slaughtered almost all of the Fox. The few survivors fled to Wisconsin, their vengeance igniting the Fox wars against the French that lasted intermittently for 25 years. Travel was hazardous along the Wisconsin waterway to the Mississippi. After peace was negotiated in 1716, the French built Fort La Baye in Green Bay to maintain the Fox-Wisconsin route. But new Fox wars erupted again from 1727 to 1738. Wisconsin trade remained in turmoil and the French looked to other trade routes.

The Fox never drove the French from Wisconsin, but they did slow their advance westward across the country. The French turned their attention to Illinois and the Ohio Valley for trading. In the Ohio Valley the French met the English colonists for their final conflict in the New World. The French and Indian War, also called the Seven Years War, was fought from 1756 to 1763 and decided who would control North America.

THE FRENCH AND INDIAN WAR

The Fox having closed expansion in the West, the

French built forts in the Ohio Valley, a region already being colonized by the English. In 1755 the English, who had aligned themselves with the Iroquois, struck back, attacking Fort Duquesne near present-day Pittsburgh. However, the French and their western Indian allies prevailed at Fort Duquesne, killing the English general Edward Braddock and 1,400 British soldiers. The following May and June of 1756, France and Britain formally declared war on each other. The western Indians, led by Charles de Langlade (who was half French and half Ottawa), fought with the French in several key battles. Langlade, a French officer from Mackinac, became one of the first permanent settlers in Green Bay.

New France was hard pressed for supplies and soldiers. Corruption within New France's government had taken its toll. British sailors waged war on Quebec and it fell in 1759. When Montreal fell the next year, Canada succumbed to the British. British sea power cut France from her claims in America, Africa, India, and the Far East. When Spain decided to ally itself with France late in the war, the British wrested Cuba and the Philippines.

Following their victory in 1763, the British claimed all the land east of the Mississippi, except for New Orleans. In the fur-rich land that had been New France, the French retained only two fishing islands off New Foundland. The Mississippi River, which the French had explored and mapped, now became the dividing line between Spanish Louisiana and England's American colonies. The French fur traders and Canadian-born settlers who wanted to trade with the Indians and develop the wilderness, chose to remain in British North America rather than migrate to French territory.

In Wisconsin there were no white residents to make a decision of remaining or leaving. The land west of Lake Michigan was untouched by settlers seeking to make homes. Wisconsin had been valuable only for its water routes to the Mississippi and also in its forts that protected the trade routes. But even though the French had proclaimed Louis XIV ruler of these lands ninety years before, the land remained Indian.

With the French government vanquished, the Indians became alarmed for several reasons. The French had been interested in trade, not land. The English, on the other hand, were colonists lured to the New World by farming. In seeking to control the fur trade,

on which they were economically dependent, the Indians could no longer play the French against the English as they had for more than a century.

The Indians revolted against the English in 1763, the year the British signed the peace treaty with France. The sudden uprising, which spread from Mackinac to Niagara, was begun by Chief Pontiac of the Ottawa, who planned a coup against the British in Detroit. Pontiac was rebuffed, but five other forts fell, including Mackinac. In Wisconsin, the English Lieutenant James Gorrell at Green Bay placated the Indians with food, gun powder, and diplomatic speeches. Elsewhere, in the bordering settlements, the uprising was unnerving to the whites who feared Indian torture.

To quell Indian fears, a line was drawn that stopped white settlement from the summit of the Alleghenies to the Mississippi River. Called the Proclamation Line of 1763, it reserved western lands for Indians that would be guarded by the military. The Stamp Act of 1765 required the colonies to help pay for the garrisons along the west. But as tensions between the Crown and the colonists grew, the British paid less attention to the western territories.

Although the British owned the Wisconsin wilderness, they were absentee landlords. The British had abandoned Green Bay to aid besieged Mackinac during Pontiac's uprising in 1763 and never formally returned. The fur trade continued in Green Bay, with Charles de Langlade and his family building a French community. Trade along the upper Mississippi thrived. One fur trader, Peter Pond, reported that 1,500 pounds of fur were sent from the Fox village of Prairie du Chien to Mackinac during the summer of 1774.

The fur trade was relatively unhampered by the Revolutionary War. Britain's yield remained higher during the Revolution than during the seven years preceding the war. There were some difficulties in transporting pelts from Mackinac to Montreal, but both the British and the traders were resourceful. The British continued to trade with the Indians not only to obtain revenue but also to secure their support during the war.

THE REVOLUTIONARY WAR

Wisconsin Indians and British fur traders were dispatched to fight in the Revolutionary War. Charles de Langlade, who had become a captain in the British Indian service, led contingents into the St. Lawrence Valley. While the Indians of southern Wisconsin were considered to be sympathetic to the Americans, the British continued their fur trade along the Fox-Wisconsin route. The bulk of trade to Montreal came from Prairie du Chien and Green Bay during the American Revolution.

The Revolution was a distant sound in Wisconsin. When the British relinquished control over the colonies in 1783, they set the Mississippi River as the western boundary of the new nation. But it took Jay's Treaty, ratified in 1795, for the British to leave their border posts and abandon their lucrative fur trade. Canadian trade was undisturbed because all fur traders—Canadian, Indian, and American—were free to travel on either side of the borders to do business.

Wisconsin's fur trade had always been tied to Montreal, whether controlled by the French or the British. The North West Company, a Canadian company headquartered in Montreal, dominated the field that included Madeline Island in northern Wisconsin and Fond du Lac on Lake Winnebago. Traders who formed small partnerships in the

Above
Rachel Grignon, of the early
Green Bay fur-trading family,
was the daughter of a
Chippewa woman and John
Law, a prominent fur trader.
Courtesy, State Historical
Society of Wisconsin

Left
Fur trader Augustin Grignon
was a member of Green Bay's
founding family. Grignon was
the grandson of Charles de
Langlade, who became
Wisconsin's first permanent
settler in 1764. Courtesy, State
Historical Society of Wisconsin

Charles de Langlade, whose
house is pictured in 1890, became the first permanent settler
in Wisconsin, and his son-
in-law, Pierre Grignon, continued Wisconsin's fur-trading
heritage with his family of five
sons, who also became fur traders. Courtesy, State Historical
Society of Wisconsin

Minnesota-Wisconsin area also prospered. The Langlade family of Green Bay were prominent fur traders in the 1790s, due to Charles Langlade's son-in-law, Pierre Grignon, and his sons. Prairie du Chien was dominated by Canadian fur traders.

Business continued to boom in furs. However, in 1809 the Non-Intercourse Act closed American ports to British and French ships. Montreal's Michilimackinac Company was banned from trade with Green Bay and Prairie du Chien. To circumvent this ban, the Canadians merged their company with John Jacob Astor's American Fur Company. The new firm, the South West Company, Americanized the fur trade in Wisconsin. Following the War of 1812, Astor created an American monopoly in the Upper Great Lakes that would last for 20 years.

THE WAR OF 1812

Relations between the American and British governments were deteriorating, and a chief dispute was trade relations. Competition for furs was keen. Along the frontier, American traders resented the freedom with which the British crossed the border and traded directly with the Indians. In Wisconsin, traders who refused to deal with Astor had to smuggle Canadian goods into the land. Many traders in Wisconsin were bitter.

Tempers among American frontiersmen were also aroused when they saw the British encourage the Shawnee chief Tecumseh. Tecumseh was gathering Indian support from Wisconsin to Alabama with the goal of ousting Americans from Indian land. Indian revolt was a dangerous threat according to Nicholas Boilvin, Prairie du Chien's Indian agent appointed by the U.S. War Department to monitor the Indian fur trade. Boilvin complained of the Canadians' large gifts of supplies to the Indians, which he saw as a sign of war. Indians continued to make pilgrimages to Mackinac, where they received gifts from the British.

Tecumseh had support in Wisconsin. The Winnebago, Sauk, and Potawatomi Indians were hostile to American claims. The governor of the Indiana Territory and future U.S. president, William Henry Harrison, became Tecumseh's archrival. In 1811, Harrison fought Tecumseh on Indiana's Tippecanoe River. Though the battle was a draw, it resulted in Tecumseh losing face among his Indian supporters and never regaining the support he needed. And although Harrison did not win the battle, he and his running mate John Tyler had a winning slogan for the 1840 presidential election: "Tippecanoe and Tyler, too!"

The Americans declared war against the British in June 1812. In Wisconsin the largely Canadian fur traders supported the British. One Prairie du Chien trader, Robert Dickson, recruited Indians for the British. Much of his time was spent finding food and keeping Indian loyalties. Indian support wavered after 1813 when the tide turned in favor of the Americans. Commodore Perry and the Americans beat the British navy in the strategic battle at Lake Erie in September 1813. A month later, at Canada's Thames River, the Americans beat the British in the battle where Chief Tecumseh was killed.

In 1814 American troops arrived in Prairie du Chien to build Fort Shelby and challenge the British along the Fox and Wisconsin rivers. On June 19, 1814, the first American flag to grace a Wisconsin building was raised. The flag's tenure was brief. A three-day skirmish that wounded eight changed the flag to British the following month. The only battle of the War of 1812 to be fought on Wisconsin soil yielded Fort Shelby to the British, who renamed it Fort Mckay after their victorious British colonel. Major Zachary Taylor later tried to reclaim Fort Shelby but was turned back by Sauk Indians at Rock Island.

No boundary changes occurred when the War of 1812 ended in a draw in December 1814. However, President James Madison did close access to the Mississippi River from Canada into American territory. British and Canadian traders were no longer welcome in America's fur trade. The dominance of Great Britain in the Great Lakes region had ended, and the British traders departed, leaving Wisconsin virtually untouched by settlement. For Europeans, Wisconsin had been valuable because of its fur, not its land. Wisconsin's water routes had connected the wilderness to Montreal in a great commercial empire. But the Europeans had always considered the wilderness Indian land. Neither the French or British had left much of an imprint, except that the Indian pathways were more worn and the fur-bearing animals less abundant.

SETTLEMENT AND STATEHOOD

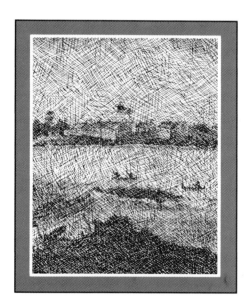

*Fort Howard, built in 1816, firmly estab-
lished American interests in Green Bay, a settlement that had been dominated by French Canadians and Indians. Courtesy, State
Historical Society of Wisconsin*

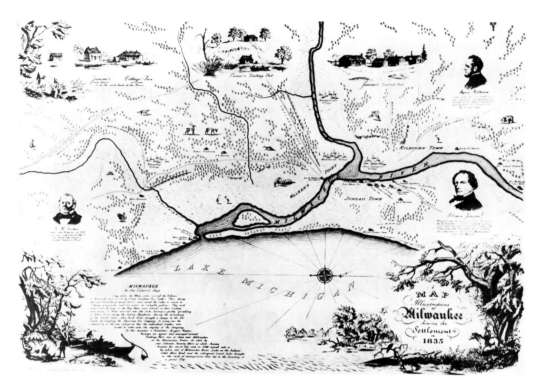

Land that Solomon Juneau bought on the east bank of the Milwaukee River in 1833 for $1.25 an acre was being sold for up to $4,000 an acre by 1836. Courtesy, Milwaukee County Historical Society

The next pathfinders into the Wisconsin wilderness would come not by canoe, but by steamboat. In successive waves, new explorers would build upon the Indian trails and eventually force the Indians out. The new pathfinders would not blend into the wilderness, as the fur traders did, but instead would try to put a Yankee stamp on it. Land, not furs, was the new bounty.

Land speculation would become a frontier fever and have devastating effects on the national economy. A crisis in banking, based on easy credit for land sales, would plunge the entire country into depression. One of the most hotly debated issues of territorial Wisconsin would be banking, an issue that would dominate political debate even through the attainment of statehood.

The storms of change were gathering, but the Wisconsin frontier of 1815 was still Indian land. Wisconsin's great frontier historian, Frederick Jackson Turner, described the course of Wisconsin's development. "The Indian village became the trading post, the trading post became the city. The trails became our early roads," he wrote in 1891. "In a word, the fur trade closed its mission by becoming the pathfinder for agriculture and manufacturing civilization." As railroads connected the coasts of the United States, a U.S. senator remarked on the evolution of the buffalo trail: "Science now makes her improved roads exactly

where the buffalo's foot first marked the way and the hunter's foot afterwards followed him."

Few frontier historians have matched the eloquence of Frederick Jackson Turner. When the U.S. Census in 1890 proclaimed there was no longer a frontier line, Turner was the first to recognize this as "the closing of a great historic movement." The American frontier, he argued, helped shape the American character: "This perennial rebirth, this fluidity of American life, this expansion westward with its new opportunities, its continuous touch with the simplicity of primitive society, furnish the forces dominating American character."

In 1815 the American frontier consisted of the Illinois Territory, which encompassed Wisconsin. The Indians who lived there were hostile to American claims. The few whites who lived in Wisconsin had allegiance to French and British Canada. One family from New York who settled in Prairie du Chien in 1816 considered themselves the only American residents in the village as late as 1827.

The upper Mississippi, which had been an enclave for the British, was a strategic waterway for the new nation. The American military built three forts along the river in 1816: Fort Crawford in Prairie du Chien, Fort Edwards at the Des Moines River, and Fort Armstrong at the Rock River. Two more forts were built in Wisconsin after a Winnebago uprising

in 1827. Fort Howard was built in Green Bay, and Fort Winnebago was built at the portage between the Fox and Wisconsin rivers.

The U.S. government, protective of its control in the fur trade, passed a law in 1816 that prohibited foreigners from trading with the Indians on U.S. land. At Green Bay and Prairie du Chien the United States government installed two trading posts, called government factories, that sold goods to Indians at prices that substantially undercut those of private traders. Since 1795 factories had aimed at currying loyalty with the Indians and forming ties against the British. In 1822, several years after the British left, the factory system that outraged private traders was abolished.

John Jacob Astor, the eastern fur magnate who had urged both congressional laws, was jubilant. He had revived the American Fur Company and bought out his Canadian partners in the American-based South West Company. The industry once controlled by the French and British would now be American. Astor forged a monopoly in furs that blanketed the Great Lakes frontier. The fur traders in Wisconsin had no choice; if they wanted to work they either had to declare allegiance to the United States, or work for Astor under a licensed clerk. Many traders did both, and they became part of the monopoly that was known as the "Fist in the Wilderness." Bad wages and job insecurity were part of Astor's grip, which lasted until his retirement in 1834.

This trading post of John Jacob
Astor's American Fur Company
was depicted in about 1820.
The company Americanized an
industry that had been controlled by the French and the British. Courtesy, State Historical
Society of Wisconsin

INDIAN LAND CESSION

By the 1830s the fur trade, a wilderness industry, was in decline. White settlement was encroaching and clamors for Indian land cessions were sounding. "The Indian must go," was the vociferous cry of many settlers moving westward. The U.S. government began its removal policy in Wisconsin in 1825 when it arranged an intertribal council at Prairie du Chien. No land changed hands, but Indian tribes were asked to identify the boundaries of their lands as the first step in treaty negotiations.

Tensions were building between Indians and whites. Tribes resented whites digging in their lead mines of southeastern Wisconsin, which they had been working years before Nicholas Perrot arrived in 1695. Miners drifting north from the Missouri mines gathered around Galena on the Fever River, an area the U.S. government had bought in 1804 from the Sauk and Fox (now Mesquakie). From there they continued to move north illegally into Winnebago territory.

Above
The 1825 Treaty of Prairie du Chien, between the U.S. government and several Wisconsin Indian tribes, marked the start of land cessions between the government and individual tribes. This treaty began the process of removing the Indians from land that could then be settled by whites. Courtesy, State Historical Society of Wisconsin

Left
Winnebago (now Ho-Chunk) Chief Yellow Thunder (seated) told the pioneer photographer H.H. Bennett in 1867 that his age was 110. Courtesy, the H.H. Bennett Studio

This Winnebago Indian camped with his wigwam and canoe in about 1880. Because Indian practices changed very slowly, this photo probably reflects how Winnebago Indians traveled and camped in earlier times. Courtesy, the H.H. Bennett Studio

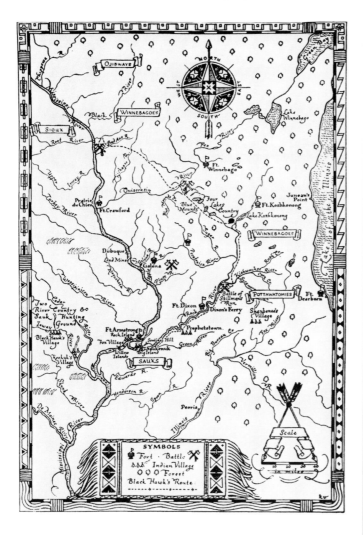

Tensions burst in Prairie du Chien when a Winnebago war chief name Red Bird murdered two white men. The military moved to quell the uprising, known as the Winnebago War of 1827, and built a fort on Winnebago land. Red Bird surrendered and a full-scale war was averted. Red Bird later died in prison, and in 1829 the lead-mining region south of the Wisconsin River was ceded to the U.S. government.

Land cessions began in southern Wisconsin in 1829, opening the way for miners, farmers, and lumberjacks to claim land. By 1848 all Indian lands had been ceded by treaty, except for negotiated Indian reservations. During the 1830s two eastern tribes, the Stockbridge-Munsee (now known as Mohican) and the Oneida, were removed to Wisconsin. These new tribes completed the present-day Indian nations of Wisconsin: the Chippewa, Potawatomi, Menominee, Winnebago, Oneida, and Stockbridge-Munsee. The Menominee of Wisconsin were able to negotiate a

Above
Chief Black Hawk was leader of the final Indian insurrection in the Wisconsin region. His defeat at Bad Axe River near the Mississippi River in 1832 ended the Black Hawk War and led to white settlement of Wisconsin. Courtesy, State Historical Society of Wisconsin

Above left
This early map of Indian tribes in the Illinois and Wisconsin region also shows the path of Chief Black Hawk in 1832. Courtesy, State Historical Society of Wisconsin

This sketch of the lead-mining region of southwestern Wisconsin appeared in Harper's Monthly in 1853. By 1836 lead mining had brought a rush of 10,000 people to southwestern Wisconsin. Courtesy, State Historical Society of Wisconsin

reservation on a portion of their original homeland, making them the oldest known continuous residents of Wisconsin.

Indian tribes anguished over leaving the homelands they revered. In Wisconsin the Black Hawk War of 1832 was a final convulsion for more than 1,000 Sauk and Fox who despaired at leaving their Illinois home. Serving in military units that pursued the aging warrior Black Hawk were Abraham Lincoln, Jefferson Davis, and Zachary Taylor. Yet no heroes emerged. Historians have viewed the Black Hawk War as a combination of bungling mistakes and ruthlessness in which almost 850 Indians were massacred while trying to surrender. Black Hawk, who escaped the army's massacre of the Indian families at Bad Axe River, explained his dilemma over land treaties in an autobiography that he later dictated:

My reason teaches me that land cannot be sold. The Great Spirit gave it to his children to live upon, and cultivate, as far as is necessary for their subsistence; and so long as they occupy and cultivate it, they have the right to the soil—but if they voluntarily leave it then any other people have a right to settle upon it. Nothing can be sold, but such things can be carried away.

Initially lead in southwestern Wisconsin was mined close to the surface of the land. But after 1840 the surface lead was depleted and the mineral needed to be brought up from deeper below the ground, as shown in this lithograph of a cross section of a lead mine in 1844. Many Cornish immigrants came to southwestern Wisconsin bringing with them the hard-rock mining techniques from England necessary to mine the remaining lead deposits. These lead miners work below the surface using hard-rock mining techniques in about 1850. Courtesy, State Historical Society of Wisconsin

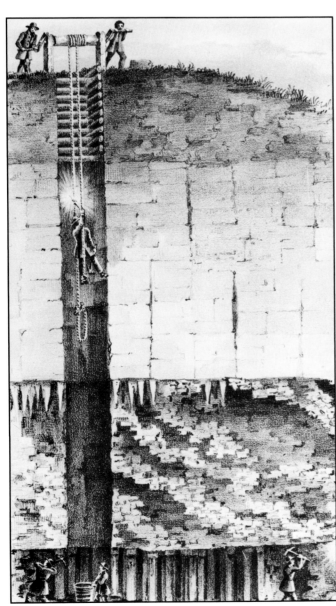

Since 1787 Wisconsin had been a part of the shifting sands of the Northwest Territory. While part of the Indiana Territory created in 1800, in effect it was controlled by the British until after the War of 1812. In 1809 Wisconsin became part of the Illinois Territory, and in 1818 was annexed to the Michigan Territory after Illinois became a state. The Northwest Ordinance of 1787 detailed the procedure by which settlers could turn the frontier into states. The government would appoint a territorial governor plus three judges, each of whom had to own from 500 to 1,000 acres in the territory. Once there were 5,000 voters in the territory, the government granted a territorial legislature. The government deemed settlers to be voters if they were male, free, 21 years old, owned 50 acres of land, and were residents of the territory for two years. Once the territory reached 60,000 voters it could petition for statehood.

In 1830 the U.S. census counted 31,600 whites in the Michigan Territory, only about 3,000 of whom lived in the land that became Wisconsin. Wisconsin had only two small villages, Green Bay on Lake Michigan and Prairie du Chien on the Mississippi River. The residents were primarily descendents of the original fur traders, a mix of French-Canadian and Indian blood.

THE LEAD INDUSTRY

The opening of the Erie Canal in 1825 connected the Great Lakes to eastern markets. Once more Wisconsin was part of an important water route. Lead ore was the magnet for much of American settlement in Wisconsin. Lead was the basic ingredient for paint and bullets, perhaps two of the frontier civilization's primary tools. The region's lead, or "galena," lay close to the surface, often exposed on hill sides and ravines. These loose pieces, called "floats," alerted miners to hidden lodes. One resident from Galena in northern Illinois noted that "mining is as simple a process as the common method of digging wells."

Lead fever sparked a rush of 10,000 people by 1836. In 1829 more than 13 million pounds of refined lead were produced by the tri-state region of present-day Wisconsin, Iowa, and northern Illinois. The government did not sell the land but instead leased permits to miners, and only licensed smelters could

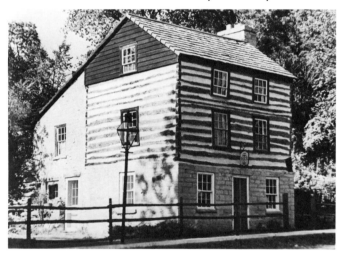

Above
Cornish lead miners settled in and around Mineral Point during the lead rush of the 1820s and 1830s. A Cornish miner's home is restored on Mineral Point's Shakerag Street. Courtesy, State Historical Society of Wisconsin

Right
Land sales swept Wisconsin during the 1830s and 1840s, and Cyrus Woodman and Cadwallader C. Washburn of Mineral Point were prominent promoters. Courtesy, State Historical Society of Wisconsin

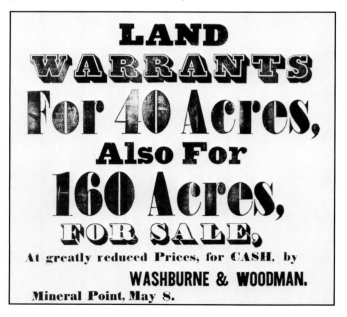

LAND WARRANTS For 40 Acres, Also For 160 Acres, FOR SALE, At greatly reduced Prices, for CASH, by WASHBURNE & WOODMAN. Mineral Point, May 8.

refine the lead ore. The government then collected 10 percent of the lead from the smelter as a royalty.

In the lead region, farming was permitted only where it did not interfere with mining. The government leasing system forbade miners to buy land; only land barren of minerals could be sold. But the lead region was also prime agricultural land. Many miners, farmers and investors wanted to buy land; there are reports that land was declared mineral-free after being examined blindfolded.

A depression in lead prices from 1829 to 1831 forced a revision in the government's land policy. With sinking lead prices and soaring food prices, many people turned to farming to make a living. In 1829 flour cost $15 a barrel, the price of 5,000 pounds of lead. The land offices that opened in 1834 in Mineral Point and Green Bay encouraged more farming. By 1847 the leasing system was dead and all land was for sale, including mineral reserves.

Lead production peaked in 1845 with 24,300 tons. However, this yield plummeted by 50 percent within five years. The accessible veins of ore had been exhausted and the deeper ore needed elaborate equipment to mine. The lead from the deep mining was mixed with what miners considered worthless zinc, which would not have a profitable market until 1900.

Though some miners were lured away by the California Gold Rush, the Cornish kept the lead industry productive after 1840, when most of the surface lead was gone. The tin mines in Cornwall, England had trained generations of miners who were used to hard-rock mining and problems with water drainage. As Cornwall's tin industry declined, about 7,000 miners were attracted to the Mineral Point region of Wisconsin by the prospect of working for themselves. Among the innovations they introduced was the safety fuse for blasting.

The lead miners are credited with giving Wisconsin its nickname of the Badger State. Before Wisconsin reached statehood a 35-page history of Wisconsin was published in 1845 called *The Home of the Badgers*. According to tradition, many miners dug holes into hillsides during the cold and, like the badger, set up housekeeping. One pioneer, Daniel Parkinson, described the hillside homes of New Diggings, a village in southwestern Wisconsin. "They usually lived in dens or caves; a large hole or excavation covered with poles, grass, and sods," wrote Parkinson in 1827. "In

Solomon Juneau, a French-Canadian fur trader, built his first trading post on what would become Wisconsin's most valuable real estate, downtown Milwaukee. In 1833 Juneau became Milwaukee's first resident. Courtesy, State Historical Society of Wisconsin

MAP OF
MILWAUKEE
SHOWING LOCATION OF ITS PRINCIPAL
BUILDINGS IN THE SPRING OF 1836
AS RECOLLECTED BY
Dr ENOCH CHASE U B SMITH & OTHERS

these holes or dug-outs, families lived in apparent comfort and the most perfect satisfaction for years, buoyed by the constant expectation of soon striking a big lead."

Just as the fur industry gave rise to Green Bay and Prairie du Chien, the lead industry gave rise to towns such as Mineral Point, Platteville, and Dodgeville. Mineral Point, well-placed between the lead metropolis of Galena and ports on the Wisconsin River, was named the county seat in 1830, and in 1834 it became the site for one of the territory's two land offices. The frontier was home to the itinerant miners who named their temporary villages Red Dog, Burlesqueburgh, Nip-and-Tuck, Hoof Noggle, Hard Scrabble, Grab, and Trespass. As the area became farmlands, many communities were renamed.

THE LAND RUSH AND THE PANIC OF 1837

After lead, the land rush was the biggest business in Wisconsin. The sparsely populated interior of Wisconsin was first surveyed around Green Bay and Mineral

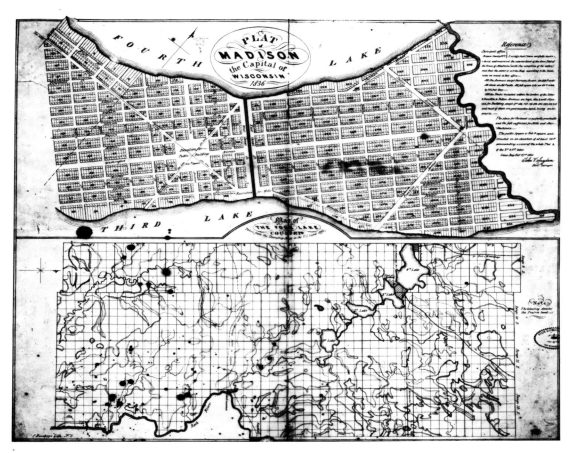

Left:
Many people were shocked when the legislators voted for Madison in 1836 as the permanent capital, because it was uninhabited wilderness. This map shows an optimistic view of the platted land, which quickly became a reality under the leadership of James Doty, land speculator and former judge. Doty would become Wisconsin's second territorial governor. Courtesy, State Historical Society of Wisconsin

Below:
When Wisconsin was declared a territory in 1836, it comprised parts of what are now Iowa and Minnesota. Courtesy, State Historical Society of Wisconsin

Henry Dodge, who became Wisconsin's first territorial governor in 1836, prided himself on being an Indian fighter in the Black Hawk War. Courtesy, State Historical Society of Wisconsin

Point. All land had to be surveyed before it could be sold for $1.25 an acre. Land speculators were the biggest buyers, but squatters also made claims to land. Many homesteaders cleared land before it was ready for public sale. Speculators with sales receipts inevitably clashed with homesteaders who were already living on the land. The Jackson administration passed four laws between 1830 and 1838 that gave some homesteaders protection. Finally, prompted by frontier agitation for a comprehensive law, the Pre-emption Act of 1841 gave all western homesteaders rights to the land they had claimed before the land was surveyed for public sale.

From 1835 to 1837 much of the country became a crazy quilt of squatters, resident landowners, and outside land speculators. The favorite targets for land speculation were the prospective towns that studded the Mississippi Valley. "Speculator," a pejorative term generally reserved for absentee owners, usually was not applied to residents buying large tracts of land. Of the 38 million acres of public land sold in the country from 1835 to 1837, 29 million acres probably belonged to speculators. In Wisconsin one active land agent, Moses Strong of Mineral Point, estimated that of the 878,014 acres sold through 1836, three-fourths went to speculators.

As land speculators tried to divine where the best land was, most promoters agreed the prime sites in Wisconsin were on waterways. Much of Wisconsin was a dense wilderness, with uncharted forests and streams separating Prairie du Chien on the Mississippi from Green Bay on lake Michigan. The Wisconsin River was the only highway between the two in 1832, during the Black Hawk War. Congress then appropriated $5,000 for a road to connect Fort Howard in Green Bay to Fort Crawford in Prairie du Chien, including Fort Winnebago in the portage between the Fox and Wisconsin rivers. Built by the soldiers of the three posts, the Military Road bridged streams and filled in swamps for 234 miles. The route it followed was south of the Fox and Wisconsin rivers, which had been heavily trafficked by the fur trade. In many places the road was no more than a lane through forests, but it attracted settlers who helped to maintain the road and keep it passable. Most settlers in Wisconsin, however, would still be attracted to the port cities.

Solomon Juneau, a French-Canadian fur trader, was astonished to discover that his fur trading post

In 1842 New Yorker Jerome I.
Case followed the wheat frontier to Racine. He brought with
him six wheat threshers, the
start of spectacular growth in
wheat threshers and harvesting machines. Case built his empire in
part by traveling through roadless Wisconsin and selling
threshers to farmers. Courtesy,
State Historical Society of
Wisconsin

was sitting on valuable land. His solitary building, surrounded by Indian wigwams, was located next to the Milwaukee River, which flowed into Lake Michigan. "His first hint of the prospective value of his location at Milwaukee came from me," recalled Morgan L. Martin, a Green Bay land speculator originally from New York. "He was so incredulous that it was sometimes difficult to prevent his sacrificing his interest to the sharks who soon gathered around him." In a verbal agreement, Martin formed a partnership with Juneau and claimed squatter's rights to 289 acres under President Jackson's 1834 pre-emption law that protected homesteaders.

The land that became downtown Milwaukee was first developed as Juneautown on the east bank of the Milwaukee River. A land surveyor from Ohio, Byron Kilbourn, built Kilbourntown on the west bank. Within three years of talking to Martin in 1833, Juneau's Indian village had increased to 50 houses and 1,208 villagers. Wisconsin writer Increase Lapham, who mapped the village in 1836, exclaimed, "Eighteen months ago there were but two families!" The land Juneau had bought for $1.25 an acre was selling for up to $4,000 an acre in 1836.

Wisconsin was declared a territory in 1836, during one of the biggest land sales in the history of the United States. Banks flooded the country with bank notes borrowed by speculators to buy public land, which they would then use as collateral to borrow more money for more land. Speculators could not afford to use hard currency for payment, but paper money was abundant. The bubble of land speculation broke in 1837.

The nationwide land speculation fever suffered a panic, following a New York City bank crash in May 1837 that spread to banks throughout the country. Banks lost confidence in bank notes and refused to accept them as payment. In July 1837 the U.S. Secretary of the Treasury issued the Specie Circular, a proclamation that required all lands sales to be paid in gold and silver only. The days of buying land on credit and with inflated bank notes were over. The Panic of 1837 destroyed almost all the banks in the Middle West, including Wisconsin. The country plunged into a severe depression that would last until about 1843.

Wisconsin became a territory in 1836 with all the optimism of boom times in land sales and prosperity of the lead rush. The next year Wisconsin felt the panic of the depression. In 1837 Wisconsin's first territorial governor, Henry Dodge, urged a one-year stay on court judgments that involved debtors. A stay of execution "would prevent the ruin of many whose property will be liable to sale at great loss," said Dodge, a flamboyant Indian fighter and faithful Jacksonian Democrat. The reason for Wisconsin's predicament was what Dodge called "the present embarrassed state of the currency in this Territory." There simply wasn't enough money around. Wisconsin's prosperity was further diminished in 1838 when the land incorporating Iowa and much of Minnesota became the Iowa Territory, removing nearly one-half of the Wisconsin Territory's industrious mining population.

The decision of where to locate the Wisconsin Territory's new capital was the first dispute between Dodge and James Doty, a Yankee land speculator who became Wisconsin's second territorial governor in 1840. In July 13 1836, Dodge chose Belmont as the temporary capital on the advice of a hopeful promoter. Belmont, off the beaten path in the southwest mining region, invoked so many complaints that Dodge promised to automatically approve the Legislature's decision on the permanent capital.

Doty had real estate interests in the area known as the City of the Four Lakes, soon to be named Madison. On July 1, 1836, on the way to Belmont's only legislative convention, he and a surveyor drew a plat of the "Town of Madison." Doty proved himself a master lobbyist, giving choice parcels of land in Madison to each legislator who promised to vote for Madison. An isolated wilderness town sitting on four lakes, Madison was virtually uninhabited, yet thanks to Doty's diligent campaigning, it was chosen as the new capital. To ensure that Madison would remain the capital, Doty quickly sold lots to prominent dignitaries, including the chief justice of the Wisconsin Supreme Court and Governor Dodge's son.

The most pressing problem in settling Wisconsin was transportation. Traveling on a stagecoach between Madison and Milwaukee, Swedish author Frederika Bremer described the well-used road in 1849: "I was shaken, or rather hurled, unmercifully hither and thither upon the newborn roads of Wisconsin, which are no roads at all, but a succession of hills, holes, and waterpools." Businessman Jerome I. Case, selling his wheat threshers throughout the region, found the roads in 1851 "soft with no bottoms in places."

The first building of the Wisconsin Marine and Fire Insurance Company, in Milwaukee, was not officially a bank. Because of the political backlash against wildcat banking, Wisconsin was bankless from 1841 to 1853. But certificates from George Smith's Wisconsin Marine and Fire Insurance Company were treated as paper money and were popularly called "George Smith's money." Courtesy, State Historical Society of Wisconsin

Another traveler described the bridges: "They get two huge trees 50 to 60 feet long, and lay across from bank to bank of creeks or small rivers. Then they lay small poles across, just to stop a horse's foot from going through, and that's all."

To stimulate financial capital for development of roads into the wilderness, the Legislature granted corporate charters for both banks and transportation companies. According to business historian George Kuehnl, of the 35 charters granted from 1836 to 1840, 7 were for banks and 11 were for canals and railroads. From 1841 to 1848, 29 of the 38 charters were related to transportation: piers, bridges, canals, steamboats, railroads, plankroads, and turnpikes. These large projects required more money than could be collected by a few investors during the depression, and canals and railroads required government land grants. By the time

Wisconsin reached statehood in 1848, no canals had been dug and no railroads had been built.

After the tremendous success of the Erie Canal, which brought Yankee settlers into the Great Lakes region, many developers dreamed of connecting Wisconsin's rivers by canals. Promoters had plans to connect the Fox River with the Wisconsin River at the portage, but the Wisconsin River proved to be too shallow. Byron Kilbourn worked to connect the Milwaukee River to the Rock River and then across land into the lead region. James Doty wanted to connect Lake Winnebago to the Rock River and then on to the four lakes of Madison, where he held substantial real estate. Competing for scarce capital, Governor Doty was able to block Kilbourn's canal route, though the dam Kilbourn constructed became a source of power for Milwaukee's pioneer flour-milling industry.

BANKING

Banking would become a highly contested issue as Wisconsin entered statehood in 1848. Much of the animosity derived from Green Bay's Bank of Wisconsin, chartered in 1835, and the Bank of Mineral Point, chartered in 1836. These frontier banks engaged in wildcat banking, the cavalier policy of issuing bank notes in high quantities regardless of actual deposits held. The trick was to keep from having the bank notes redeemed. Many of the stockholders looked upon these banks as easy ways to capitalize their land speculations. When the Wisconsin attorney general seized the assets from the Bank of Wisconsin in 1839, the hard currency in the bank's vault amounted to $86.20 compared to liabilities of $100,000. Following this episode the public remained suspicious of banks, viewing them as inventors of worthless bank notes.

Reflecting public opinion, the Wisconsin Legislature refused to charter banks, from 1841 to 1853. In 1852 Wisconsin was one of seven states that did not have any incorporated banks. Yet hard currency was scarce, and the territory's struggling economy needed basic banking services such as loans and credit.

George Smith, a Scottish real estate speculator in Chicago and Milwaukee, devised a way to bring banking services to Milwaukee. He proposed to the Legislature the formation of the Wisconsin Marine and Fire Insurance Company. This famous shadow bank was granted a charter by the Legislature in 1839 as an insurance company. The charter provided the right to accept deposits and make loans, though banking services were prohibited. Smith, ignoring this contradiction, built a million-dollar business issuing certificates that the company was always prepared to redeem in gold. As Smith's reputation grew, his certificates of deposit were redeemable in gold in Chicago, Detroit, St. Louis, and as far away as Buffalo and New York City.

Smith and his partner, Alexander Mitchell, also helped Wisconsin settlers to buy land and farmers to sell their crops. The company would buy the land in gold from the government and sell it to the settlers on a contract basis. George Smith's certificates of deposit became the pioneer's paper money. Farmers could sell wheat to New York and accept certificates of deposit, instead of waiting for the buyer to send gold after re-selling the wheat to the eastern markets.

In Wisconsin and the Middle West, the business community was grateful for "George Smith's money," as it was popularly known. However, the Legislature investigated the insurance company and in 1846 pressed for repeal of the company's charter. Alexander Mitchell defended the company by pointing out that investors received moderate returns and that the company did not engage in speculation. In addition, the company argued that the Legislature had no basis to repeal a charter unless its power to repeal was stipulated in the original charter. While this argument was supported by the Legislature's Judiciary Committee Council, the charter was repealed.

George Smith ignored the repeal of his company's charter and continued business. Four years later the attorney general ruled the repeal was unconstitutional. By 1852 the public sentiment against banking had changed among the voters, in large part due to the reputation of George Smith. The Legislature voted to allow banking again, and the Wisconsin Marine and Fire Insurance Company reorganized under the new law. George Smith sold his holdings to his partner, Alexander Mitchell, and returned to Scotland with a fortune estimated at $10 million.

IMMIGRATION

As the country recovered from the depression in 1843, New England Yankees packed their bags and moved West in search of land and new opportunities. Together with pioneers from the Middle Atlantic states, 103,000 Yankees settled in Wisconsin between 1840 and 1850; by 1850 one-fourth of Wisconsin's population was New Yorkers. While some migrants were drawn to Wisconsin by its rich, abundant farmland, many easterners had economic and political connections that helped them become entrepreneurs and politicians in the West. For example, of the largest names in land speculation, C.C. Washburn and Cyrus Woodman were from Maine, and Moses Strong was from Vermont. James Doty, Wisconsin's second territorial governor, was from New York. Wisconsin's first elected governor, Nelson Dewey, was a lawyer from Connecticut. As the 1846 state convention clamored for statehood, 46 of the 124 delegates were native New Yorkers, and 72 had some New York connection through education, residence, or business experience.

Between 1840 and 1850, Wisconsin's population increased ten-fold to 305,000. During this period sail and steam boats through the Erie Canal brought 106,000 Europeans to Wisconsin. Social reformer Margaret Fuller observed their arrival in Milwaukee in 1843: "During the fine weather the poor refugees arrive daily, in their national dresses all travel-soiled and worn. The night they pass in rude shantees, in a particular quarter of the town, then walk off into the country—the mothers carrying their infants, the fathers leading the little children by the hand, seeking a home where their hands may maintain them." Immigrants during this decade included 38,000 Germans, 9,000 Scandinavians, 21,000 Irish, and 28,000 English, Scots, and Welsh. Many of the Germans stayed in Milwaukee, and by 1850 the German-born accounted for 40 percent of Milwaukee's population.

STATEHOOD

With these sharp increases in population Wisconsin moved closer to statehood. By 1845 Wisconsin had more than the 60,000 voters required for statehood as suggested by the Ordinance of 1787. The framers of the state constitution met in 1846 to decide on government structure and conclude debates concerning boundaries between Illinois, Michigan, and Minnesota as drawn by President Polk's administration.

The most bitterly debated issue at the three-month constitutional convention was banking. While no one was in favor of wildcat banking, Whigs generally supported the concept of banks and Democrats rejected all banking. The article set before the convention banned all banks and paper money. Opponents of the article tended to agree that Wisconsin, while it did not need banks at the time, might need them in the future. Politicians ignored the business community's assertion that by forbidding paper money or banks, the article was preventing future prosperity.

Rufus King, editor of the *Milwaukee Sentinel and Gazette*, strongly denounced the proposed ban on banking, arguing in an editorial campaign that the banking article "will add immediately to the glittering heaps of those who have already amassed stores of coin. It will assuredly make the rich richer; but it will, as assuredly, keep the poor, still poor; if it does not make them poorer." King was one of many opponents who saw the need for credit and loans in a growing economy.

Persuaded by the arguments of King and others,

the voters rejected the proposed constitution. Its nemesis was the article banning banks, according to historian Robert Nesbit. In 1847 the delegates met again, anxious for Wisconsin to become a state in time for the 1848 presidential election. The new compromise gave the voters the right to accept or reject any legislation on banks by special referendum. The constitution was accepted, and on May 29, 1848, Wisconsin became the thirtieth state.

Wisconsin had become a state amid tumultuous economic times. The boom period of land speculation had crashed in the Panic of 1837, and countless businesses were ruined in the nationwide depression that followed. Upon statehood Wisconsin was bankless and virtually roadless, but European and Yankee settlers had dreams of prosperity in a wilderness of rivers, forests and rich farmland.

Cassville became a home of Nelson Dewey, Wisconsin's first elected governor. This lithograph is from a drawing by the German artist Henry Lewis, who in 1854 published an illustrated book Das Illustrirte Mississippi-thal. Courtesy, State Historical Society of Wisconsin

THE PIONEER ECONOMY

*A Norwegian family near Madison uses a
reaper to harvest wheat fields in about 1873.
Courtesy, State Historical Society
of Wisconsin*

An early photo of a log jam in Chippewa Falls in 1869 shows the dilemma loggers had when it came to unraveling the wooden gridlock. Courtesy, State Historical Society of Wisconsin.

During the years of frontier settlement, the Wisconsin economy took root in the growing wheat fields. "King Wheat," according to the *Prairie Farmer* in 1850, "pays debts, buys groceries, clothing, lands, and answers more emphatically the purposes of trade than any other crop." Even in the lead region of southwestern Wisconsin, farming gradually replaced mining.

Until the wheat belt moved westward in the late 1860s, Wisconsin was one of the nation's leading wheat producers. In 1860 farmers produced 29 million bushels of wheat, about one-sixth of the nation's total. Wheat, Wisconsin's great cash crop, commanded good prices at the Great Lakes ports. Wheat was also the ideal crop for pioneer farmers, who needed time to clear and break the land. It was easily sown and could be ignored until harvest. While the fields turned from tender green to burnished gold, the settlers could fence and build.

The problem for wheat farmers was in harvesting the crop. The basic tool, the scythe, was essentially unchanged since biblical times. The scythe was woe-

fully inadequate for large fields of wheat, which needed to be harvested within days, and gathered by hand into sheaves for storage before threshing. The farmer needed either a large workforce, which meant wages, or better tools for harvesting. During the 1840s Wisconsin inventors improved threshers and harvesters, laying the groundwork for Wisconsin's farm machine industry.

As lead mining began to decline around 1845, farming became the main occupation in Wisconsin. In 1850 the state had more than 40,000 farmers, the largest occupational group in a population of 305,000. Wheat was grown in all Wisconsin counties, with the southeastern and south-central counties being the largest producers. Oats and corn were grown for livestock and became major crops, particularly in the southwestern region. By 1840 potatos became a crop for domestic use, and by 1850 the potato yield would exceed 1.4 million bushels. Settlers continued the Indian tradition of producing maple syrup, and in 1839 more than 135,000 pounds were produced. By 1850 more than 600,000 pounds of maple syrup reached the market, coming from all but eight counties.

Location was one of the pioneer farmer's primary concerns in roadless Wisconsin. "Strangers looking for a home ought to look more to location and proximity to market than to the price," advised guidebook writer John Gregory in 1855. The best lands had a combination of forest and prairie. The woods supplied lumber for barns and fences, while the prairie was broken for crops. Forested lands were usually less expensive because the land had to first be cleared of trees and stumps. By 1850 prices for land ranged from $3 to $30 per acre based on proximity to markets and the amount of settlement on the land.

GROWTH OF EARLY INDUSTRIES

In frontier Wisconsin, business and industry were spurred by a growing population and an abundance of natural resources that didn't require large capital to exploit. Wisconsin's population more than doubled from 305,000 in 1850 to 776,000 in 1860. Settlers clustered largely in the southern counties, the sites of early manufacturing. In 1860 the counties lying south and east of Green Bay contained more than 82 percent of the state's 776,000 population and produced more than 83 percent of the $11 million in goods.

Processing raw materials, specifically wheat and lumber, dominated Wisconsin's early manufacturing. In 1850 flour and lumber mills contributed about 40 percent of manufacturing, with flour surpassing lumber. A decade later, lumber and flour would continue to dominate with 42 percent, with lumber exceeding flour milling. The average firm employed fewer than five men.

As a major industry, flour and grist mills were a natural extension of Wisconsin's bounty in wheat and water power. Every village located on a stream with enough power to turn a water wheel boasted a flour mill. Milwaukee and Racine, which emerged early as flour milling centers, drew on three advantages: water power, access to the wheat crops, and harbors that served as ports to the larger markets. Inland counties could also build markets from the local wheat fields. Jefferson County in south-central Wisconsin was in the wheat belt, and towns such as Watertown and Jefferson had thriving flour mills.

During the 1850s flour milling would gradually centralize in Milwaukee and the lower Fox River Valley, as wheat farming moved north and railroads connected Milwaukee across the state. By 1860 the villages of Neenah and Menasha would produce 50,000 barrels of flour, ranking second to Milwaukee. Wheat flour in 1860 accounted for almost 19 percent of Wisconsin's manufacturing.

The thick forests of northern Wisconsin, ribboned with rivers and streams, were a haven for Wisconsin's early lumberjacks. This was the land carved by the Ice Age. The glaciers which had formed Wisconsin's lakes and streams also pulverized rocks into sand, the soil on which white pine thrives. Most of the forests belonged to the Indians, and during the 1830s, when fur trading and lead mining dominated, there was a scarcity of building materials in the settled regions of southern Wisconsin, as logging was done only on a small scale. When the first territorial capitol was built in 1836, the lumber was imported from Pennsylvania. Land treaties with the Indians in 1836 and 1837 opened the thick pine forests of northern Wisconsin, which became the domain of the loggers. The lumber industry, which soon superseded the fur trade and lead mining, was concentrated north of Manitowoc to Portage and upward to the St. Croix River. Before the arrival of the railroads the rivers of Wisconsin divided the state into six lumbering districts: Green Bay and Wolf River districts in the northeast, and Wisconsin, Black, Chippewa, and St. Croix districts in the northwest.

The prized wood was pine, and the forest that blanketed the northern three-fifths of Wisconsin was called the pinery even though there were mixed conifers and hardwood. White pine is a softwood that cuts easily and smoothly. It is strong for its weight, and resists rot because it's resinous. Pine was the carpenter's first choice in building houses. The treeless states of Illinois, Iowa, and the Great Plains were markets for Wisconsin pine sent down the Mississippi River. The annual production of Wisconsin lumber in 1853 was an estimated 200 million board feet.

In 1831 a Green Bay entrepreneur built a sawmill on the Wisconsin River, and by 1847 there were 24 sawmills on the Wisconsin River, plus 5 on the Chippewa River and 5 on the St. Croix River. The lumber industry was moving westward, and lumberjacks from Maine and other eastern states were following. A Maine congressman complained of "the stalwart sons

of Maine marching away by scores and hundreds to the piny woods of the Northwest." Wisconsin pioneer lumber barons—Philetus Sawyer of Vermont, Isaac Stephenson of New Brunswick and Orrin H. Ingram of New York—learned the business in the East.

Lumber towns now flourished in the region once prized by Indians and trappers for beaver. Chippewa County in northwestern Wisconsin, which had only 615 residents in 1850, had more than 10,000 settlers in 1860. In 1840 the Chippewa River Valley contained an estimated one-sixth of all white pine west of the Appalachians, which translated into a potential 20 billion board feet. Eau Claire County became one of the major lumber-processing regions, and the towns of Oshkosh, La Crosse, Eau Claire, Chippewa Falls, and Stillwater developed into important sawmilling centers.

URBAN GROWTH

By the time of statehood in 1848, Wisconsin had a constellation of five urban centers: Platteville, Janesville, Kenosha, Racine and Milwaukee. The growth of these towns, each of which boasted more than 2,500

Above
Flour mills were one of Wisconsin's pioneer industries, as Wisconsin was a leading wheat producer before the 1870s. Built in Green Lake Prairie, this flour- and gristmill was moved to Alto around 1896. Courtesy, State Historical Society of Wisconsin

Right
Between the Fox and Wisconsin rivers, Portage was historically a crossroads for travelers sojourning in Wisconsin. In 1829 Army Lieutenant Jefferson Davis wrote, "I and the file of soldiers who accompanied me were the first white men who ever passed over the country between the Portage of the Wisconsin and Fox rivers and the then village of Chicago." Courtesy, State Historical Society of Wisconsin

residents, reflected the growth of the state economy.
Platteville, like its rival Mineral Point, was built near
a rich lead lode close to the Mississippi River. Surrounded by timber and growing farm lands, Platteville
became a center for Grant County's manufacturing of
flour and sawmilling in addition to lead mining. Janesville, located on the Rock River in the heart of the
wheat belt, used its water power for mills, its roads
placing it between the bustling commercial center at
Racine and the southwestern lead mining region. Kenosha, originally named Southport by the New
Yorkers who settled it, competed to become a port
city in the 1840s for exporting wheat, lead, and
lumber. Nearby Racine, whose roads into the interior
connected it to the wheat belt, became the second largest manufacturing center after Milwaukee.

By 1850 Milwaukee had been transformed into
Wisconsin's urban center. Solomon Juneau's fur post
had grown from an Indian village to a metropolis of

*Artist L.E. Blair conveyed the feel-
ing of a frontier town in this
sketch of Dodgville in 1859,
which he drew for the State Highway Commission. Wisconsin's
first territorial governor, Henry
Dodge, settled on Indian territory south of what became the village of Dodgville in the late
1820s. Courtesy, State Historical Society of Wisconsin*

20,000. Commerce was the key to Milwaukee's initial growth, just as manufacturing was the key to its future. Its largely "wheat and hog" economy used rails and lake transport to ship wheat to the East and Canada's eastern market. With the trafficking in wheat, 14 flour mills sprang up in Milwaukee by 1860. During the Civil War, Milwaukee would become the largest flour-milling city in the West.

While primarily a commercial port city, Milwaukee was setting down roots of industry. By 1860 Milwaukee County contributed more than 27 percent of the state's nearly $30 million dollars in manufactured goods. As historian Margaret Walsh noted, diversification distinguished Milwaukee industries from those of other Wisconsin towns. While other sites depended on one industry, such as lumber in northern Wisconsin, Milwaukee had a broader base. In 1850 six industries contributed to half of Milwaukee's manufactured goods: flour milling, clothing, construction material, iron, furniture, and shoes. In 1860 five in-

Above
A county fair may have been the occasion for Janesville's crowded Court and Main streets in the late 1860s. Janesville was in Wisconsin's wheat belt and by 1870 had a population of 8,789. Courtesy, State Historical Society of Wisconsin

Right
By 1860 Oshkosh had a population of 6,100 and its economy was rapidly growing, thanks to its location on Lake Winnebago and the Wolf River basin. Lumbering and sawmilling were important industries. Courtesy, State Historical Society of Wisconsin

industries provided half the output in manufactured products: flour milling, iron products, clothing, liquors, and shoes. Yet despite Milwaukee's promise of large industry, in 1860 only 7.5 percent of Milwaukee's population engaged in manufacturing.

Building materials were a substantial part of Milwaukee's early growth during the 1840s. Brickmaking became an early specialty, and the famous yellow bricks from the city's clay beds gave Milwaukee the title of "the Cream City." By 1850 there were 11 brick yards employing 95 workers who produced more than 11 million bricks. Wood manufacturing was important to the city's economy, and planed pine lumber imported from northern Wisconsin was used throughout the city.

Milwaukee dominated Wisconsin's developing meat packing industry. Wisconsin farmers were raising about 160,000 hogs and 185,000 cattle in 1850, creating a foundation for meat packing. While problems with refrigeration kept meat packing small-scale and local, by 1860 Milwaukee was responsible for three-quarters of Wisconsin's meat packing. Milwau-

The New Yorkers who founded Kenosha originally named the port city "Southport" in 1841 because it was the southernmost natural harbor in Wisconsin. By 1860 Kenosha would boast a population of 4,000. Courtesy, State Historical Society of Wisconsin

GREAT RUSH AGAIN AT BONESTEEL'S

CHEAP CASH STORE,

Since they received their

NEW GOODS

At No. 187 East Water Street,

Where they are opening a large and choice selection of DRY GOODS AND GROCERIES, adapted expressly for the Western Trade, and solicit the attention of purchasers to the examination of their stock, as they would find it very much to their advantage in making their selection, both in regard to quality and price. Their stock is new, and selected with the greatest care, and bought at a time when there were many failures in the eastern cities, and while the prices of Goods of all descriptions were continually falling, therefore they can offer greater facilities in making selections, and be enabled to sell at less prices than those who keep a small stock and sell less goods.

Above
An ad in the first Directory of the City of Milwaukee, in 1847, featured an advertisement for a grocery store, Bonesteel's Cheap Cash Store. Courtesy, Milwaukee County Historical Society

Right
This 1856 bird's-eye view of Milwaukee emphasizes its port, one of the major reasons for its growth. Milwaukee's economy was based on commerce from its port to Eastern markets. Industries such as brewing, tanning, meat-packing, and manufacturing represented only 7.5 percent of Milwaukee's economy by 1860. Courtesy, State Historical Society of Wisconsin

kee exported meat northward to lumber camps and also to eastern markets, and as railroads connected the city to Wisconsin's hinterland, cattle and hogs could be shipped to Milwaukee alive for slaughtering. The tanning of leather goods, such as saddles and harnesses, was also an important processing industry, and Milwaukee had 13 tanneries by 1860.

The German art of brewing beer expanded rapidly in the 1850s, becoming Wisconsin's fourth leading industry in 1860. By 1855 more than 50,000 barrels were produced by 20 breweries. Two years later there were six more breweries, and the total output of beer jumped to 75,000 barrels. Much of the beer was consumed locally, but Milwaukee's brewers exported as many as 35,000 barrels to Chicago in 1857.

Capital, the fuel for manufacturing, was scarce in the frontier, forcing Milwaukee to export most of its raw materials instead of manufacturing products within the city. Milwaukee and towns throughout Wisconsin created their own markets for locally produced clothing, shoes, and furniture. These businesses

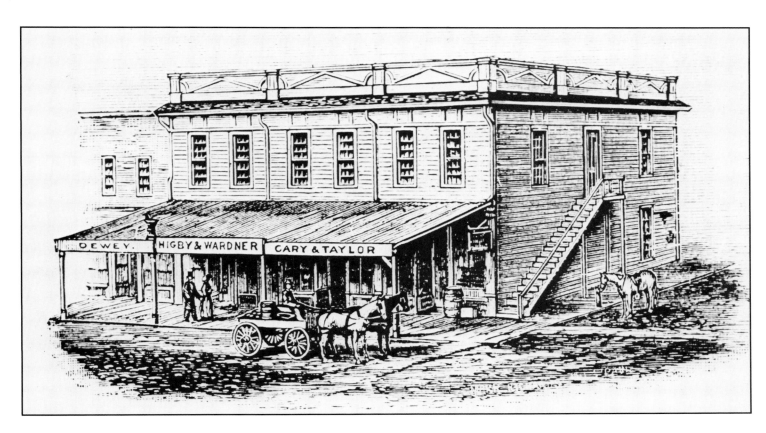

Above
The Milwaukee Sentinel re-
ported on pioneer life, and in
1848 it was the main customer
for Wisconsin's first paper mill.
The Milwaukee mill recycled
old rags for printing the news.
Courtesy, State Historical So-
ciety of Wisconsin

Right
Milwaukee's largest early German beer garden, the Milwaukee Garden, opened in 1855. Beer gardens were social centers for the German community where customs were preserved. Courtesy, Milwaukee County Historical Society

Below
A Jerome I. Case horse-powered threshing machine, produced in about 1850, enabled farmers to harvest their wheat fields quickly. Since wheat ripens all at once, harvesting became a critical time for pioneer farmers. Courtesy, State Historical Society of Wisconsin

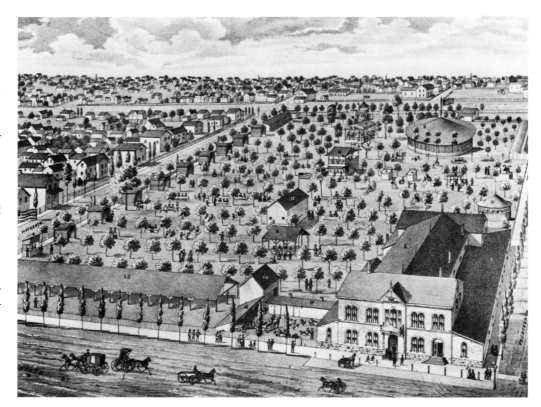

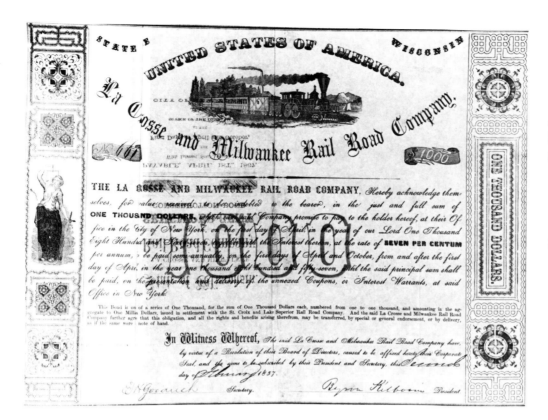

Left
From 1850 to 1857 railroads were built with the money raised by the sale of railroad stocks, as pictured here, throughout Wisconsin. Approximately 6,000 farmers mortgaged their farms in order to buy the stocks and build the railroads, but in 1857 a nationwide financial panic bankrupted every railroad in the state. Courtesy, Milwaukee County Historical Society.

developed on a small scale as family establishments. Despite a large population and promise of manufacturing, Milwaukee continued to import furniture, farm machines, wool, boots, harnesses, and stoves.

Wisconsin inventors revolutionized wheat harvesting. Jerome I. Case of Racine, who added a fan to help threshers separate grain from the outer chaff, built his own factory in 1847, producing a thresher with a two-horse tread power. Case's ten-horse sweep power threshers became the standard throughout the wheat-growing regions in the 1850s. The *Wisconsin Farmer* reported in 1850 that Case was building 100 threshing machines a year. By 1853 his market reached westward beyond the Mississippi. Case's company produced 300 threshing machines in 1860, 500 in 1865, and 1,300 in 1870.

Another Wisconsin inventor, George Esterly, produced what may have been the first successful American harvester in 1844. His Whitewater factory, built in 1857, produced reapers in Wisconsin until 1893, when Esterly decided Minneapolis was more centrally located to the railroads that served the wheat fields. Esterly is also credited with the invention of mowing machines and self-rake reapers, plus improved plows and seeders. In 1878, after years of tinkering, John Appleby of Walworth County devised the twine binder, which was adapted to harvesters to safely bind sheaves of wheat without hazardous wire. Other Wisconsin manufacturers, the Van Brunt Company

Above
Byron Kilbourn's first endeavor in Wisconsin was to develop Kilbourn Town on the west bank of the Milwaukee River in the 1830s. In 1851 Kilbourn built Milwaukee's first railroad, which ran between Milwaukee and Waukesha. Courtesy, State Historical Society of Wisconsin

of Horicon and the Rowell Company of Beaver Dam, each produced approximately 1,300 seeders by 1866.

Wisconsin's farm machinery and iron castings industries were already part of a westward regional market in 1860. These heavy-goods industries, accounting for almost 8 percent of the state's manufacturing in 1860, were the progenitors of the factory system in Wisconsin. However, growth in the Milwaukee-based iron industry, which produced castings and machinery, was slow because foundries required capital for machinery and labor.

RAILROADS COME TO WISCONSIN

Settlers, businessmen, and farmers all agreed that railroads were crucial to prosperity. In virtually roadless Wisconsin, a railroad could guarantee growth and commerce for any community. Citizens voted for revenue-raising bands in hopes of putting their town on the map. Farmers had the largest stake in rail transportation, for railroads could get their harvests to market. One historian estimated that an average harvest of 500 bushels of wheat for a Rock County farmer could require up to 20 round trips by wagon to Racine.

Milwaukee out-distanced its Wisconsin competitors in attracting railroads. Milwaukee rails stretched south to Chicago in 1855 and west to the Mississippi River. By 1860 the Milwaukee and Mississippi Company reached to Prairie du Chien and the La Crosse and Milwaukee Company reached to La Crosse. The Legislature granted charter to more than 100 railroad companies during the 1850s. A report from the Milwaukee Board of Trade observed that the proposed rails, "when laid upon the map make Wisconsin look like a spider's web." By 1860, as the Civil War broke, Wisconsin had 891 miles of railway.

Wisconsin's first rails were built in 1851 by Byron Kilbourn's company, optimistically named the Milwaukee and Mississippi. The cost was $550,000 and the tracks ran for only ten miles between Milwaukee and Waukesha when the project ran out of money. To continue Kilbourn's railroad, a Milton farmer proposed that farmers mortgage their farms in exchange for stock in the railroads. The company would sell the farmer's mortgages as collateral for its railroad bonds from eastern money markets. From 1850 to 1857 approximately 6,000 farmers mortgaged their farms, raising almost $5 million. The farmers, however, did not

know that their mortgages were sold in the East for 50 to 75 percent of their face value. The railroad promoters were not honest in their dealings with farmers, and this would have a serious impact after 1857.

Fraud riddled railway promotion. "In the history of the financial speculations of this country," said Wisconsin Governor Alexander Randall in 1861, "so bold, open, unblushing frauds, taking in a large body of men, were never perpetrated. There was, and is, no law to punish them; because such rascality could not have been anticipated." This statement was not political hyperbole. The previous governor, Coles Bashford, left for Arizona after receiving $50,000 worth of railroad bonds that Byron Kilbourn had given him. To win a charter for the La Crosse and Milwaukee Railroad, Kilbourn and Moses Strong had also bought 59 assemblymen, 13 senators, and a supreme court judge. There was a legislative investigation, but no one was punished. Kilbourn explained that competition with Chicago railroads necessitated the bribes. Kilbourn was perhaps the most flamboyant of the railroad promoters, but corruption and gross mismanagement plagued the building of all of Wisconsin's early railroads.

The railroads were riding on a gossamer of financial stability. In 1857 a nationwide panic was touched off by the failure of an eastern bank, the Ohio Life Insurance and Trust Company, causing a string of bank failures throughout the country. The Panic of 1857, which was followed by a depression, bankrupted every railroad in Wisconsin. The Milwaukee and Mississippi Railroad, for instance, carried a mortgage debt of $6 million in bonds and $3.5 million in capital stock. Revenue did not come close to what was needed to survive in a depression. In the reorganization that followed, railroad lines were consolidated despite cries of monopoly. One of the two future railroad giants, the Chicago and Northwestern, was organized in 1859. The other giant, the Milwaukee and St. Paul, was organized by Milwaukee's financier, Alexander Mitchell, in 1863.

By 1867 Alexander Mitchell had secured control of all the railroad lines running east and west from Wisconsin's lake ports to the Mississippi River, including the La Crosse and Milwaukee, the Milwaukee and Mississippi, and smaller lines such as the Milwaukee and Watertown and the Racine and Mississippi. The antimonopoly sentiment incited several incidents of antimonopoly sentiment incited several incidents of vandalism to tracks and bridges in 1865, prompting the Milwaukee and St. Paul to temporarily abandon running trains at night. To offset charges of monopoly, Mitchell pointed to his Chicago-based competitor, the Chicago and Northwestern, which ran north in Wisconsin. Mitchell's supporters preferred a monopoly based in Milwaukee rather than an outsider's financial control of rails in Wisconsin.

The railroads' bankruptcy was a calamity for Wisconsin's farmers. The farmers who had sold their mortgages to finance the railroads were left holding worthless stock, and they began receiving foreclosure notices from strangers out East. The farmers felt swindled. Governor Randall voiced their sentiment when he declared in 1861, "The railroad mortgages were conceived in fraud, executed in fraud, and sold or transferred in fraud."

A political solution to the farmers' dilemma was sought. Legislators abandoned the idea of the state assuming the farmers' debt because it would have required a state constitutional amendment. Instead the Legislature enacted stay-of-execution laws that released the farmer from debt if he could prove fraud in the contract. However, as one economic historian has pointed out, in most cases the eastern investors were innocent third parties who were unaware of the fraudulent representations of the railroad agent. Nevertheless, from 1858 to 1863 the Legislature passed 14 separate measures that released farmers, outraging the eastern investors. The state Supreme Court ruled these laws unconstitutional in 1860 and again in 1862. Many perplexed mortgageholders compromised with the farmers, but investors became less willing to support ventures in Wisconsin and capital grew even more scarce.

BANK REFORM

Wildcat banks that issued worthless paper money also discouraged capital. After banking became legal again in 1853, Wisconsin once more had problems with wildcat banking, the practice of issuing bank notes unsupported by assets. A feature of wildcat banking was having redemption centers in remote places. In less populated northern Wisconsin, there were up to 20 times more bank notes issued than around the populated areas of Milwaukee and Madison.

In 1858 45 state banks formed the Association of Banks of Wisconsin to encourage bank reform. With Alexander Mitchell as president, the association agreed that a central redemption center for bank notes was crucial. While nothing came of this resolution, a state law was ratified by voters in 1858 that required the state comptroller to issue bank notes only to banks doing business in towns of at least 200 voters. However, the state comptroller noted the existence of wildcat banks with no regular place of business as late as 1861. One bank, called the Bank of Green Bay, its name proudly bannered on its bank notes, was actually in La Crosse.

In April 1861 the Bankers' Association decided to weed out the wildcat banks, devising a blacklist of 37 banks whose discredited bank notes it refused to honor. With an eye to self-interest, the banks affiliated with the Bankers' Association immediately floated the unlucky bank notes from the blacklisted banks into their communities. Before the bank blacklist was published, however, an unusually high number of repudiated bank notes were placed in the pay envelopes of Milwaukee's labor force. Believing that their employees had been privy to inside information, angry German laborers marched to Alexander Mitchell's bank. Neither Mitchell nor the mayor of Milwaukee could appease the crowd and the two men exited, leaving four Civil War troops in training to control the crowd. A small bonfire was set to another bank's furniture, but the worthless bank notes might just as well have been tossed into the flames. Citizens were left holding worthless paper.

The ability to form a united front enabled the Bankers Association to police wildcat banking. In the fall of 1862, as business began to recover from the Panic of 1857, the Bankers Association watched for sound currency practices among new banks. Members of the association collected the bank notes of offending banks and sent the notes to Milwaukee. When a large number were collected, the notes were presented to the wildcat bank for redemption. Once the bank's assets were drained of hard currency, the remaining bank notes forced the bank to liquidate.

Despite these efforts at bank reform, the frontier economy was still considered a risk by big investors. Wisconsin's major manufacturing concentrated on the boom industries of processing lumber and wheat. The household industries such as furniture making

This sketch by Milwaukee Socialist Frederic Heath in 1897 depicts Milwaukee's bank riot of
1861. The riot was caused by
"wildcat" bank notes given to
workers in their pay envelopes
and found to be worthless. Courtesy, State Historical Society of
Wisconsin

and clothing were supported only by local markets. The promising industries of meat packing, farm machines, iron products, and brewing were constricted by elusive capital and credit. The railroads had failed to provide the panacea of easy transportation to reach new markets.

CIVIL WAR

As the Civil War broke, the frontier economy was still depressed from the Panic of 1857. Although recovery was rapid in the industrial East, growth in Wisconsin's economy was interrupted by the war, which stopped trade and commerce in the Mississippi River Valley. Immigration dropped, fewer than 100 corporations were chartered during the war, and only 130 miles of railroad tracks were built.

During the Civil War agriculture continued to dominate Wisconsin's economy. Half of Wisconsin's labor force were farmers or farm laborers, accounting for 125,000 of the 233,000 tabulated occupations. In

wheat production Wisconsin ranked second only to Illinois throughout the Civil War decade. From 1860 to 1865, Wisconsin's farmers grew 100 million bushels of wheat and exported about two-thirds of that yield.

Growth in the dominant industries of lumber and flour milling was at a standstill during the Civil War. Flour milling in Milwaukee produced more than 200,000 barrels in 1860 but output did not increase through 1865. Deprived of markets in the lower Mississippi River Valley, Wisconsin lumber was not in demand until about 1863, and prices continued to fluctuate throughout the decade.

Wood products, however, were boosted during the Civil War in the production of machine-made wooden shingles. Before 1860, German and Belgian shingle weavers in the northeastern counties fashioned shingles by hand from pine logs considered too remote in the forest to haul out. During the Civil War machine-sawed shingles became popular in Chicago, creating a market for the shingle-makers of Manitowoc and Green Bay who were close to the pineries and ports. Wisconsin became the largest shingle maker in the country by the end of the decade, producing more than 801 million shingles.

The trauma of sending young Wisconsin men to war was expressed by English novelist Anthony Trollope, who visited Camp Scott in Milwaukee during the summer of 1861: "Ten thousand men fit to bear arms carried away from such a land to the horrors of civil war is a sight as full of sadness as any on which the eye can rest." Wisconsin sent 96,000 soldiers to the Civil War; 12,216 did not return.

During the war women helped in traditional areas by making bandages and working in hospital care. However, women also entered into industry. The 1860 census records only 773 women employed in industry, but by 1870 the number had risen to 3,967. Over 360 women worked in sawmills, while others worked in light manufacturing.

The Civil War dramatically forced the spread of labor-saving farm equipment, even among those farmers who were suspicious of new fangled machines. The *Wisconsin State Journal* urged farmers to buy reapers since farm laborers, "the very bone and sinew of the harvest fields, will be called away to other fields of toil and danger." Every good reaper, the newspaper said, equaled five to ten men in the field. The Wisconsin State Agricultural Society reported that about 3,000 reapers were sold in 1860. At the beginning of the Civil War the J.I. Case company was one of the largest producers of threshers in the Northwest, selling 1,500 ten-horse threshers annually. By the end of the decade Case was one of the largest companies in the country.

Farmers responded to war-induced demands for particular crops. They grew African sorghum and Chinese imphee as substitutes for sugar cane from the South. In 1866 the *Wisconsin Farmer* reported that nearly one million gallons of sorghum were produced. However, the Wisconsin summer was simply too short for ripening the cane, and when the war ended Wisconsin could not compete with Ohio, Indiana, and Missouri in sorghum production. Beer became popular during the war and farmers responded by growing hops until the hop louse migrated from New York, plaguing Wisconsin farmers. With cotton shut out from the South, farmers experimented with flax until cotton came back after the war's end.

Clothing and feeding the Union soldier's helped to stimulate Wisconsin's economy. Wisconsin wool, with its coarse fleeces, was in special demand for the production of soldier's uniforms. Wool also replaced the North's need for cotton, and the prices continued to climb throughout the war, from 25 cents a pound in 1860 to more than one dollar a pound in 1864. By 1865 Wisconsin farmers produced more than four million pounds of wool from more than one million sheep. Wisconsin farmers looked eagerly to rivaling Ohio in the wool industry. However, peace brought back cotton, and prices for coarse wool plummeted to 29 cents a pound within two years.

The Union Army ate a diet of salted pork and beef, and this boded well for the meat packers of Milwaukee. As part of the wheat and hog economy of Milwaukee, meat packers processed 60,000 hogs in 1860 and more than 133,000 hogs in 1866. By the end of the decade Milwaukee was the fourth largest pork packing center in the country, with more than 313,000 hogs dressed for salting. Barreled pork, hams, and lard were sent to the East as well as to England. The tanneries, an extension of the meat packing industry, processed shoe leather for army boots and harnesses. In 1860 Milwaukee had 13 tanneries; by 1872 it was the largest tanning center in the West, with 30 tanneries producing more than $2.5 million in leather.

Beer became more popular during the Civil War, in part because Congress imposed a severe excise tax on whisky in an effort to raise revenue. As the tax on beer and ale was milder, Yankees discovered these beverages for the first time. The *Wisconsin Farmer* observed in 1868, "The taste for beer and ale, and the custom and fashion making it 'respectable' to drink it, is largely growing." By 1872 Milwaukee had become the largest beer-exporting center in the West, especially since Chicago's fire of 1871 had destroyed competitive breweries.

The Civil War did not industrialize Wisconsin, but it did encourage a few important industries that helped to diversify the state's economic base. From the days of settlement in the 1830s through the Civil War, Wisconsin's economy depended on extracting and processing natural resources. Lumbering would remain in Wisconsin, but the golden wheat fields were moving westward as Wisconsin soil became exhausted. Farmers eventually would rebound, but it would be a slow process.

NEW LIVES, NEW INDUSTRIES

The Joseph Schlitz brewery in Milwaukee was the third largest in the country in 1895, behind Pabst and Anheuser-Busch. Courtesy, the H.H. Bennett Studio

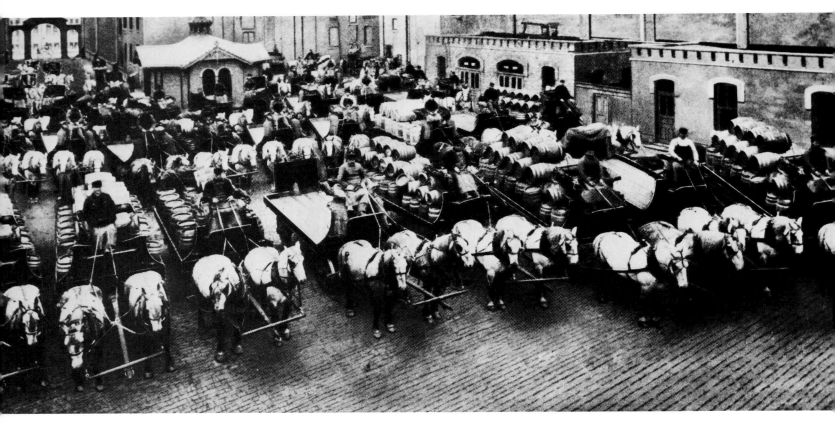

These brewery wagons lined up in the Pabst Brewery shipping yards around the turn of the century. Beer wagons were used to deliver barrels of beer to local taverns. Courtesy, Milwaukee Public Library

The younger son had returned to Germany to persuade the entire family to emigrate to America. He and his older brother were succeeding in Milwaukee, he told them. Their vinegar factory was prosperous. The younger son urged his father to move the family business to America. Times were bad in the Rhineland, but in Milwaukee 1843 had been a good year. Jacob Best, Sr., believed his sons were right, and in 1844 the family bought a factory in Milwaukee. However, the Jacob Best family business wasn't vinegar. It was beer. By 1892 their brewery would sell more than one million barrels of Pabst Blue Ribbon beer.

GERMAN BREWERIES DOMINATE WISCONSIN ECONOMY

No other ethnic culture had such a direct impact on Wisconsin's economy as did the Germans with their mastery of lager beer. Milwaukee's brewers, the first to export beer to a regional market, reigned nationally after German beer became one of the country's favorite beverages. The most spectacular growth of any Milwaukee business after the Civil War was in brewing lager beer, which by 1890 was the city's leading industry in both sales and money invested. In Wisconsin, German breweries remained family enterprises. As historian Thomas Cochran observed of the Jacob Best brewery, management was strictly a family affair, and disputes could be resolved at the family dinner table.

Jacob Best, one of the 38,000 German-born immigrants in Wisconsin in 1850, moved his family to Milwaukee primarily for financial reasons. But in a letter home to Germany in 1847, his son Philip described the political and religious freedoms found in the new land: "One beholds here how the farmer lives without worries, one seldom finds a farmer who doesn't have a newspaper in his house every week. In Germany no one knows how to appreciate the liberty to which every human being is entitled. Here officials and priests are dependent upon the people, and in Germany the people are dependent upon the officials and priests. The preacher's business is a poor trade here."

Until the mid-nineteenth century when Best and other Germans began immigrating to the United States, most American brewers were non-German. The predominant American beers, called common beer, were similar to the heavier British ales and porters. In the 1850s German brewmasters, who used a longer fermentation process, introduced a sparkling beer that was lighter than the quick-fermenting British ale. The Germans called their beer "lager" derived from the German verb lagern, meaning "to store." This light lager of German brewmasters grew in popularity after the Civil War, and by 1866 there were 216 breweries in Wisconsin.

Left
Wilhelm Strothman, Milwaukee's first German immigrant, arrived in 1835. By 1870 Milwaukee had the largest German population in the United States. Courtesy, Milwaukee Public Library

Below left
The old Plank Road Brewery in Milwaukee was purchased by Frederic Miller in 1855. He managed the brewery until his death in 1888. Courtesy, Milwaukee Public Library

Below
Frederic Miller bought the Plank Road Brewery in 1855 from Jacob Best's sons, Charles and Lorenz. Courtesy, Milwaukee County Historical Society

Milwaukee, the city made famous by its beer and advertising, listed 12 breweries in 1850. Jacob Best's brewery was the fourth largest, producing 2,500 barrels by its four employees. That same year Jacob's sons, Charles and Lorenz Best, had formed a partnership to establish the Plank Road Brewery, which produced 1,200 barrels in 1850.

In 1855 the Plank Road Brewery was sold to Frederic Miller, a German immigrant fresh from working in the Royal Brewery at Sigmaringen, Hohenzollern. On Miller's death in 1888, the Frederic Miller Brewing Company, managed by Miller's three sons and one son-in-law, was producing 80,000 barrels per year.

Milwaukee's beer production increased from 20,000 barrels to more than 100,000 barrels during the nationwide boom of the 1850s. Beer was a social product, and in German communities beer gardens flourished in breweries. Beer gardens were places where families could gather and enjoy free music, singing, and even theater. Besides providing social life, beer gardens introduced the immigrant to New World outlooks and customs.

By 1860 the four largest brewers in Milwaukee would be Charles Melms, Valentin Blatz, Phillip Best, and Joseph Schlitz. During the 1850s both Valentin Blatz and Joseph Schlitz had acquired an established

Above
The Blatz Brewing Company, a nineteenth-century pioneer in distributing beer nationally, marked its 50th anniversary in 1895. Courtesy, Milwaukee Public Library

Top
Milwaukee's Blatz Brewing Company sold beer in the 1870s to markets in New York, Boston, and Chicago. Courtesy, Milwaukee County Historical Society

brewery through marriage. Blatz married John Braun's widow in 1851 and merged with Milwaukee's second-largest brewery, becoming a leading pioneer in exporting bottled beer nationally. Milwaukee brewer August Krug had employed Schlitz for his brewery's bookkeeping. Upon Krug's death in 1856, Schlitz took over the brewery and two years later married Krug's widow, Anna. Krug's brewery was changed to the Joseph Schlitz Brewing Company in 1874, and the next year Joseph and Anna Schlitz drowned in a shipwreck during a voyage to Germany. The Schlitz Brewing Company was inherited by August Krug's nephews, August, Henry, Edward, and Alfred Uihlein.

Jacob Best, Sr., died in 1860, but like many Wisconsin breweries, his remained a family business. Jacob's son, Phillip Best, retired in 1866 and left the Best Brewing Company to the management of his son-in-law, steamer ship captain Fred Pabst, who had married Jacob Best's granddaughter Maria in 1862. Until his death in 1904, Fred Pabst steered Jacob Best's brewery to become a national producer of beer.

In 1869 Pabst bought the Charles Melms' brewery for $100,000 after Melms died. Pabst later acquired another competitor, the Falk, Jung and Bor-

chert Brewing Company, whose business operations were disrupted by fires. Historian Thomas Cochran observed that these bold decisions by Fred Pabst may have accounted for the continuing national leadership of the Best brewery, which by 1872 had become the second-largest national beer producer. In 1889 the Phillip Best Brewing Company's name was changed to the Pabst Brewing Company, by then the largest beer producer in the United States. With the name change came a new advertising slogan: "He drinks BEST who drinks PABST."

Other pioneer Milwaukee breweries included the Adam Gettelman Brewing Company and the Cream City Brewing Company. Begun in the 1850s, the Adam Gettelman Brewing Company was known for its "$1,000 Natural Process" beer and the $1,000 reward if anyone could disprove that the beer was made with pure malt and hops. The Miller Brewing Company would later buy the Gettelman family's brewery in 1961. The Cream City Brewing Company, founded in 1879, took its name from Milwaukee's acclaim as "the Cream City" built from pale yellow bricks. The

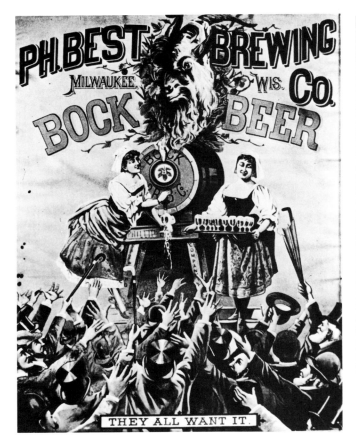

Above
An 1880s advertisement for the
Phillip Best Brewing Company
of Milwaukee, the forerunner of
the Pabst Brewing Company,
was for the brewery's bock beer,
a heavier and darker beer
traditionally made in the spring.
Bock is the German word for
goat, so the goat was used as a sym-
bol on many bock beer labels.
Although the origin of the word
bock is disputed, one explana-
tion says that the beer came
from Einbeck, Germany, in
about 1250. Courtesy, Milwau-
kee Public Library

Above right
An early ad for the Joseph
Schlitz Brewing Company
played on a slogan the company
used since the 1870s: "The beer
that made Milwaukee famous."
Courtesy, State Historical So-
ciety of Wisconsin

Left
In the late 1880s the Phillip Best Brewing Company in Milwaukee became the largest producer of beer in the country. In 1889 the brewery would be renamed the Pabst Brewing Company. Courtesy, the H.H. Bennett Studio

Facing page bottom
Frederick Pabst married the granddaughter of Jacob Best in 1862 and four years later took over the management of the Phillip Best Brewing Company. In 1889 the name of the brewery was changed to the Pabst Brewing Company. By then the brewery had become the largest producer of beer in the United States. Courtesy, Milwaukee County Historical Society

Cream City Brewing Company was operated by different groups until it closed in 1937.

Thomas Cochran suggests that Milwaukee's limited market spurred its brewers to export Milwaukee beer earlier and with more aggressiveness than other competitors. In 1870 Milwaukee had a population of only 70,000. In contrast, brewers in New York had a market of 1.4 million; in Philadelphia, 674,000; in St. Louis, 311,000; in Chicago, 299,000; and in Cincinnati, 216,000. The lack of a large local market may have pushed Milwaukee brewers into marketing their product in these more populous cities. By 1891 Milwaukee brewers were shipping 100 carloads of beer by rail daily.

Chicago was a prime market for Milwaukee beer. The Chicago Fire of 1871 destroyed many Chicago breweries, and Milwaukee brewers eagerly supplied Chicago with beer. Sales for Milwaukee brewers increased 44 percent in 1872, and production was up to nearly 192,000 barrels. After Chicago's fire Schlitz adopted its slogan, "Schlitz, the Beer That Made Milwaukee Famous." During the 1880s, the Anheuser-

Right
The ice business grew from the beer industry and also from Chicago and Milwaukee meat packing, which required several million tons of ice each year. Most ice harvesting was done on lakes closest to railroad lines. Courtesy Milwaukee Public Museum

Below right
Workers the bottling house in Milwaukee's Phillip Best Brewing Company cleaned, filled, and capped bottles. Demand for bottled beer increased during the 1880s as Milwaukee's brewers found ways to keep bottled beer from spoiling. Courtesy, Milwaukee Public Library

Busch Brewery of St. Louis would provide fierce competition in Chicago.

Competition among national brewers encouraged the development of labels, trademarks, and promotion. Pabst's "Blue Ribbon" label was promoted as early as 1892, when the company hand-tied more than 300,000 yards of blue silk ribbon around white bottles. A woman perched on a crescent moon became the symbol for the Miller Brewing Company in 1903. Brewers competed in fairs and world expositions. At the Paris World Exposition in 1878 the Phillip Best Brewing Company was awarded a gold medal along with Anheuser-Busch of St. Louis.

In 1895 Pabst, Schlitz, and Blatz ranked first, third, and seventh, respectively, in U.S. beer production, turning out a total of about 2.1 million barrels of beer. In 1900 the three brewers obtained court injunctions to stop New York brewers from advertising their eastern product as "Milwaukee beer," which enjoyed a national reputation for quality.

Milwaukee brewers were able to sustain a national market by solving the problems of transporting beer. Steaming tanks were used for heating the beer and pasteurizing it for better stability in shipping long distances by rail. They also developed techniques for large-scale bottling, which could guarantee larger markets in New York, Philadelphia, Kansas City, and New Orleans. German lager that remained sparkling in bottles was difficult to achieve. As the demand for bottled beer increased during the 1880s, the process became more mechanized to prevent bacteria contamination.

The first significant breakthrough in preventing early spoilage was the introduction of Goulding bottle-washing machines in 1884. Improvements on bottle-washing machines included the Birkholz-Theurer soak tanks, in which bottles were immersed overnight in a hot soda solution. Over 1,500 kinds of bottle stoppers competed in the bottling business, but the metal bottle cap was introduced in 1892 and later perfected.

As beer became big business, German businessmen won the respect of Milwaukee's Yankee business community. In 1865 Fred Pabst and Valentin Blatz were made members of the Milwaukee Chamber of Commerce. Charles Melms, the third-largest brewer in Milwaukee in 1865, had been the first German to be elected to the Chamber of Commerce in 1861.

The Pabst Brewing Company became one of the earliest American companies to develop a worldwide reputation for its beer. As early as 1888 Pabst was exporting several thousand quarts and pints of beer to Mexico, Australia, China, and South America. In 1893 Pabst shipped more than 600 barrels to Cuba. Until Prohibition in 1919, Pabst continued to emphasize its international market.

Successful German brewmasters outside of Milwaukee also founded breweries that have survived into the present time. Gottlieb Heileman had brewed beer in Wurttemberg, Germany before emigrating to Milwaukee. Although he was not hired as a brewmaster for the Pabst Brewing Company as he had hoped, he met his future wife Johanna Bantle, who was a domestic servant in the Pabst household. In 1858 Gottlieb Heileman became a partner with John Gund and began the City Brewery in La Crosse on the Mississippi River. The City Brewery was renamed the G. Heileman Brewing Company after John Gund left to form another brewery in 1872. Gottlieb Heileman died in 1878, and his wife Johanna headed the business until her death in 1917. When the G. Heileman Brewing Company was incorporated in 1890, Johanna Heileman became one of the first women presidents of a corporation in Wisconsin. In 1902 Johanna Heileman copyrighted Old Style Lager.

In 1867 Jacob Leinenkugel established the Spring Brewery in Chippewa Falls in northwestern Wisconsin. Leinenkugel's father, Matthias, had originally opened a brewery in Sauk City, after emigrating with his family from the Rhineland in Germany. Matthias Leinenkugel's five sons operated other Leinenkugel breweries in Wisconsin, including one in Baraboo and two in Eau Claire. In 1899 Jacob Leinenkugel's son and sons-in-law incorporated the Jacob Leinenkugel Brewing Company in Chippewa Falls. The brewery, which still promotes the fact that its water is from Big Eddy Springs, is headed by grandchildren and great-grandchildren of Jacob Leinenkugel.

The Joseph Huber Brewing Company of Monroe, in southern Wisconsin, traces its origins back to 1848. The brewery was run by different owners until Adam Blumer took over in 1891 and renamed it the Blumer Brewing Company. In 1927 the brewery hired Joseph Huber as its new brewmaster. Huber had moved from Bavaria in 1923 and worked for the Blatz Brewery. The brewery remained in the Blumer family

In the early 1900s German cooperage tradesmen made beer barrels for Milwaukee's Pabst Brewery. This turn-of-the century photo shows all stages of barrel making. Courtesy, Milwaukee Public Library

until 1947, when Joseph Huber acquired the stock of the business and renamed the brewery. The brewery remained in the Huber family until it was sold in 1985 to two former Pabst executives.

John Walter founded his brewery in Eau Claire in 1889. His brothers and their sons founded other plants throughout the state: the Geo. Walter Brewing Company of Appleton (1880-1972); the Walter Bros. Brewing Company of Menasha (1889-1956); and the West Bend Lithia Company of West Bend (1911-1972). There was also a Walter Brewing Company established in Pueblo, Colorado (1898-1975). John Walter's brewery of Eau Claire became Hibernia Brewing. Since its founding in the 1850s, the Stevens Point Beverage Company has had several German brewmasters among its many owners.

Beer was Wisconsin's third-largest industry in 1890, after lumber and flour milling. Beer production directly affected the industries of barrel making or cooperage, ice harvesting, brewery equipment, bottling, saloon furnishings, and shipping.

ICE HARVESTING

Wisconsin's brewers were the primary cause for the rise of Wisconsin's ice harvesting industry. A large natural resource in ice gave Wisconsin brewers year-round production and an advantage over other national brewers. However, Wisconsin brewers were not interested in harvesting ice; they preferred to contract separately for ice, which was used for beer production and shipping. Blocks of ice were cut and stored in large ice houses in breweries and near railroad depots. Along with Chicago and Milwaukee meat packers, Milwaukee brewers demanded several million tons of ice each year.

Ice harvesting thrived on lakes near railroads, which were the primary carriers of ice. Pewaukee Lake, because of its location just west of Milwaukee, became a prime center for ice harvesting. The primary ice carrier was the Chicago, Milwaukee and St. Paul Railroad, whose main line was 500 feet from Pewaukee Lake. In northeastern Wisconsin, on Lake Winnebago, ice was cut for railroad lines in Fond du Lac and Oshkosh. In south-central Wisconsin, Madison, built on four lakes and served by three major railroad lines, also attracted ice harvesters. Lakes Monona, Wingra, and Waubesa exported ice, while Lake Mendota was harvested primarily by local ice companies since it was farther away from the railroad lines.

Ice harvesting began to decline after 1900, when artificially made ice, using compressed liquid ammonia and local water, came into vogue. Refrigeration machinery businesses, such as Weisel and Vilter of Milwaukee, began selling machines to breweries, meat packing houses, and ice plants. Mechanical improvements eventually made artificially produced ice cheaper and safer than natural ice, which was dependent on winter's erratic chill.

Because of a tradition of apprenticeships in their homeland, Germans contributed more than beer to Wisconsin's economy. One specialty proved to be cigar making. The Herman Segnitz Cigar Manufacturing Company alone employed 700 men and women during the 1880s. By 1912 Milwaukee's city directory listed 217 cigar manufacturers, ranging from producers nestled in home attics to large halls.

One of the the many immigrants who fled Germany's turbulent politics after the revolution of 1848, Daniel Kusel, Sr., brought substantial gold with his family plus a solid background in tin and brass goods.

Kusel re-established himself in the tinware business in Watertown, according to historian Charles Wallman, and as a sideline began a hardware store. Kusel later helped to establish a Lutheran church and in 1864 a Lutheran seminary, now Northwestern College. Kusel's descendents continued the family business, which changed to sheet metal and later to the manufacturing of dairy supplies as the Kusel Equipment Company of Watertown.

"English Spoken Here," a common sign in German shops, was important in assimilating German businesses into the marketplace. German employees were also expected to be bilingual. This combination of trade skills and language assimilation helped German business owners reach a wider market than their German neighborhood. By 1900 Milwaukee businessman John Pritzlaff had built his hardware wholesale company into the third largest in the nation. Originally from Pomerania, Pritzlaff preferred German employees but assumed they spoke English, a normal expectation in Milwaukee.

Germans did business with each other, a built-in advantage when competing against Yankee businessmen. Ethnic loyalty could help a new business because the German market was so large in Milwaukee. By 1870 native Germans made up one-third of Milwaukee's 71,440 population. Although only 17 percent of Milwaukee's population was German-born by 1910, more than 50 percent of the city's 373,857 population identified with a German heritage.

TANNING

By 1872 Milwaukee had become the largest tanning center in the West with 30 tanneries, of which 70 percent were German-owned. Tanners exploited Wisconsin's abundance of hemlock bark, oak, and sumac, which were used as chief tanning agents. Leather tanneries, like breweries, tended to be family-run businesses, and nearly all the successful ones were owned and managed by German immigrants. Albert Trostel emigrated from Wurttemberg, Germany, and began his Milwaukee tannery in 1852. His two sons, Albert and Gustav, carried on the family business, which continues to the present time. August F. Gallun emigrated from Germany in 1854, and his family business continues to produce calfskin leather in Milwaukee. Similarly, Fred Vogel, Jr., and his family carried on the

Milwaukee business begun by his father, Fred Vogel, Sr.

In 1880 there were 73 tanneries throughout the state, employing 815 workers. A decade later there were only 38 tanneries, but the number of workers rose to 2,570. Milwaukee had 15 tanneries in 1890, but Kenosha, Fond du Lac, and Sheboygan were also centers for tanning. The Wisconsin Leather Company in Two Rivers built a national reputation for harness leather and shoe leather. Edward P. Allis, Milwaukee's biggest industrialist in the 1880s, was one of the early investors in George and William Allen's tannery, which claimed to be the largest tannery in the world in the 1870s.

Milwaukee tanners took advantage of their access to Chicago's meat packing industry. Chicago was the nation's hide market, and Milwaukee tanners could buy hides and process leather while still making a profit. By 1890 Milwaukee would be the world's largest producer of plain leather. In overall leather goods Milwaukee ranked fourth in the country, processing 622,456 hides.

The Pfister and Vogel Tannery of Milwaukee emerged as the giant in the field, employing more than 600 tanners in 1890. Guido Pfister and Fred Vogel emigrated from Wurttemberg, Germany, to Milwaukee in the 1840s. By 1857 they had merged their tanneries and combined their business strengths in producing and marketing leather. The reputation of Pfister and Vogel opened markets in New York and Pennsylvania, and by 1906 Pfister and Vogel had branches in Boston, New York, London, Paris, and Milan. Many other tanneries were later begun by former employees of Pfister and Vogel.

MEN'S CLOTHING

Men's clothing manufacturing was another industry in which German entrepreneurs in Milwaukee excelled; 70 percent of Milwaukee's manufacturers of men's garments were German in 1870. By 1890 clothing manufacturers employed the largest labor force in the city, including those who worked at home or in tailor shops. Milwaukee was fourth in the production of hosiery and knitted garments, the latter necessitated by the cold climate and outdoor occupations such as the lumber industry.

Many Jewish Germans who settled in Milwaukee

Right
An employee at Milwaukee's Pfister & Vogel tannery worked with calf skins. The leather-tanning industry was dominated by German immigrants, who had made Milwaukee the largest tanning center in the West by 1872. Courtesy, State Historical Society of Wisconsin

Left
In 1888 tanneries lined the Milwaukee River in Milwaukee. Courtesy, State Historical Society of Wisconsin

Below
This 1892 advertisement displayed Pfister & Vogel Tanneries in Milwaukee. Pfister & Vogel was a giant in Milwaukee's prosperous tanning industry and employed more than 600 tanners in 1890. Courtesy, Milwaukee Public Library

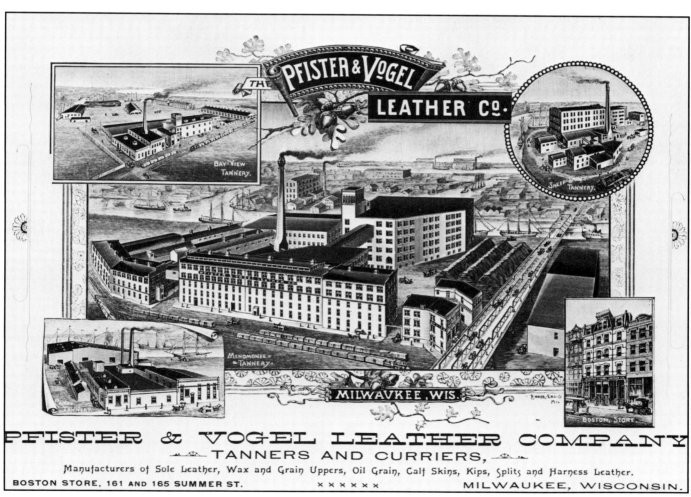

The German culture in Wisconsin was a ready market for the beer Wisconsin brewers produced. The Liederkranz singing society in Wausau in 1913 preserved the tradition of the German biergarten. Courtesy, State Historical Society of Wisconsin

became manufacturers of men's clothing. By 1880 the top three men's clothing manufacturers were owned by German and Austrian Jews, employing more than 1,400 employees. In 1847 Henry and Elias Friend, Jewish immigrants from Bavaria, began Friend Brothers, which by 1880 had become the largest Milwaukee manufacturer of men's clothing. The second-largest manufacturer, David Adler and Sons, was begun in Milwaukee during the 1850s by the Adler family, who were Jewish Austrians. Emanuel Silverman, the third-largest manufacturer in 1880, was a German Jew who had emigrated during the 1850s.

Milwaukee did not have the corner on successful clothing manufacturing. In Oshkosh, overalls would became a national symbol under the marketing of a company begun in 1895 as the Grove Manufacturing Company, and later changed to Oshkosh B' Gosh. In Sheboygan, H.J. Holman, a Russian tailor who had immigrated in 1890 made overalls in his house and delivered them to customers by horse and wagon. His 13-year-old son, George, was called "the knee pants salesman" because he also sold clothing in the family business, which later changed its name to Lakeland.

IMMIGRATION CONTINUES

Wisconsin's government actively welcomed immigrants. A commissioner was sent to New York City in 1852 to open an office that advertised the benefits of settling in the wilderness state, where there were ample opportunities fo people willing to clear the land and build towns. Wisconsin's office was maintained from 1867 to 1900, and its efforts to attract immigrants were successful. By 1870 two-thirds of Wisconsin's 1,054,670 population were immigrants and their children, half of them Germans.

Germans were keenly interested in all aspects of life in America, particularly Wisconsin and the Midwest. One book by Christian Ficker, published in 1853, was titled *Friendly Adviser for All Who Would Emigrate to America and Particularly Wisconsin*. Another book, *Hints for the Immigrant*, persuaded a German immigrant, William Rueping, to settle his leather tannery in Fond du Lac because it was "The Land of Paradise."

The influx of immigrants into Wisconsin continued, and by 1890 the foreign-born made up more than 30 percent of the state's 1,686,880 population, with Germans continuing to dominate. By 1895 there were 268,469 German-born, and 106,900 Scandinavian born. The Poles, who emigrated in large numbers during the 1890s, were more difficult to count since the country was divided among Germany, Russia, and Austria-Hungary. The census in 1900 counted 27,644 Polish or Slavic immigrants in Milwaukee County and 2,750 in Portage County in the center of the state.

The Norwegians were the earliest and largest group of Scandinavians to settle in Wisconsin. Indeed, by 1850, 70 percent of the Norwegians in the United States lived in Wisconsin. Norwegian immigrants tended to cluster into tight communities. By 1910 13,694 Norwegians in Dane County had settled in south-central Wisconsin; in western Wisconsin 7,795 Norwegians were living in Trempealeau County and almost 6,000 Norwegians in Vernon and La Crosse counties.

Over 68 percent of the Scandinavians arriving in the United States migrated to the Midwest. By 1910 there were 128,000 Norwegians, 48,000 Swedes, and 32,000 Danes in Wisconsin who were either foreign-

The Norwegians, and later the Swedes, were primarily farmers. Norwegians, who tended to be poorer than German immigrants, often were left with less favorable farmland. Nevertheless, historian Joseph Schafer credits the industrious Norwegians with building up Wisconsin agriculture. Norwegian farmers would become part of Wisconsin's dairy industry and also grew tobacco.

The British and Irish, who were also early immigrants, easily assimilated into Wisconsin's predominantly Yankee environment. The British, in particular the English and the Scottish, usually settled among the Yankees. While the Irish were the larger group with 50,000 in 1860, their numbers significantly declined

The Carl de Haas house in 1847, on Calumet Harbor in Lake Winnebago, became a familiar site to German immigrants. In 1848 De Haas wrote a two-volume book that was popular among German immigrants. It was called Nordamerica, Wisconsin Calumet, Winke fuer Auswanderer. *Courtesy, State Historical Society of Wisconsin*

born or children of foreign-born parents. Swedes settled primarily in northwestern Wisconsin from the Chippewa River basin north to Bayfield County. In 1910 the largest Danish settlement was in Racine County with 7,000. Danes also settled around Lake Winnebago in Oshkosh and Neenah.

Scandinavians tended to be parochial, preferring to isolate themselves into separate communities. English remained a foreign language to many Scandinavian immigrants. One Norwegian guide book warned that this could be a distinct disadvantage: "Before having learned the language fairly well, one must not expect to receive so large a daily or yearly wage as the nativeborn American."

thereafter. In 1850 Milwaukee's population was 14 percent Irish, but a decade later it was 7 percent and by 1890 it was down to 1.7 percent. The Irish were mobile and tended to be either small-town farmers, loggers, or urban laborers. Irish influence was felt in local and state politics, where they were devoted and savvy Democrats.

The Cornish settled primarily in the lead region in southwestern Wisconsin. In 1850 approximately 7,000 of the 27,000 British in Wisconsin were Cornish, most of whom came to mine lead. By 1850 4,319 Welsh had settled in Wisconsin, first settling in Racine and Waukesha counties and later moving northwest in search of cheaper farmland.

Above and top
At Stevens Point's Market Square, Polish immigrants buy food from farmers. Polish immigrants, who were the third-largest group to settle in Wisconsin, arrived in large numbers during the 1890s. They settled largely in the Stevens Point area and Milwaukee County. Courtesy, State Historical Society of Wisconsin

Right
Norwegians were the largest ethnic group in Stoughton. The Isham & Hale store suggests that business owners were still of German and Yankee heritages in 1890. Courtesy, State Historical Society of Wisconsin

In Wisconsin, particularly in Milwaukee, business leaders were most often Yankee, British, or German. These groups had considerable influence over jobs, since they owned or controlled key industries—metal, tanning, brewing, and meat packing. According to historian Gerd Korman, the Yankees, British, and Germans were the factory masters and foremen, and they hired and trained labor according to their ethnic preferences.

Polish immigrants, who began arriving in large numbers after 1880, were at the bottom of the job hierarchy. In Milwaukee they joined the ranks of the unskilled and semi-skilled laborers. Supervisory positions above the rank of assistant foreman were seldom accessible to Poles and other southern Europeans. The Pabst Brewing Company, for example, staffed most of its departments with Germans and reserved the most unskilled tasks in the bottling department to non-Germans, usually Polish women.

Polish workers were courted by other employers, however. In 1893 Irishman Patrick Cudahy, of the Cudahy meat-packing company, recruited 1,000 Polish workers to live and work in Cudahy's new industrial

suburb on Milwaukee's south side. He promised employment to Poles who bought land from him, and he gave land to the Catholic church's local Polish parish.

Although the largest settlements of Polish immigrants were in Stevens Point and on Milwaukee's south side, Poles also settled throughout Wisconsin, including the towns of Berlin, Menasha, Manitowoc, Beaver Dam, and La Crosse. Nearly one-third of Wisconsin's Poles were farmers.

Another central European group, the Bohemians from the Czech portion of Czechoslovakia, also settled in large numbers in Wisconsin. As with the Poles, the number of Bohemians is difficult to trace because they lacked national sovereignty at the time. Bohemians were usually counted as Austrians. By 1870 Bohemians had settled next to Milwaukee in Racine County and also in southwestern Wisconsin in Grant, Crawford, and Richland counties. In 1890 the census takers counted 11,999 Bohemians in Wisconsin, though these official figures are most likely short of the actual number.

Smaller groups of Swiss, Belgians, and Dutch formed farming communities in Wisconsin. By 1890 there were 7,000 Swiss-born in Wisconsin, concentrating primarily in southern Wisconsin in Green County's New Glarus. The Belgians clustered in northeastern Wisconsin around the Green Bay counties of Brown, Kewaunee, and Door. In 1860 there were 4,600 Belgian-born immigrants, and by 1910 there were 14,000 Wisconsin residents of Belgian parentage. The Dutch also settled in the Green Bay area and in nearby Sheboygan and Fond du Lac counties, where many grew barley. By 1910 there were 7,379 Dutchborn Wisconsin residents and 16,554 of Dutch parentage.

Wisconsin's population was on the move in the 1890s. The 1895 census revealed that one out of four Wisconsin-born residents moved outside the state, usually West. According to historian Joseph Schafer, Americans and Irish tended to leave Wisconsin more readily, taking profits in real estate ventures and land improvements. Business owners apparently were as mobile as the immigrants who searched for better farmland. In a study of Trempealeau County in western Wisconsin, historian Merle Curti concluded that 75 percent of business owners and professionals who were present in the 1870 census were missing from the 1880 census.

Immigrants who wanted to farm had fewer choices, as good land was only available further north. But the beauty of the land in central Wisconsin impressed one Scottish immigrant. Conservationist John Muir, whose family moved to Marquette County in 1849 when he was eleven, remembered "the sunny woods overlooking a flowery glacier meadow and a lake rimmed with white water-lillies . . . Oh, that glorious Wisconsin Wilderness!

IMMIGRANTS AND WISCONSIN POLITICS

As immigrants helped build industries and settle the wilderness, they also affected Wisconsin's politics. The political parties and Protestant Yankees had to contend with an emerging Catholic population. Close to half the Germans were Catholic, in addition to Catholic Irish, Poles, Bohemians, Swiss, and Belgians.

Anti-Catholic and anti-immigrant sentiment had found political expression in the nineteenth century, even in the more tolerant frontier states. During the 1850s, the nativist American Party, popularly called the Know-Nothings, advocated the exclusion of foreigners and Catholics from political office. During the height of nativism, a sermon delivered at Milwaukee's Plymouth Church in 1856 warned parishioners of great suffering if "we visit their dance-house on the Sabbath, saturate ourselves with their lager beer, and place ourselves . . . under the control of the Romanish Church."

Wisconsin had few collisions between nativists and immigrants, owing largely to the fact that the nativist was out-numbered in Wisconsin by nearly three to one in 1890. Wisconsin's ethnic community, however, did join together to fight the Bennett Law of 1889, a compulsory school law that decreed that reading, writing, arithmetic, and American history had to be taught in English. Germans saw the Bennett Law as a move to extinguish the German language; Catholics and Lutherans saw it as a threat to parochial education. Scandinavians, who usually voted Republican, allied with German Catholics and Lutherans to vote the Republicans out of office in 1890. The Republicans lost the governor's chair, the Legislature and all but one of the congressional districts. If anything else, the reaction to the Bennett Law notified party bosses about the swift fury of democracy.

V

THE AGE OF LUMBER AND METAL

East Water Street in Milwaukee circa 1890.
Courtesy, the H.H. Bennett Studio

The roar of log drives along Wisconsin rivers and the roar of blast furnaces in Wisconsin's cities were the sounds of prosperity in the nineteenth century. The state's industrial base was built on lumber and metal. In northern Wisconsin pines fell at a ferocious rate, and paper mills began to replace flour mills on the Fox River. In the southeast, Wisconsin's foundry workers forged iron and steel castings for an expanding market. No longer would Wisconsin be dependent primarily on wheat and flour. Lumbering, factories, and the dairy industry would establish an economic base that would carry Wisconsin into the modern economy of the twentieth century.

Lumber and flour milling, Wisconsin's pioneering industries since statehood, continued as Wisconsin's top two industries from 1870 to 1900. However, while the primary producers of lumber and wheat

The Reliance Iron Works was world renowned in the late nineteenth century for its production of heavy steam engines. Courtesy, the H.H. Bennett Studio

Left
One year after this Columbus Day parade was photographed in downtown Wausau, the United States economy was plunged into the panic of 1893. The worldwide depression that followed would slow business growth throughout the country. Courtesy, State Historical Society of Wisconsin

Below left
Wisconsin inventors contributed to machines of locomotion. John L. Holmes of Beloit invented this light farm tractor; however, it was never commercially produced. Courtesy, State Historical Society of Wisconsin

were moving further west, the state's producers of cheese and metal found markets that continued to expand. By 1910 metal castings and dairy products were, respectively, the second- and third-ranked industries in Wisconsin. In contrast, flour fell from second to sixth place among Wisconsin's industries and by 1920 lumber plummeted from first to seventh place.

Two business recessions slowed Wisconsin's industrialization. The Panic of 1873 was in part due to overextension of bank credit after the Civil War plus excessive speculation in stock market securities. In Wisconsin the panic touched off a depression that kept prices down for about six years. The Panic of

1893 was more severe, causing a worldwide depression. In Wisconsin 27 banks closed permanently, and many more banks closed temporarily. In Milwaukee George Smith and Alexander Mitchell's famous pioneer bank, the Wisconsin Marine and Fire Insurance Company, temporarily failed. The closing of Wisconsin's largest bank shocked residents and business leaders. Alexander Mitchell's son John and bank president John Johnston pledged their personal fortunes to reopen the bank six months later. Their bank survived to become the statewide Marine Banks of the Marine Corporation.

THE AGE OF INVENTION

The mid-nineteenth century was an age of invention. The U.S. Patent Office issued four times as many patents in the 1860s as it had since its inception in 1790. During the next two decades the number of patents doubled again. Many Wisconsin inventions were innovations of industrial machines such as Bruno Nordberg's poppet valve in the 1890s, which enabled heavy steam machines to attain constant speeds. Attracting many financial backers in Milwaukee, Nordberg ventured forth from E.P. Allis to rent space above another struggling foundry shop, Pawling and Harnischfeger. Both fledgling shops would grow into worldwide manufacturers of heavy machinery. In contrast, one

unpatented invention important to the dairy industry was first eaten in 1881 in Two Rivers. Edward Berner put chocolate syrup on ice cream for a low-priced dessert he reserved only for Sundays, later known as the sundae.

Another Wisconsin invention was inspired perhaps by Wisconsin's winters. Warren Johnson, a professor of natural science at Whitewater State College, grew tired of his classrooms that fluctuated from hot to cold. In 1883 he invented the all-electric thermostat, and in 1885 he founded Johnson Electric Service to market his invention. Johnson's curiosity led him to tinker with clock towers, invent puncture-proof tires, and build steam and electric trucks. By 1890, however, his thermostat had won renown from Germany to Spain and Moscow, and his company would become Johnson Controls, a worldwide marketer of temperature controls.

The typewriter was invented in Milwaukee by a former Kenosha newspaper editor, Christopher Latham Sholes. James Densmore, a friend and former Oshkosh newspaper editor, helped finance Sholes' invention, which went through several designs from 1868 to 1872. Densmore arranged for the gun factory of E. Remington & Sons of New York to produce typewriters, one of which was purchased by Mark Twain. The Panic of 1873 stymied sales, and Sholes, lacking confidence in the profitability of his invention, eventually sold his interest to Densmore. During the

1880s the typewriter became an office fixture. "Whatever I may have thought in the early days, of the value of the typewriter," said Sholes in 1888, "it is very obviously a blessing to mankind, and especially to womankind. I am very glad I had something to do with it."

Perhaps the most dramatic invention was electricity, evolving from Ben Franklin's rain-swept kite to Thomas Edison's incandescent lamp in 1879. In New York City on September 4, 1882, Edison switched on the first electrical power station. On September 30, Appleton businessmen, headed by paper manufacturer H.J. Rogers, turned on the second Edison power station. Driven by water, the Appleton station was the first hydroelectric plant in the country.

The electric light was a popular novelty in Wisconsin even before Edison had completed his power station. Civic leaders in downtown Oshkosh had lit the streets with electricity, and town boosters were proud of their new night life as residents strolled the streets beneath strings of lights. The *Appleton Post* reported that "the electric light is perfectly safe and convenient, and is destined to be the great illuminating agent of the near future." Daytime use was the key to profit for electricity companies. Electric streetcars would become one of the first daytime users. The first

Electric-powered streetcars, such as this 1890s Eau Claire streetcar, were one of the first daytime users of electricity. The first permanent electric-streetcar line in the nation was installed in Appleton in 1886. Courtesy, State Historical Society of Wisconsin

permanent streetcar lines in the nation were installed in Appleton and in Mobile, Alabama, in 1886.

In the mid-1880s more Wisconsin communities were exchanging gas light for incandescent lights. New utility companies entered the field, and local businesses brought electricity to their own towns. From 1887 to 1901 the Baker Manufacturing Company, a water pump and windmill manufacturer in south-central Wisconsin, supplied steam-generated electricity for the village of Evansville from dusk until 11 p.m. Throughout the state a number of electrical plants began as outgrowths of water-powered lumber mills and flour mills.

RAILROADS

Wisconsin's industrialization was fueled by heavy railroad construction. From 1872 to 1893 Wisconsin's railroads increased to nearly 6,000 miles of tracks. Wisconsin's initial 2,000 miles of tracks ran largely westward, connecting Milwaukee to Prairie du Chien and to La Crosse. After the Panic of 1857 bankrupted every railroad in the state, Milwaukee financier Alexander Mitchell stepped in to consolidate two major Wisconsin lines, the Chicago, Milwaukee and St. Paul Railroad, which ran primarily westward, and the Chicago and Northwestern Railroad, which ran primarily northward, connecting Janesville to Fond du Lac.

The flurry of construction after 1873 stretched Wisconsin's rails northward into the lumber towns. Many lumbermen and pine owners bought railroad stocks and bonds and encouraged local governments to vote financial aid. The West Wisconsin Railroad, popularly known as the Wisconsin Lumber Line, connected many of the pineries in the north with markets in Omaha. Although the Chicago and Northwestern bought a majority of its stock in 1882, the Wisconsin Lumber Line continued its separate existence.

Above right
The Chicago, Milwaukee &
St. Paul Railroad depot was pho-
tographed in Kilbourn City
(later named Wisconsin Dells).
In the 1880s tourists flocked to
this popular vacation region. Cour-
tesy, the H.H. Bennett Studio

Right
A sign near a railroad crossing
at Middleton, Wisconsin,
warned horse-drawn vehicles to
watch for railroad cars in 1883.
During the latter part of the nine-
teenth century, Wisconsin's
roads often were a combination
of mud and holes, incapable of con-
necting Wisconsin towns to the
outside business world. But be-
tween 1872 and 1893 Wiscon-
sin's railroads increased to
nearly 6,000 miles of track. Cour-
tesy, State Historical Society of
Wisconsin

The Wisconsin Central Line became another important railroad in 1877 when it completed a line from Milwaukee to Ashland, with branches to Green Bay and Portage. "Hurray for the cars of progress," was the sentiment expressed from Stevens Point as the Wisconsin Central Line first pulled into town. In 1875 Wisconsin Central built repair shops in Stevens Point, which for the next 25 years was a central stop for the line.

Railroads brought the rural populations such big-city advantages as commerce and industry, political campaigns in whistle-stop tours, and traveling theater troupes. Farm properties increased in value once the farm became accessible to an urban center. By 1890 Janesville was served by 30 trains daily, which was not unusual for cities in southern Wisconsin, according to historian Robert Nesbit. The placement of railroads was crucial to towns and businesses. When the Indiana railroads bypassed the town of Vincennes, one local department store owner and five of his brothers relocated to the boom town of Milwaukee. The family business they brought was Gimbel Brothers department store.

*Left
In 1887 the Milwaukee office of the Chicago, Milwaukee & St. Paul Railway Company was in the Alexander Mitchell building. Alexander Mitchell created the railroad company by combining a number of railroads that had become bankrupt in 1857. Courtesy, State Historical Society of Wisconsin*

The business district in Merrimac, Wisconsin, in Sauk County was little more than a few storefronts in 1890. Courtesy, State Historical Society of Wisconsin

WISCONSIN'S LUMBER BOOM

The railroads revolutionized Wisconsin's lumber industry. As historian Robert Fries observed, streams and rivers limited both the speed and quality of log transportation. Log jams were not a part of railroad transportation. But more strategically, railroads opened new markets for lumber. By 1870 much of the desirable timber had been stripped along Wisconsin's rivers. As railroads wound into Wisconsin's northern woods, trees far from rivers were no longer spared the ax. Rough logging railroads were built from remote timberlands to the main rail lines. By 1881 nearly two-thirds of the lumbermen along the pine-rich Chippewa River were shipping lumber by rail. By 1892 the railroads were carrying more lumber than the 3 million logs floated down the Chippewa River.

Chicago was Wisconsin's biggest customer for wholesale lumber during the 1870s and 1880s, receiving 85 percent of its lumber from Wisconsin and Michigan by way of Lake Michigan. As most of Wisconsin's eastern forests were exhausted by the 1890s, Chicago merchants looked to western Wisconsin for lumber, railroads overcoming the land barrier between Chicago and the Mississippi River.

Six lumber districts emerged from forests surrounding Wisconsin's main rivers. The two pineries of northeastern Wisconsin, Green Bay and the Wolf River, were Wisconsin's earliest sources of lumber be-cause of the older settlements. By the 1870s Oshkosh, "the Sawdust City," and Fond du Lac were considered old, established lumber towns. Railroads and closer markets spurred these towns to diversify in producing furniture, wagons, and doors. By 1890, however, the forests around the Wolf River were exhausted.

Four Wisconsin rivers became logging streams feeding into the Mississippi: the Wisconsin, winding down the center of the state; the Black, which joins the Mississippi just north of La Crosse; the Chippewa, which gave rise to Eau Claire and Chippewa Falls; and the St. Croix, which borders Minnesota. Enormous rafts of lumber the size of ten city blocks were not uncommon sights along the Mississippi River.

Along the Wisconsin River there were more than 100 sawmills by 1857, and the towns of Wisconsin Rapids, Stevens Point, and Wausau became early sawmill centers. The Wisconsin River district had an advantage because it had access to older settlements. As the Wisconsin River's many bends and rapids limited large-scale rafting, railroads became the main transportation in the district.

The Black River attracted lumberman Nathan Myrick, who founded La Crosse in 1841. By 1860 La Crosse had a population of 3,800, which doubled to 7,785 a decade later. The years between 1870 and 1890 were boom times for La Crosse as the lumber town grew to 25,000. In 1885 La Crosse, the state's

The Fox River had caused Green Bay to become the gateway to the Mississippi in the seventeenth century. In the nineteenth century the Fox River remained a prime waterway for Green Bay's pinery and diverse industries in paper, meat-packing, and agriculture. Courtesy, State Historical Society of Wisconsin

Above
The Wisconsin River had many dangerous passages, including the dam at Kilbourn, through which pilot Archie Young is shown maneuvering. Courtesy, the H.H. Bennett Studio

Right
Rafting pilots like Archie Smith, steered rafts that were divided into sections called "cribs" and measured 16 feet long. Cribs were then attached together to form strings or "rapids pieces" that were seven cribs long. Several of these rapids pieces could be connected to form a complete raft. Rafting pilots had to know every inch of the river, and their expertise was rewarded with wages of four dollars to $15 a day. Courtesy, the H.H. Bennett Studio

Above and left
Each raftsman built simple
wooden bunks for housing.
Blankets provided a little
warmth on cold mornings.
Courtesy, the H.H. Bennett
Studio

Above left
Another hazardous spot along
the Wisconsin River was The Nar-
rows at the Wisconsin Dells,
where turbulent water could
force rafts against the rocky
banks. Courtesy, the H.H.
Bennett Studio

Right
The Wisconsin River was famous for its shallow depths and shifting sandbars. When a raft would get lodged on a sandbar, the entire crew's effort would be required to extricate it. Courtesy, the H.H. Bennett Studio

Below right
H.H. Bennett titled this final rafting picture "Trip Finished." Early sawmills produced only rough lumber for river rafting, since water transportation damaged finished lumber. However, each sawmill had to weigh the risks of water damage against the extra profit gained from finished lumber. Water transportation, for all its dangers, was the cheapest transportation. Courtesy, the H.H. Bennett Studio

Below
These raftsmen take a drink after steering the raft oar, which required experience and strength. Courtesy, the H.H. Bennett Studio

The cook for H.H. Bennett's raft-ing photo story had an assist-ant, Bennett's son Ashley, who is the young man holding the ax. Courtesy, the H.H. Bennett Studio

largest producer of wooden shingles, and nearby Onalaska were sending out by rail an average of two million board feet of lumber weekly.

The Chippewa River, with its many tributaries, drains an area of about one-sixth the state. It extends north to within 25 miles of Lake Superior in Ashland County and reaches south to the Mississippi River above Lake Pepin where the French monarch, Louis XIV, was proclaimed king of the area in 1689. Of the lumber towns, Chippewa Falls was the chief sawmill town since 1836 when the first mill was built. By 1890 5 lumber companies in Eau Claire were producing about 20 to 40 million feet of lumber each year. The Chippewa valley timberlands contributed more than 500 million feet of lumber in 1885.

Loggers at Alma, Wisconsin, along the Mississippi River in 1890 needed to retrieve logs that had been stranded on a sandbar. The Mississippi River was a major highway for transporting Wisconsin logs to the treeless states of the Great Plains. Courtesy, State Historical Society of Wisconsin

Further north, the St. Croix River lumber district was largely held by Minnesota lumbermen, who had controlled access to the area's water power as early as 1837. On the Wisconsin side of the river the chief mill towns were St. Croix Falls, Hudson, and Prescott.

The lumber boom populated northern Wisconsin's towns and turned several lumbermen into tycoons. Orrin Ingram of Eau Claire made his fortune in the Chippewa Valley district. Philetus Sawyer of Oshkosh, who later became a U.S. senator, had also speculated in the Chippewa valley and was worth $4 to $5 million by the time he died in 1900. Isaac Stephenson of Marinette made millions in the Menominee River district.

Frederick Weyerhaeuser began his lumber empire in the Midwest, though he later became a far bigger giant in the Pacific Northwest. While in Wisconsin, he helped to settle the Beef Slough skirmishes during the 1870s. An inlet at the mouth of the pine-rich Chippewa River, the Beef Slough was used for storing and sorting logs for transport down the Mississippi River. Local lumbermen fought "outsiders" from the Mississippi River valley who attempted to control logging at the slough. Both groups tried to monopolize the slough through legislative charters. Arriving from Illinois in 1870, Weyerhaeuser sided with the Mississippi River lumbermen, overwhelming all

Above
Isaac Stephenson of Marinette became a multi-millionaire from lumber in the Menominee River district. He was later a financial supporter of Robert La Follette—in part because he wanted to become a U.S. senator, a goal he finally achieved in 1908. Courtesy, State Historical Society of Wisconsin

Above left
The Oshkosh lumber baron, Philetus Sawyer, was also a Republican party boss who became U.S. senator in 1881. Courtesy, State Historical Society of Wisconsin

Left
The United States' demand for lumber caused towns like Eau Claire to boom. Rafts of lumber lie in front of two mills that merged to become the Empire Lumber Co. Courtesy, State Historical Society of Wisconsin

competitors by the amount of capital he could pour into the lumber district. Weyerhaeuser later devised a log-sharing plan that regulated log cutting and transportation among his disgruntled Chippewa River valley competitors.

Wisconsin may have lost as many trees to fires as it did to lumberjacks. Loggers took only the choicest parts of trees while the remainder dried into kindling. Forest fires burned unchecked as people stood helpless to fight them. So great was the devastation from fires that historian Robert Fries suggested Wisconsin might have kept a thriving lumber industry if the forests' slash had been piled and carefully burned.

Between 1885 and 1891 fires destroyed more than $2 million worth of sawmills. In 1905 alone there were 1,435 fires in the northern counties of Wisconsin, creating a pall of smoke that impeded travel on Lake Michigan. On the same October night in 1871 that Chicago burned to the ground, Wisconsin had its deadliest fire. It swept through the drought-ravaged Peshtigo area, killing more than 1,000 people in a

Wisconsin Land & Lumber Company employees pose atop a pile of logs that scaled 13,562 board feet. Courtesy, State Historical Society of Wisconsin

These loggers in Barron County in northern Wisconsin used oxen to haul a load of white pine. Around 1900 it was more common for loggers to use horses for such hauling. The lumberjacks on top of the logs are shown with the canterhooks used to pull logs onto the piles. By 1900 the lumber industry, which had been Wisconsin's leading industry since territory days, was in decline. Courtesy, Milwaukee Public Library

swath 10 miles wide and 40 miles long. Over a half dozen counties were burned in the fire, and Peshtigo was razed.

Wisconsin's forests were a one-time resource. By the mid-1880s the lumber industry was moving westward to find untouched forests. Wisconsin's peak harvest was in 1892—more than four billion feet—but as the forests began to disappear, population growth in northern counties slowed dramatically. Ashland County had increased 1200 percent during the 1880s, but grew at only 9 percent during the 1890s. Eau Claire County, whose population had repeatedly doubled during the 1860s and 1870s, increased only 3 percent in the 1890s. The last log roll down the Chippewa River was in 1910. Weyerhaeuser's sawmill at Chippewa Falls, hailed as the "largest mill in the world," closed in 1911.

The lumber industry obliterated Wisconsin's pine forests, but not against the public's will. Wisconsin lumber built prairie homes throughout the treeless Great Plains. Wisconsin's northern counties were populated, railroads were finally built, and thousands of immigrants found ready jobs. At its peak from 1888 to 1893, the lumber industry paid one-fourth of all wages in Wisconsin.

The legendary Paul Bunyan had moved west. He was born in Maine, reached maturity in the Old Northwest that included Wisconsin, and he died on the Pacific Coast. But historian Richard Current points to the argument that Paul Bunyan is buried in

a grave near Wausau, Wisconsin. Paul Bunyan had a reputation for being a very large man, and the dirt on the grave piled pretty high. It formed Rib Mountain.

WOODWORKING AND PAPER MILLS

Even before the pineries disappeared, towns looked for industries to replace and augment the lumber trade. Woodworkers used Wisconsin's hardwood trees—maple, birch, oak—for a variety of new businesses. By the 1880s Oshkosh was already the country's biggest manufacturer of wooden doors, window sashes, blinds, matches, wagons, and carriages. Fond du Lac was known for iceboxes made from the hardwoods. Along Lake Michigan's ports rose the furniture-producing centers. During the 1890s Kenosha produced wooden beds, and Port Washington built swing rockers. Sheboygan manufactured so many wooden chairs that it became popularly known as Chair City.

Many present-day woodworking businesses began during the lumber era and show the diversity of the industry. The Richardson Brothers of Sheboygan Falls, which began as a sawmill business in 1848, expanded to include furniture making and remained a family-owned business. The Eggers Plywood Co. of Two Rivers was begun in 1848 by Fred Eggers, who emigrated from Germany and whose grist mill grew into a veneer and plywood manufacturing business. In 1883 Porter B. Yates began producing woodworking

POTATOES

PURE RYE
AND
BUCK
WHEAT FLOUR

ALWAYS ALL RIGHT !
H.E.M.EACHRON
PEARL
PATENT
COMPANY FLOUR KILN DRIED
GOLDEN
CORN MEAL
for Family Use
H.E.M'EACHRON Co.
GRAIN. HAY. FEED.

A

ELEVATOR.

The Cereal Mills Company and other mills called Wausau home by the turn of the century. Courtesy, State Historical Society of Wisconsin

machines such as the first successful drum sander. The Yates-American of Beloit continues to manufacture heavy woodworking machinery. In 1892 more than 30 residents of the agricultural community of Kiel formed a woodworking company to produce jobs. The Kiel Furniture Company was reorganized as the A.A. Laun Furniture Company in 1935. Begun as a community venture, A.A. Laun remains a family business. In Chippewa County in 1897, August Lotz of Boyd raised honey bees as a hobby, and he decided to use the abundant supply of basswood to manufacture wooden honey frames. Furniture parts are now the principal product of the August Lotz Company.

Wisconsin's paper industry did not emerge from the lumber trade. Wood was not a primary ingredient in papermaking until the 1890s, and by then the Fox River Valley had more than 25 paper mills alone. According to historian Maurice Branch, water power was the major factor for developing the paper industry among Great Lakes paper manufacturers during the pioneer days of papermaking, from 1834 to 1890.

Water provides the solution in which cellulose fibers form a mat which becomes paper once the water is removed.

Rags and straw were the primary ingredients for paper before 1890. These raw materials were usually in short supply for the demand, and even corn husks were considered a possible source. Clean cotton rags worked best because the yield was 91 percent cellulose, the stuff of paper.

Wisconsin's first paper mill, begun in Milwaukee in 1848, recycled old cotton rags for printing the *Milwaukee Sentinel and Gazette*. However, the paper industry quickly centered in the Fox River valley in central Wisconsin because of access to water power supplied by the Lake Winnebago reservoirs. Most of these mills developed from converted flour mills. Decreasing wheat yields in Outagamie and Brown counties, combined with the competition from Minneapolis mills, made papermaking attractive to mill owners of the Fox River valley.

In 1871 a German innovation reached Wisconsin that would eventually change the course of papermaking. Discovered in 1840, the groundwood process enabled papermakers to extract wood pulp for paper. Two Appleton businessmen began a groundwood pulp mill in 1871, using hemlock wood discarded by nearby lumber mills. Because wood such as hemlock, balsam, and spruce had to be ground first, it was not a popular choice over rags and straw until the 1890s. The sulphite process, which chemically converted wood into pulp, was introduced from Europe in 1884, but the import taxes for European sulphite discouraged growth until the 1900s.

As wood became an option for making paper, mills sprang up along the forested Wisconsin River valley and throughout northern Wisconsin. Wisconsin Rapids, Rhinelander, Tomahawk, Mosinee, and Merrill became paper mill towns. By 1910 Wisconsin would be ranked third as a national producer of paper, with 57 paper mills that employed 6,000.

FOUNDRY PRODUCTS AND HEAVY INDUSTRY

The success of one industry often spawned the demand and growth of later industries. Wisconsin foundry masters responded first to the needs of the flour and lumber industries, reflecting changing demands as Wisconsin's economy changed. During the 1850s one Beloit papermaker, Sereno Merrill, had trouble getting parts for his English-made machinery. In 1858 his brother Orson started a machine shop that specialized in repairing and making parts for his brother's papermaking machinery. As paper became an important industry, the company grew into the Beloit Corporation, which today is one of the largest manufacturers of custom-designed papermaking machines.

Agricultural machinery was one of the earliest products of Wisconsin foundries and metal workers. Entrepreneurs such as Jerome I. Case of Racine produced quality threshers for wheat farmers and later turned out steam-powered agricultural machines. By the 1900s the J.I. Case Company could proclaim, "There is not a spot in the civilized world where grain is grown that is not touched or cannot be quickly reached by the departments of our organization."

Lumber and saw milling required specialized machinery, and local foundry shops eagerly supplied the demands. Local newspapers and business leaders urged the public and business community to support new foundries. And as steam power transformed lumber and flour milling, steam engines became a Milwaukee specialty. Railroad construction also spurred new demands for iron products. Essential equipment such as rails, wheelbarrows, picks, and shovels could not be shipped economically from the East. Local manufacturers filled the orders.

From 1880 to 1910 the foundry and machine industries were Wisconsin's fastest-growing industries, outstripping brewing and even dairying. In 1880 foundry and machine shops ranked ninth among Wisconsin's industries; by 1890 they ranked fifth and at the turn of the century they had become the third-largest industry in Wisconsin. In 1910 foundry and machine shops ranked second in the state after the lumber industry, which would plummet to seventh place in the following decade. Clearly, Wisconsin's strength as a manufacturing state rested in the custom-designed engines and farm implements whose roots were present even during the early days of statehood.

Despite this industrial growth, Wisconsin was not blessed with conditions to become an industrial state. Wisconsin had no coal and would prove to have no petroleum or natural gas. The village of Oil City in southwestern Monroe County is a testimony to Wisconsinites' optimism that oil could eventually be

Above
The casting-room floor at Fair-banks, Morse and Company, a prominent Beloit manufacturing firm in 1890, was originally part of a facility producing wind-mills that was launched by a Con-gregational missionary in 1867. Courtesy, State Historical So-ciety of Wisconsin

Right
A Beloit minister invented a wind-mill in 1867 that he began manu-facturing as the Eclipse Wind En-gine Company of Beloit. A Vermont firm that made scales bought the windmill factory, and Beloit's Fairbanks, Morse and Company was launched as a large manufacturer. Courtesy, State Historical Society of Wisconsin

The North Chicago Rolling
Mills in the Bayview area of Milwaukee is pictured here in
1890. Courtesy, the H.H. Bennett Studio

This cartoon promotes the potentials of Superior in 1885. Its boosterism was backed by the brief boom in Wisconsin's iron mines and the boom in shipbuilding. Courtesy, State Historical Society of Wisconsin

found. But like the speculator's hoax that founded the city in 1866, hope soon evaporated, prompting the sentiment that "if God had designed Wisconsin to be chiefly a manufacturing state, instead of agricultural, he could have endowed her more richly for that purpose."

Wisconsin's iron mines in northern Ashland County enjoyed a brief boom in the 1880s, attracting John D. Rockefeller, who was in competition against steel masters Henry Frick and Andrew Carnegie. The village of Superior would swell from 2,700 to 44,000 people as the iron boom also gave rise to iron works and ship building. Rockefeller had acquired control of the American Steel Barge Company and an interest in Alexander McDougall's steel steamer ships, known as the whalebacks. This smooth-sailing ship also had the capacity to be used as a tanker for oil. Superior's 2,700 shipyard workers launched 27 whalebacks during the 1890s. Unfortunately, McDougall's whaleback became known as McDougall's folly after new technology made the whaleback's design obsolete for loading grain and cargoes.

Rockefeller returned to oil after losing in his bid to corner steel. Wisconsin's iron ores ran too deep and required more expensive mining methods. Superior's booming iron works disappeared although individual businesses such as the Lidgerwood Manufacturing Company, which has produced industrial hoists since 1873, managed to survive.

Wisconsin's shipwrights throughout the state returned to building wooden tugs, fishing boats, packets, and launches. For the most part Superior, Manitowoc, Sturgeon Bay, and Milwaukee shipyards would remain quiet until the twentieth century's two world wars stimulated new demand.

Milwaukee, and later southeastern Wisconsin, emerged as the state's center for foundry and heavy industry. While Milwaukee had no early advantages in power sources, it had access to iron, the essential raw material that was obtained first from Dodge County's Iron Ridge in the 1850s and later from eastern imports. With the advent of steam engines during the

E.P. Allis, the most successful foundry owner in Wisconsin during the 1880s, established the E.P. Allis Company, which made sawmill equipment and became world famous for producing heavy engines. In 1901 the company became Allis-Chalmers. Courtesy, State Historical Society of Wisconsin

1840s, coal became the main source of power for engines. Milwaukee was the chief benefactor of eastern coal because transporting the coal further west made the fuel very expensive for western Wisconsin foundries. Despite the expense of shipping, there were more than 30 foundries scattered throughout the state by 1880. Most towns seldom had more than one foundry; La Crosse and West Bend each had three. In contrast, Milwaukee had 17 foundries in 1880.

By 1880 Milwaukee had grown from a commercial port city into the country's fourteenth-largest manufacturing center, with a population of 115,587. By 1903 there were 53 foundries in Milwaukee, which had an industry-wide reputation for modern foundry equipment and progressive methods. Milwaukee founders produced some of the heaviest castings in foundry history. In 1907 Milwaukee boasted the two largest steel foundries in the country, the Falk Company and the George H. Smith Steel Casting Company.

Capital and entrepreneurial talent were the terms for survival in the foundry business, and inventiveness became the hallmark of Wisconsin's foundry masters. Adapting to the changing business climates was essential to makers of specialty machinery. John Bonnel's machine shop in Fond du Lac began as a small repair shop for local sawmills, but it continued to adapt its products to heavy-industry machine tools. Bonnel's shop grew into Giddings & Lewis, which would become one of the largest machine tool builders in the United States.

Milwaukee's most successful foundry owner, Edward P. Allis, had both imagination and access to capital, and his company would achieve national acclaim for the quality of its manufacturing in flour mills, lumber mills, and power engines. Yet when Allis entered the foundry business he knew nothing about it; his background had been in leather tanning and real estate. As historians have noted, his success was based upon a simple formula: find the men who could envision the highest state of the art and then provide them with the most modern equipment, enough money, and a free hand. Allis' factory buildings may have been flimsy, but inside no expense was spared on modern equipment and skilled personnel.

Allis escaped the Panic of 1857 unscathed—he had just sold his interest in his leather tannery. In 1861 he bought the Reliance Works and later one of his

*In the 1880s produce vendors
sold their goods wholesale in Milwaukee's North Broadway
market. Courtesy, Milwaukee
County Historical Society*

This advertisement attracted customers to John Plankinton's and Patrick Cudahy's large Milwaukee meat-packing company, the Plankinton Packing Company. In 1888, upon Plankinton's retirement, the company was taken over by brothers Patrick and John Cudahy. Courtesy, Milwaukee County Historical Society

ASK YOUR DEALER FOR

PLANKINTON'S

GLOBE BRAND OF

HAMS, BACON AND LARD,

Quality Unexcelled.

PUT UP ONLY BY

Plankinton Packing Co.,

Pork and Beef Packers,

MILWAUKEE, WIS.

leading competitors, the Bay State Iron Manufacturing Company of Milwaukee, which was twice the size of Allis' company. In the following decade consolidation and expansion forced Allis to overextend himself, and he would not escape the Panic of 1873. In 1876 Allis declared bankruptcy. His reputation as a community leader helped him through bankruptcy. His creditors, aware that he had one of Milwaukee's largest payrolls, settled his debts at a considerable discount and ensured that he would retain control of his company.

By the 1880s the Allis Company was the acknowledged giant in the field of sawmill equipment. Allis machinery had become the standard in the lumber industry. The steam engines produced by chief engineer and manager Edwin Reynolds were consistently innovative and reliable. The Reynolds-Corliss low-speed heavy engine would make the Allis Company world famous. By 1882 steam engines and pumping equipment accounted for about two-thirds of the company's sales.

As Milwaukee's largest industrialist, Allis was a risk taker who constantly expanded his company on borrowed money. When Allis died in 1889, his wisely invested life insurance policies helped absolve his debts in a company that employed nearly 1,500 workers. In 1901, the Edward P. Allis Company merged with Fraser & Chalmers Company of Chicago in order to expand production of more sophisticated engines with the advent of electricity.

As Wisconsin's only metropolitan city, Milwaukee was the leader of Wisconsin's industrial growth, contributing nearly one-half of the value of the state's manufacturing from 1870 to 1900. In contrast lumber, which contributed the majority of manufacturing, was widely dispersed throughout the state. Although most of Wisconsin's cities tended to be identified with only one or two industries, Milwaukee's industries had tremendous variety in their national markets, ranging from heavy machinery to frothy beer.

MEAT PACKING

Milwaukee's largest industry in 1880 was meat packing, adding $6 million worth of goods from seven companies. Meat packing had surged ahead of many industries during the Civil War. Salted pork and beef were shipped in barrels to Union troops by Milwaukee firms such as Plankinton and Armour, Layton and Company, and Van Kirk, McGeoch & Company.

Wisconsin's meat packers processed the hogs raised by Wisconsin farmers, who found that hogs were a perfect complement to the dairy business. The byproducts of cheese and butter—whey and buttermilk—provided a feast for portly pork bellies. Combined with dairy calves that were sold for veal, hogs helped Milwaukee to hold its own in the competition between regional meat packers.

One of Milwaukee's most flamboyant meat packers, Philip Armour, initiated a dramatic episode of speculation in pork bellies, according to historian Francis Bowman. Realizing the Civil War was drawing to a close in March of 1865, Armour convinced his partner, John Plankinton, that they should liquidate their entire stock of pork while the war prices were still high. Armour sold their pork barrels to eastern speculators for approximately $40 a barrel before the price plunged to $18 a barrel after peace was declared. Plankinton and Armour are reputed to have cleared $1.8 million from the wartime deal. Armour left Milwaukee eight years later to join Swift, Hammond and Morris in Chicago, which was growing into the meat packing center of the country.

Irishman Patrick Cudahy took Armour's place in the partnership of John Plankinton and Company. When Plankinton retired in 1888, the Cudahy brothers eventually gained control. In 1893 Patrick and John Cudahy moved their plant to their new suburban development south of Milwaukee called Cudahy. Meat packing continued to be among the top four industries in Milwaukee from 1880 to 1910, along with the Layton Company, the Peter McGeoch Company, and the Bodden Packing Company.

Although John Armour moved south to Chicago to continue his meat packing empire, one Chicago meat packer relocated north to make Madison the center of its operations. Oscar Mayer began making Bavarian-style sausages and Westphalian-style hams in Chicago in 1883. By 1900 the business had grown to 43 employees processing and selling meats throughout Chicago. His son, Oscar F. Mayer, expanded the family business in 1919 when he purchased a meat packing plant in Madison, which would grow into one of the largest and most efficient in the country. The company's headquarters were moved to Madison in 1957.

FAMILY BUSINESSES, HOUSEHOLD NAMES

Many family businesses begun in Wisconsin during the nineteenth century have survived into the twentieth century. In Janesville a teacher of telegraphy repaired his student's pens as a hobby. He felt he could make a better pen, and in 1892 George S. Parker's "Lucky Curve" debuted. In 1903 the company began its first overseas distributorship in Scandinavia; manufacturing plants later were started in European and South American countries. Parker Pen built an international reputation designing dependable and luxury-line pens before moving its headquarters to England in 1985.

Floor wax was the principal product of another family-owned business that became a household word. Johnson Wax began in 1886 when Samuel C. Johnson bought a parquet flooring company from his employer, the Racine Hardware Company. Two years later he was advertising paste wax for wooden floors in the major magazines of the day. The founder's son, Herbert Fisk Johnson, continued to emphasize advertising. "Our goal is to have the housewife so conscious of the superiority of our products," declared a Johnson Wax vice president, "that dealers need only give them a good display to have a profitable year-round business with them." During the 1920s Johnson's advertising budget reached $1 million.

John M. Kohler's foundry business in Sheboygan began producing J.I. Case's farm machines in 1880, but then branched off to produce kitchen sinks. In the following decades Kohler specialized in bathroom and kitchen designs. The Kohler family is distinctive for having produced two governors of the state, Walter J. Kohler, Sr., (1929-1931) and Walter J. Kohler, Jr., (1951-1957).

The Kohler Company is also well-known for its planned community, begun in 1900 when the company moved its factory four miles away from Sheboygan. The founder's son, Walter J. Kohler, Sr., had dreams of a garden-industrial community. In 1913 he and Milwaukee architect Richard Philipp traveled to Europe to study European cities. In England they met Sir Ebenezer Howard, a major promulgator of the theory that planned communities could avoid the congestion and slums of industrialized cities. When Kohler returned to Wisconsin he hired the Olmsted Brothers of Boston, who helped plan New York City's Central Park, and the first foundations were laid in 1917. The village differed from its European counterparts in that the Kohler employees owned their homes. The vision

110

of Walter J. Kohler, Sr., turned a large manufacturing plant into a gardened community. Perhaps English writer John Ruskin's observation, which hung in Kohler's office for 25 years, sums up the industrialists philosophy: "Life without labor is guilt, but labor without art is brutality."

Manufacturing had taken firm root in Wisconsin by the turn of the century. In 1900 there were approximately 16,000 manufacturing establishments in the state. Many of these manufacturers were isolated sawmills, but the number of companies with 100 or more employees had increased substantially during the 1880s and 1890s. In 1894 Wisconsin had 227 companies that employed more than 100 workers. The lure of success offered by business and industry inspired the growth of business schools. There were only two business schools listed in 1873; however, by the 1890s there were 20 business schools located in 14 communities. Milwaukee had six business schools, while Eau Claire had three and Janesville had two.

WISCONSIN'S BIG TOPS

For circus lovers, the world of private enterprise probably pales next to the dazzle of Wisconsin's early entertainment business. Baraboo and Delavan were both homes of the "Greatest Show on Earth." From Delavan, the earliest circus center, came the originators of the P.T. Barnum Circus, and from Baraboo rose the Ringling Brothers Circus.

In the late 1840s Ed and Jerry Mabie of New York brought their circus to their Delavan farm each winter. As the Mabies' circus grew, several employees, among them a bareback rider and an animal trainer, began their own circuses. Over the years 26 circuses were organized in Delavan and additional ones in other towns, including Portage, Beaver Dam, Watertown, Janesville, Burlington, Evansville, Whitewater, and Wonewoc.

Two Delavan circus owners, manager William Cameron Coup and clown Dan Castello, convinced Phineas T. Barnum, the world's greatest showman, to go into the circus business. P.T. Barnum, the discoverer of Tom Thumb, had never sponsored a traveling tent show. In 1871 Coup and Castello took Barnum's tent show on the road. It was Coup's idea to add a second

and third circus ring, and he set another precedent by having the circus travel by train in special railroad cars. In 1875 Barnum's decision to divide his circus into two traveling shows prompted Coup and Castello to leave. P.T. Barnum's circus was later managed by James A. Bailey, becoming Barnum & Bailey's "Greatest Show on Earth." W.C. Coup, the originator of Barnum's circus, died penniless in Florida, the owner of a dog and pony show. He is buried in Delavan.

The "World's Greatest Show" was born in Baraboo. Albrecht Ringling was the son of a harness maker from Germany, and he grew up watching traveling circuses as his family moved from Baraboo to Iowa, Prairie du Chien, and later back to Baraboo. During the 1870s Al Ringling learned to juggle and walk tightropes in a professional troupe. But his dream was to start a circus, and on May 19, 1884, Al Ringling's circus premiered in front of the Sauk County Jail in Baraboo.

Four of Al Ringling's seven brothers doubled as performers and Al's wife, Louise, was the snake charmer. Their first tour by wagon caravan took them to Black Earth, Mt. Horeb, Mt. Vernon, and New Glarus. "The boys are on the road to fortune," predicted the *Baraboo Republic* after the brothers' third year. The newspaper was right. In 1890 the Ringling Brothers Circus pulled out of Baraboo in 18 railroad cars. Five years later the three-ring circus opened in Chicago before touring major cities across North America. In 1907 the Ringling Brothers bought the Barnum & Bailey Circus from Bailey's widow for $410,000—a price earned back the following season.

The Ringling Brothers Circus continued to spend winters in Baraboo, the town Al Ringling loved, while the Barnum & Bailey circus headquartered in Bridgeport, Connecticut. Al Ringling died in 1916, and three years later the Ringling Brothers Circus train pulled out of Baraboo for the last time. The "Greatest Show on Earth" became the Ringling Brothers and Barnum & Bailey Combined Shows. In 1959 the State Historical Society of Wisconsin opened a museum to Baraboo's most glamorous business. The Circus World Museum is located on the same grounds that once housed the Ringling Brothers' winter quarters. The sound of noisy calliopes has not vanished.

This clever 1890s advertisement
for a tailor in Milwaukee employed a well-dressed boy, two
goats, and a wagon. Courtesy,
the H.H. Bennett Studio

AGRICULTURE IN AMERICA'S DAIRYLAND

Around 1890 a Milwaukee a farmers'
market provided city residents access to fresh
farm products. Courtesy, the H.H. Bennett
Studio

Cows, a cow governor, and a cow college brought Wisconsin's economy into the twentieth century. Wisconsin's dairy revolution built a modern industry based on science, marketing, and specialization. Dairying began fitfully in the 1870s, but by 1909 Wisconsin would produce almost half of the country's cheese and by 1919 almost two-thirds. The dairy farm would produce a pastoral industry that by the 1920s was Wisconsin's strongest manufacturer and the nation's largest producer of dairy products.

Wisconsin became America's Dairyland because farmers could find no other solution to the vanishing wheat fields. They had tried wool. They had tried flax and sugar. But these demands had been spurred by the Civil War. Once the South returned to the Union, these products were produced more cheaply elsewhere. Farmers had also planted hop fields, but they later watched helplessly as their crops were destroyed by the eastern hop louse.

In the 1870s, a vocal group of Yankees preached the advantages of dairying in stimulating Wisconsin's sagging agricultural economy. Wheat farmers were skeptical—cows could be as profitable as wheat? The acceptance of dairying by Wisconsin's farmers was a process of education and persuasion. "Speak to a cow as you would to a lady," advised Kenosha cheese maker W.C. White. This whimsical advice hid the difficulties facing the men and women who, within twenty years, would make dairying a Wisconsin specialty.

A loyal wheat farmer could easily object to becoming "tied to a cow." The pioneer's cow had been valued chiefly because she could produce oxen for breaking sod. If she provided milk beyond the needs of her calf, that was a happy coincidence. The job of a farmer was to grow crops; milking and butter making was considered "women's work."

Wheat had been the farmer's boom crop. Indian corn was usually the first crop the pioneer planted on his wilderness land. After breaking a few acres of sod the farmer would make ax-cuts at regular intervals, deposit a seed and step on it. "Sod corn," sometimes planted between stumps of freshly cut trees, gave the family ears of roasting corn and winter feed for oxen.

For years wheat had been the state's cash crop. "Wheat is king and Wisconsin is the center of the Empire," proclaimed the *Milwaukee Sentinel* in 1861. Yet poor soil management eventually robbed the soil of

In 1895 a promotional photo
showed a family who decided to
farm in northern Wisconsin.
The photo was included in a pamphlet, Northern Wisconsin: a
Handbook for the Home-
seeker, that promoted northern
Wisconsin's cutover region as
potentially good farmland. Courtesy, State Historical Society of
Wisconsin

nitrogen, and by the 1870s Wisconsin's wheat fields were moving westward. Alert farmers knew they had to diversify, but they resisted dairying, which required them to go into debt to buy cows and equipment. Moreover, dairy farming demanded a rigorous routine seven days a week, including holidays. Cows required milking twice a day, every day, in addition to feeding and attending them. In contrast, wheat farmers had the luxury of free time between planting and harvesting.

PIONEERS OF DAIRYING

The early leaders of dairying in Wisconsin were originally from New York. By 1850 New York produced 25 percent of the nation's butter and more than half of its cheese. Many New Yorkers who settled in Wisconsin brought with them the know-how for produc-

Above
In 1878 a rural cheese factory in the Village of Pipe on Lake Winnebago in Fond Du Lac County was an early member of an industry that would transform Wisconsin from a wheat-growing state to "America's Dairyland." Courtesy, State Historical Society of Wisconsin

Right
As the Seymour Brooks farm of 1873 in East Troy shows, not everything profitable in Wisconsin agriculture mooed. Brooks settled in East Troy in 1843 and became a breeder of cattle, sheep, and pigs. Courtesy, State Historical Society of Wisconsin

ing quality butter and cheese, skills that would help to solve the problem of marketing dairy products. The problems of pioneer dairy farmers were immense: the product was perishable, the work was seasonal, and the market was difficult to reach.

The first hurdle for Wisconsin's dairy industry was building a reputation for quality. Casual dairying was common, and the popular name for pioneer butter was "western grease," literally used as axle grease for wagons. In 1885 the publication *Prairie Farmer* illuminated the conditions of many butter-makers. Bad butter began with cows that slept in beds of manure and never knew the comforts of a brush and wash. Unclean hands would wet the teats with milk for milking, adding filth to the milk pail. Inside the house, pans of milk set out for the cream to rise shared the same space as muddy boots, family pets, wet laundry, and cooking smells. These odors became part of the butter that farm wives sold to grocers. Wholesome butter was also made, but the grocer didn't make distinctions and would combine the good butter with the inferior butter. Butter often turned rancid at the grocery store due to unclean containers and lack of refrigeration.

Butter was the most common way for farmers to market milk. Butter was easier to handle than fluid milk, and it was easy to make. Grocers traditionally accepted butter in exchange for groceries. Even with the rise of commercial creameries that offered fresh wholesome butter at higher prices, individual farms were the most common butter producers. By 1899 there would be more than 8,000 creameries in the United States, yet farms continued to produce more than two-thirds of the country's butter.

Cheese making, which required a steady supply of milk, equipment, storage space, and skill, separated the casual milk producer from the serious dairy farmer. The chemical processes involved in cheese making were still not understood. However if properly made, cheese lasted longer than butter and traveled farther in shipping. The cheese factory, pioneered in New York in 1851, improved the consistency and quality of cheese. As the milk producer concentrated on high-quality milk, the competent cheese maker divined the process of making consistent cheese. Due to bad roads and bumpy horse-drawn transportation, the cheese factory had to be close to the milk producer—a radius of not more than three miles. And in order to be economical the cheese factory needed at least 200 cows.

In 1872, recognizing the importance of dairying, seven industry pioneers met in Watertown in Jefferson County to form the Wisconsin Dairymen's Association. Their prospectus was ambitious: to improve dairy products and dairy herds; to develop markets and ways to reach those markets; and to build dairying into a permanent industry. The chief organizer, William Dempster Hoard, later became a governor of Wisconsin from 1889 to 1891. A fiery orator as well as a tireless campaigner for dairying, he is perhaps most

William Dempster Hoard was Wisconsin's governor from 1889 to 1891; however, he made his largest contribution to Wisconsin with his trailblazing leadership as a builder of Wisconsin's dairy industry. He was not a farmer but rather the editor of Hoard's Dairyman, *which campaigned for the scientific manufacturing of milk, cheese, and butter. Courtesy, State Historical Society of Wisconsin*

famous for his outstanding publication, *Hoard's Dairyman*, which he started in 1885 and which reached a circulation of 70,000 by World War I.

Though not a farmer, W.D. Hoard understood the problems besetting dairying's latent industry. Hoard never tired of promoting scientific, businesslike dairying, advising farmers to specialize in milk products, not to diversify with other agriculture. Hoard, "the cow candidate" who became governor in 1889, was defeated for re-election in 1891 largely due to the anger caused by the Bennett Law, which required that school children be taught only in English. Hoard misjudged the political climate, but he was a visionary in helping to transform Wisconsin's agriculture.

Wisconsin's white gold came from cows throughout the state. In Appleton on the Black Creek Road in 1915 a line of milk producers also marks the transition from horses to horseless carriages. Courtesy, State Historical Society of Wisconsin

One of Hoard's early campaigns was against the milk-and-beef cow. All a dual-purpose cow gave, he said, was "a little beef, a little milk and a little butter. The result is a cow whose main product is littleness all around." Gradually the beef cow disappeared from Wisconsin's dairy herds. At first the Jersey was the favorite milking breed; by 1900 the Holstein dominated, followed by the Guernsey.

Hoard experimented with alfalfa crops, a choice feed for cows, on his vacant lots in his hometown of Fort Atkinson. "Another of Hoard's notions," scoffed an agricultural expert, "alfalfa won't grow here." But Hoard was experimenting with a new yellow-flowered variety brought by Wendelin Grimm, a German immigrant, to Minnesota. Grimm's alfalfa, which thrived in Wisconsin's cold climate, not only fed the cows but also put nitrogen back into the soil that wheat had stolen.

In the 1870s dairying was still seasonal work because farmers had no way to feed milking cows during the winter. In 1879 French research on silage, the nutritious green winter feed that keeps cows milking year round, was translated into English and available to American farmers. One of the first Wisconsin silos, used for storing silage, was built by Fort Atkinson farmer Levi P. Gilbert. He built a pit six feet square

In 1929 this Plymouth, Wisconsin, cheese worker stirred Swiss cheese in copper kettles. Courtesy, State Historical Society of Wisconsin

and filled it with alternate layers of green cornstalks and rye straw. He reported that by using silage, three cows could be fed for what it had previously cost to feed one cow.

Despite well-publicized research by a few farmers and the state university, most farmers were very slow to accept silage. Farmers argued that silage would cause cattle to lose teeth, complicate calving, and eat away at the cow's stomach. As late as 1904, when Wisconsin was a leading dairy state, there were still only 716 silos. However, farmers eventually saw the advantages of silage, and by 1924 there were more than 100,000 silos, accounting for two-thirds of Wisconsin's farms. The silo had gradually taken flight from the ground to become the familiar tower.

CHEESE MAKING

While Wisconsin's farmers may have balked at silage, they were innovative when making cheese. Wisconsin's immigrants quickly introduced cheeses from the Old Country. Swiss and Limburger mingled on the market with the popular English cheddar. Two Wisconsin cheesemakers invented varieties from cheddar and Limburger. In Dodge County during the mid-1870s, Swiss immigrant John Jossi created Brick cheese, a milder version of Limburger. In 1885 Joseph Steinwald experimented with cheddar in the Black

River lumber district of Clark County. His new cheese, which was milder and moister, found an immediate market. He named this popular new cheese after his township, Colby, which had taken its name from the construction president who had built the Wisconsin Central railroad through the village. Gardner Colby's business was railroads, but his name graces one of Wisconsin's best-known cheeses.

Although the majority of Wisconsin's dairy farmers made butter in 1880, the state's industrialized dairies made cheese. By 1888 cheese manufacturing was largely concentrated in three counties: Sheboygan, Jefferson, and Green. Sheboygan County had 87 factories, Green County, 47; and Jefferson County, 36. The next three ranking counties were Walworth, Manitowoc, and Dodge. Sheboygan County built an early reputation for fine cheese, producing twice as much as its nearest rival.

Sheboygan County's newspaper reflected the importance of cheese making in that area. In 1882 the *Sheboygan County News* began a front-page column called "Dairy Notes." Beginning in 1886 the weekly printed on its masthead that it was "The Official Paper for the Dairy Interests." In 1901 the newspaper reflected the scope of its dairy coverage by changing its name to the *Sheboygan County News and Dairy Market Reporter*. The next year it dropped the first part of its name. By 1929 the *Dairy Market Reporter* alerted its audience of its final specialization by changing its name to *The Cheese Reporter,* which now publishes for the dairy industry from Madison.

A worthy rival to Sheboygan County was Jefferson County, which had developed commercial dairying before the Civil War. According to historian Eric Lampard, Jefferson County may have produced the first cooperative cheese factory. As early as 1870 a dozen farmers built a cheese factory two miles north of Lake Mills. One farmer was elected to manage the cheese maker, supplies, and accounting. Dividends were divided among the owners at the end of each year.

Green County, an enclave of Swiss immigrants, actually made very little Swiss cheese. Limburger, popular among German and Swiss, comprised half the county's total production, while Swiss cheese made up less than 10 percent. Since Green County never formed a board of trade, cheese did not become the export business that it was for Sheboygan and Jefferson counties.

To reach eastern buyers directly, the Wisconsin Dairymen's Association formed a dairy board of trade in 1872 in Watertown. They wanted to prevent middlemen from buying Wisconsin cheese and selling it as New York cheese, which kept Wisconsin from claiming its rightful reputation. In 1873 Sheboygan County, through its board of trade, began to develop a direct trade with the British and helped standardize methods of marketing.

MARKETING

Marketing was critical to pioneer cheese makers. Although Wisconsin cheese was cheaper than New York's, freight rates kept Wisconsin from being competitive. In 1874 the Wisconsin Dairymen's Association sent W.D. Hoard to Chicago to persuade the railroads to lower their rates. Hoard was successful in having the fees reduced by more than 50 percent, which allowed cheese to be shipped east on express cars in only one week. By 1880 more than 3,000 refrigerated freight cars carrying Wisconsin cheese shuttled between Chicago and the Eastern Seaboard.

England was Wisconsin's first large market, sparking the dairy revolution in Wisconsin. Cheese was regarded more as a relish in the United States, where meat was abundant. In contrast, the British considered cheese a substitute for meat. British tastes were

a salvation for American cheese makers, who during the 1870s exported nearly half their cheese to England. By 1881 national exports peaked at 148 million pounds of cheese.

The Wisconsin Dairymen's Association had achieved its goals in less than two decades. By 1890 the wheat fields had almost disappeared from Wisconsin and farmers had learned to specialize. Dairying was dominant in southern and eastern Wisconsin, and it was starting to penetrate the northern and western parts of Wisconsin. Dairy cows were replacing wheat fields, sheep, and steers. In 1890 there were more than 1,000 cheese and butter factories throughout the state.

Ironically, one of the biggest threats to cheese makers came from themselves. Across the country farmers were making skim-milk cheese and passing it off as whole-milk cheese. Also called "filled cheese," this product contained lard or oleo, which was added to replace the missing butterfat content. When very fresh it was difficult to distinguish filled cheese from whole-milk cheese. But filled cheese deteriorated very quickly, a fact that became apparent in exports. As farmers' profits rose, reputations fell. British exports fell during the 1880s as fast as they had risen in the 1870s.

In 1881 the Wisconsin Dairymen's Association pressured the state Legislature to pass a law requiring that filled cheese be properly labeled. But without enforcement powers, the law was an empty gesture. And Wisconsin filled cheese could be sold out of state and repackaged as whole-milk cheese from Wisconsin. In 1895 the Legislature prohibited the manufacture of filled cheese. Although the foreign market never recovered, the domestic market had risen to more than offset the loss of overseas trade.

For butter makers the menace of oleomargarine could not be solved through legislation. Invented by a Parisian chemist in 1867, oleomargarine was first made from a cow's udder. It tasted remarkably like the butter of the times and was cheaper. By the time the first U.S. patent was obtained in 1873, the recipe for margarine had changed. Improved oleomargarine was made from fresh sheep's stomach, ground parts of beef, carbonate of potash, milk, and water. By 1880 there were 15 oleo factories in the United States. The Wisconsin dairy commissioner reported that by 1890 four to five million pounds of oleo were sold annually in Wisconsin.

The butter maker's agitation was nationwide. In 1902 Congress passed the Oleomargarine Act, which taxed yellow-colored oleo at ten cents a pound. Dealers who mixed oleo with butter were designated manufacturers and required a manufacturing license that cost $600.

Oleomargarine sales tripled between 1904 and 1914. The public simply preferred oleo, which was becoming a more wholesome product. About 3.5 million pounds of oleo were sold in Wisconsin during 1910. Wisconsin butter makers reacted by making higher-quality butter under cleaner conditions, and Wisconsin had become the largest producer of creamery butter by 1910. Despite Wisconsin's reputation, butter sales declined nationally after World War I. In 1950 Congress repealed the Oleomargarine Act of 1902. Oleo, once a product of the stockyards, was a preferred product over more expensive butter.

Wisconsin dairies specialized in other uses for whole milk such as dried, condensed, and pasteurized

During the 1880s it was the partnership between dairy leaders and the scientists at the University of Wisconsin that built the reputation of the university's College of Agriculture. This partnership also built Wisconsin's reputation for consistently excellent dairy products. In 1906 the dean of the College of Agriculture, William A. Henry, said, "The Wisconsin State Dairymen's Association is the true parent of the Wisconsin College of Agriculture of today." Courtesy, State Historical Society of Wisconsin

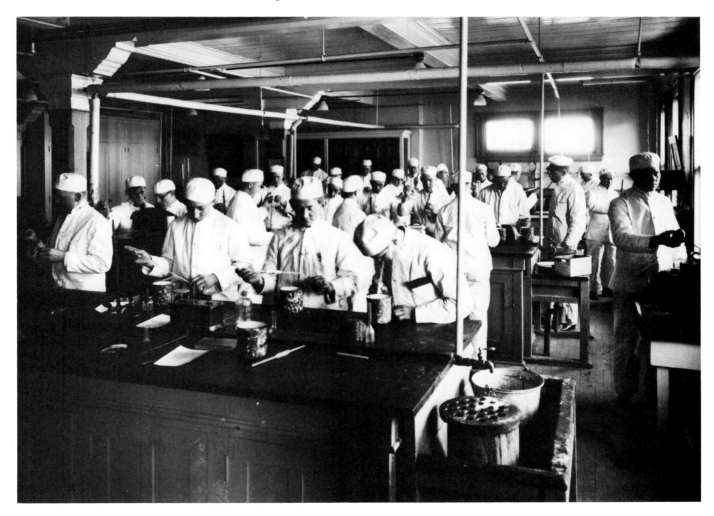

milk. In 1876 William Horlick of Racine combined dried milk with malted wheat in 1887, discovering a delicious beverage—malted milk. Horlick's Malted Milk Company later opened offices in New York City and his homeland, England. Wisconsin remained the principal home of Horlick's Malted Milk, but after World War II the English branch took control. Gail Borden opened Wisconsin's first condensery in Monroe in 1889. The New York company had 67 plants in the state by 1920, producing one-quarter of the country's condensed and evaporated milk.

AGRICULTURAL RESEARCH

During the growth of dairying Wisconsin had also become a world leader in agricultural science and nutrition. Like dairying, agricultural research had a fitful start. The College of Agriculture at the University of Wisconsin hired its first professor of agriculture in 1868; it graduated its first student 10 years later. The college had to wait another three years before its second student began school in 1881.

The dairy pioneers, who needed help in problem solving, rescued the university's program from a hostile Legislature, according to historian Robert Nesbit. In 1906, near the end of his career the dean of the College of Agriculture, William A. Henry called the Wisconsin State Dairymen's Association "the true parent of the Wisconsin College of Agriculture of today."

The detection of bovine tuberculosis was among the early scientific discoveries of the College of Agriculture and the Wisconsin Dairymen's Association. Unfortunately farmers were hostile to the tests for bovine tuberculosis because of the possibility of losing their prized herds if the tests proved positive. Pasteurization, introduced in the late 1890s, helped to prevent the spread of tuberculosis to humans, but it was not until after World War I that farmers were convinced the disease should be rooted out. U.S. pastures were not declared tuberculin-free until 1940.

The university's most famous contribution to dairying was the Babcock Test, which measures the quality of milk. Previous tests to determine the buttermilk content, which identifies high-quality milk from inferior milk, were laborious and required a chemist. The Babcock Test, which became world renowned, separated the butterfat without the aid of a

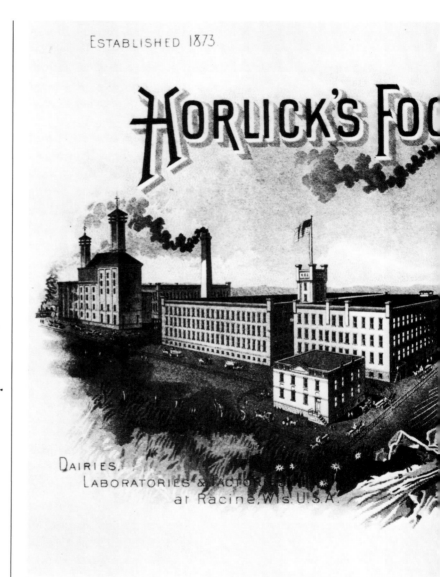

This 1890s letterhead represented Horlick's Food Company, maker of Horlick's malted milk. Malted milk was invented by William Horlick of Racine in 1887 when he combined dried milk with malted wheat. He eventually opened offices in New York City and in England, his homeland. Courtesy, State Historical Society of Wisconsin

University of Wisconsin Professor Stephen M. Babcock invented a device in 1890 that measured the butterfat content of milk. This test ensured high-quality dairy products, because milk could no longer be watered down before being sold. Babcock is shown here with his device, which he refused to patent. Courtesy, State Historical Society of Wisconsin

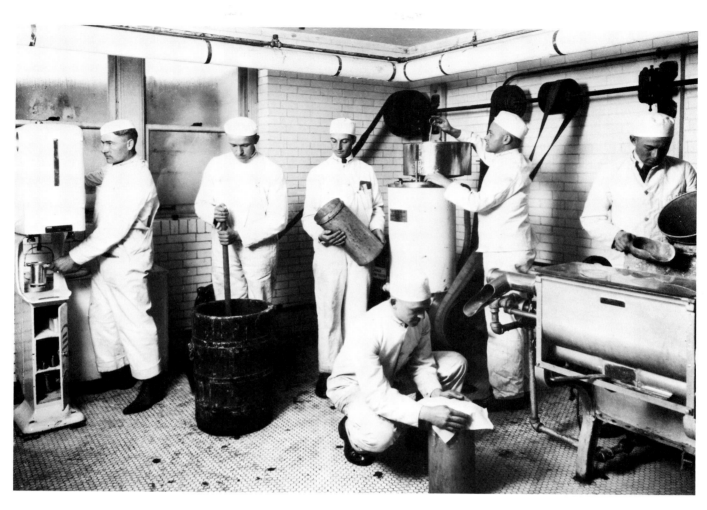

chemist.

In 1890 Professor Stephen M. Babcock discovered that sulphuric acid accurately separated butterfat from milk. When subjected to slight centrifugal force, the butterfat would gather at the neck of the gradient for easy measurement. The test, which Babcock refused to patent, was so simple and inexpensive that anyone could measure milk quality on location within five minutes. Farmers could no longer water down their milk without detection. Indeed, as one creamery owner stated, "the Babcock Test can beat the Bible in making a man honest."

In 1895 Babcock and his associates devised the "Wisconsin curd test," which measures the amount of casein in milk for cheese making. Along with Harry L. Russell, Babcock determined that this enzyme is responsible for the curing of cheese. Their experiments with curing, salting, and packing had direct results in raising the quality of Wisconsin cheese. From 1909 to 1911 Wisconsin cheese swept first, second, and third place in almost every class in the international

Students in dairying at the University of Wisconsin maintained Wisconsin's modern reputation for clean, wholesome dairy products. Courtesy, State Historical Society of Wisconsin

competitions held at the state fairs at Chicago and Milwaukee.

In his experiments with cows, Babcock realized that corn-fed cows thrived while cows fed on nothing but wheat did poorly. Some mysterious factor X accounted for the difference, he concluded. One of his assistants, Dr. Elmer V. McCollum, discovered the factor in his research analyzing milk—vitamins. He isolated vitamins A and B and later discovered vitamin D, which proved capable of curing and preventing rickets.

But vitamin D—the sunshine vitamin—was available primarily through cod liver oil, which was both expensive and bad tasting. Another of Babcock's associates, Harry Steenbock, discovered how to infuse foods with vitamin D by the simple process of ultraviolet irradiation. Now milk, cereals, bread, and oleo could be a source for preventing rickets.

Steenbock's discovery, worth millions of dollars, assured profits to fund future university research. In 1927 Steenbock sold the patent for $10 to the Wisconsin Alumni Research Foundation. Steenbock's patent earned the university $8 million in royalties by the time it expired in 1945. Among the new developments funded through Steenbock's patent were the hybridization of sweet corn, the stabilization of iodine in table salt, and the nutritional treatment of anemia and pellagra.

The catalyst in making dairying one of Wisconsin's most brilliant industries was the partnership between the Wisconsin Dairymen's Association and the University of Wisconsin. W.D. Hoard tended the growth of both. In 1907 he was appointed to the university's Board of Regents and later served as president of the board.

NONDAIRY AGRICULTURE

Not everything profitable in Wisconsin farming mooed and chewed cud. Many farmers grew hogs for the meat packing industry, as hogs conveniently guzzled the whey left over from cheese making or the buttermilk from butter. Hogs complemented dairying and corn growing in the southern counties. At the turn of the century feed crops, especially hay, rye, barley, and oats, were grown throughout Wisconsin. The College of Agriculture was developing hybrids of sweet corn that could grow in Wisconsin's short growing season.

Many farmers, including dairymen, grew peas, a good cash crop because of canning. Vegetable canning had become possible in 1874 when the first pressure

In Dodge County a German farm family poses for a portrait during their sorghum harvest of 1901. Courtesy, State Historical Society of Wisconsin

cooker appeared on the market. In 1887 Albert Landreth, a pea-seed dealer from Pennsylvania, set up a small canning plant in Manitowoc, where Dutch and German immigrants had been growing peas for years. Landreth persuaded the area's farmers to grow more acres of peas, and three years later he built another plant in Sheboygan.

Canning was still often a mystery, but Wisconsin canners improved the primitive process. In 1894, when cans of peas exploded in Landreth's warehouse, the green spray and stench inspired Landreth to seek help from the College of Agriculture's Harry L. Russell, who devised a chart of temperature, pressure, and exposure times for safe canning and sterilization. By 1900 there were 20 small canneries in the state canning peas, sweet corn, and other vegetables. Wisconsin became the largest pea-canning state in 1913, and five years later the war economy spurred more production.

Potatoes, cranberries, and tobacco became unique specialties in parts of Wisconsin. Potatoes were first grown on large scale in the central counties of Portage, Waupaca, and Waushara. Central Wisconsin also had bogs where cranberries grew wild. Summer fires were a hazard for cranberry farmers due to the peat in bogs, and early frosts were a danger in the fall. But profits were good enough for growers to overcome the difficulties of building up bogs. As cranberry growing stretched north into the central sand counties, Indians were hired for the labor-intensive picking. Wisconsin Indians also continued their centuries-old tradition of harvesting wild rice from glacial lakes and wetlands. Wild rice has since become a local Wisconsin specialty.

Tobacco was introduced by Norwegian farmers in southern Wisconsin around Edgerton and Stoughton and later west into Vernon and Crawford counties. Norwegians were indifferent to the Yankee bias that tobacco was immoral. Norwegians' large farm families were well-suited to raising tobacco, which was temperamental and needed careful cultivation. But it was a good cash crop due to the German cigar-making factories, and in 1885 farmers grew 27,000 acres.

Many immigrants from northern Europe recognized the quality of Wisconsin's soil. The Ice Age's glaciers had caused the variability of soil in both northern Europe and Wisconsin. The Old Country also had boulders, rocks, and fine glacial drift; Wisconsin's lakes and marshes resembled European homelands. The sheets of ice had been "God's great plough," according to Swiss naturalist Louis Agassiz, who in his 1876 book *Geological Sketches* first asserted that the glaciers made the land fit for agriculture.

Norwegians and their large families became associated with tobacco growing in Wisconsin, although it was not a tradition in Norway. Tobacco was a good cash crop, and this 1905 photograph of Norwegian farmers in Jefferson County shows the harvest. Courtesy, State Historical Society of Wisconsin

Above
Farm communities like Black Earth were still horse-and-wagon economies in 1909. Courtesy, State Historical Society of Wisconsin

Right
A Norwegian farmer proudly displays his grain fields, farmhouse, and barn in this 1875 photo taken in Dane County. Courtesy, State Historical Society of Wisconsin

Advertisements in the 1890s promoted the cutover lands of northern Wisconsin, an area of the state reduced to stumps by the lumber industry. Courtesy, State Historical Society of Wisconsin

THE CUTOVER

Northern Wisconsin's pine forests had been reduced to stumps by the lumberjacks. And although hardwoods would eventually rot, pine stumps remained rooted as bleak scars on the land. This land of stumps, called "the cutover," was considered by some to be potential farmland. If people could be persuaded to move north, there was a chance of turning the grim landscape into farms.

"There is no royal road to farming in northern Wisconsin," wrote Dean Henry of the College of Agriculture in 1896. His pamphlet, *Northern Wisconsin: A Handbook for the Homeseeker*, encouraged hard-working, industrious farm families to try their luck. It was not for the faint of heart, he warned, and he was right. Some farmers had to haul 20 wagonloads of rocks before a field was ready, and removing the stumps was a back-breaking undertaking. Since many pine stumps were impervious to even horse pulling, the College of Agriculture introduced the use of dynamite in 1912.

Land companies had eagerly bought land from the railroads and lumber companies in anticipation of a land boom in 1900. In their letters to prospective clients, many promoters divided sections of the cutover into districts with optimistic names: The Great Cheese Section, The Great Hay and Potato Belt, Land of the Big Red Clover. Unfortunately for the boosters, settlers did not create a land boom. Many immigrants arrived, including Finns, Lithuanians, Bohemians, and Swedes, but many others quickly departed, and those who stayed often faced foreclosure. By 1920 there were 20,000 new farms, mostly in the southern tier of the cutover, but several million acres of land were still stumps and swamps.

Farm colonization had proved a failure. The pioneer's maxim that "farming follows forests" was not true for northern Wisconsin. Although some of the soil was rich, the growing season was too short and the markets were too distant. The great tragedy of the cutover land, according to historian Lucille Kane, is that no one figured out in advance which sections of land were good farm land. By then years had been wasted trying to farm stump land that wasn't meant for diversified crop farming.

In 1929 the Legislature authorized each county to study land use for farm, forests, and recreation. By 1941 more than half the counties had adopted zoning ordinances for controlling rural land. The Forest Crop Law, passed in 1927, taxed tree growers ten cents per acre. Once the trees were cut the tax was 10 percent of the crop's value. Much of this revenue went to the tax-starved counties. Reforestation began with the federal purchases of national forests and parks. In 1925 the state authorized the federal government to buy 100,000 acres for forests that might one day draw visitors to the north.

Isolation was one of northern Wisconsin's greatest problems, however it wasn't confined to just the north. Throughout rural Wisconsin there were secluded farms and villages. Until radio began to connect these hamlets with outside culture, the county fair was the main forum for reaching isolated farmers. County fairs alerted farmers to new farming techniques. The county fair widened the agricultural world for farmers who did not read farm journals or belong to agricultural societies.

Exhibits, machinery displays, and livestock judging were small seminars for exchanging information beyond a farmer's neighbor. Starting in 1886 the state fair settled in Milwaukee, but county fairs continued to reach a larger farm audience.

From county fairs to Hoard's Dairyman, education was the key to lifting Wisconsin agriculture from its pioneer roots in wheat. The cooperation between farmer, scientist, and visionary created the dairy industry that Wisconsin has dominated for 100 years.

A stump-pulling machine is used to remove stumps from the ground in the cutover lands of northern Wisconsin on the Medford farm of Chris Paustenbach. The 1895 photo was included in a pamphlet, Northern Wisconsin: a Handbook for the Homeseeker, *that promoted northern Wisconsin's cutover region as potentially good farmland. Courtesy, State Historical Society of Wisconsin*

PROSPERITY AND PROGRESSIVISM

The Northwestern Mutual Life Insurance
Company building in Milwaukee was photographed in about 1890. The business,
founded in 1857, was the first
insurance company in Wisconsin. Courtesy,
the H.H. Bennett Studio

In 1910 workers posed in front
of the Milwaukee Harvester
Works, which had become part
of International Harvester in
1904. Courtesy, State Historical
Society of Wisconsin

In 1900 it was still the Victorian Age in England and
the age of Robber Barons in the United States. The
fury of industrialization had brought an admixture of
unparalleled wealth and sweatshop toil to nineteenth-
century America. But this era was passing, and Wisconsin would play a role in shaping the new century.
In 1900 a giant of the Progressive movement, Robert
La Follette, was elected Wisconsin's governor. In the
social reform that followed, Wisconsin would remain
competitive in an industrial society as it helped to re-
shape how society treated its workers. The Wisconsin
Idea emerged as a vague concept attached to concrete
changes such as workers compensation and university
involvement in government and industry.

Wisconsin had become a prosperous and diversified state by 1910, ranking eighth nationally in industrial wealth. Its leading industries—lumber, foundry,
and dairy—were equal in production value. Southeastern Wisconsin was becoming part of an industrial
belt with vigorous political activity. In 1910,

Milwaukee—a blend of progressivism, labor activity, and German and American socialism—elected Victor Berger the first Socialist to the U.S. House of Representatives.

Wisconsin's heavy machine industries followed the national trend of industrial consolidation, according to Richard Nesbit. Milwaukee's pioneer industry, E.P. Allis, merged with four companies in 1901 to form Allis-Chalmers, an international combine. In 1904 Milwaukee Harvester became part of International Harvester. The Milwaukee Iron Company became a U.S. Steel subsidiary. The Bucyrus Company was a combine put together by the Morgan syndicate in 1911.

The age of steam was giving way to electricity and the internal combustion engine. During the transition from steam to gas engines, Wisconsin maintained its success in building large engines for heavy machinery. By 1914 Wisconsin ranked first in the country in producing large steam and gas engines.

The change from steam to gas caused a reshuffling of the hierarchy at Allis-Chalmers, Milwaukee's largest producer of engines. According to historian Walter Peterson, as early as 1902 the board of direc-

tors at Allis-Chalmers acknowledged the need for making gas engines, especially steam turbines that produced low-cost electricity. However, chief engineer Edwin Reynolds still believed in the Reynolds-Corliss engine that he had invented in 1877. In 1904 Reynolds and Allis-Chalmers' president Charles Allis—who also supported the steam engine—were removed from their original positions, and the board of directors elected Benjamin Warren, who had worked with steam turbines at Westinghouse, as president. A year later Allis-Chalmers installed its first steam turbine in a utilities plant, and by 1906 gas engines comprised more than one-fifth of Allis-Chalmers' unfilled orders.

The gas engine revolutionized agricultural machines. Gas engines, and the hulking tractors they moved, were quickly accepted by farmers who needed power in muddy fields. The harvesting combine, which cut and threshed grain without a troop of hungry workers, also became commonplace. Charles Hart and Charles Parr, two mechanical engineering students from the University of Wisconsin, moved to Iowa to produce the "gasoline traction engine," the tractor they had designed. The Wisconsin manufactur-

The first automobile in Antigo, Wisconsin, got stuck in the mud in 1905. Wisconsin's roads in the early part of the twentieth century were generally dirt trails. The good-roads movement, which would begin in 1911, was aimed primarily at helping farmers' horse-drawn wagons. Courtesy, State Historical Society of Wisconsin

Although cars were not familiar sights on Wisconsin roads in 1901, Racine workers pave North Main Street with bricks. The pioneers' wooden plank roads had proved useless because they were slippery and rotted easily. A town's prosperity could be measured in its brick roads. Courtesy, State Historical Society of Wisconsin

ers that competed with Iowa's Hart-Parr Company included Allis-Chalmers, Milwaukee Harvester, the Van Brunt Seeder Company, and J.I. Case. The age of steam evanesced from the farm fields.

The symbol of the modern age was noisy, unreliable, and it gave a bumpy Sunday ride. Among the terms describing the horseless carriage were motor fly, electrobat, and oleolocomotive. Early cars were made from borrowed parts of steam engines, carriages, and bicycles. At the turn of the century there were simply no manufacturers of automobile parts. According to historian Victor Clark, the wide-scale manufacturing of bicycles trained many mechanics for the problem-solving of early horseless carriages.

THE HORSELESS CARRIAGE

The horseless carriages of the nineteenth century were crude toys built in the workshop. In 1873 a Racine physician, Dr. Carhart, built a steam buggy he called "the Spark." Two years later the Wisconsin Legislature, in an effort to find a "cheap and practical substitute" for horses, offered a $10,000 award to the winner of a race using public roads between Green Bay and Madison. The 1878 race attracted two hulking entries, both powered by steam engines. The Oshkosh entry was able to finish the course, but the Legislature

was disappointed in the performance, and awarded the winners only $5,000.

Wisconsin became an early center of horseless carriages. There was certainly a demand for cars, as Wisconsin granted 1,492 auto licenses in 1905, with the number increasing to 5,600 within three years. Not all car producers survived the early years of the industry. The Kunz Auto and Motor Company of Milwaukee produced cars from about 1902 to 1905. The inventor of the all-electric thermostat, Warren Johnson, produced steam and electric cars and trucks from 1901 until 1911. After Johnson's death his company concentrated on temperature controls.

The J.I. Case company deviated for a time from its threshers and tractors to produce touring cars and sports cars. J.I. Case acquired the Pierce Auto Company of Racine after the small car producer defaulted on a loan from Case. Case continued to manufacture Pierce's expensive, custom-made autos. However, J.I. Case's main customers, farmers, could not always afford the cars, which cost three times more than Ford's Model T.

Many Wisconsin businesses adapted quickly to the coming revolution of the auto industry. In Milwaukee Arthur Oliver Smith, who manufactured bicycle frames, added automobile frames to his line in 1903. In 1916 his son Lloyd began to design the automatic

The Kunz car was built in
1902 by the Kunz Auto and
Motor Company of Milwaukee,
which closed in 1905. Courtesy,
Milwaukee Public Library

The luxurious Mitchell touring car was made by the Mitchell-Lewis Motor Car Company of Racine and sold for $1,500 in 1908. The company began as a wagon maker in the nineteenth century. Courtesy, Milwaukee Public Library

assembly line, which by 1920 substituted machines for men in producing car frames.

The popularity of cars forced some Wisconsin businesses to change their products, which catered to horse owners. In 1867 Justus Luther invented a machine that rolled horse whips in one-quarter the time it took to roll a whip by hand. A Berlin glove-making company invested in Luther's machine and in 1870 changed its name to the Berlin Whip Company. Horseless carriages dried up the demand for whips, and in 1900 the company reverted to hand-stitching gloves and mittens. In 1922 the Berlin Whip Company became the Berlin Glove Company. With the disappearance of hungry horses, another company was forced to adapt its product. Since 1882 Philip Orth's company in Sullivan had milled flour and horse feed. With the advent of autos, their sales in horse feed plummeted. Orth's son switched his emphasis from flour and feed to bakery supplies, eventually adding a complete line of machinery for bakers.

At the turn of the century a successful wagon

maker in Racine, Mitchell-Lewis, began building cars in addition to wagons. Henry Mitchell, an early settler of Racine, began his wagon business in 1854 and was joined by his son-in-law, W.T. Lewis, in 1864. Though it continued to build wagons as late as 1910, the Mitchell-Lewis Motor Company produced touring cars with fashionable gray bodies and red upholstery. By 1916 the Mitchell-Lewis Motor Company employed 2,000 workers in the Racine plant, which covered nearly 30 acres. The company was later bought by another Wisconsin-based auto producer, the Nash Motor Company, in 1925.

One of Wisconsin's prized custom-built cars—the Kissel Kar—was not available to Wisconsin buyers the year of its debut. Instead, brothers George and William Kissel of Hartford sold their entire production of 100 cars to a Chicago dealer. Each car cost $1,850, not including windshield, generator, gas lamps, or horn, which were extra. A detachable top, patented in 1922, would make the Kissel Kar an all-weather vehicle. The Kissel Kar, which won the 1910 Los Angeles-to-Phoenix race, maintained its reputation for durability and sportiness. A nostalgic article in *Road and Track* magazine called the Kissel Gold Bug

"the niftiest, raciest, and classiest American production car ever to hit the highways." Kissel Kars were made until 1931, when the family business could no longer compete against assembly-built cars and the Depression.

A bicycle manufacturer became the founder of Wisconsin's most successful auto company. Thomas L. Jeffery, who built bicycles he called Ramblers in Chicago, had been tinkering with cars since 1890. Jeffery sold his bicycle company in 1900 and moved to Kenosha, where he bought the Sterling bicycle factory. In 1902 Jeffery produced 1,500 new Ramblers—this time autos, not bikes. That year Oldsmobile in Detroit and Jeffery in Kenosha accounted for 4,000 of the 5,000 cars manufactured in the Midwest.

Thomas Jeffery died in 1910, and in 1916 his son decided to sell the company. The buyer, Charles W. Nash, had served as president of General Motors for four years, winning acclaim in Detroit by rescuing the Buick line from financial difficulties in 1910. After resigning from GM over policy differences, Nash acquired the Thomas B. Jeffery Company, making Kenosha the largest producer of motor cars outside of Detroit.

Hartford's Kissel Motor Car Company built four-wheel-drive trucks for the Army during World War I. Kissel had received a special contract to assemble the trucks, which usually were manufactured by the Four Wheel Drive Company in Clintonville. Courtesy, State Historical Society of Wisconsin

In World War I women took the place of men on the assembly lines at Nash Motors in Kenosha. During the war Nash was a large producer of trucks for the Army. Courtesy, State Historical Society of Wisconsin

Thomas Jeffery's converted bicycle factory was the genesis of Kenosha's modern auto industry. In 1917 Kenosha's Rambler plant began producing the Nash, which became a prized motor car. Plants were built in Racine, Milwaukee, and Pine Bluff, Arkansas. Nash negotiated a U.S. Army contract that made the Nash Motor Company one of the largest builders of trucks, producing 11,494 in 1918. The American Motors Corporation was created in 1954 when the Nash Motor Company merged with Hudson of Detroit. American Motors survived the post-World War II shake-out that eliminated other famous car makers such as Packard, Studebaker, and Kaiser.

But American Motors would not survive the modern marketplace. Kenosha's auto-assembly plant dated back to Thomas Jeffery's bicycle factory and an 1890s five-story mattress factory, making Kenosha the oldest operating auto plant in the country. Consumer

Above
This Nash sports car of 1922 was one of Charles Nash's many successful cars that would become Wisconsin classics. In 1954 the Nash Motor Company merged to become American Motors Corporation. Courtesy, State Historical Society of Wisconsin

Left
A common sight on Milwaukee streets in the 1920s was of trucks transporting automobile bodies for Nash Motors, the forerunner of American Motors Corporation. Auto bodies were transported from the Seaman Body Corporation to the Nash assembly plants in Milwaukee, Racine, and Kenosha. Courtesy, Milwaukee Public Library

RURAL HIGHWAYS

Poor roads put the family "in a rut" and keep it there.

Good roads mean opportunity for

1 Neighborhood social life
2 Consolidated schools
3 Prompt mail service
4 Church attendance
5 Prompt medical attendance
6 Cheaper hauling of produce

In 1909 less than 17 percent of Wisconsin's roads were paved; however, Wisconsin government realized that good roads would help the farmer. Cars were not the prime motive for improving roads under the 1911 State Aid Road Law. It would take another five years for officials to realize that autos were the next mode of transportation and that gravel roads were not adequate. Courtesy, State Historical Society of Wisconsin

tastes changed in the 1970s and 1980s. Foreign car makers offered efficient small cars from state-of-the-art tech nology, and American Motors could not compete. In 1987 Detroit's Chrysler Corporation ac quired AMC and its prosperous line of Kaiser-Jeeps. Despite Kenosha's exemplary work force, Chrysler unexpectedly cut 5,500 jobs in January 1988 and effectively shut down Kenosha as an auto producer.

General Motors had entered Wisconsin in 1918 when it bought the Janesville Machine Company, a tractor producer. Tractors continued to roll out of the plant, but inside engineers were developing the prototype of the Samson, a nine-passenger car with removable seats to make room for cargo. General Motors widely advertised the Samson but never approved it for production. Instead, the Janesville plant was converted for GM's Chevrolet company, and the first Chevrolet left the assembly line in 1923.

Four-wheel drive was invented in Clintonville, a small town in east-central Wisconsin. In 1906 William Besserdich and two friends became mired in sand on a trip to Embarrass, Wisconsin. Besserdich asked his friends to move the front wheels, and the car nimbly moved out of the sand pit. Impressed by the combination of force to all four wheels, Besserdich, a prosperous mechanic, suggested to his partner Otto Zachow that they invent a mechanism that empowered all four wheels of a vehicle. By 1908 they had a patent, and in 1909 they built "the Battleship," a 3,800 pound four-wheel drive behemoth.

Besserdich and Zachow's Four Wheel Drive Company launched Clintonville as a producer of heavy trucks. World War I provided the small town with an international market. In 1915 the British government bought 288 of the 3-ton trucks while the Russian government purchased 82. By the war's end, the British government had bought 3,000 heavy trucks. When the U.S. government entered the war the company produced 14,473 trucks. After World War I, Clintonville's Four Wheel Drive Company was manufacturing trucks ranging from 2 to 15 tons.

A bicycle with an engine was the beginning of Milwaukee's Harley-Davidson Motor Company. In 1903 William Harley and the Davidson brothers, William, Walter, and Arthur, designed their first motorized bicycle. By 1907 their company was producing about 150 bikes. Their two-cylinder engine, designed in 1909, became a company trademark. During World

Above
Wisconsin roads had impeded transportation, and therefore economic growth, since pioneer days. A spring rain could easily turn a pathway into one muddy ditch. *Courtesy, State Historical Society of Wisconsin*

Left
When this accident happened in 1915 the rickety bridge was part of what was considered a major thoroughfare, Wisconsin's Highway 18. A truck from the Milwaukee-Waukesha Delivery Company broke through this wooden bridge over the Wisconsin River near Prairie du Chien and blocked the road for two days. *Courtesy, Milwaukee Public Library*

War I production rose to 18,000 motorcycles, which the military used for dispatch work.

The iron horses of the nineteenth century—trains—did not see competition from the curious autos of the 1900s. Railroads serving Wisconsin offered to help improve the feeder roads to railway depots for farmers. In 1909 less than 17 percent of Wisconsin's roads were surfaced, and farmers had difficulty in maneuvering their wagons of grain, produce, or milk for export to markets. When the State Aid Road Law passed in 1911, railroads offered to haul highway construction materials at reduced rates.

Wisconsin's good roads movement of 1911 was aimed at helping farmers, not car owners. Automobiles were still a novel luxury in 1911, and the common improved road was made of gravel. By 1916, however, the state highway commission observed that "the automobile has introduced new problems into the business of road construction. Roads fit for old horse drawn vehicles are not at all fit for use with an automobile." The horseless carriage was no longer part-bicycle and part-wagon. Cement roads were a testament to the horse's modern replacement.

The first two decades of the twentieth century saw enormous change in Wisconsin's leading industries. The 1900 census ranked lumber and flour first and second among industries for the last time. Within the first two decades of the new century lumber and flour would steadily fall as dairies, foundries, and automobiles became the top industries.

THE PAPER INDUSTRY

Papermaking became an important industry in Wisconsin despite the depletion of Wisconsin's forests. By 1910 paper products, produced by the state's 57 mills, ranked eighth in Wisconsin, ahead of the tenth-ranked auto industry. In 1911, however, Wisconsin's thriving paper industry, which produced newsprint in abundance, faced a crisis that threatened its existence. Congress passed a reciprocal trade agreement with Canada that, among other things, allowed Canada's cheap newsprint into the country duty free. Canada later rejected the trade agreement, but in 1913 President Wilson allowed Canadian newsprint to enter the country on a duty-free list. American newspaper owners were elated, but Wisconsin papermakers were faced with a fight for survival.

Adapting to this market change, Wisconsin papermakers invented new varieties of paper, creating lightweight paper, toilet tissue, absorbent wadding, and insulating paper. Glazed, glassine, and serum-resisting paper joined high-quality magazine and book paper. Kimberly-Clark introduced Kleenex facial tissue in 1924, four years after it had introduced its Kotex feminine pads. According to historian James Clark, newsprint soon became a minor product as new demands forced Wisconsin to import wood from Canada, the western states, and even from Sweden and Finland. By 1930 Wisconsin was the second leading paper producer in the country after Maine.

Wisconsin's papermakers led the industry in its innovations of paper products. The chemical laboratory of Kimberly-Clark in 1922 was one of many research labs in the state for inventing products such as glazed, glassine, and serum-resisting paper. Courtesy, State Historical Society of Wisconsin

Investment in calendaring machines that smoothed paper, such as Kimberly-Clark's in 1922, was one of the many financial commitments of Wisconsin papermakers in maintaining their leadership in the quality and quantity of Wisconsin paper products. Courtesy, State Historical Society of Wisconsin

As the paper industry expanded, one small Wisconsin business had to adapt or shut down. Henschel, a maker of wooden cigar boxes in New Berlin since 1889, was threatened by the new demands for paper boxes and paper packages for cigarettes. As sales of wooden boxes dropped, the company began coating the bronze labels of its cigar boxes, later expanding to coat other printed papers.

WISCONSIN'S LABOR AND PROGRESSIVE MOVEMENTS

While business and industry adapted to changes in the marketplace, it also had to address the grievances of labor. Rapid industrialization had created deplorable working conditions, and worker demands included the eight-hour work day, safer work places, the abolition of child labor, and fair wages. In 1893-1894 alone, 44 workers died in Wisconsin from industrial accidents; "killed, wound up on shaft" were the words used to describe eight of these deaths.

Employers would not agree to the unions' demand that employees work for eight hours but be paid for ten hours. The general public found it hard to un-

Robert La Follette was a leader of the Progressive movement, which heralded reform in the early twentieth century. The era of Progressivism was also a time of economic prosperity for Wisconsin and the United States. By 1910 Wisconsin ranked eighth nationally in industrial wealth. Courtesy, State Historical Society of Wisconsin

derstand why urban workers should work fewer hours than farmers, who worked from dawn to dusk. Strikes supporting the eight-hour work day were often met with violence. The May 1886 agitation over the ten-hour work day resulted in violence at both Chicago's Haymarket Square and Milwaukee's Bay View. Nine people died in Milwaukee when the Wisconsin militia fired into the crowd of striking workers and supporters.

Wisconsin's reform movement was fragmented. In general, Robert La Follette's Progressive movement favored farmers and small businessmen. Wisconsin's labor groups united in the Wisconsin State Federation of Labor shortly after the formation of Samuel Gompers' American Federation of Labor. WSFL deviated, however, by orienting itself with Milwaukee's

Socialist party despite Gompers' hostility to socialism. In turn, Victor Berger and his Socialist party were suspicious and perhaps envious of La Follette's success in progressivism. Victor Berger, the principal reason for socialism's success among Milwaukee's German and labor communities, advocated democratic socialism in which the people gradually voted in Socialist platforms. A conservative among the country's Socialists, Berger is credited with Americanizing socialism. Milwaukee sent Berger to the U.S. Congress four times and elected two Socialist mayors, whose party became known primarily as the party of good municipal government. Socialist Daniel Hoan was mayor for 24 years, from 1916 to 1940.

The growth of socialism before World War I was a measure of the need for reform. The magazines of

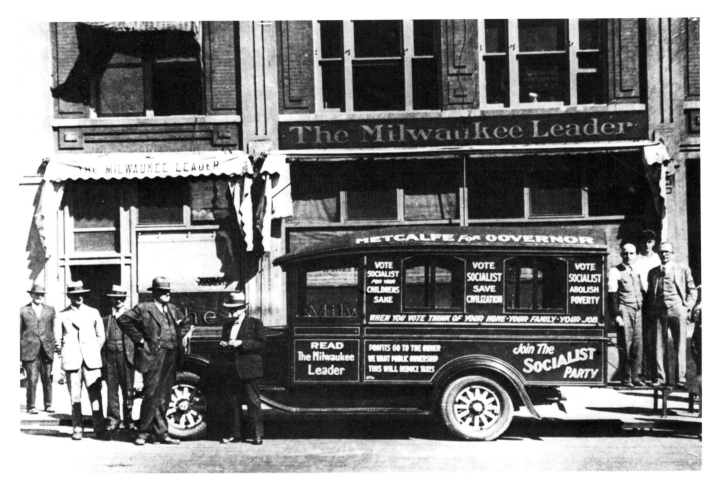

The delivery van for the Milwaukee Leader newspaper often served as a campaign billboard for Wisconsin Socialist candidates. The Leader was a Socialist daily newspaper begun by Victor Berger, the first Socialist elected to the U.S. Congress. Courtesy, Milwaukee County Historical Society

the middle class—*McClure's, Cosmopolitan, Everybody's, Collier's* and *American Magazine*—built national circulations by exposing corruption in government and big business. Insurance, the Standard Oil company, and meat packing were among the celebrated exposes. In 1906 President Theodore Roosevelt called this journalism "muckraking" and hinted that it aided socialism. The muckrakers were moralists, not radicals, but their command of facts proved that reform was needed in the industrialized nation. Progressivism was one response to the hue and cry for reform.

Robert M. La Follette, the catalyst for progressivism in Wisconsin, was governor of Wisconsin for three terms before he became a U.S. senator in 1906. Three issues dominated La Follette's gubernatorial administration: the direct primary, railroad taxation, and railroad regulation. Wisconsin's first governor to be born in the state, La Follette earned his nickname "Fighting Bob" during the battles to establish these changes. La Follette's pet issue, the direct primary, was a direct assault on the machine politics he hated. In battling the conservative Republicans who called themselves "the Stalwarts," La Follette campaigned for a slate of Progressive candidates in the 1902 election. During his last two years in office La Follette and his Progressives achieved passage of the direct primary and a railroad commission.

"The first pirates on land were the railroads," had been a common sentiment among the public. Railroads were a boon to small towns, but also a monopoly in transportation.

For all of La Follette's fire, he was pragmatic about railroad regulation. Wisconsin's first attempt at railroad regulation had been a fiasco. The 1874 Potter Law formed a commission that could only reduce rates, which proved useless when the railroad companies balked and was later repealed. In April of 1900 La Follette met with counsels of the railroads in Milwaukee, assuring them that Wisconsin's railroad commission, chaired by Professor Balthasar Meyer, would not reduce rates but only equalize them.

Lumber baron Isaac Stephenson was the Progressive party's financial angel. Stephenson, who became a millionaire in the Menominee River district, served three terms in the U.S. Congress. Angered with the Republican Stalwarts when they did not help him win the U.S. Senate seat in 1899, Stephenson became a Progressive. In 1901 he bought the *Milwaukee Free Press*, a daily newspaper that did battle with the *Milwaukee Sentinel*, owned by Stalwart leader Charles Pfister of the Pfister-Vogel tannery empire.

When Wisconsin's senate seat became open in 1905, La Follette rescinded his pledge to support Stephenson. Friends of La Follette undertook what Nesbit termed "the relatively easy task" of persuading the governor to keep the peace among Progressives by accepting the senate seat himself. Stephenson later won an expensive election to the U.S. Senate in 1908, admitting that he had spent $107,000.

La Follette and his successor, Francis McGovern, helped Wisconsin win national acclaim as a laboratory of reform. The direct primary, a successful income tax, worker's compensation, an industrial safety commission, and the legislative reference library were innovations issuing from the Wisconsin Legislature. Theodore Roosevelt wrote in *Outlook* magazine that Wisconsin was "a pioneer blazing the way along which we Americans must make our civic and industrial advance during the next few decades."

THE WISCONSIN IDEA

The spirit of reform in Wisconsin was called "The Wisconsin Idea," a vague term for trail-blazing changes. "The borders of the university are the borders of the state,"perhaps best explains scholars and legislators working together for effective reform. Although the origin of the term is obscure, the geography of Wisconsin's capital might explain the Wisconsin Idea. Bascom Hill, the seat of the university, is about one mile away from the Capitol. State Street connects these centers of learning and legislation, and the walk between them—leading to an isthmus between two lakes—is exhilirating. The Wisconsin Idea sprang from university activism. John Bascom, president of the university from 1874-1887, was "forever telling us what the state was doing for us and urging our return obligation not . . . for our own selfish benefit, but to return some service to the state," wrote La Follette in his autobiography. During Bascom's tenure, the university began the Short Course, vocational seminars for farmers. The next university president, Thomas C. Chamberlain, declared, "Scholarship for the sake of the scholar is simply refined selfishness. Scholarship for the sake of the state and the people is refined patriotism."

The next generation of leaders acting on Bascom's and Chamberlain's philosophy gave birth to the Wisconsin Idea. In his 1903 inaugural address to the university, Charles Van Hise, a friend and former classmate of La Follette, proposed that professors be used as technical experts by the state government. His proposal took fire, and by 1912 46 professors served both the university and the state. Charles McCarthy, librarian of the Legislative Reference Bureau, wrote a book in 1912 titled *The Wisconsin Idea*, which included a forward by Theodore Roosevelt. McCarthy also helped legislators write bills, including the vocational education law that established vocational schools for adults in cities with populations of 5,000 or more. Reporter E.E. Slosson observed that "it is impossible to ascertain the size or location of the University of Wisconsin. The most that one can say is that the headquarters of the institution is at the city of Madison and that the campus has an area of about 56,000 square miles.

Wisconsin's progressivism was fueled by a new source of money—corporate income taxes. In 1911 Wisconsin became the first state to tax manufacturers. Connecticut followed Wisconsin's lead in 1915, and

Construction of Wisconsin's fourth state capitol began in 1907 after fire destroyed the third capitol in 1904. By 1911 the dome was not the only Wisconsin legacy under construction. The Wisconsin Idea, the partnership between university scholars and state legislators, turned Wisconsin into a laboratory of reform. Courtesy, State Historical Society of Wisconsin

Massachusetts and New York passed corporate income taxes in 1916 and 1917, respectively. It wasn't until the Great Depression that other industrial states followed suit.

There was little disagreement with the idea of taxing manufacturers. The tax burden fell mainly on large manufacturers, exempting the railroads, utilities, and insurance companies. Manufacturers such as Allis-Chalmers, Kimberly-Clark, and International Harvester opposed the tax, which also left them subject to local property taxes. Other non-manufacturing corporations, however, supported the measure, as they hoped to see their tax burden passed along. When the conservative businessman Emanuel L. Philipp became governor from 1915 to 1921 he left the corporate income tax intact, and his taxing of manufacturers differed little from the policies of the Progressive governor who followed him.

The business community was often allied with progressivism. Although railroad regulation had a radical ring, business leaders supported it in order to equalize competition. In 1904 La Follette's Progressives elected lumber baron William D. Connor, who had helped manage La Follette's campaigns in 1901 and 1903, as chairman of the Republican State Central Committee.

WORKERS COMPENSATION AND THE INSURANCE INDUSTRY

In 1911 businessmen and progressives worked together to form one of Wisconsin's most famous innovations, worker's compensation. Until Wisconsin's groundbreaking law, workers who were injured on the job had to sue their employers and prove extraordinary negligence in order to get any compensation. Common law said that employers were not liable for their dead or injured because workers undertook an implied risk when they accepted a job.

Worker's compensation was essentially conservative reform and was written by moderates who were sympathetic to both labor and business, according to historian Robert Asher. John R. Commons, University of Wisconsin professor of economics, was the architect of worker's compensation who won approval from both organized labor and the large employers. When a worker was injured or killed, the Industrial Commission investigated the cause of the accident and then awarded money according to a fixed scale. Though worker's compensation at first was voluntary, by 1931 it was mandatory for all employers.

John Commons helped design the Wisconsin Industrial Commission, which reviewed industrial safety and sanitation. Advisory committees of employers, labor, and outside experts devised safety codes for each industry. The commission grew in power when it became responsible for enforcing the worker's compensation law, which the courts ruled the law constitutional in 1911. Commons chose Charles W. Price of International Harvester to represent management's needs. Price, who had a national reputation for industrial safety and welfare, was among the growing list of industrialists who were beginning to realize the waste involved in workers' accidents and grievances. Although employers reluctantly gave up their common-law defenses for accidents, they realized that safety laws and accident prevention were efficient and in their self-interest.

A group of Wausau lumbermen, realizing the implications of worker's compensation, designed the first mutual insurance for Wisconsin employers. Mutuals are basically cooperatives in which a group of people pool their resources to share risks and, if successful, share in investment dividends.

On September 1, 1911, the day worker's compensation went into effect, Wausau's Employers Mutual Liability Insurance sold their first policy to the Wausau Sulphate and Fibre Company, later the Mosinee Paper Company. Employers Mutual opened its first branch office in Milwaukee in 1912, but Wausau remained its headquarters. Small, hometown America became Employers Mutual corporate identity, and in 1979 Wausau Insurance Companies became its trade name. Among the safety innovations of Wausau's Employers Mutual was the hiring of the first industrial nurse in 1928 to develop on-site medical care.

In 1906, as he was leaving for the U.S. Senate, Robert La Follette asked the Legislature to investigate Wisconsin's life insurance companies. In 1905 scandal had rocked New York's insurance giants. By 1907 more than 70 insurance bills were introduced in the Wisconsin Legislature. The bills that passed required more open elections of the companies' managers, stricter fiscal reporting, curbs on salaries, and more liberal policy provisions. In response 23 out-of-state insurance companies left Wisconsin, though many

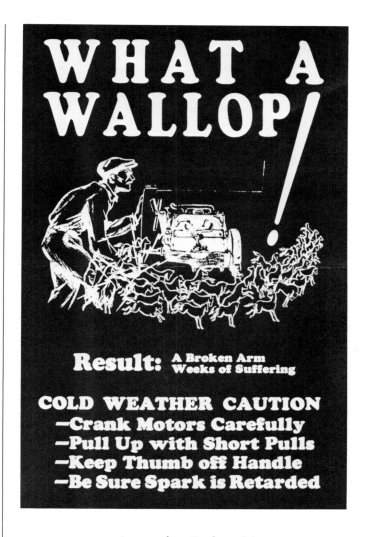

A poster from Employers Mutual Liability Insurance Company of Wisconsin was designed to help prevent accidents in the workplace. The insurance company, which began in 1911, the same year Wisconsin's Workmen's Compensation law went into effect, is now Wausau Insurance Companies. Courtesy, Milwaukee Public Library

returned in 1915.

Wisconsin's oldest and largest insurance company, Northwestern Mutual, emerged relatively unscathed from the legislative investigations. In 1907 Northwestern was the sixth largest insurance company in the country. Investigators found no corruption, and even praised Northwestern Mutual for its accounting procedures and cautious investments, though they did condemn unethical sales techniques that were common to the industry during that time.

Northwestern's name reflects Wisconsin's heritage as being the New World's original Northwest Territory. When New Yorker John C. Johnston founded the company in Janesville in 1857, Wisconsin was only six years old and still a frontier, hardly a likely birthplace for a major insurance company. However, Johnston was an eccentric with a small fortune he had earned in New York from selling insurance policies for Mutual Life of New York. At age 72 he came to Wisconsin and bought 3,000 acres of prime farm land in wheat-growing Rock County.

Johnston ignored conventional wisdom that insurance is a product of a mature economy. He was not concerned that frontier Wisconsinites had scant capital to make investments—or pay insurance premiums. In 1857, the year a financial panic bankrupted every railroad in Wisconsin, Johnston managed to gather the $200,000 worth of commitments needed to establish Mutual Life of Wisconsin, a virtual carbon copy of Mutual Life of New York.

Mutual Life of Wisconsin would grow to have more than 4,000 policy holders by the end of the Civil War, spurring its leaders to rename the company Northwestern Mutual in order to attract a regional market. The new name, "Northwestern," had the same familiar ring that the word midwestern has today.

The only snag for Johnston was the board of directors he chose. In 1859 the board of directors managed to engineer a vote that moved company headquarters from Janesville to Milwaukee. A small black trunk was enough to accomplish the move. In anger Johnston sold his interest and moved to Madison. He died in 1860 at 78, but his company, the first major insurance company born west of Philadelphia, was guided skillfully into the twentieth century by board member Henry L. Palmer.

Many of Wisconsin's oldest insurance companies were formed because of the high rates charged by eastern fire insurance companies. The widespread perception that eastern insurance companies were expensive and unfair encouraged the births of homegrown mutuals.

In 1897 two Lutheran pastors formed the Church Mutual Insurance Company in Merrill, Wisconsin. Churches were particularly vulnerable to fires because during the week they were often empty and unless a fire started on Sunday, few people would be around to notice a blaze beginning. First available only to Evangelical Lutherans or Norwegian Evangelical Lutherans, Church Mutual grew to become non-denominational and a nationwide specialist in church insurance.

Fire protection was expensive for hardware store owners because they stocked inflammable paint, linseed oil, and turpentine. But Wisconsin hardware dealers felt their premiums were too high in relation to the actual loss caused by fires. In 1904 the Wisconsin Retail Hardware Association formed a mutual insurance company in Berlin, Wisconsin. In 1912 the newly elected secretary-treasurer of the association, Peter J. Jacobs, decided to move the offices to his hometown of Stevens Point. In 1914 Hardware Mutuals joined the wave begun by worker's compensation and began to offer employers liability insurance. Later life insurance was added. In 1962 a new corporate symbol—a Revolutionary War minuteman—was introduced and in 1963 the trade name Hardware Mutuals was exchanged for Sentry Insurance.

Incensed by the high rates paid by jewelers for fire insurance, Andrew W. Anderson, secretary of Wisconsin Jewelers Association, helped found a mutual insurance group in 1913. Jewelers were grouped together with clothes-cleaning shops as bad risks because both used benzine for cleaning. However, jewelers used benzine for only cleaning watches. His Jewelers Mutual Insurance Company grew into the only insurance company devoted exclusively to protecting jewelers from fires to theft and personal jewelry coverage.

In 1927 the Farmer's Mutual Automobile Insurance Company was formed in Madison to meet the needs of farmers, who as a group didn't drive as much as urban dwellers during the winter. Their insurance premiums from Farmer's Mutual reflected this lower risk. Farmer's Mutual, like Sentry and Wausau, outgrew its initial prospect, and in 1958 was changed to

American Family Insurance.

Wisconsin's insurance industry enjoyed a unique, spectacular growth from small towns. The nature of insurance allows the industry to be located almost anywhere, which was proved by Northwestern's John Johnston in frontier Wisconsin in 1857. During the 1950s Wausau Insurance Companies began advertisements that alerted its national customers to its pride in its small-town origin and instructed them on how to spell Wausau. Carl N. Jacobs, who guided Hardware Mutuals as it swelled into Sentry, summed up why he decided to stay in Stevens Point, "I was a small-town boy, and decided to remain a small-town boy."

ALUMINUM

Wisconsin was equally an unlikely place for success in aluminum. Since 1888 aluminum had been the

Workers at the Vollrath Company of Sheboygan dipped enamel kitchenware, which was a familiar household product in Wisconsin. Courtesy, State Historical Society of Wisconsin

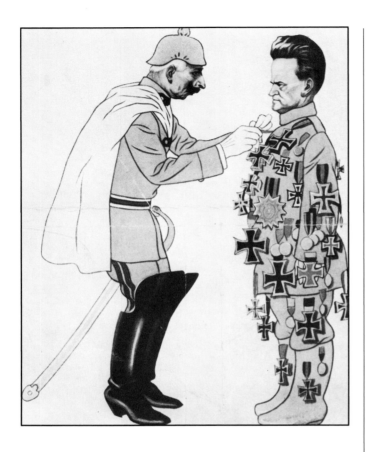

Because of the state's strong German heritage, World War I was a traumatic time for patriots in Wisconsin. Senator Robert La Follette was a vocal opponent of the United States' entry into World War I. Life's 1917 cover shows the Kaiser decorating Wisconsin's vocal senator. Resentment of German heritage even led one zealous patriot to call German beer "Kaiser brew." Courtesy, State Historical Society of Wisconsin

monopoly of the Aluminum Company of America (Alcoa) of Pittsburgh, which continued its grip on competition until World War II. Wisconsin entrepreneurs bought aluminum from Alcoa and made cookware, which by 1919 was close to becoming the most preferred cookware and utensilware. Wisconsin supplied more than 50 percent of the national market in aluminum cookware.

Aluminum was once the rare metal of kings. Denmark's King Christian X wore an aluminum crown and Napoleon III reserved an aluminum table service for special guests. Aluminum was treasured because it was extremely difficult and expensive to isolate from bauxite. Aluminum's lightness and pliability made it a luxury metal. In 1886 the electrochemical process was discovered that would eventually turn the dinner service of kings into the commonplace cookware.

Virtually unknown to the public at the turn of the century, aluminum was used for novelty items such as combs, mustache cups, cigar cases, salt and pepper shakers, and lucky pennnies ("Keep me and never go broke"). But Joseph Koenig, a German immigrant who settled in Two Rivers, was captivated by the German aluminum at the Chicago World's Columbian Exposition in 1893. Koenig spent the next two years designing machines, tools, and dies to produce aluminum novelties. He was helped by business leader J.E. Hamilton and later the city of Two Rivers, which wanted to keep the business in town. As Koenig's business flourished, several employees left to start their own aluminum enterprises. A rectangular strip from Two Rivers and Manitowoc to West Bend became the area known for Wisconsin's aluminum production.

Aluminum cookware helped to fill the vacuum created by the receding timber industries of eastern Wisconsin. Until the end of World War I only two Wisconsin manufacturers produced aluminum cookware—Koenig's company, which had merged with two of its competitors to form the the Mirro Aluminum Company, and the West Bend Aluminum Company, begun in 1911. West Bend marketed almost 50 percent of its production to Sears Roebuck and Company.

By 1920 the aluminum cookware industry was concentrated primarily in Ohio, Pennsylvania, and in eastern Wisconsin at Two Rivers and West Bend. The success of Wisconsin's aluminum industry reflected the general prosperity of the country. Although more

Chippewa (now known as Ojibwe) Indians at Reserve, Wisconsin, celebrate the return of Indian soldiers from World War I. Although Indians were not eligible for the draft, many of them volunteered to fight; and the war heroes helped publicize the economic poverty of Indians. Courtesy, State Historical Society of Wisconsin

expensive than copper or enamelware, aluminum could be bought through catalogue companies and was in demand by the general public.

SHIPBUILDING

Wisconsin's quiet shipbuilding yards were boosted dramatically during World War I, becoming the twelfth leading industry in 1920. Wisconsin built wooden and steel rescue crafts, tugs, and harbor mine sweepers. Manitowoc and Sturgeon Bay were the primary shipyards, with 6,000 workers. The Manitowoc Shipbuilding company built 32 ocean freighters during the war. After the Armistice of 1919 smaller companies such as Burger Boats returned to making custom-built commercial boats and pleasure cruisers. Beginning in 1921 Norwegian-born Ole Evinrude revolutionized motorized boats with his twin outboard motor made in Milwaukee. By 1928 his four-cylinder outboard motors were used in racing boats.

WORLD WAR I

Wisconsin's large German community was torn apart in 1917 when the United States, breaking its policy of strict neutrality held since 1914, declared war on Germany. Nine of eleven congressmen from Wisconsin voted against declaring war, and Wisconsin's fighting senator, Robert La Follette, also voted against entering the war.

The German culture that had built Wisconsin was suddenly suspect during World War I, and freedom of discussion was severely curtailed. A Madison druggist paid a $2,000 fine for his overheard remark that the Kaiser was a better friend to his people than the U.S. government was to its people. The Espionage Act gave informants the opportunity to help return 92 indictments against Wisconsinites. These indictments included different and overlapping offenses: 35 for criticizing U.S. policy; 36 for praising Germany; 32 for saying it was "a rich man's war and the poor man's fight"; 19 for criticizing the sale of war bonds; and 9 for insults to the flag.

Ten million people died in World War I. The war virtually wiped out a generation of French men from 18 to 45 years old, and in the final 19 months of the war more than 100,000 Americans died, including 3,932 Wisconsinites. The emotional costs had been staggering, but peacemakers took comfort that the Great War had been "the war to end all wars."

V I I I

PROHIBITION AND HARD TIMES

On April 6, 1933, thousands of Milwaukeeans, including hundreds at this Schlitz Brewery open house, celebrated the legalization of 3.2 beer. The final end to Prohibition came eight months later. Courtesy, Milwaukee Public Library

On January 16, 1920, the proud brewmasters of Wisconsin found their profession outlawed. Brewing beer was Wisconsin's fifth largest industry in 1920, but for the next 13 years the Wisconsin breweries that survived Prohibition would publicly sell malt syrup, soda pop, tonic water, even cheese. The pride of Wisconsin was reduced to making non-alcoholic "near beer."

Home brewing grew. Eastern Wisconsin became notorious for selling wort, the malt liquid that required only yeast and time before it bubbled into beer. One of the treasured recipes for brewing five gallons of home beer was written by the braumeister of Cream City Brewing in Milwaukee. Written on company stationery for the brewery's scrub woman, Braumeister Gustav Hanke also advised the home brewer to "omit

waukee brewer Gustav Pabst wrote an article in *Cosmopolitan* magazine in 1908 asserting "temperance is civilization and intelligence, Prohibition is tyranny." By 1911 Pabst believed that the Prohibition movement was on the wane, but World War I and its anti-German rhetoric gave Prohibitionists a sudden advantage. America's German beer became "kaiser brew" for many dry patriots. A former lieutenant-governor of Wisconsin said in 1918, "We have German enemies in this country too. And the worst of all our German enemies, the most treacherous, the most menacing are Pabst, Schlitz, Blatz and Miller." As Paul Glad observed, World War I effectively neutralized German influence in American society.

Prohibition turned saloons into speakeasies and,

A sign outside a Milwaukee milling company from 1920 called for an end to Prohibition. The wish would not be granted until 1933. Courtesy, Milwaukee County Historical Society

BRING BACK BEER
RESTORE TRUE TEMPERANCE
Lower Your Taxes

fermentation in dry territory." Sixty days in a warm room was the difference between German lager and near beer.

Prohibition was a wet affair in Wisconsin, but the length of it strangled many small breweries. When Prohibition ended in 1933, Wisconsin had lost 40 percent of its breweries. The U.S. Census had counted 132 breweries in Wisconsin in 1914 but only 80 in 1933. The Great Depression toppled another seven breweries by 1939, including Milwaukee's venerable Cream City Brewery in 1937.

Many brewers believed that reforming bawdy saloons would diffuse the Prohibition movement. Mil-

officially, German lager into near beer. Milwaukee brewers marketed several brands of non-alcoholic near beer: Pablo by Pabst, Famo by Schlitz, and Vivo by Miller. Brewers were at first encouraged by near beer sales, which then dropped during the Roaring Twenties.

One Milwaukee gin distillery quickly adjusted to Prohibition. In 1919 the National Distilling Company —called the "Gin House of America"—became the Red Star Yeast and Products Company. National Distilling had marketed Red Star yeast since the 1890s, but yeast now took center stage. When Prohibition ended in 1933 Red Star Yeast returned to making

Members of Milwaukee's Brewery Workers' Union marched in the 1914 Milwaukee Labor Day parade protesting the growing Prohibition movement five years before Prohibition became law. Courtesy, Milwaukee County Historical Society

Above
In 1928 Milwaukee's Seven Master Lock Company shipped 147,000 padlocks to New York City for federal agents to use to lock up illegal taverns. Ironically, the locks were being produced in a building in Milwaukee owned by the Pabst Brewing Company, whose brewery was closed by Prohibition. Courtesy, Milwaukee Public Library

Right
In 1919 Milwaukee men mourned, in a mock funeral for John Barleycorn, the loss of alcohol to Prohibition. Courtesy, Milwaukee County Historical Society

small quantities of gin, though gin production was discontinued four years later. The company later became Universal Foods Corporation.

Violating the Eighteenth Amendment was as easy as making a toast. As one University of Wisconsin student observed of his hometown in 1930, "There has been, is, and always will be plenty of stimulating fluids in Viroqua. Wine is a mocker, strong drink is raging, and beer—beer is two bits a quart." The editor of the *Burlington Standard-Democrat* observed that "a beerless Milwaukee is like a beanless Boston—it can't be done."

Prohibition was in part a reaction to immigrants and their foreign ways. The Irish of the nineteenth century were often stereotyped as whiskey-loving drunks. Moreover, drinking openly on Sundays was a special sin to a great many Americans—and a cherished custom among Germans. Whether Lutheran or Catholic, German-Americans did not consider Sundays in the biergartens as sacrilegious.

During the Dry Decade Wisconsin had a resurgence of nativist activities—only this time members wore white sheets. The Ku Klux Klan attracted as many as 40,000 members in Wisconsin. The Klan

This Milwaukee freight-hauling truck had originally been used for bootlegging. It was confiscated by federal agents as it was delivering a shipment of beer to Manitowoc. Courtesy, Milwaukee Public Library

Zahringer's Malt Products Company's business went flat in 1919, because beer, which uses malt in the brewing process, could not be produced legally. Courtesy, Milwaukee Public Library

preached "100 percent Americanism," which appealed to nativists who objected to Wisconsin's large immigrant and Catholic population. The strongholds of the Ku Klux Klan were in Milwaukee, Kenosha, and Racine counties, which had received the twentieth-century influx of Polish, Italian, and Russian Jewish immigrants. Many German Socialists who opposed the Catholic clergy joined the Klan to the embarrassment of Socialist leader Victor Berger and Milwaukee's Socialist mayor, Daniel Hoan.

Madison was also an active Ku Klux Klan center in reaction to its Little Italy neighborhood, according to historian Robert Goldberg. Italian laborers had settled in Madison at the turn of the century during the construction of the State Historical Society and the Capitol. During Prohibition the Greenbush neighborhood, a community of about 500 Italians, was known for its bootlegging. In 1924 six men were killed in the neighborhood during what local newspapers called a "rum war." The Ku Klux Klan promised to bring law and order to Madison and even burned two crosses along Lake Mendota in 1924. The anti-Catholic rhetoric failed to sustain passion, however, and by 1927 Wisconin's Ku Klux Klan had died out for lack of members.

THE GREEN BAY PACKERS

Even as Wisconsin's communities appeared splintered along ethnic lines, a new business was forming that united communities against a common foe. It inspired conversation among strangers and sparked enthusiasm that cut across ethnicity, class, and gender. In 1919 Curly Lambeau organized a football team.

Green Bay is known more for football than for being part of the historical waterway to the Mississippi River. Son of a Belgian-born building contractor, Earl Louis Lambeau spent most of his freshman year at Notre Dame playing football for Knute Rockne. When he returned home to Green Bay, Lambeau persuaded his employer, the Acme Meat Packing Company, to pay for the uniforms of a new football team. Lambeau was coach and star player. During their first season of 10-1, the players each earned $16.75 from the hat passed among the fans.

In 1921 the meat packing company paid the $50 needed to join the year-old National Football League, and Lambeau's team became the Green Bay Packers. They had winning seasons for the next eight years and won three league championships in 1929, 1930, and 1931. When their team was struggling financially in 1925, Green Bay residents bought 1,000 shares of stock at $5 a share, turning the football team into a community-owned enterprise.

Green Bay would continue to be the smallest city in the National Football League, and the fans were steadfast regardless of the Packers' record. In 1949 the city once again bought shares of stock and raised $100,000 to help its losing football team. The new community stockholders agreed not to receive stock dividends, preferring that profits be saved for bad times.

Curly Lambeau resigned in 1949 after a coaching career of 31 seasons, making way for a committee that steadily steered the team from one loss to the next. From 1948 to 1958 the Green Bay Packers were the goats of the league despite a multi-million dollar stadium subsidized by Green Bay in 1957.

In the 1960s, however, the Packers would bring honor to Green Bay. A Brooklyn meatcutter's son would make the Green Bay Packers the winningest team in football history. His approach to success would be simple—winning was not the main thing, it was the only thing. In 1959 Vince Lombardi would come to town.

URBAN GROWTH AND THE GENIUS OF FRANK LLOYD WRIGHT

The prosperity of the twentieth century belonged to the cities, and many rural Americans were leaving the country for urban life. In Wisconsin the urban population grew 163 percent from 1900 to 1955. In contrast the rural population grew only 26 percent during those years. The greatest population centers remained in the 13 counties of southeastern Wisconsin, the center of industry and jobs. In 1900 one-sixth of Wisconsin's two million population resided in Milwaukee County. However, by 1950 more than one-quarter of Wisconin's 3.4 million population lived in Milwaukee County alone.

One young man from rural Wisconsin went to Chicago although he would hate city life. However,

he earned a fortune in the city and it enabled him to return to the land he loved. In the process he made Wisconsin internationally famous.

The low, lean lines of Frank Lloyd Wright's architecture influenced design throughout the world. Together with Louis Sullivan, Frank Lloyd Wright was a fresh American voice from the prairie. Wright's Prairie Houses would reconstruct how Americans looked at homes.

Frank Lloyd Wright made his reputation in Chicago, but his nesting instincts drew him back to southern Wisconsin. Born in Richland Center in 1867, Frank Lloyd Wright spent his youth in Spring Green and Madison. It was in the Wyoming Valley near Spring Green that Frank Lloyd Wright worked on his first building, Unity Chapel, for his Unitarian minister uncle. When Wright was 20 he began working for Chicago's most innovative architect, Louis Sullivan, whom Wright referred to as "Dear Master." He learned from Sullivan that in design, form follows function, a philosophy evident in Wright's distinctive Prairie House, his signature in which a house grew organically from its environment. The elements of water, fire, and earth haunted Wright. At the center of many of his homes were cavernous fireplaces surrounded by interiors of bare brick and stone and unpainted wood. "Architecture . . . is no less a weaving and fabric than the trees," he wrote. Frank Lloyd Wright was always trying to escape the traditional rectangles of modern architecture, according to Peter Blake. The goal of Frank Lloyd Wright was breaking down "the insufferable limitations of the box."

In 1911 Frank Lloyd Wright returned to the Wyoming Valley and built a home he called Taliesin, the name of a Welsh poet that invoked Wright's Welsh ancestry. "I turned to this hill in the Valley as my grandfather before me had turned to America—as a hope and haven," said Wright in his autobiography. The Wyoming Valley is in Wisconsin's Driftless Area, the craggy, diverse region in southwestern Wisconsin that was not chewed and flattened by the Ice Age glaciers.

Taliesin was a haven for Wright, but in 1914 it became a nightmare. While Wright was in Chicago on business his Barbadian chef went beserk and burned Taliesin to the ground, killing seven people. Among the dead were Mamah Cheney, the woman for whom Wright had left his first wife, plus Cheney's two

Above
Although Frank Lloyd Wright
became a famous international
architect, he returned to his child-
hood home of Spring Green to
found his school for architects,
the Taliesin Fellowship. Courtesy, State Historical Society of
Wisocnsin

Right
Frank Lloyd Wright's genius
for using wood, stone, and light
created his celebrated Prairie
Houses. At Taliesin in Spring
Green in 1957, Wright sits at
his desk. Courtesy, State Historical Society of Wisconsin

Facing page
In Racine the Johnson Wax Company commissioned Frank Lloyd
Wright to build a research
tower in 1946, a decade after
Wright designed Johnson Wax's
administration building. Courtesy, State Historical Society of
Wisconsin

children and four workers.

In 1923 Wright's genius was confirmed internationally when a devastating earthquake hit Japan. One hundred thousand people died and Tokyo was left in rubble—except for Wright's Imperial Hotel. A telegram from the hotel chairman informed Wright, "Hotel stands undamaged as monument of your genius—Hundreds of homeless provided for by perfectly maintained service—congratulations." In 1932 Taliesin, which Wright had rebuilt, became in part a school for architects called the Taliesin Fellowship.

Wisconsin's Johnson Wax Company commissioned Wright to design their Racine administration building in 1936 and a research tower in 1946. His last grand project was the Guggenheim Museum in New York City. Frank Lloyd Wright died in 1959, two months before his ninety-second birthday. He was buried near Unity Chapel, the first building on which he had worked. In 1985 his remains were transferred to Arizona to be interred next to his widow, Olgivanna, at their western home near Phoenix called Taliesin West.

Frank Lloyd Wright had retreated in comfort to the country after he had made his reputation in the city. It was a privileged choice born from his genius. However, few people had such unrestricted mobility.

WISCONSIN'S MINORITIES

Wisconsin had its share of inequalities. Wisconsin's Indians, isolated in reservations in central and northern Wisconsin, lived in rural poverty. Since 1890 Indians have consistently accounted for less than one percent of the state's population, their economic resources becoming increasingly scant. During the 1920s the Menominee tribe, living on an undivided reservation, owned a forest and lumber mill that could provide regular employment. The remainder of Wisconsin's tribes—the Chippewa (Ojibwe), Winnebago (Ho-Chunk), Oneida, Potawatomi, and Stockbridge-Munsee (Mohican)—did not fare as well, according to anthropologist Nancy Oestreich Lurie. For most tribes, work was seasonal and frequently piece-meal.

During World War I many Indians, not eligible to be drafted, volunteered to fight. As some Indians became war heroes, the deplorable conditions of the reservations were publicized in the newspapers. In 1924 Congress granted Indians full citizenship and suffrage, although some traditional Indians were suspicious of this symbol of assimilation.

Just as Indians were overwhelmingly rural, Wisconsin's black population was primarily urban. Many of Wisconsin's first blacks had arrived as slaves of Southerners migrating to the lead region during Wisconsin's territorial days. By 1900 there were only 2,486 blacks in the state, but the 1920s saw a new influx of blacks from the South. Wisconsin's heavy industries in Milwaukee and Beloit encouraged migration during the 1930s despite the Depression, and there were nearly 9,000 blacks in Milwaukee just before World War II.

Like new immigrants before them, blacks got only the dirtiest jobs such as blast furnace work, according to labor historian Robert Ozanne. However, once white immigrants had learned English they were often promoted to foremen, whereas black Americans remained in the foundries. Labor unions were not agents of change for blacks until the 1930s. In fact during the nineteenth century blacks were often considered strikebreakers since few were allowed in unions, according to historian Robert Nesbit.

During the Great Depression blacks and other minorities would become first-class union members. In 1935 and 1937 both the federal government and Wisconsin passed labor relations acts that prevented employers from spying on workers and dismissing workers who led or organized labor unions. Collective bargaining was now sanctioned by law. In 1936 the Congress of Industrial Organization (CIO) and the American Federation of Labor (AFL) competed for votes in becoming a local union's representative. The competition for votes elevated blacks, women, and immigrants within the ranks of unions, according to Robert Ozanne.

The surge of unionism during the 1930s gave blacks better pay and benefits, but they were still given the least desirable jobs. However, blacks were often staunch supporters of unions. Although very few blacks were union officers, one black steelworker in Beloit did become a union officer in 1937.

Working women in Wisconsin had been traditionally employed either in domestic service or industries such as clothing manufacturing and cigar rolling. Their hours were just as long as men—60 hours a week —but their wages were usually half that of men's pay. It was presumed that women worked only until they could find a husband, and their employment was dismissed as transitory.

Because of their low wages women often were considered threats to unions. In 1898 the Oshkosh Woodworkers' Council asked the seven woodworking companies to stop hiring women. Refusing to acknowledge the fact that women and girls were replacing men at lower pay, the union wrote: "Believing that a woodworking factory is no place for the employment of either women or girls we respectfully ask that female labor be abolished." Women joined unions in large numbers during the 1930s, but wage and job discrimination against women continued in both blue-collar and white-collar jobs according to Ozanne.

When jobs became scarce married women were often fired. During the Depression women teachers who were married had a difficult time hanging onto their jobs. While the leadership of the Wisconsin State Federation of Labor opposed firing married women, local trade unions such as the Green Bay Federated Trades Council often were active in barring married women from teaching during the late 1920s and 1930s.

Discrimination also came in separate pay scales. During the 1920s and 1930s Wisconsin school boards often had three separate salary scales: one for women, a higher one for men, and the highest pay for married men. However, because women dominated the teaching profession, unionization eventually destroyed discriminatory pay scales. Women who worked in factories were not helped until the 1964 Civil Rights Act, which prohibited race, age, and sex discrimination in the workplace. After 1964 both unions and employers quickly adopted single pay scales.

Ironically Wisconsin's most famous strike occurred, not in the radical 1930s, but in the 1950s. The gardened company town of Kohler, Wisconsin's first planned community, was the site of worker unrest. In 1954 contract talks broke down at the Kohler Company, and approximately 1,400 workers went on a strike that lasted for six bitter years. Kohler's plumbing supplies were nationally recognized, and the conflict on the streets of Sheboygan and the village of Kohler attracted national attention. In 1958 a U.S. Senate committee, the McClellan Committee, held hearings in Washington, D.C. that lasted five weeks. In 1960 the National Labor Relations Board ruled that the Kohler Company had refused to bargain, and the

company paid $4.5 million in back pay and pension credits.

THE GREAT DEPRESSION
The 1920s had been a time of laissez-faire. During the Roaring Twenties, tax rates were low and the national debt was decreasing at a satisfactory rate. Many believed that the management of the Federal Reserve System had made depressions a thing of the past. When the stock market crashed on Black Thursday, October 24, 1929, many business leaders thought the business slump was only temporary. They were gravely mistaken.

Banks failed. In 1930 Wisconsin had 933 banks; by 1933 it had only 445. More than 500 banks were suspended, while 90 banks consolidated. Recovery was slow. From 1934 to 1936 there were 10 more suspensions and 43 more consolidations. Eventually nearly 200 suspended banks reopened their doors, but banking in Wisconsin would not exceed its pre-1929 strength until 1942.

Manufacturing plummeted. About 1,500 Wisconsin businesses shut down between 1930 and 1932. In 1929 the value of manufacturing in Wisconsin was $960 million, but in 1933 it fell to $375 million.

Unemployment skyrocketed. Within a dizzying three years, from 1929 to 1932, Wisconsin factories lost nearly 56 percent of their workers—from 264,745 workers to 116,525. Milwaukee alone lost about 44 percent of its wage earners. There were 117,658 employed in Milwaukee in 1929, but by 1933 there were only 66,010 with jobs.

Farmers struggled. Wisconsin farm income fell from $350 million in 1930 to $199 million in 1932. Using 1929 as the base index for farm commodities, prices dropped from 100 to 43 by 1932. Drought hit the Midwest in the early 1930s, and the 1934 drought became the most severe ever recorded in Wisconsin.

Dreams evaporated. The bottom fell out of the 1920s with such ferociousness that it scarred an entire generation of Americans. People who lived through the Great Depression tell stories of fear and insecurity that never quite healed. Some blocked the memories entirely. "We weren't affected," said a woman vaguely who failed to mention she took in boarders. The children of the 1930s grew up with such movie classics as the Wizard of Oz and Gone With the Wind—but

The bustling appearance of Appleton's Fox River belies the realities of the period when this air view was taken, the decade of the Great Depression. In 1929 the value of manufacturing in Wisconsin was $960 million, but in 1933 it fell to $375 million. Wisconsin factories lost more than 50 percent of their workers —from 264,745 workers in 1929 to 116,525 workers in 1932. Courtesy, State Historical Society of Wisconsin

Wisconsin farmers dumped an estimated $10-million worth of
milk during their 1933 "milk
strikes," which protested falling
milk prices. Courtesy, Milwaukee Public Library

these children could also see breadlines and soup kitchens and the shantytowns of the homeless once called "Hoovervilles."

Apple vendors became a symbol of the depression in the summer of 1930 as a bumper crop of Oregon and Washington apples reached the country. Across the nation the unemployed sold apples for a nickel a piece. The vendor's profit for the day amounted to less than a dollar—if the vendor sold all the apples. Shoe shiners and street vendors became legion, selling everything from rubber balls to cheap neckties.

Drought and a decade of falling prices made Wisconsin's farmers desperate. Milk strikes in 1933 and 1934 showed the turmoil of the dairy farmers, revealing an underlying hostility between dairy farmers and dairy manufacturers. Most of Wisconsin milk was manufactured into dairy products such as cheese, butter, and ice cream products. As prices dropped, the dairy farmers of the radical Wisconsin Milk Pool in the Fox valley called three milk strikes in 1933 that tried to prevent milk from reaching the manufacturing plants. Two larger groups, the Farm Holiday Association and the Wisconsin Council of Agriculture, refused to join the strikes.

Milk was Wisconsin's white gold. As striking farmers poured their milk onto the ground they made a powerful statement. Two men died in the May strike of 1933, and Governor Schmedeman called in the state troops. One striker remembered, "Scenes of violence were being enacted elsewhere in the State, notably around Shawano and Appleton, and blood from noses was flowing almost as freely as milk." Although violent, the strikes were largely ineffective, as farmers could not agree on a unified strategy. The milk strikes were an angry release against an enemy no one could point to.

Beginning in 1933 Congress passed two bills designed by Franklin D. Roosevelt to help industry and agriculture. The National Industrial Recovery Act was largely a failure, falling victim to inside quarreling and outside criticism from both business and labor. The Supreme Court later invalidated the controversial act.

The Agricultural Adjustment Act (AAA) tried to curtail the abundance that caused falling prices. It identified nine basic crops and paid farmers to decrease acreage. This program helped some farmers, but small farmers or those who grew crops outside the chosen nine found themselves just as badly off, according to historian Paul Glad. In Wisconsin four AAA programs reached farmers—tobacco growers were paid to reduce their acreage by half, wheat growers were asked to reduce their yields about 15 percent, and corn and hog farmers reduced their yield approximately 30 percent.

Hunger and want in America's land of plenty was the Great Depression's greatest paradox. Critics of the New Deal could not forget the image of the the government buying six million pigs and having the meat butchered—much going to relief agencies—but much being dumped.

The Depression also emphasized the large disparity between urban and rural life. In 1930 only one in six Wisconsin farm homes had access to electrical power lines. Although 84 percent of Wisconsin farm families had automobiles, only 16 percent had indoor plumbing. The New Deal's Rural Electrification Administration began to provide electricity to rural areas, thus partially closing the gap between urban and rural dwellers.

Radio became America's new entertainment. The families that gathered around the large wooden radio were listening to the sounds of the modern era. Financial stability and better programming had made radio a mass advertising medium by 1929, and radio drew large audiences during the Depression years as people sought relief from their troubles. One of the longest-running shows sponsored by one advertiser was Johnson Wax's Fibber McGee & Molly, a comedy show that ran from 1935 to 1950.

As advertising hit the airwaves, people became more aware of the power of promotion. In 1932 Wilbur Carlson, a Wisconsin promoter attending an agricultural conference in Washington D.C., heard a representative from Maine talk about how the Pine Tree State was promoting itself as the Potato State. As Carlson listened, it struck him: Wisconsin was America's Dairyland. Carlson returned home and began lobbying. By the early 1940s Wisconsin's famous slogan was on its license plates.

The Depression years were not favorable times to start a print shop, let alone one that used the little-known process of photography to make smooth printing plates. During the 1930s most print shops and newspapers still used virtually the same process that Gutenberg had used to print his bibles in the fifteenth century—letterpress—where cast lead directly pressed onto paper. But W.A. Krueger, who opened his Milwaukee print shop in 1934, bet on the new photographic offset method, which dominated printing until the digital revolution of computer technology in the 1990s.

Children became the market for two of Wisconsin's oldest printers during the 1930s. In Menasha, the George Banta Company was launched as a leading publisher of "skill and drill workbooks for elementary school children. In Racine, the Western Publishing Company signed an innovative contract in 1933 with cartoonist Walt Disney to print storybooks, and Disneyland's first castles nestled in the imaginations of the readers of Big Little Books.

Fascinated with letterpress printing, a young George Banta collected unwanted metal type from his hometown newspaper in Franklin, Indiana. After marrying a Menasha woman in 1886, he hand-printed an 1888 book of family-written stories and poems called *Flying Leaves*. Begun in 1902, his small shop printed insurance forms and in 1908 began to print college fraternity and sorority magazines. Scholarly works, with their demands for precision and accuracy, formed the Collegiate Press during the 1920s, and in 1929 Banta began printing disposable workbooks for school children.

The Three Little Kittens and *The Little Red Hen* were two of the greatest hits of the Little Golden Books of Racine's Western Publishing Company. The print shop, begun in 1907, accidentally fell into book marketing when a Chicago publisher could not pay its printing bill. Western Publishing easily sold the unpaid inventory of children's books. First published in 1942, the 25-cent books with the gold foil spine became a familiar sight in household toy boxes. The one-billionth Little Golden Book was printed in 1986. The ubiquitous Betty Crocker's Cookbook had been published by Western since the early 1950s.

WORLD WAR II

During the hard times of the Depression, war clouds gathered in Europe. In March 1938 Hitler's armies marched into Austria to proclaim the union of the German Reich. By July 1940 Germany occupied most of Europe, including Poland, Czechoslovakia, Denmark, Norway, Belgium, the Netherlands, and more than half of France, including Paris. Japan signed a Tripartite Pact with Germany and Italy in September 1940 that pledged mutual support.

The United States remained cautiously neutral until the morning of December 7, 1941, when Japanese warplanes attacked Pearl Harbor, leaving 3,500 servicemen dead. America's entrance into the war galvanized the nation's economy. Mass production and the country's assembly lines were crucial to the country's war effort, and after more than a decade of unemployment the United States now had a labor shortage. Government contracts were awarded only to businesses that could guarantee the required labor needed to meet the contract deadlines.

Wisconsin's largest single wartime industry was shipbuilding. The shipyards of Superior, Sturgeon Bay, and Manitowoc produced primarily small naval vessels. The Manitowoc Shipbuilding Company employed 7,000 shipbuilders to produce 28 submarines. Since the subs were too large for the St. Lawrence River and Erie Canal, they sailed to Chicago and then were towed via the Illinois Drainage Canal to the Mississippi River. The subs were floated downriver on pontoon docks until reaching the Gulf. Of the 28 submarines produced, only three failed to return at the end of the war.

The automobile industry throughout the country halted production on new cars in 1942 and began making tanks, aircraft, engines, weapons, and ammunition. Chrysler became a major builder of Sherman tanks, while General Motors became the country's largest single producer of weapons. Nash Motors of Kenosha, which merged to become American Motors in 1954, built aircraft engines for Pratt & Whitney. The plant in Janesville built shells, and a popular slogan at the plant was "Keep 'Em Firing."

World War II brought women into the factory jobs once reserved only for men. Rosie the Riveter became the symbol of women working in the foundries and on the assembly lines. In Wisconsin small business owners such as Jefferson's Ben Schweiger were forced to hire women for the first time. Schweiger's furniture-making business would soon comprise 400 workers, half of whom were women. Discovering that attention to detail was a trait found not only in men, Schweiger continued to hire women after the war. In 1943 the Wisconsin Legislature abandoned its 40-year-old prohibition against hiring female clerks. By the war's end, 35 percent of the national workforce was female.

The farmers of Wisconsin helped feed the U.S. armed forces. Wisconsin's farmers were the major producers of the cheese, vegetables, and dried and evaporated milk that were sent overseas. The canning industry boomed. In 1941 alone the government bought one million cases of Wisconsin canned peas for the army and navy. In 1945 Wisconsin, the leading producer of vegetables for canning, produced 15 million cases of peas and nearly 12 million cases of sweet corn, beets, and beans. After the war about 150 canneries continued to operate.

Wisconsin's industries sent diverse goods overseas, from mess kits and raincoats to guns and trucks. Many of the military's combat boots were made of Milwaukee's Trostel leather. In 1938 Albert Trostel, Jr., had visited Europe and was convinced that war was imminent. On his return to Milwaukee Trostel immediately converted production from calf leather to the tougher side leather in anticipation of the need for combat boots.

One Wisconsin company changed products because of World War II. The Green Bay Soap Company had been making soap since 1881, but soap's major ingredient—glycerine—was needed for explosives. Edward Meyer and his family began processing other animal byproducts such as tallow and cured hides. By 1950 the Green Bay Soap Company would discontinue laundry soap, and in 1978 it changed its name to Anamax.

Wisconsin sent 375,000 citizens into service during World War II, and the number of Wisconsin casualties at the war's end was 7,980. With the returning GIs, Wisconsin would be part of the boom in education, buildings, and babies. An expanding middle class would shape the tastes and patterns of a new, prosperous economy.

The Wisconsin Products Exposition of 1922 in the Milwaukee Auditorium proudly displayed the auto, dairy, and manufacturing products that had helped bring the Wisconsin economy into the twentieth century. Courtesy, State Historical Society of Wisconsin

THE WISCONSIN IDEA CONTINUES

Fleets of rowboats carried tourists and guides on the Wisconsin River in the 1870s at the Wisconsin Dells. The main attractions of the area are the many bluffs and rock formations along the shores of the river. Courtesy, the H.H. Bennett Studio

The full moon rises above the Silos on this productive Wisconsin farm. Photo by R. Hamilton Smith

The pathways of the glaciers and ancient Indians, fur traders, and settlers are still alive in Wisconsin's newest major industry, tourism. Modern highways have replaced the Wisconsin River for getting around, but forest trails and crystal lakes still allow travelers to explore the land described by Nicolet and mapped by Marquette and Joliet in the seventeenth century.

Wisconsin's natural resources have allowed tourism to become part of Wisconsin's economic Big Three: manufacturing, which by 1986 produced approximately $59 billion in annual sales; agriculture, with a total annual product of $20 billion; and tourism, which brought in about $4.1 billion in 1984.

By the mid-1980s tourism in Wisconsin was a big business built on small and medium-sized establishments. Southeastern counties contributed to half of the state's total tourism, but in the northern one-third of Wisconsin tourism was the leading industry. Statewide the nearly 15 million visits by travelers created approximately 130,000 jobs in 1985.

Water, and its promise of renewal, was Wisconsin's first attraction for tourists. In the 1870s the springs in southern Wisconsin became buried treasure as entrepreneurs, doctors, and quacks promoted the miraculous powers of mineral water. "Taking of the waters" was the genteel remedy for ailments and frazzled nerves throughout the nineteenth century.

Waukesha, which became famous for its mineral spas, was trumpeted as "the Saratoga of the West," after New York's lavish Saratoga Springs where the wealthy and powerful came to sip. Waukesha's fame began in 1868 when one rich New Yorker, Colonel Richard Dunbar, drank from a spring and felt unusually refreshed. A diabetic, Dunbar felt so rejuvenated that he moved to Waukesha and bought 40 acres of land surrounding the spring he called "Bethesda," referring to the biblical house of mercy. In 1869 Dunbar pronounced himself cured of diabetes. Two Chicago promoters built a dazzling hotel, Fountain Spring House, launching Waukesha as a watery haven for affluent visitors throughout the country, especially the South. One newspaper editor in 1873

Above
In the 1880s the tourist steamer Dell Queen *docked on the Wisconsin River at the Wisconsin Dells near Kilbourn City. The well-known Wisconsin pioneer photographer H.H. Bennett is pictured third from the left. Courtesy, the H.H. Bennett Studio*

Left
The tourist steamboat Alexander Mitchell sailed on the Wisconsin River near Kilbourn City (later called the Wisconsin Dells) in the 1880s. Courtesy, the H.H. Bennett Studio

The Bethesda Spa in Waukesha
was known in the 1880s and
1890s as a fashionable resort
where people came to drink the
curative waters. In its heyday
Waukesha aspired to be the
"Saratoga of the West." Courtesy, the H.H. Bennett Studio

"The Pride of Waukesha!"

FOUNTAIN SPRING HOUSE

In the 1870s the Fountain Spring Hotel helped launch Waukesha nationally as a fashionable mineral spa for visitors, especially these from the South. Waukesha became the "Saratoga Springs of the West," as its pure groundwater was recommended for curing frazzled nerves, diabetes, and other ills. Courtesy, State Historical Society of Wisconsin

Finest Summer Hotel West of Saratoga Springs.

A New Hotel !   Elegantly Furnished !

Accommodations for 800 Guests

described a Sunday evening walk as a concentration of "at least $200,000 worth of jewelry, silks, satins, ribbons, laces, hair bustles, etc." Dunbar collected more than 1,000 orders for barrels of mineral water, providing area coopers with a beverage other than beer for filling their barrels.

Fashionable spas and bottles of Wisconsin water were not founded on a hoax. Wisconsin has some of the purest groundwater available because of its rock formation bequeathed by the glaciers. The Ice Age deposited vast amounts of sand and gravel mixed with snow. The porous sandstone rocks that formed were water bearers, or aquifers, which excell at transmitting clean groundwater. Sandstone covers most of Wisconsin, except for northern Wisconsin that has harder rock and the Driftless Area in southwestern Wisconsin where the glaciers did not form.

Wisconsin's clean, abundant groundwater gave competition to Dunbar's Bethesda Park. Healing springs were promoted in Sparta, Palmyra, Beloit, and Appleton. In Madison the Tonyawatha Springs Hotel on Lake Monona drew visitors. In Beaver Dam, the owner of the Vita Spring Pavilion, Dr. George Swan, declared, "I name this water Vita—or life—life to the whole urinary economy." Nine more springs discovered around Waukesha were given such fanciful names as Hygeia, Vesta, Lethean, Arcadian, Fountain, Clysmic, and Glenn. The well-known White Rock

continued to bottle Psyche mineral water after most resorts closed down at the turn of the century.

The railroads were the first to extensively promote vacations to Wisconsin. The Milwaukee Road claimed that its "palace cars" brought 8,000 to 10,000 passengers to Waukesha annually, and in the 1900s it advertised Lake Delavan as a vacation spot for Chicago tourists. In northern Wisconsin, the Wisconsin Central built the Chequamegon Hotel in Ashland and made a profit with its trainloads of vacationers and sportsmen. By 1915 the Milwaukee Road's "Guide to Summer Homes" featured 63 Wisconsin locations.

The crown jewel for vacationers to Wisconsin was Kilbourn City on the Wisconsin River, located amid eerie rock formations called the "Dalles" by the French fur traders. "Dalles," which means "a swift stream of water running between the high banks," was changed to "Dells" after the founding of Kilbourn City in 1856. Few settlers had seen these primeval vistas before the 1850s except for lumber raftsmen trying to survive the wild Wisconsin River. Parlour-room photography advertised the Wisconsin Dells and Devil's Lake long before Kilbourn City became a tourist spot. The Dells were captured in vivid three dimensions in double photographs called stereographs, which gave a startling sense of depth.

Kilbourn City's portrait photographer, Henry Hamilton Bennett, became one of the country's great

Right
The Lake Lawn Hotel was one of Delavan's retreats for Chicago tourists in 1900. Nearby Lake Geneva and Delavan have continued to attract Chicagoans eager to leave the city on a three-hour ride by train. Courtesy, State Historical Society of Wisconsin

Below right
The bluffs surrounding Devil's Lake were formed by the Ice Age and became a tourist attraction for vacationers also visiting Kilbourn City (later renamed Wisconsin Dells). Courtesy, State Historical Society of Wisconsin

RATES.

Per Day...........$ 2.00
Per Week........ 10.00

A Pleasant Summer Resort.

W. B. PEARL, PROPRIETOR.

CLIFF HOUSE, DEVIL'S LAKE, WISCONSIN.

Above
Madeline Island is the largest of the Apostle Islands of Chequamegon Bay, a popular spot for Ashland's tourists. Courtesy, State Historical Society of Wisconsin

Left
The Wisconsin Central Railroad advertised Ashland's Chequamegon Hotel in the 1880s. At the entrance to the Apostle Islands of Lake Superior, Ashland had a population of five in 1872. However, railroad surveyors and investors saw the tourist potential, and more than 200 buildings were constructed in the spring of 1872. Courtesy, State Historical Society of Wisconsin

A Wisconsin era ended with the last of the lumber rafts floating down the Mississippi River in 1915 at Prairie du Chien. Courtesy, State Historical Society of Wisconsin

landscape photographers. "You don't have to pose nature," said Bennett, "and it is less trouble to please." According to biographer Sara Rath, Bennett invented camera parts to simplify the bulky, complicated process of on-site photography. In 1886, using a shutter that could freeze action, he documented the active life of lumber raftsmen on the Wisconsin River, producing what is probably the first photographic essay.

By the 1870s Kilbourn City was a growing summer resort mainly because of Bennett's exciting stereographs. Bennett and Kilbourn City's tourism enjoyed a symbiotic relationship; the more tourists, the more portrait commissions for Bennett, who traveled with the sightseeing boats. In 1874 Bennett reported that he had sold more than 20,000 stereographs. Bennett was later hired by the Chicago, Milwaukee and St. Paul Railroad to photograph the scenery along the rail lines to attract railroad passengers. In 1931 Kilbourn City changed its name to Wisconsin Dells so that tourists could readily identify the town from railroad timetables and brochures.

Wisconsin's tourism evaporated each autumn, prompting resort owners to promote Wisconsin as a winter playground. In the 1920s Model-T Fords were converted into snowbuggies by exchanging wheels for skis. In 1927 Carl Eliason, of Lost Lake Resort in northern Vilas County patented a motorized toboggan that he called the "autoboggan." The modern snowmobile was designed in Canada in 1958, and Wisconsin became home to 6 of the 23 major producers. With its extensive trails and races, northern Wisconsin billed itself as the snowmobile capital of the world, and Wisconsin tourism became a year-round business.

After World War II Door County became one of the Midwest's most popular tourist destinations. Its 250-mile shoreline on Lake Michigan and its seacoast appeal also attracted artists, many of whom stayed to build art studios and galleries. Tourism gradually eclipsed commercial fishing and lumbering, which had sustained settlers and the large colonies of Belgians in the nineteenth century. The popular fish boils and active shipyards of Sturgeon Bay remind visitors of the peninsula's nautical past. Bountiful cherry trees and apple groves have also kept Door County a farming community.

The active State Historical Society of Wisconsin has helped protect Wisconsin's heritage, preserving the state's frontier architecture and Indian effigy mounds. In 1987 there were more than 1,000 Wisconsin listings on the National Register of Historic Places, including more than 80 historic districts.

Visitors can retreat to Wisconsin's pioneer past in historic sites preserved by the society. Madeline Island in northern Chequamegon Bay ventures back in time to the fur traders. In Baraboo the circus business is preserved in live performances at the Circus World Museum. Lead miners and the Cornish cut their presence at the Pendarvis and other Shake Rag Street sites in Mineral Point. The most elaborate site is Old World Wisconsin in Eagle, where nine farmsteads are traditionally farmed on 576 acres. Ethnic festivals during the summer add more color to Old World Wisconsin's celebration of the past.

The preservation of Wisconsin's unique Ice Age landscape was begun by citizens and private donations in the 1960s. In 1980 Congress declared it a National Scenic Trail, a designation given to famous pathways such as the Appalachian Trail. The 1,000-mile Ice Age Trail winds through bowl-shaped kettles, snake-like mounds called eskers, and elongated hills called drumlins. The trail follows the extensive mounds called end moraines that clearly outline the glaciers' last pathway into Wisconsin more than 70,000 years ago. Five of the nine units of the Ice Age National Reserve established in 1971 are open to the public: Horicon Marsh, Devil's Lake State Park, Interstate Park, Mill Bluff State Park, and the northern unit of Kettle Moraine State Forest.

Wisconsin was the first state to establish a park system, setting aside 50,000 acres in Lincoln County called "the State Park" in 1878. The land was later sold to lumber companies, but in 1900 Interstate Park was established along the St. Croix River, becoming Wisconsin's oldest park. During the 1930s the federal government purchased land that became the Nicolet and Chequamegon national forests, and by 1942 Wisconsin had eight additional state forests. By 1987 Wisconsin had 48 state parks, 9 state forests, 11 state trails, and 3 recreation areas.

In 1961 Wisconsin became a pioneer in conserving its natural resources, especially its single most important geological gift—water. The Outdoor Recreation Act Program (ORAP) pledged $50 million for cleaning the environment and buying land. Wisconsin's sand and gravel aquifer, which covers most of the state, is at the land's surface and therefore is particularly vulnerable to pollutants from industry, municipal waste, farm fertilizers, pesticides, landfills, and some types of mining. Water pollution became ORAP'S primary target, and by 1984 almost half of the total $332 million program had been spent on cleaning Wisconsin's water.

Two governors of the Great Lakes states have likened clean water of the Great Lakes to the oil boon.

When this picture of Fish Creek in Door County was taken in 1950, the 250-mile peninsula was quickly becoming one of the Midwest's most popular tourist spots. The lumber and fishing traditions of the nineteenth century were replaced by artists' studios and galleries and hotels. Courtesy, State Historical Society of Wisconsin

Logging had built Chippewa
Falls into a prosperous town by
1900, although the lumber industry was moving west. The challenge for logging towns was to
build a manufacturing base to replace the lumber trade. Courtesy, State Historical Society of
Wisconsin

"Water will be for the Midwest almost like oil is to the OPEC countries," said former Michigan Governor William G. Milliken. In 1987 Wisconsin's Governor Tommy Thompson described Wisconsin's strength in terms of water. "We have an abundance of natural resources, clean air and clean water," he said after bristling at the notion that Wisconsin is part of the "Rust Belt." Speaking to the Wisconsin Farm Equipment Association, Thompson said clean water is going to be "the new petroleum of the future."

Many of Wisconsin's industries, such as food processing, require abundant clean water. By 1983 Wisconsin industries were using 133 million gallons of groundwater each day. The six major industries that require clean water are pulp and paper, fruit and vegetable processing, cheesemaking, brewing, meat processing, and electroplating.

Wisconsin's paper industry, one of the chief polluters of water, has become a corporate leader in preventing the pollution that contaminates water and kills fish. Since the 1970s it has spent more than $450 million in environmental protection equipment, with operating costs for cutting pollution exceeding $115 million annually. Since the 1970s papermakers have cut 80 percent of BOD (biochemical oxygen demand) and 90 percent of TSS (total suspended solids) discharged—while increasing paper production more than 46 percent. By 1983 production of each ton of paper required 60 percent less water than the amount needed in 1960, and production of each ton of paper used 22 percent less energy than it required in 1972.

However, a new challenge for science and technology is unraveling the exact source of toxic waste pollution in water and providing dependable tests that measure toxic levels of pollutants such as PCBs and dioxin. Research and cooperation from municipalities and industry is crucial. In 1986 Neenah's Biodyne Chemicals and the University of Wisconsin-Madison were experimenting with a revolutionary sulfur-free paper process, which could help reduce acid rain and one source of water pollution.

Wisconsin's careful stewardship of its lakes, rivers and forests is essential for the growing tourist industry. Old World settlements in a glacial land of lakes make Wisconsin distinctive when competing for tourist dollars and business travelers. In 1986 business travel was beginning to eclipse pleasure trips in traditional resort towns such as Lake Geneva. Convention centers were built in cities such as Green Bay and Oshkosh with an eye to accommodating business travel.

The continued growth of Wisconsin tourism will rest on general prosperity plus the perception that Wisconsin is indeed a desirable place to trek. Wisconsin's unique landscape and ethnic history is one formula for positioning Wisconsin in the minds of vacationers and business travelers. The diversity of Americana is something Wisconsin has preserved in abundance—or often overlooked in many of its small cities and towns.

RECESSION AND RECOVERY

During the 1970s Wisconsin was such a prosperous state that in 1977 the *Wall Street Journal* called it the "Star of the Snow Belt." Wisconsin gained manufacturing jobs from 1970 to 1979 and matched the national growth in manufacturing jobs. The national newspaper asserted that Wisconsin could compete with the Sun Belt states because of its quality of life, low unemployment, and strategic business tax cuts.

And then the recession hit in 1979, and by the early 1980s Wisconsin's manufacturing economy was in a depression. Job layoffs in automobile and nonelectrical equipment boosted the state unemployment to 7.8 percent, causing Wisconsin to exceed the national level for the first time since 1958. Economists noted that Wisconsin's recovery began later and moved more slowly than the nation's during the recesssion years of 1980 to 1983. The continued downswing of manufacturers such as Allis-Chalmers indicated that Wisconsin's manufacturing was in a painful transition.

In 1984 Governor Anthony Earl formed the Wisconsin Strategic Development Commission, a group of corporate leaders and state officials, to evaluate Wisconsin's economic future. The 1985 final report, which concluded that manufacturing would continue to be the foundation of Wisconsin's economy, identified the strengths and weaknesses of Wisconsin's major existing industries. The commission believed that part of the key to preserving the existing job base lay in the Wisconsin Idea, the partnership between activist scholars and leaders in government and industry. In effect, argued the commission, the Wisconsin Idea could "improve the working relationship between faculty and private industry" through such programs as industrial-funded faculty chairs, expanded partnerships in the University-Industry Research Program

(UIR), and additional research for entrepreneurs and small business.

The markets that had fueled Wisconsin manufacturing— construction, farm, auto, mining, and oil machinery— remained in a stupor during the mid-1980s. Wisconsin's nonelectrical machinery industry, which produced farm and heavy machines for international markets, was Wisconsin's largest employer in 1983 with 92,000 workers, down from 1979's peak of 135,000 jobs. In other sectors, electrical machinery manufacturers employed about 49,000 people in 1984, a loss of about 10,000 jobs. The primary and fabricated metals sector, which employed about 65,000 people in foundries in 1983, lost nearly 25,000 jobs during the recession.

Recovery remained elusive. Modernizing industries was one costly avenue of recovery pursued by Wauwatosa's Briggs & Stratton, which invested $230 million in modernizing its production of small gasoline engines. The modernization by Briggs & Stratton, which reportedly had 60 percent of the U.S. market in small engines, helped to rejuvenate Wisconsin's strong tool and die makers. Tool and die makers are the ultimate machinists since they make the machines that make machines.

In competing for international customers, Wisconsin's Department of Development opened offices in Frankfurt, West Germany, and in Hong Kong. The department also began the Mentor-Mentee program which paired experienced Wisconsin exporters with new companies that needed advice on how to enter the exporting business.

The hard times of the 1980s brought one of Wisconsin's oldest manufacturers to its knees. In 1987 Wisconsin's pioneer mogul in heavy engines, the Allis-Chalmers Corporation, filed under Chapter 11 of the Bankruptcy Code for reorganization with a reported debt of $248.4 million.

PAPER AND PUBLISHING

During the devastating recession from 1979 to 1983, only the paper industry in Wisconsin achieved growth. Wisconsin's 46 mills produced 3.7 million tons of paper annually, or 11.6 percent of the nation's total, the highest of any state. The forest products industry—lumber, wood, and paper—was the second largest employer in the state in 1985, with 76,000

jobs, and the largest in 28 counties; in some northern towns a paper or pulp mill was the only employer.

Wisconsin also ranked first in the diversity of its paper products. Wisconsin's papermakers led the nation in the production of writing paper, laminated and coated process paper, and sanitary tissue products. Wisconsin's Consolidated Papers was the country's leading producer of high-quality coated paper used for magazines and commercial printing. Wisconsin's Fort Howard Paper Company invested $42 million in 1984 to operate the world's widest tissue-making machine.

Recycled paper, which has about 50 different grades, constituted about 25 percent of Wisconsin's papermaking. In 1985 Wisconsin became the national leader by producing 1.4 million tons of recycled paper, the majority of which was cardboard. As early as 1925 there were 13 recycling mills in Wisconsin—6 were rag mills and 7 used paper stock.

The dearth of valuable softwood trees for papermaking remained a concern of Wisconsin's forest industry. Wisconsin was blanketed with softwoods during the nineteenth century, but lumberjacks and forest fires eliminated most of the white pine, spruce, and fir. Modern forest management is by definition a patient industry, since it takes 30 to 40 years to grow trees for commercial use. By 1987 about 42 percent of Wisconsin's land, or 14.5 million acres, was commercial forest land, of which 82 percent was hardwood used for construction millwork and furniture. Only 22 percent of Wisconsin's softwood demands were supplied by Wisconsin's forests, forcing papermakers to import 155 million cubic feet of softwood from Canada or other states.

Wisconsin's leadership in paper was a perfect complement to one of the state's strongest emerging industries—printing and publishing. Wisconsin's industry grew 30 percent from 1969 to 1983, while nationally it grew 17 percent. The majority of Wisconsin's 1,200 companies, which provided 33,000 jobs in 1983, employed about 20 workers, reflecting the national trend. The largest sector was commercial printing, with 13,800 jobs in 1983, followed by newspapers, with 10,700 jobs, and book publishing, with 3,200 jobs. Weekly magazines such as *Time, Newsweek,* and *Sports Illustrated* filled the presses of one of Wisconsin's largest commercial printers, Quad/Graphics. Established in 1971 by Harry Quadracci of Pewaukee, Quad/Graphics demonstrated an ability to

Above
Established in 1867, the Leinen-
kugel Brewery of Chippewa
Falls had prospered with the
lumber town. Times would
change after World War I with
Prohibition. Courtesy, State
Historical Society of Wisconsin

Left
The Whiting paper mill in Mena-
sha was part of the rapid
growth of paper and pulp mills
in Wisconsin during the late nine-
teenth century. Courtesy, State
Historical Society of Wisconsin

meet weekly deadlines, enabling it to quickly become a major printer of national magazines.

BEER, CHEESE, AND "BRATS"

Although Wisconsin's economic base remained in manufacturing, Wisconsin's national reputation rested on its beer, cheese, and brats. Wisconsin's pioneer reputation for beer and cheese survived into the twentieth century, although beer was no longer the family business it was in the nineteenth century. By 1983 dairy products led food production with more than 17,000 jobs, while meat packing provided 13,400. The beverage industry and the preserved fruits and vegetable sector each employed 9,800 people in 1983.

Modern consumer tastes had changed Wisconsin food production. By 1985 the poultry industry was expected to outpace meat shipments, although high-quality processed meats, such as the proud bratwursts of Sheboygan, still had markets. Madison's Oscar Mayer hotdog, promoted since 1963 by the famous "wiener jingle," continued as a national product. Wisconsin's canning industry was also changing. One of Wisconsin's oldest canning companies, the Larsen Company of Green Bay begun in 1890, began adapting to the consumer's growing preference for frozen vegetables. By the mid-1980s its nine Wisconsin plants were working to meet the goal of a 50-50 mix of frozen and canned vegetables.

Milwaukee's pioneer elixir—beer—had changed the most. National competition and fewer beer drinkers reshaped the beers that made Milwaukee famous. Consolidation turned many of Milwaukee's family breweries into historic anecdotes. Pabst was sold to a California millionaire in 1985; Schlitz's brewery was bought and closed by Stroh's of Detroit in 1982; the Miller brewery was bought by the Philip Morris Company in 1971; after closing in the late 1950s, Blatz was brought back by G. Heileman in 1969. In 1987 G. Heileman was bought by an Australian brewery.

Wisconsin remained a national beer producer in 1986 with Miller, Heileman, and Pabst breweries producing more than 15.6 million barrels. Miller, which ranked second in production after Anheuser-Busch, in 1987 planned to invest $12 million in a new hops plant in Watertown. However, the number of brewery jobs fell during the 1980s, largely due to the Schlitz closing and increased automation. By 1984 Wisconsin breweries employed 5,635 workers, down from 8,814 jobs in 1980.

The brewery begun in the hinterlands of Wisconsin in 1858, G. Heileman's of La Crosse, emerged as the fourth-largest brewer in the country by the mid-1980s. In 1960 the 39th-ranked brewery began acquiring more than one dozen small breweries across the country at favorable prices. By 1983 its breweries were producing about 26 million barrels of beer from Baltimore to San Antonio and Seattle. Combined with its bakery and snack food products, G. Heileman became one of Wisconsin's leading food and beverage producers.

The taste of Europe, which built Milwaukee into Beer City, began returning to some of Wisconsin's small breweries in the 1980s. These boutique beers were made in small batches and sold at import prices, tapping the Wisconsin tradition of pride in the hometown brew. G. Heileman decided to keep Blatz a small producer of custom-made beer, as was Sprecher Brewing of Milwaukee. Hibernia of Eau Claire and Capital Brewery of Middleton produced European-style beers, while Joseph Huber of Monroe became a regional producer of its Augsburger brand. Point Brewery of Stevens Point and Leinenkugel of Chippewa Falls had been well-established local breweries since the 1860s.

Cows remained big business in Wisconsin. In 1985 America's Dairyland produced 1.8 billion pounds of cheese, 35 percent of the nation's total. Wisconsin also led in butter production with 295.6 million pounds, and in condensed milk and whey products. Wisconsin's food processors in 1985 were a diverse group of nearly 1,100 companies, the majority of which employed less than 30 people.

Wisconsin's agricultural prosperity of the 1970s was not expected to return during the 1980s. Overproduction continued, food prices fell, and a strong dollar crippled farm exports. Dairy surpluses caused Congress to cut dairy supports, and farm income spiraled down. In 1983 Wisconsin ranked eighth nationally in farm receipts—small comfort for Wisconsin farmers, who earned an average of $12,756. In three harsh years Wisconsin lost 9,000 farms—in 1982 there were 92,000 farms and by 1985 there were 83,000. More and more farmers sought part-time jobs in the struggle

Ginseng was a closely guarded
secret for Marathon County
farmers, who began exporting
the temperamental root to the Orient as early as the 1900s.
Growing ginseng is labor intensive and requires four years for
each harvest. Courtesy, State Historical Society of Wisconsin

to keep their farms. Wisconsin's agriculture was based on medium-sized farms, the average being 213 acres compared to the 1985 national average of 433 acres.

The country's farm crisis also depressed makers of farm machinery, which stymied many Wisconsin manufacturers. Nearly one in four jobs in Wisconsin could be traced to the state's farms, since Wisconsin was also a leading producer of farm machinery and processed food.

In the 1980s Wisconsin farming entered the computer age, where skillful management and marketing was almost as crucial as rain. The traditional jargon of business—capital, cost reduction, demographics, new technology—would be part of the farms that survive, according to the task force that studied agriculture for the Wisconsin Economic Development Commission in 1985.

Some farmers had turned to specialty crops. While only 22 percent of farm revenues came from crops, Wisconsin was first in corn for silage and led the nation in green peas, beets, cabbage, and sweet corn for processing. Wisconsin ranked second in cranberries and third in maple syrup, with mint another specialty.

Some farmers turned to the Orient and invested in ginseng and shiitake mushrooms. Wisconsin's wild ginseng was domesticated by farmers in Marathon County during the early 1900s. Farmers guarded their secrets and exported the temperamental plant to New York and the Orient. By 1985 Marathon County had become the country's ginseng capital, producing more than 1.1 million pounds. Prized in the Orient for medicinal powers, ginseng sold for about $60 a pound in 1980, and farmers were willing to buy the expensive roots and invest the four years it took to produce the first crop. By 1986 overproduction had driven the price of ginseng down to approximately $30. Despite the drop in price, Marathon County exported 97 percent of the nation's ginseng to markets such as Hong Kong and Singapore.

Some agricultural officials were optimistic that shiitake mushrooms could grow into a billion-dollar industry nationally during the 1990s. Wisconsin had the oak suited for the exotic mushrooms, and in 1987 about 300 growers were investing in the spawns, which new techniques allowed to grow within six months. The success of shiitakes would ultimately depend on convincing the American consumer that they tasted better than familiar mushrooms—or that they cut cholesterol levels, as the Japanese believed.

Mink farms remained another Wisconsin specialty. In 1984 Wisconsin led Utah and Minnesota, two leading mink producers, with its 241 mink ranches, which produced 1.2 million of the 4.2 million pelts in the country. It required approximately 40 to 50 mink to produce one full-length mink coat.

BUSINESS GROWTH AND R&D

During the prosperity of the 1970s Wisconsin was considered by many business leaders to have a poor business climate, specifically because of its higher taxes. With the recession the criticsms grew sharper, and in 1983, after vocal criticism about Wisconsin's business climate, Darwin Smith of the venerable paper giant Kimberly-Clark moved his company's world headquarters from Neenah to Dallas, Texas.

Academia rallied to the defense of Wisconsin's business climate. According to William Strang, business professor at the University of Wisconsin-Madison, by objective standards Wisconsin's business climate in 1982 was average—"at worst." Peter Eisinger, professor of political science at the University of Wisconsin-Madison, found in a 1982 study of Fortune 500 companies that there was no clear relationship to tax rates and decisions to move—44 percent of the companies went to areas with lower tax rates, while 44 percent went to areas with higher rates.

Wisconsin was a top-ranking state for many new business opportunities, according to new criteria for measuring business climate devised by the Corporation for Enterprise Development that premiered in 1987. Wisconsin's high employment and income levels made it a good place to work. Although Wisconsin's financial resources such as venture capital were relatively scarce, its work force was high quality, making it more desirable for new and incoming businesses. The report concluded that Wisconsin needed a better partnership between business and state government, but the biggest need for improvement was entrepreneurial energy as measured by self-employment, new business growth, and women and minority business ownerships.

The newer criteria for business climate suggested that perhaps Wisconsin could recapture its "Star of the Snowbelt" stature. The Wisconsin Strategic

Development Commission, the partnership of business leaders and state analysts, concluded that Wisconsin should advertise its exemplary strengths in work force, education, natural resources, and quality of life. Wisconsin residents received a high standard of living in services, schools, and vocational education. The strong work ethic from the early immigrants survived in Wisconsin's reputation for productive workers and squeaky clean government.

Many Wisconsin analysts hoped that if the nation's service industries grew more prominent in the Midwest, Wisconsin could offer quality of life as its trump card. Wisconsin had preserved its natural beauty in parks, ranging from northern woods to city parks and historic preservations. Wisconsin's clean environment and pure groundwater could be found throughout the state, including the industrialized southeastern region. Its tradition of clean government had continued, following the earlier examples set by Robert La Follette's Progressives and Milwaukee's Socialist mayors.

Quality of life also meant that daily life was easier in Wisconsin, according to business professor Dowell Myers at the University of Wisconsin-Madison. Myers, who moved from Texas in 1986, observed that Wisconsin's quality of life made it easier for young families to pursue the American dream. Wisconsin's quality of life included diversity in leisure and recreation, low cost of living and housing, low crime rate, and even the low "hassle factor" of traffic.

The explosive growth of high-tech business was expected to continue in specific industries through 1995, according to analysts for the Wisconsin Strategic Development Commission. The commission pointed to the University of Wisconsin's international research reputation plus its dominance in attracting research funding as obvious advantages for high-tech firms.

In 1984 the National Science Foundation ranked the University of Wisconsin-Madison third nationally among universities in expenditures for R&D firms. Most firms were clustered in Dane County, where the University of Wisconsin-Madison is located. The campus had more than 5,000 research projects, and Wisconsin firms such as Agracetus, Agrigenetics, and Astronautics drew on university resources.

The university's Biotechnology Center, established in 1984, coordinated more than 150 faculty

In 1903 Charles Van Hise, the new president of the University of Wisconsin, proposed that scholars use their knowledge to help state government in problem solving. His proposal was not original; it echoed the advice of two earlier university presidents, John Bascom and Thomas Chamberlain. The Wisconson Idea was born during Van Hise's tenure. Courtesy, State Historical Society of Wisconsin

members in 15 different departments to explore new technology such as food processing and medical technology. Fitchburg's Nicolet Corporation, just south of Madison, worked with faculty in its advancements in hearing aids. In 1983 Fitchburg's Promega Corporation became the first biotechnology company to enter into a joint venture agreement with the People's Republic of China for establishing Chinese manufacture of enzymes.

The university's Wisconsin Center for Applied Microelectronics used faculty research for specific projects of several Wisconsin manufacturers. Dodgeville's Silicon Sensors received help in making devices that transform light into electrical energy. The center also designed new ways for monitoring flashlight batteries for Madison's Rayovac Corporation. Milwaukee's Rexnord Company received help in its pioneering process called X-ray lithography, while researchers were helping to modernize specific instruments of Milwaukee's Johnson Controls.

High-tech seeds also fell in northern Wisconsin. In 1984 two-thirds of the world's renowned supercomputers were designed and built in Chippewa County. Seymour Cray began Cray Research in his hometown of Chippewa Falls in the early 1970s. Although Cray moved his corporate headquarters to Minneapolis, supercomputer building in Chippewa County employed 1,700 people in 1987, rejuvenating the county's sagging economy. In Marinette, Cade Industries made aerospace component parts, and in 1987 Cade Industries was ranked by *Inc.* magazine as fourteenth of the 100 fastest-growing small public companies.

Not all businesses chose to locate in Wisconsin because of the university. Gary Comer of Dodgeville's Lands' End, a successful clothing and catalogue company, explained that he moved his firm from Chicago because "I fell in love with the gently rolling hills and woods and cornfields and being able to see the changing season."

The Old World heritage is still a part of Wisconsin. A 1970s survey revealed that 5 percent of Wisconsin residents were either born in Germany or had parents from Germany. However, 50 percent of the respondents claimed to be of German ancestry. Scandinavian ancestry is also above the national average throughout Wisconsin—La Crosse, Eau Claire, Stoughton, and Mt. Horeb are Norwegian, while Racine has been described as "the most Danish city in America." Wisconsin also has the nation's seventh-largest Polish population, centered mainly in the Milwaukee and Stevens Point areas.

Some of Wisconsin's small businesses have carried on the nineteenth-century tradition of pride in custom work. The W.C. Russell Moccasin Company, which has made handmade boots since its founding in 1898, was bought by Berlin's Bill Gustin in 1927. Resisting the trend of automation, his shoemakers have adapted styles for specialty catalogue companies such as L.L. Bean. In Kewaunee, Joseph Svoboda from Bohemia made church furniture in the 1880s, and a century later the family business, Svoboda Industries, specialized in traditional grandfather clocks; five different styles of clocks were named after Svoboda children. In Sturgeon Bay the Palmer Johnson company gained prominence as the world's largest builder of custom sailing yachts, their reputation for attention to detail impressing such clients as King Juan Carlos of Spain.

Wisconsin's strengths helped to cushion the economic turbulence of the 1980s in business and industry. The state's self-examination that culminated in the Wisconsin Strategic Development Commission reconfirmed the partnership between scholars, state government, and the risk takers of business. The Wisconsin Idea continued to create pathways as divergent as the tastes and opinions of Wisconsin residents.

Wisconsin's greatest strength lies in its diversity, from industry to landscapes and ethnic traditions. The people of this glacial land preserve Wisconsin's Old World values, but they also rely on Wisconsin's progressive tradition of experimenting with new ideas. Wisconsin is still a frontier state of opportunity. Perhaps Wisconsin's most enduring legacy is the pioneer's love for excellence and the optimism that all things are possible if one works hard enough.

A round barn in Vernon County pictured on a crisp, autumn day.
Photo by R.J. and Linda Miller, courtesy,
Wisconsin Department of Tourism

Left
Fall colors reflecting in a peaceful lake are a pleasant sight enjoyed by Wisconsin residents and visitors alike. Photo by R. Hamilton Smith

Facing page left
A clear blue sky frames this photograph of Julian Bay in the Apostle Islands. Photo by R. Hamilton Smith

Facing page below
A bright sun sparkles through the trees above Trout Lake in Northern Highland State Forest. Photo by R. Hamilton Smith

Below
A Wisconsin sunset is framed by overhanging trees in this R. Hamilton Smith photograph.

Above
A farmer and his threshing machine work a field in Old World Wisconsin. Photo by James L. Sernovitz, courtesy, Wisconsin Department of Tourism

Left
Visitors to the popular Flake Out Fest enjoy a sleighride during a wintery day in Wisconsin Dells. The festival features snow sculpting, a snowman-making contest, Eskimo Pie eating contest, tricycle races, ice carving, kite flying, hot air balloons, ice skating, sleigh rides, and cross-country skiing. Courtesy, Wisconsin Department of Tourism

Facing page
A rustic, winter scene in rural Wisconsin. Photo by R.J. and Linda Miller, courtesy, Wisconsin Department of Tourism

Facing page top
Roger's Street Fishing Village in Two Rivers, as it appears from Lake
Michigan. Photo by R.J. and Linda Miller, courtesy, Wisconsin
Department of Tourism

Facing page bottom
The picturesque Madison skyline features a spectacular view
of Lake Monona. Photo by Joe Demaio, courtesy,
Wisconsin Department of Tourism.

Above
A striking view of the Wisconsin State Capital from State Street.
Photo by Zane Williams, courtesy, Wisconsin Department of Tourism

Above
An Abbotsford barn, like many barns in Wisconsin, becomes a canvas as well as a place for dairy cows. Courtesy, Wisconsin Division of Tourism

Left
Wisconsin's agriculture land is some of the most productive in the nation. Photo by R. Hamilton Smith

Above
Birch trees cast soft shadows while the sun sets behind a Wisconsin pasture. Photo by R. Hamilton Smith

Right
Clouds promise rain above the windswept Cuex Meadow Wildlife Refuge. Photo by R. Hamilton Smith

Above
Stonefield Village near Cassville in western Wisconsin preserves a nineteenth-century town and the pioneer industries that helped build the frontier. Maintained by the State Historical Society of Wisconsin, this outdoor museum leaves behind the modern world.
Photo by Hubert Franks, courtesy, Wisconsin Division of Tourism

Right
A visitor to a traditional pumpkin farm peruses the aisles for the perfect jack-o-lantern. Courtesy, Wisconsin Department of Tourism

Below
An Amish farmer leads his hay wagon across a field. Photo by R.J. and Linda Miller, courtesy, Wisconsin Department of Tourism

A vendor at this popular Dane County Farmer's Market sells fresh vegetables and flowers to local patrons. Photo by Gary Knowles, courtesy, Wisconsin Department of Tourism

Above
Avid bicyclists circle the State Capitol during the Dave Kagy Wheels on
Willy Criterium race in Madison. Photo by Jim Bach, courtesy,
Wisconsin Department of Tourism

Facing page top
The popular Milwaukee Marina is a picturesque accent
to the city's skyline. Photo by Dave LaHaye, courtesy,
Wisconsin Department of Tourism

Facing page bottom
Boating enthusiasts enjoy a gorgeous day during the Lake Mendota
Regatta in Madison. The regatta runs for a week and features more than
200 boats and 2,500 racers. Photo by Donald R. Johanning, courtesy,
Wisconsin Department of Tourism

Above
Skiers enjoy the fresh snow at Lake Geneva in Walworth County. Photo by Donald S. Abrams, courtesy, Wisconsin Department of Tourism

Left
Avid skiers hit the slopes at the Rib Mountain Ski Area which has the second highest vertical drop in the Midwest. Photo by Doug Alft, courtesy, Wisconsin Department of Tourism

The annual American Birkebeiner race, held the third weekend in February, attracts 6,500 skiers from around the world and 15,000 cheering spectators. Photo by Philip G. Olson, courtesy, Wisconsin Department of Tourism

Tribal dancing is one of the many attractions at Milwaukee's Indian Summer Festival. Courtesy, Wisconsin Department of Tourism

The Old Schlitz Brewery *was commissioned by the New Deal's Federal Art Project, which employed artists during the Great Depression. Painter Paul Lauterbach apprenticed as an artist in Germany before coming to the United States in the 1920s and exhibiting at Milwaukee's Layton Art Gallery. Courtesy, Charles A. Wustum Museum of Fine Arts, Racine*

Above left
Oktoberfest originated as a popular way to mark the end of the crop harvest. Today, pubs and festivals are a popular destination to celebrate this German-inspired holiday. Courtesy, Wisconsin Department of Tourism

Above
A popular Farmer's Market surrounds the State Capitol each weekend as sellers showcase their vegetables, flowers, and other fresh items. Photo by Gary Knowles, courtesy, Wisconsin Department of Tourism

Left
The Great Circus Parade is a tradition dating back to 1963. Due to financial restrictions, parade planners expect to discontinue the event in 2004. Photo by R.J. and Linda Miller, courtesy, Wisconsin Department of Tourism

Above
Jimbo and Jolly pose for a picture as the train arrives carrying circus props and fellow clowns. Photo by Zane Williams, courtesy, Wisconsin Department of Tourism

Left
The Hudson Hot Air Affair is the premier winter ballooning event and winter festival in the Midwest. Thousands of visitors head to the St. Croix Valley community every year on the first full weekend in February. Photo by R.J. and Linda Miller, courtesy, Wisconsin Department of Tourism

Left
Long before he "discovered" water skiing, Tommy Bartlett was well-known throughout America for his popular "Welcome Traveler" broadcast show. Born in 1914 in Milwaukee, Bartlett started offering water skiing shows back in the 1950s. Audiences gathered daily from Memorial Day to Labor Day at Wisconsin Dells to watch the spectaculars, which continue to this day. Courtesy, Wisconsin Department of Tourism

Below
Snowmobile racing and Eagle River have become so deeply intertwined for the past 40 years that the names are practically synonymous. The first Eagle River race took place in 1964. Photo by Philip G. Olsen, courtesy, Wisconsin Department of Tourism

The American Birkebeiner race in Cable, Wisconsin
attracts thousands of elite and recreational skiers.
Courtesy, Wisconsin Department of Tourism

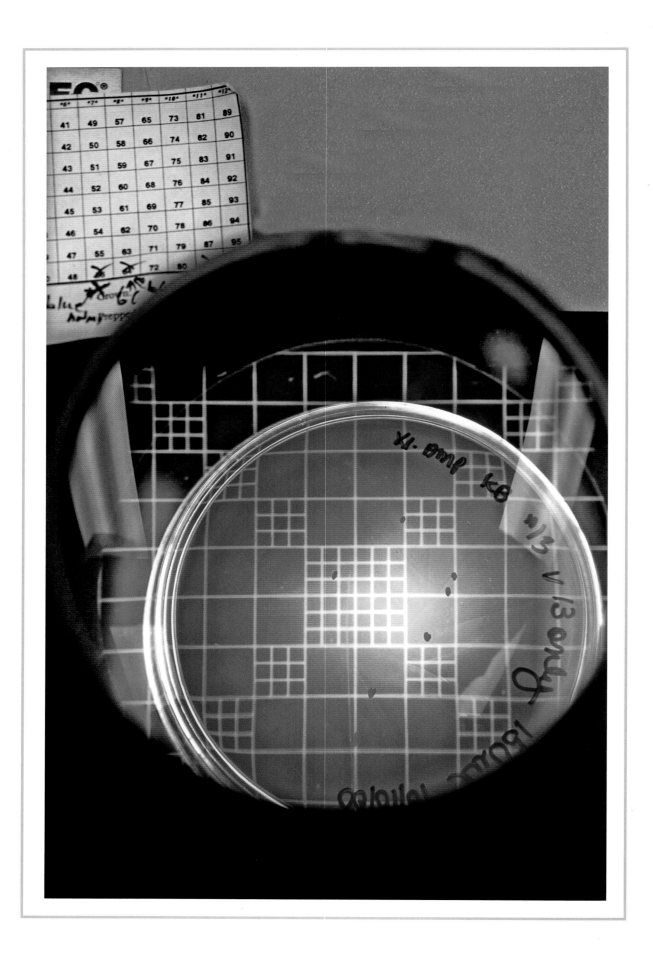

FULL CIRCLE: WISCONSIN'S ANCIENT HERITAGE AND HIGH-TECH FUTURE

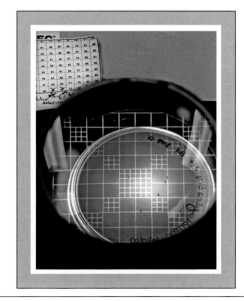

Counting bacteria colonies to use for genetic DNA sequencing in the Blattner research lab. Photo by Jeff Miller, courtesy, University of Wisconsin-Madison

Fishing fed his family. It also fed his spirit. And in the cold darkness the light from his headlamp illuminated the waters filled with spawning walleye. Over two centuries earlier, brightly lit torches on evening lakes gave his Ojibwe people the French name, Lac du Flambeau or "lake of torchlight."

"Someone could easily shoot me in the head," Nick Hockings thought, as angry shouts cut the night air. As he stood tall in his boat—light on his head and spear in hand—he tried to ignore the protests from the shoreline. But Nick Hockings could not ignore the anger, often mixed with hatred, and always clouded by fears that Indians would claim all the prized walleye. A gun fired into the air. He was alone in the boat except for this bright beacon perched on his head. *Just how angry were these protesters?*

Only the brave fished Ojibwe-style in the mid-1980s. As hundreds of protesters shouted or threw rocks, it was not unusual to hear a gunshot from the shorelines. Tribal drums sounded support to spearfishers, but ugly slogans also filled the cold spring air. By 1989 spearfishing was as much a political act as a cultural one.

It took 10 years before the U.S. Supreme Court ruled and upheld the Ojibwe's treaty right to spear fish within the tribe's ceded territory. And it took almost as long for residents to realize that spearfishing would not destroy northern Wisconsin's sports fishing economy. This was no small fear since tourism is one of Wisconsin's "Big Three," after agriculture and manufacturing.

However, stakes were higher in northern Wisconsin because tourism was, and still is, the leading industry. Throughout the struggle over fishing rights, tribal leaders tried to tell frightened whites that Indians were not taking all the fish, that they had strict rules for a "safe harvest," and meticulously counted each fish take. Fishing in northern Wisconsin would remain tourism's centerpiece, especially with the conservation work of the newly formed Great Lakes Fish and Wildlife Commission (GLFWC) working with the state to monitor fishing limits.

Ironically, the ugly protests themselves dampened Wisconsin's tourism—but with all the shouting who could hear? Television cameras followed the angry protests, and news reports added to the confusion every time a headline proclaimed, "Courts *give* Indians *new* rights." Eventually the media learned that courts did not give Indians any new rights; instead, the tribes retained rights protected by their treaty with the U.S. government. As journalist and historian Patty Loew observed, northern Wisconsin was often called "the Mississippi of the North."

It was a rocky start for cultural renewal. For Wisconsin's tribes, spearfishing was part of the larger challenge: explaining American Indian sovereignty. As Larry Nesper documents, the Walleye Wars were fought on the lakes, in the courts, and in public and media gatherings throughout the state. It began when the 1974 Voigt decision first upheld Indian treaty rights for off-reservation fishing. And for the next 25 years Indian

Northern Wisconsin would lose its summer soulfulness if the common loon did not remind listeners of its 65-million-year-old ancestry. The haunting cries pierce the evening light as loons nestle in lakes and tend to their newborn. Courtesy, Wisconsin Department of Tourism

leaders reached out to non-Indian groups to explain why these rights are still legally binding. In 1999 the U.S. Supreme Court cast the final affirmation of treaty rights and ended the fishing wars.

Culturally, the state of Wisconsin was finally realizing its true Indian heritage. Ojibwe peoples never forgot their peace treaties with the U.S. government. Yet for most Wisconsin residents, the rhythmic reciting of treaty years—1837, 1842, 1854—conjured no recognition or understanding. Indian cultures were not taught in schools, and so Hollywood movies of cowboys and faux Indians easily filled the knowledge void.

"We are the *invisible* minority," said Margaret Clark-Price, of Wyandotte and Shawnee descent, and author of the 1980s *Native American Annual*. But many Indians refused to stay invisible.

For Nick Hockings and dozens of Indian activists and supporters, the solution was clear: education. These educational warriors were in good company once they left the landing docks of northern Wisconsin. There were sympathetic ears in Wisconsin, but it required relentless outreach that needed to be supported by a news media, newly versed in the facts of treaty rights. Educators and environmental groups gradually learned the finer points of Indian sovereignty.

Above the protests, new voices emerged. The rise of the tribal press in the mid-1980s added another dimension to sovereignty. Indians were telling their own stories to their own communities—and beyond. Early on, Indians rode the wave of new computer technology. The new Indian storytellers wielded digital cameras, laptop computers, and microphones.

The first computer revolution was not the Internet, but desktop publishing. Seemingly overnight, the power of the press extended to anyone curious enough to master the computer mouse—including the tribes of Wisconsin. In 1987 Oneida/Ojibwe journalist Paul DeMain used desktop publishing to start one of the first independently-owned Native newspapers, *News From Indian Country*. From the Lac Courte Oreilles reservation near Hayward, DeMain proved there was a national audience across Indian Country.

Wisconsin's Native journalists helped educate mainstream journalists. They were active in the fledgling press association, the Native American Journalists Association (NAJA) founded in 1984. Observing the leadership from Wisconsin, Paul DeMain wondered aloud, "What is it about Wisconsin—the water?" DeMain

Known as the "City of Festivals," Wisconsin's Indian tribes gather each September for Milwaukee's Indian Summer Fest along Lake Michigan's shoreline. Drums, dancers, and tribal songs fill the air along with the aroma of buffalo burgers and traditional fry bread. Themes for other Milwaukee summer festivals include African World, Asian Moon Fesitval, Cajun Fest, and Irish Fest. Courtesy, Wisconsin Department of Tourism

Ice fishing shanties dot Wisconsin lakes throughout the winter as walleye, northern pike, and sturgeon try to outfox the warm-blooded anglers. There are three distinct ice fishing seasons: first ice, mid-winter, and late ice. Courtesy, Wisconsin Department of Tourism

had a point. Many of NAJA's leaders were from Wisconsin's tribes: Paul DeMain (Oneida/Ojibwe) and Karen Lincoln Michel (Ho-Chunk) are past NAJA presidents; Mark Anthony Rolo (Bad River Ojibwe) and Mary Annette Pember (Red Cliff Ojibwe) are former executive directors; Keith Skenandore (Oneida) and Patty Loew (Bad River Ojibwe) joined NAJA's board of directors.

American Indian education expanded both within and outside the reservation. Lac Courte Oreilles Community College opened its doors in 1982. The College of Menominee Nation opened in 1992, and now has a pilot program to send its graduates to the University of Wisconsin-Madison to complete studies in sustainable development. In 1989 Wisconsin's public schools, through Act 31, started requiring K-12 curriculum and teacher training in the diversity of Wisconsin Indian nations.

Cultural education fits naturally into Wisconsin's tourism economy. Along with the Wisconsin Historical Society the state actively promotes its past, from the Ice Age Trail to the immigrant cultures of Old World Wisconsin. Since 1994 the inter-tribal cooperative, Native American Tourism of Wisconsin, alerts visitors to reservation pow wows, cultural villages, museums, and Indian-owned trading posts.

Nick Hockings, who once wondered whether he'd be shot spearfishing, now owns a cultural center at Lac du Flambeau. Wa-Swa-Goning, "the place where they spear fish by torchlight," is a re-creation of an 18th century Ojibwe village on 20 acres of forest overlooking Moving Cloud Lake. Wa-Swa-Goning earned a 1999

Wisconsin Historic Preservation Award, and *Wisconsin Trails Magazine* named it a prime cultural site. The *New York Times* went a step further, calling it "the Ojibwe tribe's answer to Williamsburg."

Despite a controversial beginning, Wisconsin tourism expanded with the assertion of treaty rights. Beginning in the 1990s tourists had a new destination: gaming and casino resorts. Although Wisconsin Indians are not wealthy, gaming revenue has created more than 35,000 jobs for both non-Indians and Indians alike. As Nancy Lurie observed, tribes were building needed infrastructure in tribal housing, schools, community centers, health services, and elder care. Tribal-state compacts vary by tribe, but all agreements require a percentage of gross revenue to the state and by 2004 revenue sharing increased to a reported $100 million.

Wisconsin's environmentalists are well aware of gaming revenues. After a 25-year battle over the proposed Crandon mine that threatened to poison the Wolf River, an alliance of over 30 anti-mining groups witnessed environmental history. In 2003 two tribes stepped forward to purchase the mineral rights. The Forest County Potawatomi and the Sokaogon Ojibwe (Mole Lake Chippewa) acquired the mine for $16.5 million, a sum undreamed of before the shouting began over spearfishing. A gala pow wow in Green Bay celebrated this environmental precedent and brought together environmentalists from many cultures, walks of life, and even a few button-down lawyers flying in from Washington D.C.

Today many tribal members quietly spearfish like their ancestors. The ugly protests are gone, and in Wisconsin there is more cultural understanding. As Patty Loew observes, many Wisconsin tribes are experiencing "a cultural renaissance" in the rescue and renewal of Native languages, traditional ceremonies and ancient art forms. Many tribes are investing in traditional Indian crops such as cranberries or protecting the lakes where wild rice grows. And the Ho-Chunk tribe is bringing back the buffalo to the Wisconsin landscape.

Environmentally, tribes are setting new standards. The Menominee are nationally known for their sustainable forestry of 223,000 acres which, on part of their original homeland, represents over 5,000 years of continuously tending to one small part of Wisconsin. The Bad River Band of Ojibwe are protecting the Kakagon Slough, the watery home to waterfowl, wild rice, and many endangered species. And as stewards of Wisconsin's most precious resource, tribal standards for water quality often exceed those of the U.S. Environmental Protection Agency.

WISCONSIN'S TRADITIONAL BASE

Despite increases in international sales, however, the 2001 recession devastated Wisconsin workers in the state's traditional industries. The national downturn increased Wisconsin unemployment from 3.5 to 5.6 percent, the first time Wisconsin unemployment was as bad as the nation's. UW-Madison researchers Laurel Dresser and Joel Rogers discovered that manufacturing jobs were hit hardest from 2001 to 2003 with 54,000 jobs lost—almost 10 percent of total employment in manufacturing. However, the Department of Workforce Development reported a grimmer number: 80,000 lost jobs. African-Americans were hit hardest with more than 19

percent unemployed. Elsewhere salaries stagnated. Surprisingly, Dresser and Rogers found that Wisconsin's college graduates experienced only a 2 percent unemployment rate.

Like manufacturing workers, Wisconsin farmers were also hit hard. Farm income decreased to $888 million in 2001, a loss of $404 million from 1999. The number of farms declined to 77,000, from a mid-1930s peak of nearly 200,000 farms. The remaining farms grew slightly larger, with an average of 206 acres. The number of cheese plants fell by more than 60 percent from the 1980s, largely in cheddar cheese plants.

Still, Wisconsin farmers are resourceful. Dairy products accounted for 55 percent in cash receipts with meat animals providing more than 14 percent, and crops adding more than 13 percent. UW professor Edward Jesse estimates that 80 to 90 percent of Wisconsin's milk is funneled into cheese. America's Dairyland ranks first in cheese production, producing 2.2 billion pounds of natural cheese—about 27 percent of the U.S. total. No wonder Wisconsin cheeseheads are easily recognized at sporting events.

America's love for pizza drives Wisconsin's current cheese market. Wisconsin's tradition of dairy cooperatives such as Foremost Farms, spends considerable time analyzing and responding to America's changing dairy tastes. Wisconsin's 364 dairy plants make a range of products, but the big winner is mozzarella cheese with a 240 percent increase since the 1980s. Cheddar and mozzarella account for more than 60 percent of natural cheese although Wisconsin is the leader in varieties like American, Italian, Brick, and Muenster. Wisconsin is second to California in milk and butter.

In 2003 crop production, Wisconsin retains its top rankings. The state is first in cranberries, corn for silage, cabbage for German kraut, and snap beans for pro-

On the Troy Gardens CSA (Community-Supported Agriculture) farm on the north side of Madison, farm manager Claire Strader, undergraduate April Johnson, and member Beulah Lee (pictured from left to right) harvest soybeans during summer. The 31-acre garden is the site of an outreach project in sustainable agriculture research and education, led by the College of Agriculture and Life Sciences. Photo by Michael Forster Rothbart, courtesy, University of Wisconsin-Madison

cessing. Wisconsin is among the top five nationally in producing oats, potatoes, tart cherries, carrots, sweet corn and green peas for processing, maple syrup, and cucumbers for pickles.

NEW PLAYERS
IN WISCONSIN

In the last 30 years, treaty rights taught Wisconsin leaders one important fact: Indians are more than cultural partners. The tribes are powerful players in Wisconsin's economic, political, and environmental future. And so are Wisconsin's scientists.

Over the past 20 years scientists and hundreds of high-tech startups have driven Wisconsin's new economic growth. The scientific impact on Wisconsin's economy is partly a continuation of the Wisconsin Idea, which claims the borders of the university are the borders of the state.

Some science will create more than jobs. In 1998 University of Wisconsin-Madison scientist James A. Thomson isolated the process that creates, in the book of life, the "first blank page." Scientists call this primal blank page "stem cells," which is not the same as cloning. The stem cells that James Thomson and his lab developed cannot grow into a fetus. Instead, stem cells remain pliable with the potential to turn into specific kinds of cells. They are unique written pages in the book of life that say "heart," or "brain," or "bone." Thomson's scientific breakthrough capped 17 years of investigation among international scientists. Now researchers looking for cures to Parkinson's disease, paralysis, or cancer have a new arena for discovery. Almost.

For some, including the U.S. government, the response was uncertainty and even fear. At the heart of the debate is the earliest stage of the human embryo. Days after fertilization, a small cluster of about 140 cells form a hollow ball called the blastocyst. It's the 140-celled blastocyst that yields stem cells. In the mid-1990s James Thomson convened a UW ethics committee to oversee his work, step by step. The committee determined that using the consciously donated, yet discarded, fertilized eggs from in-vitro fertilization was ethical in the quest for potentially life-saving research.

Ethical questions, however, will remain part of new technology—from media ethics of digital computers to scientific ethics of high technology. Few scientists dismiss the continuing need for ethical dialogues. New technology can raise as many questions as it answers. Computers are not a magic wand, and neither are petri dishes. What it means to be human, healthy, and prosperous are societal, as well as scientific questions.

In high technology, there are cultural questions as well. Wisconsin's potato farmers might welcome a genetically-modified plant that can save their potato harvests from devastation. Yet Minnesota's attempts to genetically engineer wild rice are not the same thing. Native peoples in Wisconsin and Minnesota have an ancient, even spiritual, connection to wild rice. Ojibwe activists like Winona LaDuke question how scientists can patent an indigenous grain and then keep it from spreading to wild plants.

Some biotechnology communities express social concerns in a code of ethics. The Wisconsin Biotechnology Association pledged that members are "committed to the *socially responsible* use of biotechnology to save or improve lives, improve the quality and abundance of food, and clean up hazardous waste."

Just as the past 25 years reflected a public education in Wisconsin Indian sovereignty, the next 25 years will reflect a public dialogue in high-tech trends. The mass media will play a crucial role in this. The media was part of the early problems in public understanding of Indian sovereignty; in turn, it can elucidate important science stories or fuel confusion. Environmental and science reporters, along with health communication experts, have an important role in a full public dialogue.

When biology met high technology during the 1990s, Wisconsin became a national leader—without an identity. One Wisconsin journalist noticed and ventured into unknown waters. In the best sense, Tom Still is a high-technology geek with a journalist's eye for a good story. A former associate editor of the *Wisconsin State Journal,* he argues that "the Wisconsin story" is a secret. Currently president of the Wisconsin Technology Council, Tom Still looks at the national picture and notes the state's income average is about 96 percent of the national average. On the West Coast, he sees how Stanford University fueled the growth of Silicon Valley and how its high-tech bubble reached down to San Diego. On the East Coast, he sees how Duke University and North Carolina-Chapel Hill forged the Research Triangle Park.

And then there is the heartland. Wisconsin is—surprisingly—a third coast. It can even boast shorelines of two Great Lakes and the nation's longest river. This third coast is already part of the new economic cycle.

Economic growth always has cycles. Tom Still observes that Wisconsin's 19th century economy was driven by bigger and better farms. Wisconsin's 20th century economy had bigger and better factories. However in the 21st century, he argues, Wisconsin's economy will be dominated by bigger and better ideas. Some experts predict the U.S. economy will be driven by healthcare, biotechnology, and life sciences. Wisconsin's high-tech companies provide a solid base in all three areas. If only the third coast was not such a secret.

THE I-Q CORRIDOR

Wisconsin is not an island on the third coast. Instead, Wisconsin lies in the middle of what Tom Still calls the "I-Q Corridor." This is a 400-mile stretch between two giants of the national economy, the Twin Cities of Minneapolis and St. Paul and winding down Interstate 90-94 to Chicago. The I-Q Corridor of the Midwest, however, is not the white-knuckle commute found in California. According to Still, the four "I's" of the I-Q Corridor are ideas, intellectual property, innovative spirit, and the more elusive component, investment capital.

America's Dairyland is home to a variety of farms that produce a wide selection of livestock, dairy, vegetables, crops, and nursery stock. Its farm heritage and agribusiness outreach keeps Wisconsin among the top ten agricultural states in the nation. Although dairy dominates, farmers grow apples in western Wisconsin, cherries in Door County peninsula, potatoes in central Wisconsin, and cranberries in northwestern Wisconsin. Courtesy, Wisconsin Department of Tourism

Wisconsin has a tradition in the first three and, like all markets, always needs more of the last.

At the geographic center of Still's I-Q Corridor, Wisconsin offers well-documented quality of life. The four "Q's" of the I-Q Corridor include quality of environment, schools, recreation, and people. From the Twin Cities on Interstate 94, high-tech clusters are forming in the Chippewa Valley and extending to the Fox River Valley, Milwaukee, and Madison. Heading toward Chicago, clusters in Janesville and Beloit are reaching into

northern Illinois. Although Wisconsin's metropolitan areas might compete for high-tech companies, the actual marketplace is now also global. In Chicago, the 2003 Midwest-Japan Biotechnology Summit revealed Japanese awareness that the third coast is another potential partner.

International statistics from the Wisconsin Department of Commerce support Tom Still. Despite the national recession, Wisconsin's international trade increased 1.86 percent in 2002 compared to a national decrease of 5.17 percent. Wisconsin's 2002 exports totaled $10.68 billion with the top two customers, Canada and Japan, growing more than 4 percent and 30 percent respectively. The next leading international clients were Mexico, Germany, and the United Kingdom. Industrial machinery, including computer equipment, remained the top export commodity growing to $3.6 billion. Medical instruments ranked second, with an increase of more than 3 percent to $1.6 billion. An additional $2 billion dollars flowed into Wisconsin from sales in transportation equipment, electrical machinery, and paper manufacturing.

In the nineteenth century Wisconsin's scientists and dairy farmers united to build an agricultural economy on cheese and its blue-ribbon quality. Inspectors continue a tradition that is over 100 years old. Courtesy, Wisconsin Department of Tourism

HIGH-TECH GROWTH IN A GLACIAL LAND

According to Tom Still, the next wave of high-tech success will be interdisciplinary such as biotechnology, medical devices, and information. Wisconsin is forming a similar clustering of alliances within the Marshfield Clinic, the Medical College of Wisconsin, and Madison's University Research Park. The I-Q Corridor is more than a branding slogan, argues Still. A clustering of similar high-tech ventures are emerging in this region that share geography, history, and Midwestern values.

The groundswell of Wisconsin biotechnology is largely in Madison. Nationally, the University of Wisconsin-Madison ranks second in annual research spending with about one-half of its $600 million funding directed at life sciences. According to the Wisconsin Association for Biomedical Research and Education (WABRE), the state has 248 biotech companies that produce nearly 20,000 jobs and $5 billion in revenue. More than half are nestled in Madison's University Research Park.

As Baby Boomers age, healthcare will remain a growth industry. Central to Wisconsin's biotechnology community is the philosophy of "science focused on saving lives." From medical devices to drug development, much of Wisconsin biotechnology comprises medical research and includes the engineering of "error-free hospitals." Madison's partnerships reach to the Marshfield Clinic, where new research is combining personalized medicine with information technology. The clinic is probing how knowledge of a patient's individual genetic history can improve the efficacy of drugs, potential diagnoses, and prognoses.

At the epicenter of Madison's high-tech growth are patents. The highly-successful Wisconsin Alumni Research Foundation (WARF) is the independent, non-profit manager of UW patents. WARF began in 1925 after UW Professor Harry Steenbock rejected $1 million from the Quaker Oats Company for exclusive use of his ultraviolet process for Vitamin D. Instead, Steenbock believed that UW research belonged to the people of Wisconsin. Steenbock's philosophy still guides WARF where more than $700 million has returned to UW science labs in a renewable loop of discovery, profit, and innovation. Hundreds of WARF patents have seeded start-up companies, which in turn attracts more scientists. Among WARF's well-known patents are the 1997 isolation of human embryonic stem cells by James Thomson; the 1989 organ transplant storage solution by Folkert Belzer and James Southard; and the 1985

The University of Wisconsin-Madison's University Research Park nurtures start-up companies in high-technology and, at the Mirus Corporation, research in biotechnology. Photo by Jeff Miller, courtesy, University of Wisconsin-Madison

MRI technology (Magnetic Resonance Imaging) by Paul Moran.

Milwaukee is still a center for beer, brats and cheese—and also information technology. A 2004 directory of high-tech companies in southeastern Wisconsin revealed that Milwaukee has an emerging mix of information technology and life sciences companies. There are 500 information technology companies clustering in Milwaukee, Waukesha, Ozaukee, Port Washington, Racine, Kenosha, and Walworth counties that employ more than 21,000 workers with a $1.2 billion annual payroll.

Above right
Just 40 miles west of Madison, the American Players Theatre is the second largest outdoor classical theater in the United States and boasts more than 1,100 seats. Since 1979 audiences have enjoyed Shakespeare, Chekhov, Moliere, and the evening calls of the whippoorwill nestled in the hills near Frank Lloyd Wright's Taliesin home along the Wisconsin River. Courtesy, Wisconsin Department of Tourism

Right
A Mississippi River town known to fur traders and lumber barons, La Crosse now celebrates its Fourth of July at the historic Riverside Park which was created by nationally known architect John Nolan. Courtesy, Wisconsin Department of Tourism

Biotechnology may also benefit Wisconsin's potato farmers. In 2003 UW professor John Helgeson successfully developed potatoes that are genetically resistant to the devastating pathogen that causes potato blight. Like Ireland's terrible 1840s potato famines, late blight can destroy entire harvests such as Wisconsin's 1994 potato crop failure. A gene-resistant potato plant could reduce spraying multiple waves of fungicides and chemicals.

Biotechnology is also helping Wisconsin's paper industry. Biopulping is the high-tech process of removing the natural "glue" that keeps wood strong. Lignan holds together cellulose fibers in wood and biopulping adds fungus that feast on lignan. By treating wood chips before pulping, a special fungus eats wood's natural lignan but does not disturb the papermaking cellulose. The Energy Center of Wisconsin reported that biopulping experiments at a Wisconsin pulp mill found energy savings up to 30 percent while improving the strength of its paper. Paper manufacturers in Wisconsin have a record of welcoming innovations in efficiency, safety, and water quality controls. Indeed, Wisconsin's paper industry grew step by step with the Information Age.

KNOWLEDGE WORKERS IN WISCONSIN

Peter Drucker was among the first to study the emerging Information Age, and in 1969 dubbed its professionals "knowledge workers." Drucker included knowledge-intensive industries such as high technology, financial services, legal, and healthcare. Are these knowledge workers different?

Richard Florida studied the demographics of knowledge workers and the urban centers they clustered in—and he talked to a lot of geeks. He saw something more than knowledge; he saw the rise of creative workers. In his 2002 bestseller, *The Rise of the Creative Class,* he argues what makes creative workers different—and why cities should care. Florida collected empirical data to construct a creativity index based on a city's patent applications; occupations including high-technology; education levels; and diversity scales. Research universities drive the creative economy, Florida observed, and he argues that the core industries are research and development, high-tech sciences and engineering, education, media, and the arts.

Madison, Minneapolis, and Chicago—the centers of Tom Still's I-Q Corridor—scored high as creative centers. Madison ranked Number 1 in creativity for its size, a score of 925 out of a possible 1,000 points. Minneapolis ranked 10th among large cities and Chicago, like the golden oldies, was in the Top 40.

Richard Florida is an economist fascinated by how beauty and art add to a city's economic growth. He argues that creative workers, which include scientists, are driven less by money and more by intrinsic rewards such as new ideas, innovations, flexible work schedules, and a celebration of diversity. In fact, Florida suggests that creativity and inventiveness fuel high technology more than venture capitalism. Creativity attracts the knowledge workers renown for prizing quality of life and work schedules, over punch-clock salaries.

Florida asserts that cities need a "people climate" even more than they need a business climate. Creative workers often use location as their first criterion for getting a job. Florida highlights the three most important contributions of creative centers: technology, talent, and tolerance. Truly creative communities attract a rainbow of diverse groups.

Culturally, the third coast has a diverse heritage. Numerically, Wisconsin's population grew by 472,000 on the threshold of the new millennium. The 2000 U.S. Census reported 5,363,675 residents in Wisconsin and although still very white, Wisconsin had a modest increase in racial diversity. Hispanic/Latino populations more than doubled and now represent 3.6 percent of Wisconsin residents while African Americans represent 6 percent. Of Asians, the Hmong from Laos and Thailand grew to 34,000 in Wisconsin. The suburban rings of metropolitan areas grew fastest where lakes and forests beckon, such as around the Fox River Valley, circling Milwaukee County or ringing the Twin Cities in St. Croix and Pierce counties.

Tom Still reflects the values of Wisconsin's creative class. Although he is a high-tech advocate by day, he is also author of the book, *Hands On Environmentalism.* If Richard Florida is correct, the creative class

Celebrating the New Year, Wisconsin Hmong women observe their traditional dress and festivals. Their population in the state jumped to 33,791 in 2000, a 106 percent increase over the previous decade. Hmong represent one-third of Wisconsin's total Asian population. Courtesy, Wisconsin Department of Tourism

in Wisconsin will absorb the environmental, often progressive values of Wisconsin's heritage. High-technology is a national economic movement; Wisconsin's leadership can shape the new century much the way progressivism shaped the last century.

In the autumn, scarlet colors blaze among the trees in Wisconsin's forests and cranberry bogs. First in the nation in production, Wisconsin's cranberry growers have supported professional associations as far back as 1887. Courtesy, Wisconsin Department of Tourism

RETURNING TO WISCONSIN'S HERITAGE

It's not surprising that the founder of Earth Day is a former Wisconsin governor and U.S. senator. Gaylord Nelson's vision continues as a bipartisan commitment to Wisconsin's bounty of water and forests. Before he left the governor's office, Republican Governor Scott McCallum declared 2003 as the "Year of Water." In turn, Democratic Governor Jim Doyle declared 2004 the "Year of Wisconsin Forestry." Water and forests built the state's first economy and remain key to its economic and quality-of-life future.

Wisconsin is a water-rich state with 15,000 lakes, more than 5 million acres of wetlands, and 44,000 miles of streams. Groundwater and watersheds have long been part of land-use plans in communities even when tempers flare and locals learn the fine art of conflict management. Wisconsin remains an effective stew-

ard of water quality even with paper manufacturing. The Great Lakes water pollution is largely under control, although PCBs in the Fox River and Green Bay still require watchful monitoring. Water reminds us that land use and water quality are interconnected. Lawn care, agriculture, and drainage issues are not only local issues; they are all part of the larger ecological web. Human behavior, from perfect lawns to leaf raking, contributes to Wisconsin's water quality.

Nearly half of Wisconsin—a verdant 46 percent—are forests, a total of 16 million acres. Wisconsin's native trees such as red and sugar maples, red and white oak, pine, and aspen are protected by sustainable forestry that began earnestly in the 1930s. The treeless cutover of nineteenth century lumber barons was replaced by educated cooperation among scientists, conservationists, and lumber professionals.

Trees come with limits now, much like fishing for walleye and other wildlife. Each year loggers take 332 million cubic feet of wood, enough to preserve a careful balance. Forest products account for more than 16 percent of manufacturing, employing 103,000 people from loggers to sawmill workers and papermakers. Wisconsin lumber products lead in the production of fine paper, sanitary paper, children's furniture, millwork, and hardwood veneers.

Forests also contribute to tourism and to magical walks in autumn and the primeval calls of loons on northern lakes.

CLUSTERING: BUILDING ON WISCONSIN'S STRENGTHS

California's wine region can teach us much about how business grows organically. Essentially, no one can do it all. Instead, they form alliances around clusters. California wines have poetry-invoking clusters: grape growers, wine cask makers, bottlers, and wine experts who can publicize and create a sub-media that promotes California wines. There are tours, bed & breakfast inns, festivals, blue ribbons, in short: a community. It's not that everyone knows everyone else; but they do know who is in their cluster. From wine clusters come musical incantations of Napa, Sonoma, Mendicino; sparkling, cabernet, chardonnay.

It works nearly the same in high-technology clusters, only the pictures are far less romantic. The concept of technology clusters is both geographic and commu-

Since 1973 the International Crane Foundation in Baraboo is home and sanctuary to Sandhill Cranes, as well as the world's other 14 crane species. With a wingspan of six to seven feet, Sandhill Cranes create heavenly silhouettes in the Wisconsin skies. Courtesy, Wisconsin Department of Tourism

In 1972 Madison hosted its first
Farmers Market near Capitol Square.
Now among the largest in the country,
the Dane County Farmers Market
takes place every Saturday morning
from late April to early November.
Courtesy, Wisconsin Department
of Tourism

nity-based. By nurturing—not ignoring—Wisconsin's key industries, new clusters can join to solve common problems in suppliers, distributions, and workforce development. The Wisconsin Technology Council promotes clusters using research centers as their starting point. Knowledge is shared, and science migrates from lab to business and back again. Wisconsin clusters might not produce blue-ribbon wine, but it can tap blue-ribbon talent and create its own community and specialized media.

Clustering might provide the bridge between old and new economies. In the fall of 2003 panelists on the Wisconsin Economic Summit IV recommended that Wisconsin invest not only in emerging high-technology companies, but also in Wisconsin's traditional industries. In manufacturing, the Bureau of Labor Statistics reports that Wisconsin ranks third nationally in its reliance on manufacturing, trailing only Indiana and Michigan. According to the Department of Commerce, Wisconsin's top five industries are dairy products, motor vehicles, paper, meat products, and small engines. If scientific knowledge is the next economic resource, then new ideas in clustering can yield innovations in Wisconsin.

Wisconsin residents understand culture and community. Wisconsin's Old World immigrants built communities from a work ethic that still resonates. Belgian Walloons settled in Door County, Racine is Danish, New Glarus is Swiss, Stevens Point is Polish, Mineral Point is Cornish, Milwaukee is German, Stoughton is Norwegian, and everyone is Irish, or can be, if they wish. Culture is community, and a scientific or arts community can create networks associated with creative metropolitan centers. The world-class architecture of Frank Lloyd Wright's Monona Terrace in Madison regularly attracts business, artists, and the local community.

Whatever urban problems Wisconsin cities may face, its history shows that solutions are seldom found in the lone leader. Clustering around groups is something very organic to Wisconsin economics. The act of raising cows expanded to cheese science; lumber along Wisconsin's wild rivers led to sawmills and later, paper-making; farming led to inventions of farm machinery; heavy machinery lead to innovations in light engines. Of course, it's not a linear line; behind the numbers are hard work, broken dreams, and stubborn pride.

Perhaps as a third coast, Wisconsin will create new wealth in the interplay of cultural and geographic diversity. Wisconsin history gives us some clues. The glaciers carved Wisconsin into a water-rich land of four seasons and ancient cultures. Its immigrants built Wisconsin into a state nationally known for progressive and environmental solutions. Historic preservation is as much a Wisconsin tradition as its reputation for a squeaky clean government.

Wisconsin's optimism for the future is deeply rooted in its past. In fact, optimism is an original Wisconsin idea. Legend has it that in 1851 Wisconsin's first governor sat down on the steps of a New York City bank and pondered his new state's motto. Since printing was not yet a Wisconsin industry, Governor Nelson Dewey was in New York—not yet the Big Apple—to drop off Wisconsin's seal to the engraver. The governor chanced upon a fellow Wisconsinite, Edward Ryan, the future chief justice of the Wisconsin Supreme Court. Ryan objected to the proposed Latin motto, "Excelsior," meaning "higher, ever upward." Perhaps Ryan didn't like Longfellow's 1841 poem by that name or maybe it was because New York claimed the motto. Excelsior was also a trade name for thin shavings of curly softwood used for packing and stuffing cushions. Apparently Dewey had second thoughts, too. On the steps of Wall Street they designed a new Wisconsin seal and, on the spot, they chose Wisconsin's simple, direct motto: "Forward."

Culturally, Wisconsin's Indian nations also ponder the future except they often use the philosophy "Seventh Generation." Found in the Great Law of the Iroquois Confederacy, this Native value urges decision makers to first consider how an action will affect the welfare of the seventh generation to come. As environmental reporter Ron Seely observes, the seventh generation approach is an ancient solution to modern conservation. Or perhaps any social issue. A new generation begins, for a sociologist, approximately every 20 years. Therefore, the seventh generation, arguably, spans roughly 140 years.

In a sense, we belong to the seventh generation living under Wisconsin's motto, "Forward." Like the stories our grandparents told us, each generation worked hard to build a better future for their children. Each generation contended with the politics and resources available to them. Creative ideas and resourceful solutions have a way of becoming legacies, if not community stories or family legends. Wisconsin's legacy can remind us to look at Wisconsin's future with optimism—but also with a shared connection to those who follow in our footsteps.

XI

CHRONICLES OF LEADERSHIP

America's Dairyland is still a land of cows and natural beauty—and also known for its bragging rights over quality of life, quality of education, and quality of workers. Why not? Culturally, activists still work to preserve the architecture and history of Old World Wisconsin in its cities and towns. Politically, conservation in land, water, and forests is usually a bipartisan affair, much like mom and apple pie. And a multicultural ethic is growing as Wisconsin's tourism embraces its Native American heritage and newer immigrant groups like Hmong and Hispanic peoples. The land of cows is also the land of vibrant voices.

"The Wisconsin Idea" has changed a little, too. In the past 20 years, University of Wisconsin scientists and faculty created the new ideas that fueled the rapid growth in biotechnology and computer-driven high technology. This high-tech growth is somewhat invisible to the Wisconsin landscape. It's less bucolic as dairy cows or imposing as factory smoke stacks. However, high-tech growth is highly visible to scientists, civic leaders, and state economists.

When people talk about doing business in Wisconsin, some points come up over and over again. The availability of good employees is one; the Wisconsin work ethic is another. Wisconsin's natural beauty and resources are also a boon. "You couldn't get us out of here with dynamite," said Robert Cervenka, president of Phillips Plastics, back in 1988. His company is still here—and still going strong.

Much of Wisconsin's growth is deeply rooted. America's Dairyland remains a top producer in milk and the national leader in many cheeses. Wisconsin businesses have also shown resourcefulness in growth. Wisconsin's lumber industry of the nineteenth century created a foundation for paper industries. The clustering of paper manufacturing led to a clustering of printing services. The computer technology revolution during the 1980s allowed printing innovator Harry Quadracci to put Pewaukee, Wisconsin on the map for many national media companies. Quad/Graphics printed national magazines ranging from *Newsweek* to *Defenders of Wildlife*.

But it is more than high-quality and good ideas that allow businesses to thrive in Wisconsin. The people who make the products are also a rare find—hard working, well-educated, and skillful. Businesses within Wisconsin have changed and grown throughout the years, and as they do they will continue to make their mark on the future of this great state.

ARIENS COMPANY

Like thousands of communities across the country, Brillion, Wisconsin, was hit hard by the Depression of the early 1930s. Henry Ariens, a resident of the town and the son of Dutch immigrants, owned the local ironworks. When his customers couldn't pay their bills, the bank called in the loan that Ariens had taken out on his business. Ariens' business, the Brillion Ironworks, was forced to close its doors in 1932. Many business owners never reopened, but Henry Ariens seized the opportunity to start all over again, and used his skills to venture into the manufacturing of tilling equipment. Today, more than 70 years later, the Ariens Company is still a family-run business and one of the leading manufacturers of lawn and garden equipment in the United States.

Back in 1932 Henry Ariens had heard of a rear tine rotary tiller that was being manufactured in Europe. He thought such a product might be good for the local farming business and managed to get one to test. Ariens felt the product could stand some great improvements and, along with his son Mando "Steve" Ariens, he decided to redesign the tiller. They worked in the basement of Mando's home and enlisted the help of a neighboring town's machine shop to make the parts. Once finished, Henry and his three sons Mando, Leon, and Francis incorporated the business on September 11, 1933. They then started selling their first product, the Model A Tiller, out of Henry's garage. The Ariens Company was the first business to manufacture the revolutionary rotary tiller in North America. However, it took many attempts to redesign the piece of equipment before the new product was introduced.

Henry first tried using a water-cooled engine, but was unhappy with the results. At the time Mando was working for the Works Project Ad-

The garage where the Ariens Company began in the early 1930s.

ministration (W.P.A.) in Madison when Leon was contacted by a firm in Milwaukee, which later became Wisconsin Engine. The Milwaukee company had been developing an air-cooled engine and offered their engine as a possible solution. The Ariens redesigned part of their tiller to adapt to the engine and the result was highly successful. The first big test in the product's marketability was when Ariens took the 800-pound tiller with its 30-inch tilling width to a nursery in Grand Rapids, Michigan and demonstrated it in the nursery beds. The tiller was so exceptional at pulverizing the soil that the James Vis Nursery bought ten of them on the spot.

With the 14 horsepower Ariens Rotary Tiller the company was off and running. It proved much more efficient than typical plow machines in preparing the soil, and quickly became a workhorse for nurseries, landscapers, and gardeners. Together, Henry Ariens and his sons made a perfectly balanced business team. Mando was the inventor, while his father had the perfect acumen for sales. Leon was the financial brain and Francis thrived on the manufacturing end. By 1935 the company

came out with a second tiller, the Model B Tiller, which also was highly successful. The Model B had a 20-inch tilling width, was lighter in weight, and easier to handle. The company became successful enough with their new products to finally purchase their own property. In 1935 they moved into their first facility, with approximately 8,000 square feet of space, on Calumet Street in Brillion.

By 1940 Ariens had sold the tillers to nearly all the greenhouses in the Grand Rapids, Toledo, and Cleveland areas. Rotary tillage was considered to be the saving grace for the greenhouse business and vegetable growing industry. One of the major reasons for this was the way the tiller solved the tremendous problem with nematodes (worms) that often decimated the roots of vegetables and other plants. The soil was typically treated by running steam in tiles under the surface, until the temperature reached 180 degree. However, normal plows did not break up the soil enough for the steam to penetrate it. The rotary tiller did the job and drastically increased yield and profitability for

Current Ariens plant.

vegetable growers, as well as the profit margin for the Ariens Company.

During World War II nearly 90 percent of the Ariens plant facility was devoted to ordnance and other related war production. Throughout the war years the company manufactured many products for the war effort. These included M3 tank eccentric spindles, engine lift eyes, fine lock nuts for 250 bombers, transmission jack shafts for five-ton Army trucks, torpedo tube turntables for PT boats, 8-inch naval shell bases, and naval fire direction equipment. The Heil Company was making tanks for the U.S. Army at this time and called on Ariens to machine the eccentric wheel axles for the tanks. The contract required the manufacture of 300, 75-millimeter shell buggies. Ariens had only three weeks to design and manufacture the units, but by working night and day the task

was accomplished. The Ariens shell buggies were used in the Air Force's aerial invasion of Sicily. As a result of the company's outstanding performance, the Ordnance Department of the U.S. Army awarded it the Ordnance Flag. Ariens was one of the very few to be awarded this honor in Wisconsin.

In 1945 Ariens introduced the Tillivator, an offshoot of a smaller

tiller the company was developing called the Jitterbug. The idea for the Tillivator was initiated by a local vegetable grower who needed a larger version of the jitterbug that could be adjusted to the row width of carrots, onions, and lettuce. Mando Ariens made five of the tiller units to attach

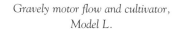

Gravely motor flow and cultivator, Model L.

to the grower's Model B tractor and it turned out to be an astounding success. It rapidly became one of the more useful products for vegetable growers through the United States.

On July 30, 1956, Henry Ariens died at the age of 91. He was a man whose life accomplishments were enumerable. In addition to founding his original ironworks company and the Ariens Company, he was the Brillion village president for more than eight years. He was credited with creating such innovative products as the Brillion gasoline engine in 1912 and the front wheel pull tractor in 1916. Henry Ariens would not be forgotten.

Throughout the 1950s Ariens continued to develop and manufacture a number of innovative products. The Jet Tiller, a smaller consumer version of the company's larger in-

serious gardener. It became known for the thorough job it did preparing the soil and for cultivation. At the same time Ariens launched its first two-stage, four horsepower, self-propelled snow thrower.

By the early 1960s the family-run business had expanded so much that it required a larger facility. In 1963 Ariens opened its 23,000-square-foot plant on West Ryan Street in Brillion. Shortly after, the company lost another of its founders, Leon Ariens, who died in 1965. Throughout his years with the company Leon had been vice president, treasurer, and director up until 1964. Other changes also took place during the 1960s. Mando (Steve) Ariens became chairman of the board in 1969 and his son, Michael, took on the role of president of the company. That same year the Ariens Foundation

Beginning in the 1970s Ariens began to acquire other businesses that would complement its line of products. Its first acquisition was the New Holland Company's lawn and garden division in 1974, which allowed for further development of Ariens' lawn and garden tractor line. It was also the year the company lost another of its original founders; the inventor behind many of the Ariens line of products, Mando "Steve" Ariens died in 1974. Mando had been elected chairman of the company in 1969.

In 1977 a new fabrication plant was built, bringing the company's total manufacturing space to 600,000 square feet—1,600 times the size of

Ariens employees gathered in front of the original company plant, during a company picnic.

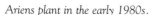

Ariens plant in the early 1980s.

dustrial-sized tillers, was introduced in 1958. It was a small front tine tiller that could break ground and also cultivate vegetables. At about the same time the company introduced their first riding lawn mower, the Imperial Riding Mower. The Imperial was a five horsepower mower with a 28-inch cutting deck, which carried riders on a cushioned seat mounted to a massive tubular steel backbone. In 1960 the company introduced The Rocket, a rear time tiller, which was designed for the

Ltd. was created under the leadership of Francis Ariens. The foundation offered scholarships to local high schools, as well as supporting local charities.

Francis Ariens was also responsible for starting a field training program in the 1960s. In the beginning, he used 35mm slides and index cards for his presentation at schools. He also went to distributors and dealers around the country with his field training program. Additional staff was added and today field training is offered to company clientele throughout the world.

Henry Ariens' garage where it all began. By 1982 Ariens made one of its largest acquisitions with the purchase of the Gravely Company. Gravely, a North Carolina manufacturer of lawn maintenance products, had a history dating back to 1926. As a result of the acquisition, Ariens began designing and marketing a new line of commercial lawn care products. The commercial mowers produced under the Gravely brand name continue to be one of the company's most successful products. The following year Ariens received the 1983 Governor's New Product

Award for its 21-inch Walk-Behind Lawn Mower and the HT 16 Tractor. In 1985 Ariens added Promark to the Gravely line, a, manufacturers of commercial chippers and vacuums.

In 1992 Michael Ariens was named chairman of the board and David Vander Zanden was named president. The company also continued its acquisitions efforts, purchasing the Stens Corporation in 1995. Afterwards, it introduced the revolutionary EZ Rider mower. This 15 horsepower, 40-inch, zero-turn mower used hydrostatic transmissions, replacing the disc and gear system. It also utilized an electric clutch, which replaced the manual one on Ariens earlier models.

In 1998 Michael's son Daniel Ariens became the fourth generation in the family to serve as president. Previously, Daniel had served as vice president of the parts and accessories division and president of Stens Power Equipment Parts, Inc. In 1998 Daniel's brother, Peter, who had been the Stens national sales manager since 1996, was named president of Stens.

In 2000 Ariens lost its last surviving founder of the company, Francis Ariens. In 1983 Francis had been honored for his contribution in building one of the industry's best service training facilities at Ariens Company. The first generation had passed and now the fourth generation was in charge, keeping the business alive and thriving.

In 2003 the company introduced a full line of new hydrostatic commercial and consumer zero-turn mowers and riders. Ariens also officially opened the Ariens Company Museum in 2003, located on the company's original property on Calumet Street. The museum chronologically details the history of the company and its products, and includes many of the original machines dating back to the company's beginnings. In addition,

Ariens' Plant 1 in the 1980s.

the museum showcases the latest technology and products in the Ariens and Gravely lines.

Ariens Company products, which are now sold worldwide, continue to offer tillers, walk-behind mowers, tractors, and "sno-thros" for both commercial and consumer use. The company has been a mainstay of the local economy, a major source of employment, and an involved supporter of the Brillion community. Today Ariens still holds onto the same set of core values that it did when it first began doing business from Henry Ariens' garage back in 1933: be honest; be fair; keep commitments; respect the individual; and encourage intellectual curiosity. Those core values are evident in all that the company undertakes, from its continuing innovation to the quality of the award-winning products it manufactures. Now with 800 employees, Ariens Company still makes a special effort to ensure that each employee feels that they are part of one large family.

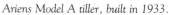

Ariens Model A tiller, built in 1933.

BARTHENHEIER CONSTRUCTION, INCORPORATED

Barthenheier Construction is located at 231 Buffalo Street in the newly gentrified sector of Milwaukee, aptly referred to as the "Renaissance Neighborhood." Rebirth in the design and architecture of the neighborhood is largely due to the admirable work of Barthenheier Construction. In fact, the company also worked on the building from which it operates, restoring it to its original beauty. The quality of the old building's renovation is representative of Barthenheier's proficiency in architectural design and construction. Dennis Barthenheier, owner and visionary of the company, utilizes the artistry and fine craftsmanship of the past and applies it to the construction and architectural challenges of today.

The company was started in 1976 by the father and son team of Charles and Dennis Barthenheier. But the story does not begin there. Prior to that time, Charles worked as superintendent for several well-known and established construction firms in the Milwaukee area. Noticing his son's interest in reconstructing everything from bicycles to transistor radios, Charles decided to bring

Dennis Barthenheier at the beginning of a two-level riverwalk walk. A derrick and crane are anchored, ready to drive new pile.

Dennis to construction sites where projects were creative on a larger and more challenging scale. Dennis became enamored with the construction process. He was only 12 when he began working summers for his father's employers.

Even though Dennis was only given simple tasks such as rearranging the supply truck or pulling nails from planks, he did each job with vigor. His fellow employees were

impressed with his diligence and attention to detail. Soon he was given more responsibility and his interest and curiosity grew in all aspects of construction. "I learned the trade working alongside my dad," remembers Dennis, fondly. "Let me try that!" became his mantra in those early years and Dennis's proud father, Charles, was accommodating. A new piece of equipment would be introduced on the job, like a bulldozer or backhoe, and Charles would place his son in the driver's seat while he protectively sat behind, supervising his son's movements. Eventually, his dad allowed him to drive the equipment on his own. By 16 years of age, Dennis could operate any piece of machinery on the job site.

Working gave Dennis a keen sense of responsibility. He was up every morning by 5:30 a.m. and on the job no later than 7:00 a.m.. He was paid well and the work was guaranteed. "I knew as soon as school let out, I would have a job; no question about it," says Dennis. The work required hard physical labor, which allowed him to stay in shape for football season when he returned to school. But the best part was working with the team of experts on the job and learning all aspects of the building process. These men were artisans. They did not believe in the modern view of "value engineering" and did quick work as cheaply as possible with no attention to the finished product. His mentors were mindful of classic methods. They utilized updated tools, but still created intricate designs that were reminiscent of old-world quality. They started with the highest grade of materials and ended with sophisticated design and detail. These were work methods that Dennis admired and would eventually emulate in his own business.

In 1971 Dennis was drafted during the Vietnam War. Toward the end of his term of duty he signed up for

This warehouse loft was converted into office space and featured in Wisconsin Architect.

a class in cement masonry, designed to prepare students for work after returning to civilian life. The class instructor spotted Dennis' honed skills immediately and promoted him to assistant instructor after just two days. Upon leaving the service, his proficiency and experience allowed him to return to work promptly.

In the spring of 1976 while working on a job site, Dennis encountered some creative differences with his employer. He realized it was time to try something new. He took a risk and ventured out on his own in the construction industry. He asked his father to join him and the two enthusiastically embarked upon a joint business endeavor, Barthenheier Construction.

Enthusiasm ebbed as the two struggled in the new business for close to three years. "I fell behind on my mortgage," recalls Dennis. With a wife and two small children, pressure grew and a change in approach was necessary. Dennis and Charles were both excellent craftsmen, but they lacked the business acumen of writing proposals and generating new business. In 1979 an opportunity arose which transitioned the company from residential work to the commercial construction world. Ray Wilbur, an expeditor and old business acquaintance of Charles Barthenheier, offered the floundering company a chance to work its first commercial job. Not only did they complete the work in a timely manner, they brought the job in under all other contractor bids. Wilbur asked the Barthenheiers if they were willing to do more commercial work. They were. Wilbur agreed to share his expertise in writing estimates and contracts and the Barthenheiers agreed to deliver excellent craftsmanship for less money than the larger, more established, construction companies. Barthenheir Construction has grown steadily ever since.

One of Barthenheier Construction's crews, standing from left to right: Charles Barthenheier, Joe Rohs, Chris Lutink, and Eric Barthenheier. Kneeling: Dennis Barthenheier and Steve Frye.

Today the number of employees ranges from 10 to 20, depending on the specifications of each job. Many have been with the firm for years and are "like family." Low overhead and no advertising have enabled Barthenheier Construction to deliver quality work without compromise in materials or craftsmanship. The company has become known for its classic detail in design, its competitive pricing, and the diversity of jobs completed. Barthenheier is able to offer variety because it outsources creative positions on a job-by-job basis. Hiring different architects, designers, and engineers to do a variety of jobs keeps ideas fresh. "There are a million ways to build a mousetrap," Dennis explains. "If you have the same mindset for each project, things become stagnant."

There is no risk of things becoming stale at Barthenheier Construction when the owner of the company prefers a challenge over rote. "I get bored. I like to take on things that are just not normal," Dennis

quips. This business approach is explored in the many stories that have been written about the company in publications such as *The Wisconsin Architect* and *Western Builder.*

The company takes on jobs that other larger companies are afraid to even bid upon. For instance, Barthenheier created a two-level parking facility and office building out of an old abandoned power plant. Other construction companies refused the job complaining the basement was too low for a two-level parking structure. Barthenheier, however, had a plan to create an opening and ramp system along with special column spacing. Dennis was convinced the job could be done. Barthenheir Construction won the job and completed it with success.

A new generation of Barthenheiers has joined the company. Dennis' son, Eric, follows closely in his father's footsteps. "He likes to dig in the dirt, just like I do," claims Dennis. Charles, although retired, still visits job sites and offers advice and opinions. After all, it is the experience and artistry of the past which is the very foundation of Barthenheier Construction and its future.

The Milwaukee Ale House Microbrewery, constructed by Barthenheier Construction.

BELOIT COLLEGE

Beloit College provides a learning and living environment dedicated to the cultivation of liberally educated persons. Students are prepared for intelligent and responsible participation in the contemporary world of action, and asked to think carefully, communicate clearly, and cultivate international and interdisciplinary perspectives on ideas and issues. Their lives are enriched by broad exposure to the arts, humanities, social sciences, natural sciences, and mathematics.

Beloit developed from the vision of seven New Englanders in early 1844. Their plans led to a series of four conventions involving both clergy and laity from northern Illinois and southern Wisconsin. Known as Friends of Education, these participants considered proposals for a frontier college. Eventually, they accepted an offer of $7,000 in supplies, materials, labor, and cash from the village of Beloit. This was the backbone of the College's corporeal form. Members of the third and fourth conventions chose a board of trustees, who adopted a charter that was enacted into law by the Territory of Wisconsin Legislature on Feb. 2, 1846.

Beloit's curriculum emphasizes the benefits of "hands on" experiential learning opportunities.

Stephen D. Peet, William C. Hooker, and Joseph Collie were the first graduates of Beloit College—members of the class of 1851.

The foundation for Beloit College's main building, now known as Middle College, was laid in 1847 and classes began that fall. The College graduated its first three students in 1851.

The school's early curriculum was cast mainly in the Yale mold. Aratus Kent, chairman of the Beloit College board of trustees, along with the first faculty members Jackson J. Bushnell and Joseph Emerson, built a solid casing with Yale mortar before another Yale graduate, Aaron Lucius Chapin, accepted Beloit's first presidency in December 1849. He served until 1886, and during this time the College became widely known for its scholastic excellence.

From its founding, the College showed both a solid classical tradition and a penchant for innovation and experimentation in curriculum. Under the administration of Edward Dwight Eaton, Beloit's second president, the institution departed from the Yale curriculum by adding courses in philosophy and science. Students were given greater latitude in the selection of courses, and the first women students enrolled in 1895.

New courses and other innovations flourished under Melvin Brannon's administration after World War I. The Brannon era saw substantial growth in the endowment assets of the College and a refurbishing of the physical plant.

Irving Maurer, of the class of 1904, returned to his alma mater as president in 1924 and served until his death in 1942. President Maurer's administration put renewed emphasis on the liberal arts and spiritual values, and continued resistance to the post-war demand for the "practical."

More than two years later, when World War II sharply reduced enrollment and presented many other problems, Carey Croneis became president in 1944. The nine-year administration of Beloit's fifth president saw an influx of veterans swell enrollment to more than 1,000 and

additional buildings and other campus improvements were completed.

The administration of Miller Upton, who served for 21 years, was marked by far-reaching curricular changes, enrollment growth, and extensive development of the physical plant. The building period included a new library, science center, performing arts center, anthropology building, and seven more residential buildings. The College's world outlook program was inaugurated in 1960 and continues today as an exemplary international education program. The innovative "Beloit Plan" of year-round education, introduced in 1964, brought increased national recognition to the College, and many elements of that program continue today.

During the latter 1970s—under Beloit's seventh president, Martha Peterson—the College responded effectively to smaller enrollments, an altered pattern of student interests, and the demands of an inflationary economy. A traditional two-semester academic year was restored, extracurricular life was enhanced, improvements to the campus were completed, and endowment resources were expanded. A long-range plan for the 1980s was developed.

Roger Hull was elected president in 1981 and during his administration the College's enrollment and endowment increased. The Hull years saw accelerated physical plant improvements including new facilities for music and economics; extensive renovation of residence halls; the creation of a campus center and sports-fitness center; a multi-million-dollar library renovation; and the establishment of the Center for Language Studies, a summer immersion program that offered intensive instruction in critical and less commonly taught languages.

In 1991 Beloit's ninth president, Victor E. Ferrall, Jr., arrived in time to oversee the $100-million sesqui-

Classes sometimes relocate to the expansive lawn in front of historic Middle College.

centennial campaign. He directed major renovations of the Logan and Wright Museums and Strong Stadium, increased size and diversity in the faculty, and oversaw the installation of a fiber optic network.

With the new millennium came new leadership, and in 2000 John E. Burris became Beloit's tenth president. He welcomed students into newly renovated residence and dining halls and initiated a process of strategic planning for the next decade. In his first years, applications to the College increased dramatically

Beloit College has offered an outstanding liberal arts education for more than 150 years

and the Moore Hall townhouses were built at the north edge of campus.

In recent years more than 60 percent of Beloit's graduates have continued their education in graduate school or with professional training. A significant number work with domestic and international service organizations, while others share their talents within their professions and communities. Noteworthy graduates include legendary explorer Roy Chapman Andrews, '06; civil rights activist Jim Zwerg '62; disability advocate Marca Bristo '74; United States Ambassadors Robert C. Strong '38 (Iraq, 1963–67), Adolph Dubs '42 (Afghanistan, 1978–79), and Peter Tufo '59 (Hungary, 1997–2001); designer Robert Lee Morris '69; still-photographer Ray Metzker '53; film director John Pasquin '67; journalist/writer Stephen Hall '73; ABC television network president James Duffy '49; environmentalists Mark Moffet '79 and Judy Logback '95; cartoonists Jay "Ding" Darling 1899 and Warren K. Miller '60; medical researchers Robert Nowinski '67 and Dr. Roy Bakey '71; and geologist Thomas Casadevall '69.

Throughout the years Beloit College has stressed the value of individual concern and growth, the students' desire to learn and flexibility in that process, and a rigorous academic program in the best tradition of the liberal arts. Today Beloit remains dedicated to the liberal arts, active learning, and the ideal of responsible participation in the contemporary world. Despite its changes, the College's central character as an institution of concentrated personal discovery and intense learning carries through.

OSCAR J. BOLDT CONSTRUCTION COMPANY

Recognized as the largest general contractor and construction management firm in Wisconsin, Oscar J. Boldt Construction Company has risen to prominence through the inspired leadership of four generations of the Boldt family. A true American success story, the company has withstood world wars, the Great Depression, and numerous recessions to become the construction giant it is today. The Appleton-based firm is credited with an extensive list of building projects throughout the nation including hospitals, schools, stadiums, and industrial buildings like pulp and paper mills; power generation, automotive, and aviation plants; and mining operations.

Oscar C. Boldt, the chairman of the board, has served in a variety of positions: as president, director, CEO, and chief operating officer, during a career that has spanned more than half a century at his family's company. Now 80 years old, he still goes to the office each day and is passionate about his work. "I was four years old when I decided that construction was what I wanted to do," says Boldt. "I would love to be 20 years old again so I could do more of the same."

O.C. Boldt has been with the company for 50 years.

Boldt's grandfather, Martin, started the company in 1889 as a small carpentry shop on West College Avenue in Appleton. Charging an hourly rate of fifteen cents, Martin Boldt built wooden tanks and cabinets and created decorative wood moldings for windows and doors. With help from his beloved horse, Billy, Boldt delivered the finished products by wagon to his customers.

The company was renamed Martin Boldt and Sons around 1910 when his three boys, Oscar J., Robert, and Arthur joined the business. Oscar J. showed promise as an innovator and problem-solver. On weekends

he enjoyed dismantling cars and reassembling them, just to see how they functioned. He also patented a bowling pin design in 1917. "My father (Oscar J.) was an ingenious person who could have been an inventor rather than a contractor," observes Boldt.

Oscar J. became president of the company in the 1920s and the name was changed to Oscar J. Boldt Construction in 1931. A housing boom following the end of World War I brought moderate success to the business. Weekly wages at the time were $15 to $20. Under his leadership, the company branched out into commercial construction and renovation projects.

As the Depression deepened, however, construction jobs grew scarce in the Fox Valley area. At one point, the company's total sales amounted to only $9,000. Out of necessity Oscar J. sought work elsewhere, and was fortunate to negotiate a contract for the construction of a canning factory in Illinois. This assignment was the company's first large construction project outside the state.

During World War II the construction industry remained stagnant. Boldt Construction redirected its focus to the war effort, building ammunition boxes for the Department of Defense. Waste from the large crates was used to make smaller ammunition boxes. By the end of the war, the company had manufactured thousands of these boxes without any rejections.

While Oscar J. served his country on the home front as an ammunition box manufacturer, his son Oscar C. was a navigator and bombardier in the 15th Air Force unit based in Italy. After two-and-a-half years of military service, Oscar C. returned to the University of Wisconsin at Madison and earned a bachelor of science degree in civil engineering.

In 1948 Oscar C. joined the family construction business. With the

The original Boldt shop in the 1900s.

Tom Boldt, fourth generation CEO of Boldt Construction Company.

death of his grandfather in 1939 and his father's career-ending accident in 1950, Oscar C. assumed the reins of the company. Drawing on skills he learned in the Air Force, he quickly became a smart, decisive businessman who would take the company to a whole new level. "As a navigator, I had to get the airplane back on the ground. I learned to not make many mistakes under those circumstances," says Boldt.

His first objective was to focus on commercial construction. Success in that area led to industrial projects. Soon the company was building gas stations, churches, schools, and factories. Machinery installation, particularly in the paper industry, became an important segment of the business. By 2003 Boldt Construction was ranked by *Engineering News Record* as the 104th largest general contractor and the 56th largest construction manager in the nation.

The fourth generation of Boldts, represented by Oscar C.'s sons, Chuck and Tom, settled into positions of authority in the family business in the mid-1970s. Trained as a civil engineer like his father, Chuck worked at the company for 14 years before spreading his own wings elsewhere. Tom,

after graduating from St. Olaf College with a bachelor of arts degree in French and English, took part in the construction of an equipment repair facility in Riyadh, Saudi Arabia for the Saudi Civil Defense. After gradually taking on more responsibilities, Tom was named CEO of the company in 1999.

The company outgrew its headquarters on Badger Avenue and moved operations to the Appleton Center in downtown Appleton in 1985. Five years later, Boldt built a new corporate facility at Northeast Industrial Park on Roemer Road. Its first regional office opened in 1971 in Wausau, Wisconsin. Additional branch offices were established during the next three decades in Waukesha, Stevens Point, Madison, and Milwaukee, and in Cloquet, Minnesota; Oklahoma City, Oklahoma; Augusta, Georgia; and Chicago.

With the retirement of Warren Parsons as president in the late 1990s, Robert DeKoch assumed the roles of both president and chief operating officer. His organizational and interpersonal skills solidified the company's leadership core, as Boldt Construction continued to gain national recognition.

Today Oscar J. Boldt Construction is part of a holding company called The Boldt Group, which includes The Boldt Company, Boldt Technical Services, Boldt Consulting Services, and Paper Valley Corporation. The organization has 1,800 employees and generates more than $400 million in construction, consulting, and machinery installation each year.

"We have been blessed with good luck, a good family, and good employees," says Oscar C. Boldt. "We have

A power generation plant under construction by Boldt.

known our share of adversity, but we are building on a firm foundation. The future looks extremely bright."

Oscar C. Boldt has served on the boards of numerous civic, industrial, and academic institutions. In 2000 he received the Distinguished Constructors Award from the American Society of Civil Engineers and was inducted into the Paper Industry International Hall of Fame. He has been awarded honorary degrees from Lawrence University and Ripon College.

President and Chief Operating Officer Robert De Koch is in charge of all corporate operations at the Boldt Company.

BRAEGER COMPANY OF WISCONSIN

Ever since he was a young boy, Bob Braeger was fascinated with cars—the gleaming chrome, the smooth leather interior, and the hum of a perfectly tuned engine. On his way home from school the outgoing lad would stop at all the car dealerships to admire the new vehicles and pocket any brochures on hand. Lucky for Bob, one of those car dealerships belonged to his father Oscar Braeger.

Oscar had been a bookkeeper at a Milwaukee Ford dealership where he worked during the day. In the late afternoons, the industrious Wisconsin native would tend the flower garden for his landlord, not because he was asked to do it but because he enjoyed it. When an opportunity arose to purchase a Chevrolet dealership in 1923, Oscar turned to his landlord for a $5,000 loan, and the gentleman was happy to comply. Oscar's business partner James King came up with the other $5,000 and the King-Braeger Company was born.

Call it providence or a simple twist of fate, but that was the same year Oscar's son Bob was born. From the beginning, Bob seemed destined to be part of the business. As a child, he

Bob Braeger and his wife Deanna in 1999.

was always hanging around the dealership marveling at the sleek new cars. By the time he was 16 the energetic teen with the infectious smile was working summers, running errands and washing and delivering cars.

While Bob was in college at the University of Wisconsin-Madison, the bombing of Pearl Harbor took place. The proud American enlisted in the U.S. Army Air Corps in 1943

to serve in World War II. Serving as a navigator, Bob flew 30 missions in a B-24 *Liberator* bomber over enemy territory. Among those were two particularly dangerous ones over Normandy on D-Day. For flying so many successful missions, Bob and his squadron were awarded the Distinguished Flying Cross. Unfortunately, Bob missed the ceremony and didn't receive his medal, something that always gnawed at him.

In 1945 Bob left the Army Air Corps as a first lieutenant and returned to Milwaukee to his first love: his father's Chevrolet dealership. The following year he began working full-time and held numerous positions in an effort to understand every aspect of the business. By 1963 Bob took over as president, and Oscar shifted to chairman of the board.

In 1967 Oscar and his partner James parted ways. Each of them had a son working in the dealership, and they both wanted to eventually hand over ownership of the company to their own son. In an amicable split, Oscar maintained the original dealership and changed the name to its current title, Braeger Chevrolet, Inc.

For about 10 years after Oscar retired he would still come into the dealership to talk with the employees and the customers, and to share his thoughts with Bob about running the company. It wasn't until Oscar's health declined in the 1970s that he stopped making his regular visits to the dealership. When Oscar died in 1979 the entire company mourned his loss.

When Bob took over as president, he geared up to expand the business. His roadmap for growth included moving the dealership to a more prominent location on South 27th Street, acquiring additional dealerships, and advertising. Bob was a

King Braeger Chevrolet at 18th and Forest Home Avenue.

*Bob Braeger and his father,
Oscar Braeger, in 1950.*

firm believer in the power of publicity and helped create and star in several TV commercials. Although most of the ads were sincere in nature, the company did have fun with one of them. Bob's wife of 31 years, Deanna, recalls, "We did one ad with Bob, me, and our dog. The poodle jumped through a hula hoop and we said, 'We'll jump through hoops for you." The ads worked and helped drive sales on cars, parts, and service to $30 million in 1984.

To speed up expansion, Bob started buying other dealerships located on South 27th Street. First it was an AMC franchise (the manufacturers of Jeep). Next was a Chrysler dealership and finally a Ford franchise. Today, Braeger Company of Wisconsin owns three dealerships on the same busy street: Chevrolet, Chrysler-Jeep, and Ford.

Throughout the years, Bob was always concerned with much more than just the bottom line. His commitment to outstanding quality, service, and customer satisfaction helped earn him the prestigious *Time Magazine* Quality Dealer of the Year Award in 1983. On top of that, he felt that the most important reason he was in business was to create jobs for people. The staff he hired seemed more like an extended family than employees to him. He loved doing things with them and hosted several picnics and outings, including a dealership-wide bash for the company's 75th anniversary in 1998.

Keeping the business in the family was also important to Bob. His wife

Deanna worked a couple days a week and attended Chevrolet Dealership Management School in the mid-1980s. Later Bob's daughter Amy and her husband Todd Reardon joined the company.

In 1994 Bob took the title of chairman of the board, and Todd took over the day-to-day operations as president. But just like his father before him, Bob still came into the dealership to chat with customers and often stayed until 9:00 p.m. when they closed. Although, lately, he's had to curtail his visits due to his health.

Although Bob was dedicated to the car business, he managed to find time to volunteer in the community as well. From 1972 to 1974 he served as president of the board of trustees for the Boys & Girls Clubs of Milwaukee. He acted as co-chair of the War Memorial Center in Milwaukee from 1997–2003. He was on the founding committees for both the Fox Point Lutheran church and the America's Freedom Center, a proposed education center about the wars the nation has fought. On the professional side, he was active in the Wisconsin Automobile & Truck Dealers Association as an officer and board member, the Automobile Dealers Association of Mega Milwaukee, and in various automotive advertising associations.

After accomplishing what he set out to do with the car enterprise, there was only one thing left in his life that was missing. He was disappointed that he had never received his Distinguished Flying Cross. Through his association with a veterans group, he was able to produce the necessary records and prove he deserved the medal. Finally, in 2002 in a gala ceremony at the War Memorial Center, Bob received the medal he had earned so long ago. For a man who has such numerous accomplishments, this remains one of his proudest moments.

BUCKSTAFF COMPANY

A young man's ambition and pioneering spirit is what began the strong legacy of the Buckstaff Company, which has been crafting quality woodwork and furniture for more than 150 years. In 1849 John Buckstaff, Jr. left New Brunswick, Canada to explore his opportunities in the newest state of the union, Wisconsin. This land of opportunity was filled with flowing rivers, rich territory, and an abundance of trees which Buckstaff promptly decided to harvest into cedar logs. He wisely crafted shingles from the logs, sold them and gained a return of $400, a sizable sum for that time. Thus, the profitable and long-lasting association between the Buckstaff name and wood crafting began.

Enthusiastic about his success and the opportunities that were waiting for him in the new land, John Buckstaff, Jr. returned home to his father in New Brunswick to share the news of his good fortune. John Buckstaff, Sr. was so influenced by his son's passionate description of Wisconsin; he decided to relocate his entire family to the new state. In 1853

John Buckstaff, original founder, 1825–1900.

the senior Buckstaff bought a farm in Algoma just outside of Oshkosh. The land was as rich as his son had promised and John Buckstaff, Sr. started a profitable logging business.

In 1865 the nation was in the throes of reconstruction following the effects of the Civil War. The need was great for lumber and other construction materials, to repair and rebuild what was lost. John Buckstaff, Sr. along with his two sons, John Jr. and James, did their part by construct-

ing a shingle mill—and The Buckstaff Brothers Company was formed. The mill was so successful, an additional sawmill was built to supply the quickly expanding shingle business.

As the company grew, a partnership was formed with a well-known lumberman named James Chase. In 1872 the name expanded to Buckstaff Brothers & Chase. In addition to running a sawmill in Oshkosh and a shingle mill at Mannville, the company began working in the fast-growing logging industry. The newly formed company was instrumental in aiding the rebuilding of Chicago after the great fires of 1871.

In 1882 another transition of ownership came about when John Jr. and his sons, Noel and Daniel Clyde, joined forces with businessman R.H. Edwards. The new entity, then called The Buckstaff Edwards Company, shifted its focus from raw wood materials to finished consumer goods. Its specialty was well-crafted wood chairs and Buckstaff Edwards soon became known for crafting the best selling childrens high chair in the country. John Buckstaff Jr. saw the effectiveness of working directly with the consumer sector. When the opportunity presented itself, the company made a purchase of a nearby casket making company. Adding this necessary consumer good to the company's existing product line served a distinctively different but just as profitable market.

Buckstaff Edwards grew in status and in size. In 1889 the company was incorporated with John Buckstaff, Jr. serving as president. His strength of character and reputation was known well beyond the community and he was characterized in the 1924 publication of *Wisconsin, Its History and Its People*, as a man of, "...dependability, a capacity for hard work and exacting labor, a keen power of analysis and promptness, and firmness in decision—all traits that mark men for

Drayage crew heading to the local freight depot to ship furniture to customers.

John Buckstaff, Jr. (IV), current president and CEO.

leadership of men and movements." John Buckstaff, Jr. served his company well until his death in 1900. His precepts of quality, reliability, and service carry on in the Buckstaff Company to this day.

After John Jr.'s death, his son George Angus became president and R.H. Edwards sold his interest back to the company. The name changed to the Buckstaff Company in 1912. When George Buckstaff died in 1927 a new generation joined the firm, John Buckstaff Jr.'s grandsons Ralph N. and John D. Buckstaff.

For the next 25 years, Ralph N. and John D. Buckstaff led the firm through volatile changes in the nation's history. Not only did the brothers survive the testing times of the Great Depression, they responded promptly to the needs presented by World War II. The company used its resources to manufacture necessary items for the war effort. They constructed anti-aircraft gun mounts for military cargo haulers and manufactured equipment boxes for electrical generating units that were shipped overseas.

In 1958 Ralph Buckstaff retired from the business, and just two years later John D. Buckstaff died after serving his company for over 50 years. John D's sons, John D. Jr. (IV) and Clyde Buckstaff, had only been with the company for a short time, but true to their heritage the two pioneered through the transition with ease. The brothers continued with lines introduced by the company in the early 1950s and added their own ideas and expertise to grow the business to a new level of output. They successfully phased out the casket line and focused on commercial markets in the areas of education and institutional furniture needs. The company concentrated its efforts on manufacturing high quality furniture for libraries, restaurants, schools, and other institutions. This new direction in the commercial market proved successful and continues to this day.

Clyde Buckstaff sold his interest back to the company, to his brother John D. Jr., in 1976. That left John D. Buckstaff Jr. (IV) as the only family member in the business. He then became the only sole shareholder in the company's 150 year history. To this day, he is president and CEO of the company. His engineering background and expertise enables him to successfully integrate modern technology with the traditional values and heritage of his forefathers.

John D. Buckstaff, Jr. (IV) and his vice-president, Frank Yench, manage over 200 employees. They surround themselves with wood crafting engineers and other manufacturing experts who ensure that Buckstaff remains on the cutting edge of progress in the high-end institutional furniture market. John D. Jr's employees respect his business philosophy of profitability first and size second. Many have been with the company for over 20 years and take pride in the reputable Buckstaff name and the company's longevity.

Buckstaff is located at 1127 South Main Street in Oshkosh, the same location where the company began in 1850. The plant now covers over 10 acres of land and still utilizes some of the original building structures from its inception. However, that is not all that has remained intact. Its reputation for building furniture with quality and durability continues to this day. Creating lasting impressions has been the goal for four generations, something the Buckstaff name has helped to achieve for more than 150 years.

Installation at a school library.

CEDAR VALLEY CHEESE

Thirty-five miles outside of Milwaukee and a mile down the road from Random Lakes is a 104-acre piece of land, home to Cedar Valley Cheese. The company has made its name-brand cheese since 1947, despite fluctuations in industry demands and other external circumstances. To meet these challenges, the business has developed a pattern of facing difficulties head on. Not only has the company overcome obstacles, it has learned from them and thrived. Each new hindrance has provided a foundation on which to build success.

The first of the challenges the company faced "plowed through" in the late 1950s. It was Highway 57, a two-lane road expansion that crossed the planes of Belgium, Wisconsin that would cut directly through the Cedar Valley Cheese Company's small processing plant. Ralph Hiller, founder and owner of the firm, had two choices: find another business or move his existing one out of the pathway of the oncoming road. He chose to move—600 feet to be exact. Ralph, along with his son, Bill Hiller, constructed a new plant at the junction of Jay Road and the new two-lane highway. Not only was the new building larger and more modernized,

Cedar Valley Cheese production line.

it was now perfectly located for easy access to farmers who made daily milk deliveries. At that time, the company had only two "employees," Ralph and his son Bill worked 7 days a week processing milk into cheese.

Days were long, but the milk had to be processed before it was given a chance to spoil. It arrived at the plant in 10-gallon cans at the rate of about 60 gallons a day from each farmer. The Hillers unloaded the milk, weighed it, and poured it into a compressor that pushed it into a small holding tank. That milk had to start and finish the pasteurization process before the delivery cycle began again the next day. Even though the work was arduous, the results were worth it. Buyers grew in number as did the deliveries of fine American cheese from Cedar Valley.

A dramatic shift in the cheese industry occurred in the 1960s. Buyers became more interested in Italian cheeses which could easily be used in a large selection of frozen and ready-to-cook entrees. The market for Ameri-

can cheese plummeted. Thus, the Hillers faced a new challenge: how to give customers what they wanted. The answer was right down the road.

Just seven miles away, a first generation Italian cheese maker, Gino Boccotti, had his own small cheese processing plant. He had generations of recipes for fine Italian cheeses such as mozzarella and provolone. What Boccotti didn't have was customers. Cedar Valley Cheese, with its established reputation, had no problem supplying interested buyers. The solution was obvious; the two plants would work together. The Hillers brought Boccotti on board and a partnership was formed under the name of Cedar Valley Cheese. The number of employees grew from two to six, and the new processing changes were put into motion. Tragically, Boccotti died in a car accident in 1971. However, his memory lives on in his coveted recipes which continually contribute to the success of Cedar Valley Cheese.

Ralph Hiller retired in the mid-1970s selling his half of the family business to Gary Cline, his son-in-law. Bill Hiller remained owner of the

Back row, left to right: Terry Krahn, Jeff Nett, and Scott Krahn. Front row, left to right: Ron Beck, plant manager; Ken Nett, master cheese maker; Dion Degnitz; Don Eischen; and Jeff Hiller, owner.

Jeff Hiller, owner (left) and Rick TeStroete, trucking manager (right).

other half. That same decade, a third generation of Hillers joined the company. Bill Hiller welcomed aboard his son, Jeff. A high school-aged kid on his summer breaks, Jeff Hiller began working at the plant just as any other new employee. Pay was minimum wage, but the number of hours he worked proved profitable for the penny-wise 14-year-old boy. His last two years of high school, Jeff even put in hours before and after classes. "My day would start at 4:30 in the morning. At 6:30 I'd go home, shower, and head to school," remembers Jeff. Yet his work day was not over. He returned to the plant after school and worked until 8:00 at night. He loved every aspect of the cheese making process, but he also had his eye on the future. "I always thought of it as, someday, being mine."

Jeff Hiller had learned all aspects of the cheese making process from milk deliveries to packaging. He also had a hand in customer relations, getting to know buyers on a first name basis. By 1986 Jeff was managing the company. In 1988 at the age of 24, he purchased his uncle's half of the company. Jeff managed close to 20 employees and the company pro-

duced approximately 9 million pounds of cheese, with sales reaching $10 million annually.

In 1992, with his father's financial backing and strong encouragement, Jeff secured a bank loan and purchased his father's remaining stock in the company. Bill Hiller continues to serve as a consultant for Cedar Valley Cheese.

In 1995 the company completed its biggest expansion which more than doubled its production. Larger facilities and new equipment, including five milk storage silos, created greater processing capabilities with the ability to produce larger quantities of product. However, an inevitable outcome of the increased pasteurization process was a vast increase of waste water. At 30,000 gallons a day, the waste water loomed as an issue. True to his innovative heritage, Jeff approached the problem by turning it into an opportunity. The company purchased 50 acres of land on which the waste water was sprayed at certain designated times during the year. The water irrigated the

grass crops which were harvested and fed to neighboring farmers' milk cows, the same milk producers which provided Cedar Valley Cheese with its daily fresh milk supply. The hindrance, to Hiller, was simply seed for opportunity.

Today, the company manufactures more than 30 million pounds of cheese per year. Eighty-five percent is made into mozzarella; 14 percent into provolone; and one percent is String Cheese, winner of the Wisconsin State Fair's *Seal of Excellence Award* five of the last six years. Cedar Valley Cheese has more than 45 employees which include eight licensed cheese makers, each with an average of 26 years experience. The company's customers are widespread in the United States, Canada, and Mexico; its products are a mainstay in the frozen pizza, frozen entrée, and shredded and sliced cheese industries.

The future looks bright for Cedar Valley Cheese whose owner and employees are proud to be a part of the industry which ranks Wisconsin as the number one cheese producer in America. But even if the future looked dim, Jeff Hiller and his expert team would find a better way to make cheese out of milk.

Aerial photo of Cedar Valley Cheese in 2004.

CLEMENT MANOR

Clement Manor groundbreaking in 1987.

In 1981 the Milwaukee School Sisters of St. Francis made a decision to expand their involvement in the healthcare field by sponsoring a new facility that would be dedicated to providing continuing care for seniors. Named Clement Manor, this new enterprise rose up on the grounds of an old farm just southwest of Milwaukee in the town of Greenfield. Like most long-term care enterprises, the goal of the new endeavor was to enhance and enable the healthy aging of residents. But what set this facility apart from others was, and still is, its devotion to the Franciscan values of respect, service to the poor, and care for one another.

Over the years Clement Manor has remained true to its ideals of respect, collaboration, and quality service. Originally the facility housed 98 apartments for independent living and 168 beds in the nursing home. Expansion in 1986 increased the number of apartments to 201 and took the number of beds in the nursing home down to 166. The expansion included the construction of a new building adjacent to the original facility on the 20-acre campus. The new structure housed the additional

apartments as well as new services, including adult day care and child day care.

Other new services were eventually introduced and today Clement Manor includes 71 assisted living apartments, 130 independent living apartments, 166 nursing home beds, adult day care, child day care, and life-long learning opportunities for the older adult. In addition to its own property, the organization also manages other residences and nursing homes under the Clement Manor Inc. umbrella. The firm's involvement with one such nursing home, Mount Carmel, exemplifies its deep-rooted Franciscan values of respect and service.

In 1998 Mount Carmel, the state's largest nursing home, was mired in regulatory troubles. Unfortunately that meant that 520 elderly residents were going to be forced out of their homes right around Christmas time. The mere thought of seniors being displaced in this manner didn't sit well with the folks at Clement Manor. They moved into action quickly in an attempt to prevent the evictions.

With only a few hours to go before the seniors were forced out, Clement Manor formed an alliance with another healthcare provider based in Duluth, Minnesota. Together they were able to go in and take over management of Mount Carmel before any residents were evicted. "Working together in collaboration, we were able to come up with a solution to the problem. We were able to keep the people there and improve their quality of life and the quality of care they were receiving," says Richard Rau, president and CEO of Clement Manor Inc.

Clement Manor came to the rescue on another occasion as well. For many years residents took advantage of continuing education classes offered by a nearby Milwaukee organization. The classes covered a wide variety of interests including Russian history, art, and even aquatics. When that company was forced to close due to financial difficulties, Clement Manor stepped up and created its own educational programming. That way its residents were able to continue to take advantage of learning opportunities. The classes offered on the Clement Manor campus are also available to seniors living in the area, representing just one of the many ways Clement Manor interacts with the local community.

It's this kind of caring attitude and dedication to quality service that has earned the organization its accreditation by the Joint Commission on Accreditation of Healthcare Organizations. Normally reserved for hospitals, accreditation is somewhat rare among long-term care facilities. The fact that Clement Manor has

earned this accolade is a testament to its overall mission.

In addition to accreditation, the continuing care center was also tapped for a national quality award from the American Health Care Association. The firm is also following the required steps that could potentially lead to the coveted Malcolm Baldridge National Quality Award, often referred to simply as the Baldridge Award. This national prize is given to one organization per year in each of the fields of manufacturing, service, small business, education, and healthcare. "That's a ways off though," admits Rau. "It's a three-step process and we're currently attempting to move on to step two. Once we get there, then we get to the Baldridge criteria."

The quality of service is reflected throughout every aspect of the business. From the bright, airy apartments and chef-prepared meals to health and wellness classes and skilled nursing, Clement Manor endeavors to meet the various needs of its residents.

Daily church services in a beautiful chapel meet the spiritual aspects while activities like movies, musical performances, and shopping outings satisfy other interests.

The venture's dedication to its residents is mirrored in its commitment to its employees. In an effort to make sure employees are the best they can be, the firm encourages ongoing education and has affiliations with Alverno College, one of the leading all-women colleges in the nation. And like Clement Manor, the college is sponsored by the School Sisters of St. Francis. However, Clement Manor's educational ties go beyond religious-based institutions and include the University of Wisconsin, Marquette University, and Milwaukee Area Technical College.

One thing that has remained constant at the organization is its strong connection to its sponsor, the School Sisters of St. Francis. Several sisters work in various capacities on the campus and a few sisters will soon become residents as well. Although

In May 1987 Clement Manor expanded its Continuing Care Retirement Campus with an addition of independent apartments for active seniors, complete with an indoor swimming pool.

Clement Manor is a religion-based facility, employees and residents are not required to be Catholic. In fact, in an effort to embrace people of other religions, non-Catholic religious services are offered on a regular basis.

Throughout its history, the organization has routinely identified community needs and sought ways to fulfill them. That tradition is expected to continue in the future as Clement Manor Inc. evolves into other arenas. Future endeavors could possibly include the management of additional facilities, hospice services, expansion of the assisted living services, and increased opportunities in lifelong learning. No matter what direction it takes, Clement Manor is sure to do so with respect, collaboration, and quality service.

FIRST BANK FINANCIAL CENTRE

The history and heart of First Bank Financial Centre can be summed up in one simple motto: Dedication to enriching the communities it serves. Established in 1859, the roots of First Bank run deep. As tourists traveled west into Wisconsin and were attracted to the beautiful lakes and countryside, towns were established and businesses began. Even before Oconomowoc officially became a city, Summit Bank, the forerunner to First Bank, opened its doors. It operated out of one of the first brick buildings in the town, with six shareholders and $25,000 in capital ready to serve the burgeoning community. The spirit of independence and community service which existed then is still evident to this day.

The bank's customer base has grown each year since its inception. "We remain one of the few banks that is truly community-based," says Mac Dorn, president of First Bank. "The very nature of our business makes us the hub of the communities we serve and service is what we care about most. We must be doing something right—we've been around for 144 years." Most recently the bank earned $3,324,000 in 2003 and in-

Mac Dorn, president of First Bank.

creased its dividend for the 37th consecutive year.

The bank's first location was at the site of the Old Oconomowoc Library on North Lake Road. After surviving an unsuccessful burglary in 1868, they moved to their former location at the corner of Wisconsin Avenue and Main Street. A new name, Bank of Oconomowoc, was established in September of 1889. By then its capital base had grown to $50,000 and the bank incorporated in November of that same year.

Even through the difficult Depression era, Bank of Oconomowoc was able to remain open while many others were forced to close. Adapting to constantly changing environments

has been integral to its success. "Across the years," Dorn says, "The bank has been able to keep up with changes. Regulations have impacted banking a lot and so has technology. We've been able to stay abreast of both." An innovative response to the changing environment around them was reflected in 1963 when the bank leased the Rand Building on South Main Street and remodeled it into a TV drive-in auto bank. This was the first installation of a TV drive-in unit in the state of Wisconsin, which made banking more accessible as the culture transitioned from pedestrian to automobile traffic. In August of 1982 the Bank of Oconomowoc opened a drive-in branch at West Wisconsin Avenue which featured five car lanes, a customer lobby, a night depository, and the bank's first automated teller machine. Customer service continued to be the bank's competitive advantage.

Adapting to growth as always, in September of 1998, First Bank of Oconomowoc changed its name to First Bank Financial Centre. This change was brought on by continued growth which included adding seven branch locations in surrounding communities. Today, First Bank's commitment to the Oconomowoc community remains strong as evidenced in the bank's recent renovations to their headquarters at 155 West Wisconsin Avenue in the heart of downtown Oconomowoc.

Many may think of banking services as standard operations with little variation from bank to bank, but that's not so for First Bank Financial Centre. They recognize themselves as a bank with a heritage that specializes in discerning customer's needs and helping them reach their goals. "We enjoy the daily interactions with our customers," Dorn remarks. "My door is literally always open, and anyone can drop by to see me at any time." However, it isn't uncommon

Summit Bank, 1870–1889.

for the all the officers at First Bank to go the extra mile. "Our success is based on getting to know our customer's hopes, dreams, and aspirations both personal and business; then getting our staff involved to assist in making them happen." One real life example of "making dreams come true" involved Mac Dorn, the president himself. He met a customer at a house the gentleman hoped to buy and analyzed the premises with him as they walked the property. They were then able to arrange the finances to make the dream a reality. "These days, people are understandably wary about where they invest their money," Dorn says. "To us, banking is not just a robotic process. We take the time to get to know our customers, build a rapport, and ultimately earn their valued trust. Our customers know we are looking out for their best interest." First Bank prides itself on providing better service, whether that means a quicker turn-around on transactions such as loans, or a personal touch in addressing financial concerns.

Another example of the bank's determination to go the extra mile involved meeting a widow who had been a long-time customer of the bank. Numerous papers needed to be signed and understood and the woman felt uncertain. "I simply went out and sat with her through the signing," Dorn explains. "People need compassion, simple assurance that they are doing the right thing."

Clearly, at First Bank Financial Centre doing the right thing within the community matters too. "We believe we have an opportunity to fulfill certain needs in the communities we serve," Dorn says. In 2003 employees of the various branches of First Bank were given a chance to take part in a food drive. First Bank then matched each food item and monetary donation, totaling more than $1,000 and over 900 items. First Bank

Newly remodeled First Bank headquarters at 155 West Wisconsin Avenue, in the heart of downtown Oconomowoc.

was also a major contributor to a new building for Oconomowoc's YMCA. In addition, First Bank donated computers to the new public library in Germantown.

Most recently, an area foundation which provides grants to local charitable and civic organizations was started. Dorn and First Bank Financial Centre made an initial contribution to assist in its development. The foundation addressed five basic needs: caring for children, developing youth, helping the less fortunate, preserving the environment, and enriching the community both culturally and economically.

Last, but not least, there is Mac's Café! Mac's Café is a recent addition in the downtown Oconomowoc branch. It provides customers with a place to enjoy coffee and a snack while learning about the bank's many

TV drive-in auto bank, 1963.

services. It, too, has done its part for the community in raising over $1,000 for many local charities.

The bank's success is a reflection of the commitment from employees and the community at large. Mac Dorn says often, "I'm only successful because of the wonderful people I work with and the members of this community." Many employees of First Bank certainly can boast of a strong track record and outstanding longevity. It isn't uncommon to find employees with 30 or 40 years of service at the bank. One vice president recently broke the record with 50 years of service within the organization.

From a small bank with six shareholders and $25,000 in capital, to a Financial Centre serving numerous communities in southeastern Wisconsin with $26,887,000 in capital and $335,700,000 in assets, First Bank Financial Centre continues to expand and strengthen with each passing year. "Our heritage as a community-based bank is what drives our success," Dorn says. "We intend to keep it that way and will continue to adapt and grow with the people of the communities we serve."

DAVID J. FRANK LANDSCAPE CONTRACTING

It is rare to find an individual who can say that he started his own company—a business that is worth millions today— at the age of nine. However, that is exactly what David J. Frank, the owner and founder of David J. Frank Landscape Contracting, Inc., did. Living with his parents and siblings in the Shorewood area of Wisconsin, David started a neighborhood gardening and lawn service. He reached out to the older residents, as well as others, who were eager to employ his services. Now, 45 years later, David J. Frank Landscape Contracting, Inc. has developed into a diverse landscaping business. It offers a wide range of services and has earned numerous national, regional, and state awards including being named as one of America's "Top 25 Landscaping Firms."

David recalls balancing rakes, hoses, and gardening tools as he pushed a lawn mower to the homes of his clients. At the age of nine he was, of course, too young to drive and could hardly wait for the advent of his license to make transporting equipment easier. Even when he was as young as 12, David employed friends, schoolmates, and his brother in the business. He applied for the

David J. Frank, president.

appropriate state and federal employee I.D. numbers and began withholding taxes for the working crews he was managing.

By the eighth grade David had teams of workers to help with the 30 accounts he had acquired. Once he was in high school he was subletting a garage to store his equipment, and furthering his marketing efforts by placing 5,000 advertising fliers into local mailboxes each spring. His advertising paid off because by his senior year in high school and freshmen year of college he was servicing 150 accounts weekly—and managing a team of four lawn crews to meet the growing demand.

David credits the generosity of business people in the community, as well as excellent role models and mentors, to a large part of his success. He recalls one mentor in particular, Earle Rose, with great fondness. In high school David was responsible for various gardening projects on Mr. Rose's property. Every Sunday morning like clock work, Mr. Rose would get on his riding lawn mower and drive around the premises. He would then call David at 9:30 a.m. sharp and give him a report, letting him know what he had done well and what he had overlooked. Each week, David recalls, Mr. Rose would say to him, "David, do you want to know the secret?" David would respond, "Yes, Mr. Rose." Again he would repeat, "David, do you want to know the secret?" Once more, David would answer in the affirmative. This went on until finally Mr. Rose would say, "David, the secret is…you have to write things down!" Invariably, David would have forgotten some little job he had said he would do. This was Mr. Rose's way of drilling into his mind the need to be scrupulous in his efforts to keep his commitments.

Obviously, this and other lessons were learned well as David J. Frank Landscape Contracting, Inc. now employs 320 people with a payroll of $7 to $8 million, revenues of $15 million, and profit margins between 5 to 10 percent annually. The company specializes in a wide range of services for both residential and commercial properties. "We can help all types of property owners improve the utility, appearance, and value of their property," David says. The design/build model is a very effective one and David J. Frank Landscaping has assembled all the necessary players to achieve the desired results. They have 11 landscape architects on staff, carpentry and masonry crews, commercial contracting departments, and earth-moving and grading services.

David J. Frank Landscape's corporate office has been located in Germantown, Wisconsin since 1973.

David Frank presenting information at the annual staff company meeting.

The company also added irrigation, interior landscaping, and lighting design and installation lines.

The firm is an industry leader in utilizing the latest in cutting edge technology, whether it is state-of-the-art tools in the field or computer aided design (CAD). "CAD is the most remarkable," David exclaims. "With it, we can show clients exactly what the finished product will look like three-dimensionally. Technology has become a driving force in our business and we are heavily computerized from scheduling to design."

One of the unique elements at the company is the work force David has hired. Many of the crews have been with him for 25 years—a rarity in a field which is largely comprised of temporary labor. His employees are career people who have made landscaping their life's work. To that end they are licensed professionals affiliated with organizations such as Nationally Certified Landscape Technicians; The Center for Irrigation Technology; The International Society of Arborculture; and The Associated Landscape Contractors of America. David is proud of the people he employs. "Despite what people think, the work ethic is very alive in this country," he says. His teams bring an incredible focus to

their clients with a passionate drive for quality and excellence. Naturally, like any business, they have also faced obstacles ranging from adverse weather conditions to difficult deadlines and site challenges. But David's philosophy in the face of obstacles is an inspiring one: "One of the things we are blessed with in this life is the obstacles. They challenge us as human beings and make us grow. Without them we would be destined for mediocrity."

That quality of optimism and positive change is reflected in the firm's commitment to community service. The staff has provided landscaping services for many parks and schools and have been leading participants in Arbor Day projects. The Zeidler Memorial Park, which was dedicated to the industrial workers of Milwaukee, was just one beneficiary of David J. Frank's services and generosity. Additionally, many of the firm's staff participate in the annual "Great American Clean up Day" where volunteers join together to restore various public properties in need

The firm's landscape architects work closely with home and business owners to create beautiful gardens.

of beautification. David is on the board of Keep Greater Milwaukee Beautiful and has served as past president as well. As advocates of environmental education, many of his staff members volunteer by leading seminars and discussions in local public schools.

Clearly, it is a company with a proud heritage. Some of the customers that David started with 45 years ago—as a nine-year-old in 1959—are still with him today. His brother Michael Frank has been with the company for 44 years and recently his son, David Robert joined the business. "David Robert had offers from numerous investment banking houses," David beams. "But after graduating in three and a half years from the prestigious Wharton School of Business, he chose to join us." David Robert was the number four sales person last year and is a leader in information systems and technology applications for the firm.

Reflecting on the years behind him and looking towards those ahead, David J. Frank states, "Landscaping is very tangible work. It's gratifying to drive around the community and see the work that we've done over the years. Or to have customers call up and say, 'Our garden is more beautiful than ever.' We're living in the birth of the environmental era. There's a desire to restore and revitalize areas that have been damaged by the industrial age and we get to be a part of that revitalization." As gardening continues to flourish, listed as America's number one hobby, clearly David J. Frank and his staff of licensed professionals will be ready to lead the way and make their clients landscaping dreams come true.

GALLAND HENNING NOPAK

"Time without change produces only age." This is a motto that the manufacturing firm of Galland Henning Nopak lives by. It has been a master at anticipating and adapting to change with each passing decade.

Hermann Nunnemacher should know. He's been a part of the family business nearly all of his life. When he was in high school in 1930, he initially served as a worker in the shop earning 35 cents per hour. Now, at age 90, he's in the office four days a week serving as CEO and treasurer, a position he's held since President Peter Weil retired in 1992. While today Galland Henning Nopak primarily produces air and hydraulic linear actuators, pneumatic valves, and scrap metal baling presses, the company began in an altogether different manufacturing and malting equipment business.

The Galland Henning Nopak story actually goes back to 1843 when Jakob Nunnemacher emigrated from Switzerland to America. Previously working as a journeyman butcher throughout southeastern Europe,

Nopak cylinders displayed at 75th anniversary by Henry Nunnemacher and son.

Jakob arrived in Milwaukee three years before Wisconsin became a state. Milwaukee's community of European immigrants needed experienced, industrious artisans and Jakob's butchering skills met with instant success. As his slaughterhouse and meat market prospered, Jakob

bought a large tract of land and had cattle barns and a distillery erected to supply beef and corn whiskey to the growing Milwaukee population.

In the mid-1840s Jakob married a northern German immigrant, Catarina Barjenbruch. Together they had four sons and a daughter. As they got older, Jakob established each son in a different industry: Herman, the oldest, in real estate; Rudolph in banking; Jakob in entertainment (Jakob built the Nunnemacher Opera House, forerunner to the Pabst Theater); and the youngest son, Robert, he set up as a grain broker. At the time, Milwaukee had the best harbor facilities for shipping grain to milling centers in the eastern states.

In 1886 a European patent agent arrived in Milwaukee. He negotiated with Robert Nunnemacher to license a patent held by the parent Galland Henning Company of Germany, for the American manufacture of malting drums and kiln turning machines. The 300-bushel slowly rotating drums converted barley into malt by drawing warm, moist air through the germinating barley while it was gently tumbled. It was then dried as it turned on the kiln's floors. Nicholas Galland and Julius Henning had been very successful with their company in Europe. However, the machinery was too ponderous to transport which led them to license its manufacture in America. Two years later in 1889, due to the astounding acceptance of this revolutionary technology, the firm incorporated.

In the late 1880s there were roughly 3,600 breweries in the United States, most having small adjacent malt houses. As the successful breweries grew—Schlitz, Pabst, Blatz, and Miller in Milwaukee; Anheuser-

Six-hundred bushel malting drum produced by Galland Henning.

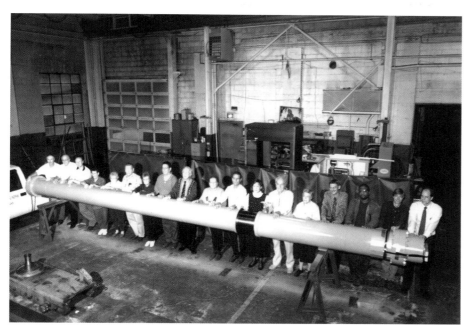

*Galland Henning Nopak employees prior to
shipping a 14" x 300" gate cylinder
for the Panama Canal.*

Busch in St. Louis; Jacob Ruppert in New York; etc—all bought malting equipment from the Galland Henning Manufacturing Company. Overall, business for the two men couldn't have been better until ...Prohibition.

From 1920 to 1933 Prohibition gripped the nation. Breweries shut down and malt house design and construction came to a halt. Galland Henning Nopak now labels those years as "the dismal days of desperate diversification." Yet with that shutdown, other possibilities emerged. The machine shop equipment, which previously produced the malting machinery, had the capability to manufacture hydraulic baling presses to process scrap metal. Another product line Galland Henning developed was the rotating lapped disc valve which directed the flow of air to linear actuators. Both of these products proved to be paramount to the future of the company.

As if Prohibition wasn't severe enough, yet another disaster struck in October 1929—the Stock Market

crash, which was followed by a decade of depression. Like most companies, Galland Henning was forced to cut back to survive. At its lowest point, its staff dropped to nine employees; six in the shop and three in administration. Additionally, they owed over $300,000 to the First Wisconsin National Bank. The company would not have survived without frequent infusions of working capital from Louise, widow of the late founder, Robert Nunnemacher.

Hermann Nunnemacher, Robert's grandson, still remembers Franklin D. Roosevelt campaigning against Herbert Hoover in 1931, stating that if elected he would "bring back beer." Anticipating the repeal of the 18th Amendment, President Irving Uihlein of Schlitz called on William Peterman, manager of Galland Henning, to refurbish its malting equipment—which had been idle through the 11 years of Prohibition. Galland Henning agreed and similar work orders flooded in from Pabst, Anheuser-Busch, Stroh, and other breweries. Once the amendment passed, people mobbed the breweries for jobs. By the end of 1933 Milwaukee beer sales were in excess of $30 million.

In the depression years, the firm looked ahead and improved the design of its machinery to process scrap metal. This led to the company's major post-World War II product, metal balers. These "monster machines" revolutionized scrap metal reclamation, swallowing whole junked autos and squeezing them into neat bales for re-melting. Today Hermann Nunnemacher comments that they don't bale up the total bodies of cars as they did with the Model As, Model Ts, or the Chevys of the '30s and '40s. Cars of today are produced with more than 50 percent plastic material. The remaining metal, after the plastic is discarded, can be baled. Instead, Galland Henning Nopak has developed smaller balers for processing aluminum scrap.

As the baler size grew, the need arose to replace the manual, lever-operated, hydraulic, directional control valves with pneumatic pilot circuitry. From this employment of pneumatic cylinders, the NOPAK brand name emerged as the company began marketing NOPAK linear actuators, popularly referred to as double-acting cylinders. "Of course one might not think about it, but 'push-pull' cylinders are used in all kinds of equipment," one company employee comments. "The giant, automatic gates that open at various amusement parks—they use our cylinders. In fact, I once looked up at a roller coaster in one of those parks and underneath was a component with our name."

It was the development of the scrap processing equipment and the NOPAK cylinder lines that enabled the struggling company to survive the demise of Wisconsin's brewing and malting industries. Today the production of pneumatic and hydraulic cylinders represents 80 percent of Galland Henning Nopak's sales volume.

Hermann Nunnemacher can certainly attest to the many changes and trends he has seen in his own family business, and the world at large, across the past 90 years. He graduated from Marquette University in 1936 with a degree in business administration. He worked in the shop at Galland Henning Nopak until 1942 where he acquired a thorough understanding of the company's operations. In 1942 he was named manager of the NOPAK products division. His father, Henry J., semi-retired in 1960.

Nunnemacher assumed the role of board chairman in 1979, and continues in that position to this day. He is passionate about the tenets that made his company survive. Galland Henning has been without debt of any kind since 1939. "We are an original equipment manufacturer. Our product is sold to distributors. We are also very proud that Galland Henning Nopak has the oldest profit sharing plan in Wisconsin for *all* of its employees—not just a few."

Yet with all the progress the country has made, Hermann Nunnemacher laments the loss of manufacturing jobs and the demise of small, family businesses in America. "It's important that as Americans we buy American products and think of our country first," he says. "Otherwise we're gutting our very selves, depleting our own industry, and making our nation weak." He is most concerned about the "globalization" of our economy and the short-term decision making that fails to take into consideration long-term effects—such as exporting jobs. "Whenever possible, everything our company buys is made in the United States or Canada," he proudly states. "And I am always asking my employees and friends to please buy American."

Galland Henning Nopak has been operating for 117 years as a family-owned manufacturer. "Original equipment manufacturers make up

only 30 percent of the American economy, and we're glad to be a part of that," Nunnemacher states. Having survived the many challenges progress has brought, he remains optimistic about the future. One of his sons works in the firm's sales department and another is completing his degree in engineering. This company surely knows that "time without change produces only age," and if history is any indication of what to expect, Galland Henning Nopak will see the future coming and once again find unique and creative ways to adapt and meet the challenge.

One of a broad line of dual compression metal balers.

A farmer and his threshing machine work a field in Old World Wisconsin.
Photo by James L. Sernovitz, courtesy, Wisconsin Department of Tourism

GUNDERSEN LUTHERAN HEALTH SYSTEM

For more than 100 years, people in 19 counties throughout western Wisconsin, northeastern Iowa, and southeastern Minnesota have relied on Gundersen Lutheran Health System for their care. While medicine has changed since Adolf Gundersen founded Gundersen Clinic in La Crosse in 1891, the organization's mission to provide high-quality, compassionate medicine has not. Gundersen Lutheran has been named among the top 100 hospitals in the nation four times, most recently in 2004.

Gundersen Lutheran's more than 5,500 employees, including nearly 400 physicians and 150 associate staff, provide primary and specialty healthcare in 42 clinical locations, allowing patients to receive care close to home. With a broad range of highly-specialized services, Gundersen Lutheran cares for people with all but the rarest diseases or disorders.

The comprehensive Gundersen Lutheran healthcare network includes one of the nation's largest multi-specialty group medical practices, regional community clinics, hospitals, nursing homes, home care, behavioral health services, eye clinics, pharmacies, and air and ground ambulances. More than 1.3 million

Dr. Adolf Gundersen founded Gundersen Clinic in La Crosse, Wisconsin in 1891.

patients visit Gundersen Lutheran's clinics and medical center each year.

Gundersen Lutheran offers treatment in a wide range of medical specialties, and patients benefit from some of the most advanced healthcare technology available today. Some specialty centers include the Gundersen Lutheran Heart Institute, Cancer Center, Neuroscience Center, Norma J. Vinger Center for Breast Care, Eye Institute, Plastic and Reconstructive Surgery Center, Orthopaedics Center, Trauma Center, and Outpatient Surgery Center.

Gundersen Lutheran has been providing comprehensive care for patients with heart disease for more than 40 years. As the largest and most comprehensive cardiac program in the Tri-State region, the Gundersen Lutheran Heart Institute offers services for people of all ages and includes preventive care, rehabilitation, high-tech interventions, and surgery. Dedicated to continually improving care, Heart Institute physicians participate in nationally and

internationally-recognized research studies with clinical testing for devices, procedures, and pharmaceutical agents.

Gundersen Lutheran's cardiothoracic surgeons and cardiologists perform a number of procedures including heart valve repair and replacement, coronary artery bypass grafts, endovascular vein harvest, aortic surgery, cardiac catheterization, pacemaker insertion, and drugcoated or bare metal stent insertion. The Heart Institute performs nearly 4,000 invasive procedures in the cardiac cath lab each year, as well as more than 400 open-heart surgeries.

A long-standing reputation for cardiovascular excellence, along with premier diagnostic and therapeutic capabilities, enable Gundersen Lutheran practitioners to treat the most complex and high-risk cardiac patients. As a result, the institute was twice recognized, in a nationwide study, as a "Top 100" cardiovascular hospital.

The Gundersen Lutheran Cancer Center brings all aspects of cancer care under one roof. Located in the East Building on the La Crosse campus, it includes adult and pediatric

Dr. Adolf Gundersen, researching treatment options for appendicitis, circa 1894. Gundersen and his colleagues were among the first to study the effects of surgery on the disease.

The Gundersen Lutheran Heart Institute performs nearly 4,000 procedures in the cardiac cath lab each year.

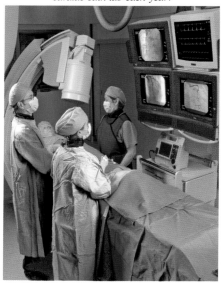

hematology/oncology; chemotherapy; radiation oncology; the Norma J. Vinger Center for Breast Care; the Sanctuary, which provides patients and their family and friends with a place of meditation; Ronald McDonald Kid City for children, which is the first of its kind in the nation; and a clinical research area.

Patients in Gundersen Lutheran's Cancer Center benefit from its interdisciplinary team approach to care and its integrative cancer support services. The goal of these professionals is to work together to help the "person within the patient" by addressing all of the needs and concerns related to their illness, not just the illness itself. For example, when a child has cancer and is preparing to return to school, a member of the pediatric oncology team will visit the child's classroom and educate the students about the disease, easing the child's adjustment back into school life.

Gundersen Lutheran Health System's main campus is located in La Crosse, Wisconsin.

Gundersen Lutheran's East Building opened its doors in 2003 and houses the Cancer Center, Neuroscience Center, Eye Institute, Plastic & Reconstructive Surgery Center, and Outpatient Surgery Center.

The Health System's participation in both regional and national research groups allows it to offer many of the same leading-edge treatments as the best-known names in cancer care. More than 165 national and international treatment protocols in oncology, hematology, radiation oncology and surgery are available at Gundersen Lutheran. The Gundersen Lutheran radiation oncology department is one of six facilities in

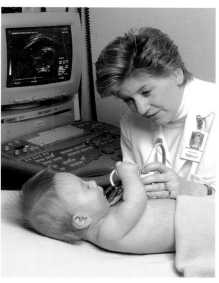

Gundersen Lutheran pediatric cardiologist Susan MacLellan-Tobert, MD uses state-of-the-art technology to care for children with heart problems.

the state and 157 nationwide accredited by the American College of Radiology (ACR). This distinction attests to the quality of care the facility offers its patients.

One of the Cancer Center's most highly-advanced treatments for cancer is MammoSite™ for breast cancer. Gundersen Lutheran was one of the first 30 centers nationwide authorized to offer the MammoSite Radiation Therapy System. Treating breast cancer from the inside out, the FDA-approved treatment delivers a carefully-localized radiation dose through a catheter and directly to tissue where cancer would be most likely to recur. Gundersen Lutheran also offers a number of other new technologies that have moved from the realm of science fiction into reality, offering more effective and less invasive ways of treating many cancers.

New state-of-the-art technologies have also changed the way members of the medical staff and patients receive information. Gundersen Lutheran has a "Clinical Workstation," which has computerized patient medical information, making the patient's experience more streamlined. Staff at any Gundersen Lutheran location in the 19-county service area can access necessary medical information. The Picture Archiving and Communications System, known as PACS, also connects healthcare providers across the system. PACS is an online system that allows providers in different locations to see patients' medical images at the same time—making diagnosis easier, more precise, and dramatically more efficient. Instead of patients having to carry their files from appointment to appointment, their physicians can call up their medical imaging results in a matter of seconds.

Employees at Gundersen Lutheran are more than just doctors, nurses, therapists, or technicians. They're also teachers, sharing their expertise with resident and student doctors, student nurses, paramedics, and other health professionals. Gundersen Lutheran views teaching as an opportunity to influence the next generation of practitioners and constantly improve the quality of patient care.

With the support of Gundersen Lutheran Medical Foundation, medi-

cal and education programs help more than 1,400 students—from high school students to medical/nursing school students and graduates—pursue their training in healthcare at Gundersen Lutheran each year. Residency and training programs are offered in many medical specialties including internal medicine, general surgery, oral and maxillofacial surgery, and podiatry.

Gundersen Lutheran is also part of one of the best physician assistant programs in the nation, a collaborative effort with other regional educational institutions. The average scores of the program's graduates on the physician assistant national certifying examination consistently place the program in the top 20 percent of programs nationally.

Gundersen Lutheran physicians and midwives deliver more than 1,500 babies each year.

Experts at Gundersen Lutheran provide primary and specialty care in a variety of services.

In addition, Gundersen Lutheran has been designated as both the Western Clinical Campus of the University of Wisconsin Medical School and the Western Campus of the University of Wisconsin-Madison School of Nursing. Students from these premier medical and nursing education programs receive training at Gundersen Lutheran each year.

Registered nurses at Gundersen Lutheran also have the opportunity to participate in a unique nursing education and research fellowship program. An average of 16 nursing fellows are chosen each year to participate in educational and research projects, and then publish their results.

From the very beginning, research has been one of the most important aspects of Gundersen Lutheran's mission. In the late nineteenth century Dr. Adolf Gundersen and his colleagues, Dr. Edward Evans and Dr. Christian Christiansen, were among the first to study the effects of surgery on appendicitis. The results of their study led to the widely-held belief that the only successful treatment for appendicitis is early surgery.

Pioneering research continues to be a major part of the work done at Gundersen Lutheran today. Staff members have, and continue to, publish countless studies in the top medical journals in the United States, which consistently rank the clinic as a premier health center. The research is

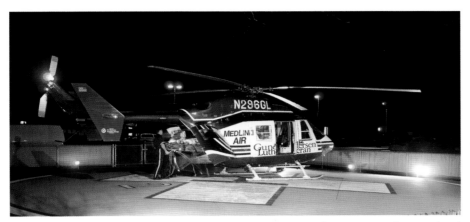

*Gundersen Lutheran MedLink
AIR emergency medical helicopter
transports critically-ill patients
directly from the scene of an accident,
or referral hospitals, to its tertiary
care center in La Crosse.
MedLink AIR has provided
care in the air since 1992.*

made possible through the administrative and financial backing of Gundersen Lutheran Medical Foundation.

Clinical research conducted in Gundersen Lutheran's patient population has helped establish protocols now common in many disciplines. By collaborating with schools such as the University of Wisconsin, national societies, and other healthcare organizations, the researchers at Gundersen Lutheran are able to make major contributions to the medical community across the country.

Gundersen Lutheran's microbiology research team is internationally renowned for its early and unrelenting attention to Lyme disease. The team began in 1985 with the goal of understanding the disease, aiding vaccine research, and improving diagnostic testing. Their successes include being awarded three U.S. patents for developing more accurate

*Thanks to its less confining design and interior
air movement, patients examined in
Gundersen Lutheran's shortbore MRI usually
require little or no sedation for anxiety or
claustrophobia. This state-of-the-art imaging
equipment is also used for highly-sensitive
breast MRI studies to determine cancer's
true extent before treatments or surgery.*

diagnostic tests and an effective canine vaccine. Today researchers continue their groundbreaking work in Lyme disease; cancer, surgical, cardiac, and clinical research; cholesterol studies; congestive heart failure; and more.

Gundersen Lutheran is committed to improving healthcare through a wide range of health and wellness programming, educational services, support groups, and screenings. It collaborates with other organizations in the region and state to improve the health of the community members it serves. The Health System is part of the La Crosse Medical Health Science Consortium, a unique partnership among the area's regional medical systems and institutions of higher education. Its mission is to enhance healthcare, strengthen health science education, and encourage applied research initiatives.

Gundersen Lutheran helped form the Wisconsin Collaborative for Healthcare Quality Inc., a voluntary statewide consortium of healthcare organizations working to improve the quality of healthcare in Wisconsin. The collaborative serves as a model for the nation in terms of how organizations can make useful information publicly available. The group is developing a common set of measures of healthcare quality outcomes by publicly reporting the performance of healthcare organizations against these measures. All data is independently verified. These measurements include evaluating the entire spectrum of medical care from office visits to hospital stays.

Gundersen Lutheran Health System has experienced significant growth and changes since Dr. Adolf Gundersen founded his small clinic more than 100 years ago. However, one thing remains the same. Gundersen Lutheran's quality results continue to make it the proven leader in healthcare in the Tri-State region.

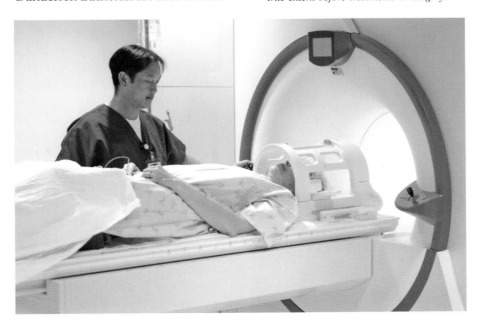

HAWKS NURSERY

Wauwatosa, Wisconsin was first settled in 1835 along the banks of the Menomonee River, just west of Milwaukee. From the Civil War into the 1870s, thousands of European immigrants were attracted to Wisconsin's many lakes and natural beauty, and many chose to start their new lives in Wauwatosa. The Industrial Revolution was then taking the nation by storm, and many of the town's citizens prospered from the new opportunities. A new upper-middle class formed in the area, and they imitated their East Coast predecessors by building rows of elegant Victorian houses, adorned with sweeping lawns and splendid gardens. The burgeoning trend also created a growing need for gardening and landscaping services, and a few farsighted New Yorkers stepped up to fill it.

Charles H. Hawks Sr., Arthur F. Moser, and Theodore J. Ferguson started Hawks Nursery in western New York in 1875, in the city of Rochester. The area was known for its fertile soil, plentiful moisture, and a climate that was well-suited for the landscape and nursery business. It was

Theodore Ferguson and his daughter at the production facility.

also along the railway lines, which made the transportation of plants to many of the developing markets a much easier task. Ferguson, who had family ties in Wauwatosa, knew the town was a perfect place for a branch of the company and that same year opened a second Hawks Nursery in Wauwatosa. He moved there to run the new branch, opening offices at the Loan and Trust Building. By the late 1800s there were more than 200 salesmen working for Hawks Nursery between the New York and Wisconsin locations. Most of them traveled between the cities, towns, and rural farms covering hundreds

of miles by rail, horse and buggy, or by foot. In the early days Hawks was particularly known for selling fruit and shade trees serving the needs of farmers and urbanites west of the Appalachians. In little time, orders from the Wauwatosa nursery began to represent the bulk of the company's business.

By about 1910 the company had purchased a 20-acre parcel of land from J.D. Gilbert, one of Wauwatosa's major landowners. The property gave Hawks Nursery the space to propagate a large amount of stock to answer the continually growing demand for its product. After a stint overseas fighting in World War I, Charles Hawks, Jr. joined the company as supervisor of shipping. About the same time one of the company's business partners, Arthur J. Moser, passed away. The Hawks family bought up Moser's interest in the nursery and shortly afterwards Hawks, Jr. joined Ferguson in Wauwatosa. By 1921 new administrative offices were opened on State Street, with a suite overlooking the river.

Theodore Ferguson retired from the company in September 1925, sell-

Charles Hawks, Theodore Ferguson, and office staff at the turn of the century.

*Joseph Kresl, current president
of Hawks Nursery.*

Hawks' retail facility, which opened in 1994.

ing his share of the business to the Hawks family. Upon his retirement, after 50 years with the nursery, Ferguson was quoted in the local newspaper:

"In my estimation there is no better farming land in the world than that close around Milwaukee. As for climate, I find it most suitable for general nursery work. The winters are perhaps too cold for the successful raising of seedlings and for certain other usual southern stock, but for all else, it is unequaled."

Business was booming in the Roaring Twenties, and the nursery's capacity was soon outgrown. Realizing their need for more land to meet the rising demand for greenery products, the company sold its Swan-North Avenue property in June 1927. The original land was subdivided between Hawks, Sr.; his son; and an associate, A.W. Ritter. By September they finalized the purchase of 38 acres of land from W.S. Robbins at 122nd Street and Watertown Plank Road, where the company is still located today.

Hawks Nursery was hit hard by the depression in the 1930s. Cities which were experiencing rapid growth before, now slowed almost to a halt. The company's salesmen struggled to obtain orders from existing clients to keep the nursery out of bankruptcy. The company also saw a drastic reduction in orders from farmers for fruit trees, one of Hawks' main products. Charles Hawks was sure they would all end up in the "poor house," but he also felt that being part of a business like Hawks had distinct advantages. "The satisfaction of working outdoors and eating a sandwich on a summer day in the shade of a huge Carolina Poplar," he said at the time, "was enough for many to counterbalance the lower wages paid."

Instead of buckling under their losses, the company partners put their heads together. They decided to move in a new direction and offer services and products in ornamental landscaping, for both businesses and homeowners. It turned out to be the saving grace for the company and the area for which Hawks Nursery is most widely known today.

After World War II John Orton and Jim Bennett were hired to bring

*Hawks' sales yard
and information gazebo.*

new blood and fresh ideas into the business. Along with the post-war Baby Boom and the general expansion in both residential and commercial development in the Wauwatosa area, Hawks' business grew rapidly in the early '50s. The company sold 28 of it original 38 acres in 1956, turning from growing their own stock to purchasing a wider variety of products from outside vendors. They also

formed Hawks Landscaping, Inc. in 1969 which gave the nursery the ability to bid on union contracts, while still allowing it to perform in the non-union sector. In 1972 Charles Hawks sold his interest to Orton and Bennett, though he did continue to visit the nursery on a regular basis. The two men carried on the traditions of the business and took it in prosperous new directions. Most notably, they were responsible for taking the company into large commercial projects such as the landscaping of Northridge, Southridge, and Brookfield shopping centers, as well as continuing the residential business. They also purchased new vehicles and equipment for the nursery.

After almost half a century of successful cultivation of the company, Orton and Bennett decided to sell the business in 1993. They found a buyer in Joseph Kresl, a successful landscape architect who had designed projects in Madison, Milwaukee, and Minneapolis. Running the business proved a daunting task for Kresl. The buildings on the property were in such disrepair that they had been nearly condemned by the city. Kresl made every effort to save the old structures, bringing in engineers to assess the possibilities. Unfortunately they were beyond repair. At that point he decided to build a new nursery structure which was, and still is, considered state-of-the-art in the business. The new $1.5 million building, which opened in 1994, covers 22,000 square feet and consists of a three-tiered, gazebo-type atrium; a large arbor structure; an information gazebo; and several vignette gardens where customers can see the types of landscaping for which the company is known. Kresl also incorporated a "presentation" concept in the 1990s, designed to sell products by creating beautiful arrangements of all types of flora.

The Hawks Nursery production facility, then located at Highway 100 and Burleigh, circa 1920.

Today, customers entering the garden center will find any number of Hawks specialists ready to serve them. Horticulturists, landscape designers, architects, floral designers, maintenance, and construction crews, as well as salespeople make up the company staff of 180. They are available to answer questions, help with design needs, and offer expert advice on product choices. Kresl notes that the demand from the public for the expertise of Hawks horticulturists is so great, they often feel more like a university extension. More than 1,500 calls come into Hawks every day and Kresl believes that providing information to the public is a key to the company's continuing success. Hawks also offers classes in gardening, landscaping, maintenance, and floral design for a fee of $5 per class.

Hawks now has three main profit centers: landscape design and construction, landscape maintenance, and the garden center. Seventy percent of the company's design/build business is in residential work, while 30 percent is commercial. In the maintenance area, 60 percent of their work is in commercial and 40 percent is residential. This area includes services such as tree trimming, snow removal, spring clean ups, and lawn care.

The nursery wins numerous awards each year for its landscape design projects. Most recently, Hawks won the prestigious Judges Choice Award presented by the Wisconsin Landscape Federation. This is quite an honor as the federation is made up of landscaping professionals throughout the state.

After more than a century, Hawks Nursery continues to be known for its quality of service, diversity of plants, wide variety of gardening supplies, and knowledgeable employees. The company is also highly-respected for its deep roots in the Wauwatosa community. Kresl says that is one of the most enjoyable parts of owning Hawks Nursery. Third and fourth generations of families are still coming to Hawks for their gardening, design, and maintenance needs. For Kresl, that longtime connection to the community is one of those Milwaukee traditions that is especially rewarding, and one that he plans to continue for many years to come.

A vendor at this popular Dane County Farmer's Market sells fresh
vegetables and flowers to local patrons. Photo by Gary Knowles,
courtesy, Wisconsin Department of Tourism

HOLY FAMILY CONVENT

On a hill, gently rising from the north shore of Silver Lake in Manitowoc, Wisconsin, stands Holy Family Convent, the home of the Franciscan Sisters of Christian Charity. Founded in 1869, just 21 years after Wisconsin became a state and four months before the village of Manitowoc was incorporated as a city, the Franciscan Sisters' history reaches back to the pioneer days of the area. A flood of immigration from 1850–1870 swelled the population of the city of Manitowoc from 756 to 5,168, and Manitowoc County from 3,702 to 33,364.

In 1866 a young priest, Father Joseph Fessler, was appointed pastor of a newly formed Catholic parish in Clarks Mills, Wisconsin, about ten miles west of Manitowoc. In an effort to provide the children of the rural area with a teacher, Father asked Theresa Gramlich to take on the task. She provided religious instruction in a summer vacation school and then taught the children again in the fall.

In 1867 a group of people from Ohio came through the area on their way to a settlement in Minnesota. Three of the women met Theresa and were impressed with the work she was doing. They joined her, taught in the area and, as they became acquainted, found they shared an interest in forming a religious community. Father

Three of the five foundresses of the Franciscan Sisters.

Earliest photo of Holy Family Convent, 1879.

Joseph Fessler became their guide and spiritual director. Bishop Henni of Milwaukee approved the intentions of the women. In May 1868 Father Fessler was appointed to a larger parish, St. Boniface in Manitowoc. He built a combination school and living quarters for the women who continued teaching and preparing their new community. They chose to follow the Gospel way of life of St. Francis of Assisi. On November 9, 1869, the four, and Father Fessler's sister, were received as women religious —and the Franciscan Sisters of Christian Charity was established. Even today, it remains the only religious community based

in Manitowoc County. Theresa Gramlich then became Sister Gabriel; the other four, Sisters Odelia, Coletta, Hyacinth, and Seraphica.

That same year, Sisters Gabriel and Hyacinth were sent on a collecting tour to the east to raise money to build a convent. For five months they traveled through many towns including Philadelphia, Baltimore, and New York, bringing home about $2,000. Sisters Odelia and Seraphica continued teaching at St. Boniface School.

The following school year the Sisters were invited to accept their first school away from home in Potosi, Wisconsin, in the southwestern part of the state. Sisters Gabriel and Seraphica left for the new assignment in November, beginning a long list of parish schools where the Franciscan Sisters would eventually serve.

Dire poverty plagued the small religious community from its founding, but the Sisters had incomparable riches of joy and trust in God. Their humble, dedicated lives spoke to and inspired others. A wonderful problem soon faced them. By 1872 the original five Sisters had grown to 12, plus nine candidates, requiring larger living quarters. From the beginning they had cherished the hope of "a real motherhouse." The need was now there.

Franciscan Sisters at grotto of the Blessed Virgin (habit style worn from 1869–1929).

One day the superior, Mother Odelia, on her way to tend to community business in a nearby village, passed a small lake surrounded by wooded land about four miles from Manitowoc. What a beautiful location for a convent! The thought would not leave her. Upon her return, she spoke with Father Fessler. He found the land could be purchased for just less than $30 an acre and bought 40 acres for the Sisters. A midwest architect, Adolphus Druiding, willing to serve poor and middle income institutions and use more modest materials and designs, was hired. Delighted with the location of the convent-to-be on Silver Lake, he drafted a plan that was accepted by Father Fessler and the Sisters. Due to limited finances, only one wing of the plan would be built. Generous settlers in the area helped haul materials for the building, asking only that the Sisters pray for them. Construction began in spring 1873. The building, dedicated to the Holy Family, was ready for occupancy less than a year-and-a-half later.

The community continued to grow steadily as did the demand for teachers in the pioneer state. By fall 1874, in addition to the schools in Manitowoc and Potosi, the Sisters were teaching in small Catholic schools in Cleveland, Hollandtown, Alverno, and Cross Plains, located throughout rural Wisconsin, and in Chillicothe, Ohio, their first out-of-state mission.

A surprise came to the Sisters in fall 1875. A teaching community of 28 Franciscan Sisters from Gieboldehausen, Germany, forced to leave their homeland because of the policies of Prince von Bismarck, was referred to the Sisters in Manitowoc, who now numbered 27. The Sisters needed a home while they decided their future in the United States. True to their title, Franciscan Sisters of Christian Charity,

Holy Family Convent in Manitowoc, Wisconsin.

the Manitowoc community heartily welcomed the Sisters. Days were not easy as the two cultures met, but the Sisters worked out their difficulties.

Within one year the German Sisters decided to amalgamate with the Manitowoc Sisters, doubling the membership and enabling further extension of the community's teaching apostolate. Between 1876 and 1879, the Sisters accepted five more small Wisconsin schools at Kaukauna, Lima, Schleisingerville, Paris, and Francis Creek. They also responded

Fire from lighting destroyed the convent on September 1, 1881.

to the request of a large school in Manistee, Michigan.

The increased membership—plus new candidates—brought the number of Sisters to about 70, requiring the construction of a second wing of the architect's plan. The Superior of the German Sisters returned to Germany for three months to settle business, sell property there, and beg for money for the addition in Manitowoc. Her trip was successful. The new wing was completed in spring 1879.

Faith formation and professional training of the new members was always a concern of the community. Holy Family Academy, Holy Family Normal School, and an in-service program for teachers were established at the convent.

Always ready to fulfill the needs of the community around them, the Sisters realized another need in Manitowoc. The city had no hospital and a few of the German Sisters had some health care training. In spring 1881, with the encouragement of a Manitowoc pastor, Reverend Henry Jacobs, and the help of the county, the Sisters opened a 12-bed hospital which received high praise in the coming years.

While poverty still plagued the Sisters (the salary of teachers at the time was $20 a month), the future looked bright as the community and its apostolates continued to grow. On the night of September 1, 1881 a terrible electric storm raged in Manitowoc. A deadly bolt of lightning struck a gable on the north side of the convent, igniting wood between the ceiling and the roof. The fire was uncontrollable and by morning the building was in ruins. The Sisters lost nearly everything. Because the imposing brick structure was considered fireproof, the Sisters had little insurance on it. In addition, they still had a $16,000 debt on the building. It was a devastating experience, seeming like "the graveyard of their hopes." A memoir says, "There was a great outpouring of compassion and help from the citizens of Manitowoc and the neighboring areas."

Group of Franciscan Sisters in front of Holy Family Convent.

Hand-carved altar in St. Francis Chapel at Holy Family Convent.

Mother Odelia said, "A star of hope still shone in the convent sky." The Diocese told them to go among the people and solicit funds. Monetary help and offers to loan money, interest-free, permitted the Sisters to rebuild. And they did—on the same spot and according to the same plans. The new building was dedicated in December 1883.

The Franciscan community was abundantly blessed. By 1891 the membership had grown to 182. They were teaching nearly 4,450 students in 40 schools—30 in Wisconsin and 10 in Illinois, Michigan, Missouri,

and Nebraska. Enrollments ranged from 40 to 350. In the golden jubilee year, 1919, there were 449 Sisters, 53 schools (41 in Wisconsin), and three healthcare institutions. Growth in numbers required additions to the convent structure in 1890, 1910, 1912, 1922, and 1925. The 1890 wing contained the first large chapel in the convent. An employee, John Falbisoner, in gratitude to God for his gift of wood-carving, carved the entire large gothic altar which continues today as an inspiration to the Sisters in their prayer.

The fine arts have been a part of the life of the Franciscan Sisters since their foundation. Music and art were offered in their convent educational institutions and Sisters were sent to schools for advanced work. In 1925 the Sisters opened Holy Family Conservatory of Music and Art in Manitowoc which has served thousands of people, from children to adults, in Manitowoc County.

As the country grew and developed, so did education. Requirements for teachers increased. The Sisters had been pursuing bachelor, masters, and doctoral degrees since about 1915. The Depression of the 1930s made costs of travel, room, board, and tuition at outside schools nearly impossible. New members had to be prepared for their apostolic works. In 1935, with courage and vision and at great sacrifice, the Superior of the community, Mother Generose Cahill, proceeded to have a final wing constructed at Holy Family Convent—a college. Degreed members staffed Holy Family College, training fellow Sisters for their professional services. This college served the community for 25 years and was the forerunner of a new and extended facility built on property just west of the convent in 1960. In 1957 the college had begun to accept lay women and became coeducational in 1969. Known since 1972 as Silver

*Group of Franciscan Sisters
at Holy Family Convent.*

Lake College, it continues its liberal arts and professional degree emphases, serving students from all parts of Wisconsin and beyond. The Franciscan Sisters sponsor the college.

The healthcare apostolate of the Sisters had expanded since the opening of the 12-bed hospital in Manitowoc in the 1880s. Insufficient funds for a new and adequate structure caused the closing of that facility in 1888. In response to requests of local citizens in Manitowoc and other areas, healthcare facilities were opened over the years which have grown phenomenally with the times. All are sponsored by the Sisters. Two are in Wisconsin: Holy Family Memorial in Manitowoc, which began as Holy Family Hospital in 1899; and St. Paul Elder Services in Kaukauna, established in 1943 as the result of a request to care for one elderly woman. The Sisters' health ministry also extended to Zanesville,

Ohio in 1900, and continues there as part of the Genesis Health Care System. An elder care home in West Point, Nebraska was accepted in 1905, and a hospital was constructed in 1950. Today the two form Franciscan Care Services in West Point.

The 1950s brought tremendous growth in the community and a new focus on deepening faith formation and preparation for ministry. On June 13, 1957 the Franciscan Sisters' membership reached 1,013. Their number peaked at 1,126 in 1966. The 1960s held a new experience in religious communities—many members left and fewer joined. However, many more stayed than left, and others did enter. While numbers have decreased and works of the community have had to be reduced, the religious commitment and the spirit of dedication and service continue.

The Franciscan Sisters have a proud history of growth with, and commitment to, the people of Wisconsin and beyond. They have taught in 104 schools in the state and served many people through healthcare and other ministries. They have carried the

*Franciscan Sisters teach at all levels—
children through adults.*

name "Manitowoc, Wisconsin," to citizens of 13 other states and Lima, Peru.

Currently, there are just over 400 Franciscan Sisters serving in seven states (in addition to Wisconsin). They continue their works of teaching from preschool through college and sponsor and serve in several state-of-the-art healthcare institutions. Some are engaged in parish ministries and catechetical work. They have expanded their programs for the poor and elderly. They serve Hispanics, African Americans, Native Americans, and immigrant people. The retired Sisters support the ministries of the community by their prayer.

Much has changed in the lives of the Sisters since the founding days in the 1870s. A sketch of the community in *A History of the Catholic Church in Wisconsin* reflected upon the difficulties the Sisters experienced in the early days, and made a prophetic statement. "*But in spite of all, the Order grew and thrived; slowly at first, it is true, yet with healthful and positive assurance that it would live to succeed …Gradually, in proportion to their increase in numbers, the field of activity also expanded, until today the influence of their labor is felt throughout the land.*" And so it is.

HOLY FAMILY MEMORIAL HEALTH NETWORK

Holy Family Memorial Health Network is a place of healing and caring. Serving the people of Manitowoc for over 100 years, the hospital's mission has not varied although the practice of medicine certainly has. The hospital has adapted and changed throughout the years to accommodate the progressive requirements of Manitowoc and its surrounding communities. Holy Family Memorial has grown from a single building, built in 1899, to the sophisticated healthcare network it is today. This advancement could not have been possible without the dedication and eternal hope of the Franciscan Sisters of Christian Charity.

In 1898 Mother Alexia Fullmer weighed a request made by Manitowoc citizens who wanted a hospital, against the pressing needs of her existing responsibilities. She was the superior general for the convent, which was already heavily in debt. However, after much consideration and prayer, she was convinced the Sisters should embark upon the project. Although facing financial obstacles they forged ahead, banking on faith alone.

Holy Family Memorial Medical Center, during its very early days. The Sisters who operated the hospital worked in the garden, shown on the lower left, which provided produce for the patients, nursing students, employees, and the Sisters from 1901 to 1961.

Mother Alexia Fullmer, superior general of the Franciscan Sisters of Christian Charity in 1898.

The completed structure was dedicated as Holy Family Hospital on September 28, 1899. Later, Mother Alexia said this about the experience: "Under such trying circumstances, it was evident that human means were not to be the foundation of the edifice in question. No—it was to rest upon a foundation more solid and more secure than earthly goods, trust in Divine Providence."

The first decade was not an easy one for the Sisters. The magnificent new building was well-staffed and ready for patients to fill its 45 available beds. However, patients were reluctant to come. People saw the impressive building and were intimidated by the prospect of what unfamiliar modern practices might take place inside. Also, the prevailing view of hospitals at that time was that they were places to die and not places to get help, become well, and continue living. Only 189 patients were cared for the first year of operation, but Mother Alexia did not become discouraged. "This house will build up and be a wonderful place some day. The city will also build up, and we will have more work than we can do," she stated in a memoir.

By 1909 attitudes about hospitals had shifted. People realized they could benefit from the modern facility and welcomed the opportunity to do so. Throughout the 1920s the hospital's positive reputation continued to grow as more patients were served. In fact, many in the community believed the hospital was doing so well that they did not realize it was actually operating at a deficit. The Sisters were deeply in debt as their income was below their expenditures, which included interest of more than $15,000 per year. The Sisters and an advisory committee embarked upon a campaign to raise community awareness about the hospital's situation and the need for an expansion in order to accommodate the growing number of patients being admitted for treatment. The people of Manitowoc County generously supported the building project which was dedicated on April 2, 1929, just before the full force of the Depression.

True to their commitment to service, the Sisters continued to provide healthcare and help meet the needs of many during the years of the Great Depression. There were 320 families living in the city in 1931 and many of them had five to ten children. Men—destitute, hungry, and unable to find work—often showed up at the hospital's back door. Because of the Sisters' continuous labor in the hospital's gardens, no person was turned away hungry.

The facility's history is marked by other impressive deeds of service which were direct responses to the needs of the time. A nurses program, established in 1920, turned out 38 graduate nurses who served in the Armed Forces during World War II. A nurses cadet program, which started in 1943, produced graduates who helped in veteran and civilian hospitals in Wisconsin and other neighboring states.

The polio epidemic presented new challenges in the mid-'40s. The hospital responded by creating a polio isolation unit in August of 1946. In addition to the physical needs, there were great emotional and spiritual needs of patients and family members suffering through the polio crisis. The staff of Holy Family Hospital created an atmosphere of respect and compassion for each patient who faced a future of uncertainty. Nurses and doctors cared for and nurtured even when they could not cure.

Over the next several decades continued advancements were made, both technologically and structurally, to the hospital. The Manitowoc community recognized the value of these changes and participated politically and financially. The Sisters, who had

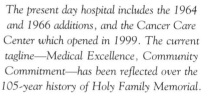

Shown from left to right: the 1929 addition which added 100 beds to the 1898 building; the 1949 pediatric and administration wing; and the 1898 original hospital building.

been governing hospital operations for over 60 years, realized the need to invite lay people in the community to help govern and oversee future changes. A new board of directors was created consisting of four Sisters and seven businessmen from the community who were devoted to the hospital's mission.

One of the most significant changes in the hospital's history was the merger of Holy Family Medical Center with Manitowoc Memorial Hospital on May 1, 1991. The new entity became Holy Family Memorial honoring the history of both established institutions. The cooperative change went smoothly and an impressive 92 percent of the employees of both institutions received their first choice in job placement.

In 1993 Holy Family Memorial began affiliating with physician clinics, changing its composition

The present day hospital includes the 1964 and 1966 additions, and the Cancer Care Center which opened in 1999. The current tagline—Medical Excellence, Community Commitment—has been reflected over the 105-year history of Holy Family Memorial.

from an inpatient only facility to a total healthcare network. Today there are 14 physician clinics ranging in service from primary care to specialty care. They are all part of Holy Family Memorial and share in the vision for a successful and healthy community. "We hold our obligation to the community as being sacred," remarks Mary Maurer, vice president of professional services. In 2003 almost 20 percent of the total network expenses were dedicated to community services such as healthcare classes, blood pressure checks, charitable treatment, and providing care through government programs.

Holy Family Memorial is the largest employer in Manitowoc County with over 1,300 employees and 300 volunteers. Whether someone is an employee or a volunteer, the entire network team is committed to their community. "We live here and share in the challenges faced by our community," says Mark Herzog, president and CEO of Holy Family Memorial. "The blueprint we have designed for tomorrow's Holy Family Memorial incorporates the very foundation of our mission—serving people."

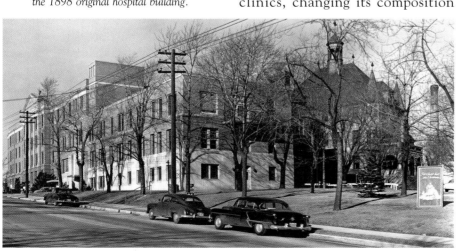

KIKKOMAN FOODS, INC.

Kikkoman Corporation of Japan, the world's largest producer of soy sauce, began a concerted effort to develop the U.S. market through the importing of product in the early 1950s. Demand grew so strongly that a subsidiary, Kikkoman International, Inc. was established in San Francisco in 1957 to oversee North American sales.

Later in 1968, bottling of Kikkoman soy sauce and production of Kikkoman Teriyaki Marinade & Sauce began in California. Soy sauce was transported from Japan to California in large stainless steel containers and then packaged.

Sales demand continued to grow until it became economically feasible to consider a U.S. plant location. A U.S. based plant would provide significant advantages to Kikkoman in penetrating the American mass market. The savings on freight would be substantial in terms of the raw materials (soybeans and wheat) grown in the United States and then shipped to Japan, as well as the finished goods which then had to be shipped back again to the United States. Moreover, periodic dock strikes, which could interrupt supply, could be avoided. Finally, in addi-

Kikkoman Foods, Inc., Walworth, Wisconsin.

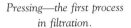

Pressing—the first process in filtration.

tion to growing sales which would support a U.S. plant, the declining value of the U.S. dollar relative to the Japanese yen encouraged investment in the United States.

Once the decision was made to expand to the United States, Kikkoman made a detailed study of where to locate the new production facility. Walworth, Wisconsin was chosen for a number of reasons. With markets on the west and east coasts, the Wisconsin location provided easy access to both market areas and was in a central location for the purpose of physical distribution. It was also close to the raw materials needed for the production of soy sauce—soybeans and wheat.

Walworth offered additional advantages over other potential sites. The community itself was tranquil and friendly, electricity was reasonably priced, and there was a good supply of fresh water—an important ingredient in making soy sauce. The local labor force was mainly made up of rural employees who were accustomed to working hard and felt comfortable working with soybeans and other agricultural products. In all respects, Walworth was the right location.

On a cold day in January 1972, a Shinto priest blessed the new home for Kikkoman in the United States. Even though the Wisconsin earth was frozen and hard as steel, the groundbreaking went on. Kikkoman became the first Japanese company to build a full-process manufacturing plant in the United States.

Between the time of the groundbreaking and the opening of the new plant, a lot of work had to be done. There were cultural issues that needed to be addressed, but there were also concerns from the locals that the new plant would be the beginning of the end for southern Wisconsin's rich farmlands.

The management used a grassroots approach to the community's concerns. Instead of taking a corporate stance, they went out to the community, visiting local churches, hosting coffee groups, and educating the citizens about the process of making soy sauce. They also allayed any fears the people might have about the environment. Another potential problem was that, up until the arrival of the new families, no Japanese had lived in the county. Since 20 Japanese families would be living in the area, Kikkoman was adamant about not placing the families all together thus creating the image of a "Little Tokyo." Instead, the company spread the families throughout five local communities, integrating them into Wisconsin life, as well as helping locals get to know the new arrivals.

The plan proved to be very successful and by June 1973 the 100,000-square-foot plant was up and running. Kikkoman Foods Inc., a subsidiary of Kikkoman Corporation of Japan, was finally born. By the end of that year more than 1.7 million gallons of product had been produced. The company was under the leadership of Yuzaburo Mogi, whose new title was president and executive managing director. It had been his dream to have a U.S. operation.

Today Kikkoman Foods, Inc. ships out approximately 30 million gallons

Raw material preparation.

annually in the United States, and through steady and consistent growth, has become the second largest facility producing soy sauce in the world. Kikkoman Foods has grown steadily since its first days in Walworth. The physical plant has expanded continually and now covers some 700,000 square feet and has more than 150 employees.

The company also prides itself on one fact that separates it from its competition. Since its founding in Noda, Japan, their soy sauce has always been naturally brewed. That tradition continues today in its Walworth plant. Unlike the chemical "soy sauce" of its competitors, Kikkoman's natural process requires several months to complete. The results are in the flavor. This is the major reason why Kikkoman is number one in the soy sauce market today.

Bottling—the final step in the production process.

The company is proud of its successful integration into the local community. This is evident in the many ways in which Kikkoman has reached out and supported both state and local activities. Most recently, the company's foundation donated $1 million to the University of Wisconsin-Madison for its Bio-Star project, which includes the creation of the Kikkoman Laboratory of Microbial Fermentation.

The decision Kikkoman Corporation made to expand to Walworth is a decision it has never regretted. The same business advantages it saw then, are just as valid today. As a result, the company plans to continue the expansion of its Wisconsin facility to meet the growing demand for Kikkoman products.

MARSHFIELD CLINIC

In 1916 a revolutionary idea was born in the Wisconsin town of Marshfield. The plan—unusual for its day—called for a group of doctors to join together to form a clinic. It was a radical proposal that would forever change how medicine was practiced in cities throughout the U.S.

It all began with a German immigrant physician and surgeon by the name of Karl W. Doege, who is thought to be primarily responsible for making the "group practice" concept a reality. Named after the town where the organization was formed, Marshfield Clinic is recognized today as one of the five leading clinics in the country.

Dr. Doege was traveling by train in 1890 to his family home in Thorp when a railroad conductor happened to mention that Marshfield was in need of a doctor. Marshfield was a thriving center for railroad commerce that served five different freight and passenger lines. The Marshfield depot saw more than 40 daily rail arrivals and departures. It was almost unthinkable that a bustling hub like that was without a doctor, and Doege decided it was the perfect place to hang his shingle. Doege was absent from

Marshfield Clinic, 1926.

town for a brief period when he traveled to Vienna, Austria to expand his medical knowledge, but by 1897 he was firmly ensconced at his practice in Marshfield.

By 1916 Marshfield had a substantial number of doctors and Doege brought five of them together to discuss his unusual, and somewhat controversial, idea for a group practice. The group included Dr. Victor Mason, the son of a Marshfield photographer, who had a medical practice in town since 1909; Dr. H.H. Milbee, a Canadian internist who moved to Wisconsin in 1901; Wisconsin native Dr. Roy Potter, a general practitioner who was schooled in pharmacology and medicine; and Dr. William Hipke, also

a Wisconsin native who earned his medical degree at the University of Illinois and who studied ophthalmology and otolaryngology in Vienna, Austria. The youngest of the six doctors was Walter Sexton. Sexton, a Marshfield native, received his training in surgery and gynecology at Johns Hopkins University and the Hebrew Hospital.

The clinic's biggest challenge would be to win over the citizens of the area who distrusted this new style of practice, fearing they would be forced to pay higher prices and have fewer options for treatment. To allay the public's concerns, the group of doctors took the unusual step of preparing a statement that appeared on the front page of the *Marshfield News Herald* on December 23, 1916. In their statement the six doctors made clear that the aim of the new practice was to offer "better and more efficient service to the public and to do it in a scientific way. Each member of the firm, besides his usual work, will do reading and study in a special field. He will thus gain more expert knowledge by reason of such study and will, through this extra knowledge, assist and help his colleagues in diagnosing especially difficult cases."

The founding fathers, from left to right: Dr. William Hipke, Dr. K.W. Doege, Dr. Victor Mason, Dr. Walter Sexton, Dr. H.H. Milbee, and Dr. Roy Potter.

Marshfield Clinic, 2004.

They also successfully dispelled people's suspicions that the clinic would charge higher fees or limit their choice of doctors.

Marshfield Clinic was incorporated in December 1916 and officially opened its doors to patients on January 2, 1917, on the second floor of a building, at the corner of Central Avenue and Third Street. In addition to the six doctors, the new corporation had an office manager and four employees. All the doctors were employees of the corporation and each

Pictured below, from left to right:
Dr. Russell Lewis, Dr. Ben Lawton,
and Dr. George Magnin.

had purchased a $1,000 share of non-transferable stock under the articles of incorporation, with each stockholder having one vote. The terms of issue, which never changed, kept control of the organization solely in the hands of actively-practicing physicians.

After World War I, Dr. Doege's son, Karl H. Doege, became part of the medical group. Shortly after, Dr. James Vedder, Sr. and his brother Harry, also a physician, and Dr. Lyman Copps joined the clinic, bringing the total number of doctors to ten. The group began hosting scientific meetings for other doctors. This quickly became a tradition at Marshfield, one that has endured and helped to shape the character of Marshfield Clinic. By 1924 the clinic formally became part of the Univer-

sity of Wisconsin's first medical preceptor program. This was the beginning of Marshfield's growing commitment to medical education, which is still evident today in both its residency and fellowship programs.

The clinic faced the first major challenge to its existence in 1929 with the stock market crash. The income of Marshfield Clinic plummeted, but the dedication of its doctors stayed solid. Patients paid for treatment through in-kind services: canned goods, poultry, beef, eggs, vegetables, and fruit. Some patients even paid with live animals. Despite the severe financial challenges, the clinic survived.

In the years between the great wars, Marshfield Clinic continued to grow. It added new members to its roster of physicians and with them

came new medical skills. For the first time the clinic also instituted a policy which required all physicians to be certified, as well as eligible for their specialty boards. In addition, the group formed an educational sabbatical program as well as a formal governing board.

During World War II, the organization faced yet another daunting financial challenge and was nearly forced to dissolve in 1944. It was at this time that several of the clinic's doctors were called to military service. The facility's management had decided to pay these colleagues their regular salary, less their military pay, while they were called to service. As during the great depression, medical care was given regardless of the patient's ability to pay. The wartime economy was very difficult. However, as with other challenges, members of the clinic worked together and the corporation survived.

In 1950 the clinic's own Dr. Dean Emanuel received the first federal grant for Marshfield, for his major study of Farmer's Lung Disease. He was also the lead researcher on the Maple Bark Disease discovery. Both of these led to the establishment of the National Farm Medicine Center. In 1959 Dr. Stephan Epstein, a clinic dermatologist, established what is now the Marshfield Clinic Research Foundation, a division of the clinic.

Additional physicians joined the medical group in the '50s including Dr. George Magnin, an internist; Dr. Russell Lewis, an obstetrician; and Dr. Ben Lawton, a thoracic surgeon. Dr. Magnin was not only an outstanding clinician, he was also one of the clinic's finest teachers of medical students and residents. Through their

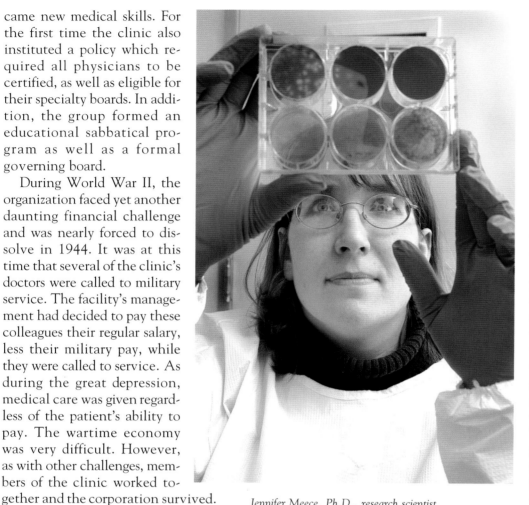

Jennifer Meece, Ph.D., research scientist.

years with the practice, both Dr. Lewis, the clinic's first medical director, and Dr. Lawton, had a major impact on the course the clinic took. Both men also became president of the organization at different times.

Dr. Lewis is considered the architect of the Greater Marshfield Community Health Plan, one of the earliest HMOs in the U.S. and the predecessor of the current Security Health Plan Inc. Dr. Lawton would later serve on the Board of Regents at the University of Wisconsin and later became a presidential appointee to the National Institute of Medicine. Dr. Lawton was a major advocate for service to the underprivileged, as well as for research and medical education. For his unwaver-

ing dedication to social advocacy he was given the pen that President Lyndon Johnson used in 1965 to sign Medicare into law.

By the end of the 1960s more than 80 doctors were part of Marshfield Clinic, offering nearly 20 areas of specialty. The immense growth that the clinic was experiencing made it necessary to abandon the downtown clinic for a more suitable space. An eight-acre parcel of land was purchased and the new clinic was built adjacent to Saint Joseph's Hospital—which included a connecting corridor between the two facilities. The 212,000-square-foot building was officially opened in 1975 with a staff of 135 physicians. Two major additions were added to Marshfield Clinic in 1984 and 1989, and in 2003 a new east wing was completed, which is now home to both the ambulatory surgery and gastroenterology departments.

Under the leadership of Dr. Frederic P. Wesbrook, president, and Reed E. Hall, executive director, today's Marshfield Clinic is the largest private group medical practice in Wisconsin and one of the largest in the United States. The practice offers the services of nearly 750 physicians and 5,700 additional staff who are employed throughout the clinic's 40 regional centers. There are nearly 2 million patient encounters on an annual basis, and people travel from 25 different countries, every state in the nation, and every county in Wisconsin for the clinic's primary and specialty care.

Marshfield Clinic offers care in 86 medical specialties including:

Mosinee Center, the clinic's first regional facility.

• Neurosciences (neurology, neurosurgery, neuropsychology)—Marshfield's neurology specialists take care of a wide variety of medical conditions that affect the brain, spine, and nervous system (epilepsy, Alzheimer's disease, multiple sclerosis, movement disorders, etc.). Because clinic doctors are also involved with research they employ the latest techniques, technology, and medications to diagnose and treat conditions such as Parkinson's disease, Huntington's disease, brain tumors, cerebral palsy, multiple sclerosis, headaches, and stroke.

• Oncology—Marshfield Clinic's oncologists provide state-of-the-art care for patients with cancer, including many on research protocols. Cancer treatments also cross many specialization boundaries at Marshfield Clinic involving pediatrics, pain management, orthopaedics, otolaryngology, dermatology, surgery, pathology, and neurology.

• Cardiology/Cardiovascular Surgery—Because heart disease is a growing problem in the United States and especially in Wisconsin, cardiology and its related fields are among the most important areas of specialty at Marshfield. Clinic specialists include pediatric cardiologists, echocardiography, interventional cardiologists, and cardiovascular surgeons.

• Pathology—Medicine relies heavily on laboratory analysis (pathology) for diagnosis of disease and other conditions. Marshfield Clinic Laboratories is a large regional referral laboratory servicing much of Wisconsin, and even clients nationwide. An 80-route courier system picks up specimens daily for analysis at Marshfield. Laboratory results are immediately available via computer.

• Food, Safety Services, Veterinary Diagnostic services, and Toxicology Testing—Marshfield Clinic is the only institution in the world that combines these services to such a degree. This allows the clinic to contribute to public health in unique ways.

At the core of Marshfield's network of patient records and other important data is a regional Electronic Medical Record (EMR). The EMR serves as the legal medical record for 42 clinics and three hospitals that comprise the clinical component of the Marshfield EMR network. It is utilized by 6,700 internal users and contains files on all procedures, insurance claims, and laboratory results dating back to 1985. It also has a file of more than 72 million patient diagnoses dating back to 1960.

Marshfield Clinic and its research foundation have been credited with several major discoveries. As recently as 2003, Marshfield Clinic received international acclaim for discovering the first case of Monkeypox in the Western Hemisphere. This vital discovery permitted early treatment of patients and quickly stymied the spread of the disease.

The Center for Medical Genetics was established in 1994 as a new research unit within the clinic's research foundation. It was responsible for the "Marshfield Maps," a key component to the Human Genome Project. Although a wide variety of research activities are underway within the center, research focuses on the hunt for genes which influence human health disorders. Identification of these genes is an important first step in improving disease prevention and treatment.

Since its beginnings as a clinic, Marshfield has created and participated in numerous community outreach programs including free clinics, public lectures, health fairs, support groups, sponsorships for various health-related charities, and educational programs. The clinic has also won many awards and commendations.

Marshfield Clinic's mission remains to serve patients through accessible, high-quality healthcare, research, and education. The clinic's physicians and staff will continue to strive to be where the future of medicine lives.

MARTH INCORPORATED

The Marth Companies are a three generation, family-run business which utilizes one of nature's most valuable, renewable resources—trees. The owners of the companies are doubly resourceful in using by-products of the tree, wood shavings, and sawdust, which to some are considered the "leftovers" or by-products of the tree. This was not so for Milton and Geraldine Marth, founders of the company, who saw the potential to capitalize on a marketing and sales opportunity that others had overlooked.

The company's story began in 1958. Milton and Geraldine Marth —a hardworking couple of German decent and work ethics, with strong Christian values—were turkey farmers on their 40 acres of land just north of Marathon, Wisconsin. At the time, turkey farms and lumber mills were two prominent businesses in the area. And Milton Marth found a way to bring the two together utilizing the resources of one for the benefit of the other. He realized, as a turkey farmer, that bedding was a necessity for all of his neighboring farmers. He also knew that manufacturing plants and saw mills were producing the by-

Aerial view of the Marth's Marathon location, 2004.

product that could be used for that bedding. Assuring the mills of the efficient removal of by-product gave the Marth's the opportunity to concentrate on production and growth. The idea worked and the company was off to a solid start.

Geraldine Marth was skilled in accounting and clerical details and handled that aspect of the business, while Milton kept his eye on future opportunities. He knew that selling bedding for the turkey and livestock industries was only the beginning. Sawdust and wood shavings had greater potential and Milton Marth was determined to push forward and

discover what the possibilities were. He contacted manufacturing plants who were using the wood by-product for things such as particle board, toilet seats, and salad bowls. He began marketing his new found resource to these companies and his client base broadened instantly.

Marth Wood Shavings was growing in size and reputation. Marth applied to the Public Service Commission of Wisconsin to become a licensed carrier to transport his wood shavings and sawdust to his customers. Ironically, the commissioner determined that wood shavings was a garbage product and did not require a permit. However, Marth was persistent and the request was granted. He was issued a permit on August 17, 1971. This gave him the advantage when it came to growing the business.

In December of 1972 Marth Wood Shavings grew in another way—internally. Geraldine and Milton Marth's daughter Paulette and her husband Kenneth Natzke moved from Milwaukee to join the family business. In addition to buying stock in the company, the two took a hands-on approach and went right

The on-site shavings mill.

to work doing what was necessary to help expand the company. Kenneth began loading and delivering shavings and managing equipment maintenance. He was also responsible for contract negotiations. Paulette took over all the financial and legal responsibilities for the business. Because of this additional help, the business expanded greatly. Buildings were added to the plant, as well as new equipment and extra employees.

By 1984 the sawdust and shavings products were being screened and a sorting system made it possible to customize customers' requests. A bagging system was installed so the products could be compressed and bagged, which made handling and storage compact and convenient. Customer growth demanded that a second bagging system be added and two shifts packaged about 3,600 bags per day.

Geraldine and Milton Marth dedicated their lives to the growth of their business for close to 30 years. In 1984 they decided to retire knowing that they were leaving the business in good hands. Paulette Natzke became president of Marth Wood Shavings and Kenneth Natzke was named president of Marth Transportation. This additional business not only allowed Marth to expedite the transport of Marth Wood Shaving products, but it also presented the opportunity to move cargo efficiently for other manufacturing companies. The idea, again, was a winner and the company today has 31 employees and 8 owner operators. It also boasts a fleet of 25 tractors and 240 semitrailers. Marth Transportation, Inc. brings in 20 to 25 semi loads of shaving from mills each day and delivers 70 to 80 tons of sawdust to farms for bedding, and another 80 tons of sawdust for industrial usage.

The Marth ingenuity persisted through the second generation of ownership and Paulette and Kenneth

Wet sawdust entering the tumble drying process.

found another resourceful use for their tree by-product—fuel. Natzke's son Jerome convinced them that wood pellets would be a future source of fuel in pellet stoves.

Wood pellets are formed by a process which mixes sawdust with water, compresses it, and forms it into small sphere-shaped pellets. In addition to being efficient, the hardwood pellets are clean; easy to work with; and environmentally-friendly, meeting low emissions standards. Wood pellets are also used as bedding for animals, including reptiles.

Shavings and wood pellets remain Marth's two strongest sources of income. Other seasonal sales are landscaping chips, gardening shavings, and meat smoking maple shavings.

A third generation is now a part of the Marth team. Paulette and Kenneth's two children, Jerome and Julie, grew up in the business. They began working for the company as teenagers. They received their educations and then returned to the family-business full-time.

Jerome is general manager of shavings and president of Marth Manufacturing in Athens, Wisconsin. The plant he oversees was established in 2000 and manufactures

wood flour which is used in composite wood, animal filler, plastics, and automotive components. Julie heads up public relations, handles payables, and dispenses payroll for all three companies. Even though the Marth descendants have their separate job titles, they work together and run all three companies jointly.

Although Geraldine and Milton Marth have retired, they stay close to watch the business grow and enjoy babysitting the fourth generation of their offspring. The company they began almost 50 years ago supports not only their family, but the families of their valued employees. This is all possible because of the Marths' ingenuity and the renewable resource of trees. "If you cut down a tree, you can grow another one," states Paulette Natzke. "We are surrounded by trees and lakes. We want the land and the water to stay friendly for our children, grandchildren, and future generations." The Marth's way of doing business will help ensure that.

MURPHY ENTERTAINMENT GROUP

The Evening Telegram Company, primarily doing business as Morgan Murphy Stations, is a third generation, family-run business. It is trademarked by its owners' willingness to experiment with new communication technologies and venture forward into unchartered media arenas. The tenacity, creativity, and innovation of its founding owner John T. Murphy lives on in his granddaughter Elizabeth Murphy Burns, who serves as president of the company, and grandson John B. Murphy, chairman of the board. The firm has always emphasized serving the community over earning higher profits. Its roots reside in the newspaper trades, but its present owners now focus on the future of communication in broadcast media.

The story began over a century ago with John T. Murphy's father, Daniel Murphy, who emigrated from Ireland to flee the devastation of The Great Famine of 1845–1849. He moved to America to begin his new life in the land of hope and opportunity. He and his wife, Abigail, settled in Greenfield, Massachusetts and soon after began their family.

John T. Murphy was born on September 7, 1860, a year that was also

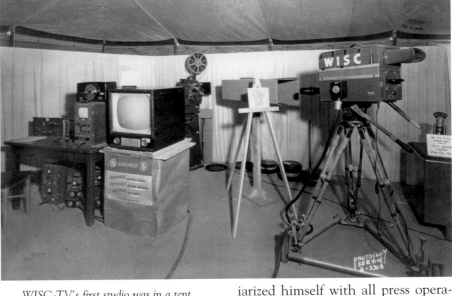
WISC-TV's first studio was in a tent.

eventful for the nation. In 1860 the Pony Express began its run from Missouri to California and Abraham Lincoln was elected president of the United States. Both events would prove crucial in the developing communications business to which John T. Murphy would dedicate the vocational part of his life, as well as an ample portion of his heart and soul.

At age six, the precocious John T. Murphy wanted to work. His first job was as a printer's assistant where he helped with various jobs and famil-

iarized himself with all press operations. Loving the work, John soon enrolled in North Adams Academy where he continued to pursue his interest in the newspaper business. While in school, John began working at the *North Adams Transcript* as an apprentice. There he learned typesetting and press runs, as well as accompanied reporters on assignments. Upon graduating from the academy, John worked at the *Transcript* full-time and was promoted to associate editor on his 21st birthday.

John was, at heart, an explorer and seeker of adventures. The same gumption that led him to begin his newspaper career so early in life was present throughout his early adulthood. He traveled to various cities, journalism being his passport along the way. He moved to Springfield, Massachusetts and joined the Bowles' family newspaper business. Then he was off to New York working for the Associated Press. There he became familiar with the big-city excitement of the newspaper business and covered stories from world sporting events to entertainment icons. After short stints in Chicago, Missouri, and Canada, John T. Murphy landed in Minnesota working for the *St. Paul Globe*.

WISC-TV's early office building and studios.

By the late 1920s John T. Murphy had established himself as a major presence in the newspaper publishing industry.

As circulation manager for the *Globe*, his work took John to Duluth, Minnesota and Superior, Wisconsin where he established the paper as the best-circulated, out-of-town newspaper in the fast-growing twin port cities. It was in Superior that John realized he had enough experience and drive to venture into another realm of the newspaper business—ownership.

On April 21, 1890, at age 29, John T. Murphy purchased the *Superior Telegram* and set up shop in a small, wood-framed office at 1805 Winter Street in Superior, Wisconsin. Business was competitive as three other weekly and two daily newspapers were within the same circulation area as the *Telegram*. John T. Murphy's dedication to journalism and his community prevailed and by the early 1900s the *Telegram* was firmly established as the "Voice of Great Superior." It was just the beginning for John as he branched out to build a chain of publications. His acquisitions included the *Fort Myers Press*, the *Lafayette Advertiser*, the *Chippewa Falls Telegram*, and *Manitowoc Times*, the latter two located in Wisconsin.

The legacy continued as Elizabeth Flynn Murphy, John's wife, gave birth to Morgan—the first heir of the Murphy media holdings—on May 28, 1903. Morgan Murphy attended college at the University of Wisconsin and finished his education at the Harvard University Graduate School of Business. Morgan Murphy's academic achievements, along with his good fortune of growing up in his father's shadow in the newspaper business, made him the logical successor to the expanding family business.

John T. Murphy died on December 14, 1932 at age 73. At age 29, which was the same age his father had been when he first bought the business, Morgan Murphy took over the *Telegram*—at that time a multi-publication corporation. Morgan Murphy, well-schooled by his father in entrepreneurial endeavors, promptly expanded the enterprise into a chain of Northland newspapers and embraced the emerging media technologies of radio and television.

Just 10 years earlier, in 1922, John T. Murphy had taken his son to the Superior studios of radio station WFAC and introduced him to Walter C. Bridges. Bridges was not only the chief engineer and co-owner of the station, he was considered an electronic genius of the times. He not only operated the radio station, he also manufactured and sold radio receivers, which were just emerging in popularity then. Meeting Bridges would prove momentous for Morgan Murphy who later partnered with him to form the Head of the Lakes Broadcast Company, with the radio call letters WEBC.

Their radio station in Duluth, Minnesota featured everything from musical programs to church services. Its popularity grew, and the two young entrepreneurs pursued more acquisitions. In the 1940s Bridges and Murphy established the Arrowhead Radio Network in Minnesota and Wisconsin. Soon, a third media technology was on the horizon—television.

The acquisition of television stations was a bit more challenging to Morgan Murphy as VHF (very high frequency) television licensing rights had to be awarded by the FCC. Understanding the incomparable potential of the television medium, Morgan Murphy was tenacious in his pursuit. In December 1955 his diligence paid off and he built WISC-TV in Madison, Wisconsin.

An editorial that followed the death of Morgan Murphy.

Morgan Murphy, like his father, was recognized as a man who realized the potential of innovations in the media industry and was fearless in exploring all possibilities. Prior to his death, he had built, or was in the process of building, four cable television systems in Northern California. He built or acquired eight television stations during his life.

Also like his father, Morgan Murphy found time to give back to his community through civic and church-related contributions and commitments. He wished to serve the community not only in his broadcasts and newspaper circulations, but also in his personal life. "He believed in his community, invested in it, and realized immense joy in seeing it progress," was a quote that appeared in an editorial about him the day after his death.

For the following 12 years until her death, Morgan Murphy's widow, Elizabeth, maintained the media business until her children Elizabeth and John B. were ready to devote their full energies to it. Both Elizabeth and John were raised in the family business and worked for the company in varying degrees while completing their schooling. John graduated from the University of Wisconsin-Superior in 1976 and the following year joined the family business full-time. He became manager of the *Telegram*'s commercial print division. In 1980 he advanced to president and publisher of the Evening Telegram Company. While John focused on the newspaper side of the corporation, Elizabeth found her stride on the broadcast end of the business.

After attending the University of Arizona, Elizabeth began her broadcasting career at age 21 by working for KGUN-TV in Tucson. She continued her hands-on education at several other television stations and she also owned a radio station before she moved to Madison, Wisconsin

Seeing the growing need to expand, John T. Murphy purchased the Maryland Block building on the northwest corner of Tower and North 13th Street.

in 1975. She brought a spirit of community service and business acumen to the family's broadcast business and her skills were a perfect compliment to her brother's publishing experience. The two worked in tandem, operating and growing the media business.

Wanting to continue the innovative and experimental ways of their parents in new media, the Murphy's—in partnership with others—operated a successful, long distance, educational satellite system that delivered classes to rural areas in subjects that were not offered locally. The courses were primarily secondary classes and interactive via phone. This division, RXL Communications, also co-produced educational/entertainment programs with Beijing TV that were broadcast in most of the major cities in China for more than five years. It currently operates as a video production company in St. Louis.

Other projects included the expansion of the newspaper division to include 12 publications in northern Wisconsin and northern Minnesota. On the electronic media side Morgan Murphy Stations operates Channel3000.com, one of the most highly viewed local websites in the nation. They also operate the UPN network on Channel 14 over local cable systems. *Madison Magazine* was purchased a number of years ago

and remains in the "family." Another division of the company, Murphy Entertainment Group (MEG), creates original programming for cable networks including *Wildlife Detectives* on Animal Planet and *Billion Dollar Disasters* on the Discovery Channel.

Other than WISC-TV and UPN14 in Madison, Morgan Murphy Stations also owns WKBT-TV in LaCrosse/Eau Claire, as well as five radio stations in southwestern Wisconsin. They also own three television and seven radio stations in eastern Washington and northern Idaho.

In 2003 the family made an emotional decision to sell the newspaper subsidiary of *The Evening Telegram*. Its roots will always be respected and remembered. As the company moves into the future of advanced technological media its mission will remain constant. "Our focus is the same—to inform, educate, and entertain our friends, neighbors, and the communities we serve," says Elizabeth Murphy Burns. Indeed, it is a philosophy that has touched everyone in the state of Wisconsin—and beyond.

A popular Farmer's Market surrounds the
State Capitol each weekend as sellers showcase
their vegetables, flowers, and other fresh items.
Photo by Gary Knowles, courtesy, Wisconsin
Department of Tourism

PHILLIPS PLASTICS CORPORATION

On any given day millions of Americans unknowingly use products containing parts that have been manufactured by Phillips Plastics Corporation. Whether it's turning up the volume knob on a car radio, pressing the "on" button on a dishwasher, hitting the "start" button on a dryer, operating a riding lawn mower, accessing a computer, taking a puff from an inhaler or using a hand tool, people come in contact with dozens of items on a daily basis that have passed through the manufacturing facilities of this storied company. This Wisconsin-based manufacturer currently churns out hundreds of thousands of plastic, metal, and magnesium parts every-

For more than 35 years Phillips Plastics Corporation has partnered with the most respected medical device original equipment manufactureers in the industry.

day. It boasts $211 million in annual sales, has 14 facilities, and employs 1,600 people.

Robert Cervenka, the company's founder and current CEO and chairman, says the business philosophies behind that extraordinary success are simple. They include a commitment to innovation, as well as a pledge to achieve an average annual growth of 20 percent and a return on equity of 20 percent. The other element is something Cervenka calls the "People Process Culture," which emphasizes the value of working together as a team. These concepts, which have stimulated growth at Phillips Plastics for the past 40 years, took root right from the start.

Phillips Plastics' debut in the fall of 1964 was decidedly humble compared to its current status. In fact, Cervenka never dreamed the busi-

ness would reach the kind of success it has today when he and partner Louie Vokurka launched the venture. "I was just hoping to have enough income so I could go hunting and fishing every weekend," says Cervenka. The founder's starting salary of $7,500—meager even by 1964 standards—barely allowed him to indulge in those hobbies.

The company's founders had to scramble to scrape up the money to fund the enterprise. Cervenka used $6,000 from a home he sold. Vokurka borrowed $25,000 from his mother. Together they also convinced several local businessmen to take a chance on them by investing in the start-up. From all those sources combined, the pair raised $52,000 in seed money. Cervenka admits that "even with the dollar value in the 1960s that wasn't very much money, so we had to be really efficient."

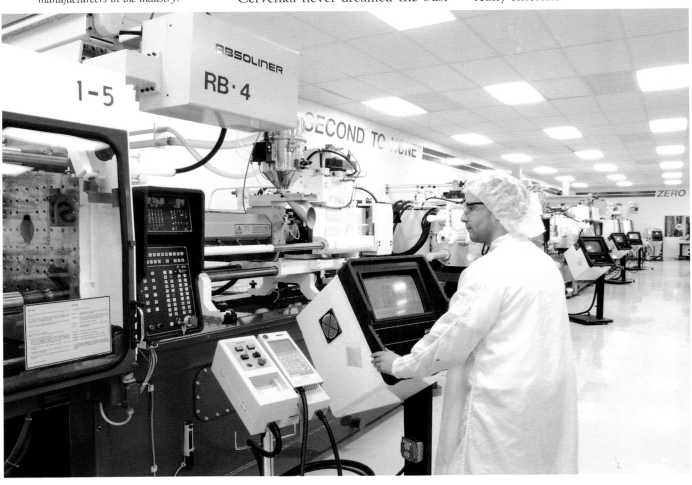

To make the most of that initial investment, Cervenka set up shop in the former Laabs Creamery Cheese Factory—an abandoned building off Main Street in the small town of Phillips in northwestern Wisconsin. The lease on the building was only $200 a month. To get the business up and running, Cervenka bought a used injection-molding machine for $4,000, about half the cost of a new machine at the time. With that, Cervenka was ready to take on customers. His first orders included making the clear crystal faces for analog clocks used in car dashboards and making soap dispensers and rack rollers for dishwashers.

The upstart firm had to be innovative to land customers and to earn a profit. One particularly memorable job during those early years shows just how important it was for Cervenka to think on his feet. When a large order for Batman figurines came in, the crew couldn't get them spray painted fast enough. To get the job done on time, he rounded up dozens of local people who took the figurines home and hand-painted them. Mission accomplished.

Finding customers and meeting deadlines in those early days weren't the only challenges for Phillips Plastics. Hiring employees wasn't easy either. As a start-up with minimal funding, the venture was considered risky. But Cervenka and Vokurka managed to convince a few people to leave their secure manufacturing jobs to take a chance with the new firm. the men's enthusiasm and vision also attracted some high school graduates who otherwise would have left the small town to find jobs in a bigger city. Cervenka credits these daring individuals with helping to create an environment of risk-taking that remains with the company today.

With just a few employees at the time, job titles didn't really apply. Everyone pitched in on every project,

including Cervenka and Vokurka. No task was considered too small or too menial for the hard-working partners. Cervenka routinely took his turn as typist and even janitor when he wasn't acting as engineer, estimator, or press operator among his many other duties. It didn't take long for Cervenka to realize that hiring and retaining employees with a can-do attitude was going to be the key to long-term success.

To create a sense of teamwork and ensure satisfaction among employees, Cervenka created a policy of open-management and chose to keep staff members informed about the company's sales performance, profits, and expansion plans. That policy still stands today and Phillips currently keeps employees updated with a weekly email newsletter, a bimonthly news magazine, facility-specific newsletters, internal marketing campaigns, annual reports, and frequent team meetings. Dedicated to retaining quality employees, Phillips Plastics also offers a profit-sharing retirement plan, merit increases, and bonuses tied to performance. In addition, there is a "promote from within" policy that offers opportunities for

What was once considered a remote location is now a sought after destination by many of Phillips' Fortune 500 customers who seek the confidentiality that comes from a supplier with plants located in rural Wisconsin.

employees to grow in the field and gain more responsibility.

That notion of teamwork, along with a commitment to innovation, set the framework for rapid growth. It didn't take long before the start-up outgrew the creamery facility and needed to expand. Cervenka could have moved the burgeoning business to a metropolitan area where large facilities were more readily available. Instead he made a vow to remain in the small town of Phillips where he had been born and raised. One reason was his admiration for the local people's work ethic. In addition, he noted that the town was losing a lot of its brightest high school graduates to Milwaukee where there were more career opportunities in manufacturing. Cervenka hoped to provide jobs in Phillips so locals wouldn't have to leave town to make a decent living.

With that in mind Cervenka broke ground in 1967 on the north end of town on what would become "The

Custom Facility." The 12,000-square-foot building was completed that same year and 30 employees moved into the building over the Labor Day weekend. Since that time, Cervenka has remained true to his vow to provide opportunities in small towns. Over the years Phillips Plastics has opened more than a dozen additional facilities, most of them in small towns throughout Wisconsin.

That growth hasn't been without incident, though. In 1977 a huge windstorm struck the Phillips Plastics headquarters building. Cervenka recalls that the wind hit hard, blowing down one entire wall of the plant where the water main was connected. The impact severed the main, creating a minor flood, which took several hours to get under control. Despite the turmoil, Cervenka and his crew were determined not to grind operations to a halt. They managed to keep the presses rolling—albeit at diminished capacity—until repairs were made.

The company's current facilities bear little resemblance to the original creamery. That building's low ceilings, lack of windows, and single bathroom (shared by men and women) didn't make for ideal conditions. Plus, with all the presses running in the hot and humid summers, the building could reach sweltering temperatures. With the corporation's new facilities, Cervenka was determined to offer his employees a more pleasant working environment.

Today, Phillips Plastics employees enjoy natural lighting, windows, heating, air conditioning, efficient workstations, and pleasant break rooms. In fact, Phillips Plastics won the *Business Week* Architectural Design Award for two of its buildings—the Custom II plant in Phillips and the Origen Center in Menomonie. This prestigious award is given to only 10 companies annually and recognizes those organizations that

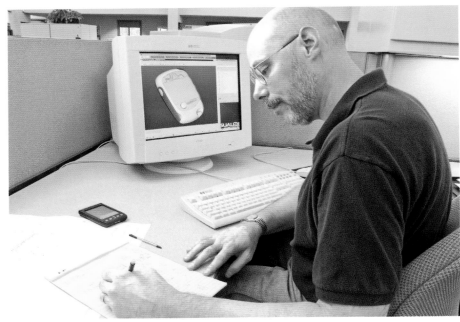

From the beginning of every program, Phillips' engineers apply their knowledge of multiple process technologies to create the optimum design for manufacture.

understand architecture's ability to solve corporate problems, increase worker productivity, and boost the bottom line. The firm's facilities also feature glass walls, which Cervenka believes encourage curiosity and communication. The "factory without walls" concept creates a seamless flow between the factory floor, management, and other departments. It also serves to help break down barriers between manufacturing and office workers.

As the business expanded into new facilities, its sales figures ballooned as well. Year after year, Cervenka has tried to maintain his initial goal of growing sales and return on equity by 20 percent annually. Although he admits that Phillips Plastics fell short of that goal a few times, he adds that other years had so much growth it made up for the difference. A quick look at the firm's sales figures throughout the years shows how that lofty goal has translated into big numbers.

It took 13 years for the venture to reach $10 million in sales but after that, things really took off. Sales doubled to $20 million in 1983. Just two years later, that number climbed to $42 million. By 1990 Phillips Plas-

tics was bringing in $80 million. The company reached just under $100 million in sales in 1992 and hit the $200 million mark in 1999.

Diversification into new products and services as well as the acquisition of existing manufacturing entities are what drove growth throughout the '70s, '80s, and '90s. The enterprise that got its start with custom injection molding of plastic parts for the automotive and home appliance industries eventually branched out. It moved on to producing parts for manufacturers in the durable consumer goods, electronics, industrial, lawn and garden, medical, recreational, and telecommunications markets. The firm has also sparked growth by adding services such as design development, metal injection molding, and magnesium injection molding to its core plastics business.

Throughout its 40 year existence, Phillips Plastics has distinguished itself in the marketplace for its attention to quality. Almost from the start, the business adopted the creed "Quality is a Given." To make sure that the company achieves total customer satisfaction on every order, Cervenka insists on something called "continuous improvement." This includes constantly reviewing and updating procedures, technologies, and work practices in an effort to eliminate errors and defects. Increases in national and global competition in the custom injection-molding field have made quality assurance more important than ever.

At Phillips Plastics, quality control is an ongoing process that never stops. To ensure top quality, three elements come into play: product design, employee performance, and equipment maintenance. Designers work with customers to modify and optimize product designs for maximum efficiency. The business takes great strides to make sure all employees are aware of the importance of quality and that equipment maintenance remains rigorous.

Phillips Plastics operates its presses 24 hours a day, seven days a week, since start-up and shut-down would generate scrap. The presses, which range in size from 7 to 935 tons, are frequently evaluated by a computer for accuracy. The computer automatically compensates for any inaccuracies in the molding process and provides a frequency of adjustment record. Because accuracy declines with use, Phillips has adopted an aggressive eight-year replacement policy for all of its presses.

At Phillips Plastics the commitment to continuously update and improve resources applies to more than just equipment. Cervenka is a firm believer in making sure employees have the skills and training necessary to be the best they can be. Each facility boasts a Learning Center where employees can bone up on the latest software and learn job-specific tasks, processes, and technologies. For example, one computer software program simulates an injection-molding machine and allows users to set up the controls to run a press just like they would on the factory floor. The software simulates an actual run as the worker has programmed it and shows the quality of the part that would result.

Each year Phillips Plastics dedicates 3 percent of payroll to training, including workshops and seminars for employees. The company even has an entire building—the Origen Center—that is dedicated to training. With several classrooms, an auditorium, and hands-on technology labs, the Origen Center offers classes to employees throughout the year on a variety of subjects ranging from injection-molding techniques to interpersonal skills. Going beyond that, the manufacturer actively encourages its employees to seek out additional education and technical training, and offers generous tuition reimbursement.

Cervenka's devotion to education goes beyond the walls of Phillips Plastics and into neighboring communities. Its innovative Partners in Education program provides local school districts with resources to enhance the learning experience. On top of that, Cervenka and his wife endow a chair at the University of Wisconsin-Stout in Menomonie to teach a course on the "People Process Culture." Now in its fifth year, the class attracts undergraduates, graduate students, and people already in the work force.

A commitment to education is one of the ways Cervenka repays the community that has been so instrumental in the corporation's long-term success. The AnnMarie Foundation, named after Cervenka's and Vokurka's mothers, has given $4.5 million in grants and scholarships since 1974. The foundation provides funds for college scholarships, local volunteer fire departments, sports teams, and cultural institutions.

There's no question Cervenka is very proud of the ways Phillips Plastics gives back to the community. However, ask him what he's most proud of and he doesn't hesitate to answer. "That's an easy one," he says. "We've provided excellent security for our people and opportunities for them to grow and be prosperous."

Phillips Metals, LLC, located in Menomonie, is one of the most comprehensive and experienced metal injection molding suppliers in the nation.

PORT OF MILWAUKEE

Since its inception in 1835, the Port of Milwaukee has become a major commercial and shipping hub which handles millions of tons of product annually. In June 2004 the Port marked one of its greatest achievements in its nearly 170-year history when it launched the nation's first high-speed ferry service, connecting ports within the continental United States. The 68-mile trip across Lake Michigan between Milwaukee, Wisconsin, and Muskegon, Michigan takes only two and a half hours on the new *Lake Express* ship. That's less than half the time of a conventional ferry. Traveling at a speed of about 34 knots (about 40 miles per hour), the 192-foot long vessel can transport 46 cars and approximately 250 passengers on each of its daily trips during the summer and fall.

Speed isn't the ship's only appealing feature, however. The ferry's computer-controlled stabilization equipment provides a smooth ride and virtually eliminates any concerns about seasickness. A climate-controlled passenger area is equipped with comfortable seating, video monitors, full restroom facilities, food service, a special play area for kids, and even a conference room for meetings of up to 50 participants.

The Lake Express *catamaran arrives at the Port of Milwaukee to begin the first high-speed, auto-passenger service in the country on June 1, 2004.*

Sailing ships berthed in the Milwaukee River during the 1800s when shipping activity was concentrated at docks along the riverbanks.

Its sleek catamaran design also boasts many modern safety features.

The *Lake Express* service is particularly appealing to tourists, business people, and travelers going long distances across the United States. One of the many advantages of crossing Lake Michigan by ferry is the ability to avoid chronic traffic delays through the Chicago area. Another plus is the fact that tourists and business people are able to use their cell phones, laptop computers, and other electronic devices throughout the voyage. *Lake Express* isn't the first ferry service to connect Wisconsin and Michigan, though. Car ferries began traversing the lake well over 100 years ago. In the mid-1900s ferries routinely carried over one-hundred thousand passengers across the lake each year to various destinations in Michigan.

The most famous ship to ferry passengers between Milwaukee and Michigan was the *Milwaukee Clipper*. With a capacity of up to 900 riders and more than 100 automobiles, the

Clipper crossed Lake Michigan regularly between 1941 and 1970. The only ferry service operating across Lake Michigan over the last 10 years is the S.S. *Badger*, which runs a slow-speed coal-fired ship between Manitowoc, Wisconsin and Ludington, Michigan. However, ferry service is only one of the many services the Port of Milwaukee has been providing since its inception.

Milwaukee began as a Great Lakes port in 1835 when the first commercial cargo vessel called at the struggling new village on the west shore of Lake Michigan. Settlers and traders were drawn to the site because of its Indian population and its access to the "western frontier" afforded by three separate streams—the Milwaukee, Menomonee, and Kinnickinnic Rivers—which flow into Lake Michigan at a central point in Milwaukee harbor. The streams were originally of interest to fur traders because they afforded transportation to the interior by canoe. Over the years they have been intensively developed with dock facilities and expanded by dredging and channel improvements.

The first major development in converting the harbor from its original natural condition came in 1857 when the "Straight Cut" or new harbor entrance was completed. This project involved abandonment of the actual mouth of the Milwaukee River and construction of a new outlet half a mile to the north. This project not only diverted the Milwaukee River from its natural course, but also caused somewhat of a revolution in the city's port development. The commerce originally handled through lakefront wharves was diverted to new docks along the riverbanks throughout the downtown area.

The rapid growth of lake commerce and the steady increase in the size of lake vessels created a strain on Milwaukee River docks and downtown street traffic. A wharf that was planned and built for small schooners and steamers was obviously not ideal for navigation by large bulk freighters, which by the turn of the century were being built to dimensions unheard of 50 years earlier. Milwaukee officials therefore devised a comprehensive plan to acquire strategic lakefront areas and to develop an outer harbor on Jones Island.

In June 1920 the Board of Harbor Commissioners was created to oversee operation and maintenance of the harbor, including its expansion plans. Mayor Daniel W. Hoan appointed five citizens as members of the board for a three-year term. The board of harbor commissioners has functioned continuously since that time. Taking advantage of the favorable prices available during the Depression era, the board carried out an extensive construction program during the years 1931 to 1933. The project included the dredging and docking of the Municipal Mooring Basin, the creation of 65 acres of new land on the outer harbor, the construction of Transit Shed Number 1, and the completion of South Pier Number 1.

Another historic milestone came in 1938 with the city's purchase of

Ships loading cargo for export during the 1990s at the Port of Milwaukee's South Pier 2.

the Illinois Steel Company's property on Jones Island for harbor and terminal development. The negotiations for this strategic lakefront property were initiated nearly 20 years earlier in 1919. In 1908 harbor officials had begun looking into the cost of acquiring Jones Island and the feasibility of establishing harbor terminals on those lands.

In addition to being a center for traditional commerce, the Port of Milwaukee played an important role in World War II. Huge quantities of strategic cargo were funneled through the harbor on their way to U.S. armed forces. Shipbuilding and transportation services for the military provided another significant contribution to the war effort.

Successful completion of the many expansion projects throughout the years has transformed the Port of Milwaukee into a thriving hub for commerce. Today it serves as a regional transportation and distribution center handling an average of two to three million tons of commerce and welcoming 250–300 vessels into its docks annually. Primarily serving the states of Wisconsin, Illinois, and Minnesota, the Port of Milwaukee also reaches Iowa, the Dakotas, Nebraska, Missouri, and Indiana, as well as the western Canadian Provinces of Alberta, Saskatchewan, and Manitoba.

More than 330,000 square feet of covered warehouse space is reserved for a diverse mix of general cargoes and steel. General cargoes include forest products, bagged materials, heavy machinery, farm and construction machinery, and project cargoes. Exceptionally heavy cargoes are no problem thanks to a stiff leg derrick capable of lifting a total of 440,000 pounds at a 52-foot radius.

The expansive Port of Milwaukee also devotes more than 50 acres to dry bulk storage and handling facilities, including four domes totaling 50,000 tons of storage. Dry bulk handling services include storage and stock piling, direct transfer truck/rail/ barge, vessel loading and unloading, packaging, palletizing, and processing. A wide variety of dry bulk materials are handled, including salt, construction aggregates, coal, fertilizers, cement, and grain products.

By adding the new high-speed ferry to all of these existing services, the Port of Milwaukee is entering into a bold new chapter in its extraordinary history. This new era promises to be one of growth and prosperity for the outstanding lake port.

Turn of the century shipping activity at the Port of Milwaukee's inner harbor reflected the early industrial growth of the city. A Kaszube fishing village is pictured in the foreground.

THE REDMOND COMPANY

One might wonder what Walgreens, Roundy's, and Johnson Bank could possibly have in common—but The Redmond Group knows. Each of these organizations looked to the Group to meet its real estate and construction needs. Redmond has grown into one of the Midwest's most successful firms, extending into a six-state area. Mark Redmond, the owner of the firm believes, "If you can produce leaders and develop people, you're going to be the best in your field." Clearly at Redmond, that's what they seek to do and continually achieve—both within their own organization and externally in the communities it serves.

The Redmond Group began in 1976 with a father-son construction team, then named Redmond Construction Company. Tom Redmond, the founder, had worked his way from carpenter to partner in one of Milwaukee's leading construction firms. He decided to venture out and

Mark Redmond, owner and CEO of The Redmond Company; Redmond Commercial Development Corporation; Redmond Residential of Wisconsin, Incorporated; and MRED Management, Incorporated.

Redmond utilized fast track scheduling techniques to demolish an existing 80,000-square-foot building and build this 76,000-square-foot grocery store in less than four months—40 percent faster than the competition.

go into business himself. Mark Redmond, his son, had recently graduated from Marquette University with a degree in finance. After considering graduate school, Mark decided to join his father instead and learn the business side of construction.

"Our office was located at Watertown Plank Road and Highway 100 in the old State Sand Gravel office," Redmond recalls. "We were rent free that year because my father's friend owned the building. He had gone bankrupt and he let us use the space." Together the father and son team brought in $90,000 worth of work in one year. Steadily, they began to grow their business into a strong, highly-regarded, local company.

By the mid-'80s, Mark recognized an opportunity for growth in the form of vertical business expansion. "I became inspired to create a company that could provide services to clients from the initial stage of a project—the idea, all the way through to managing occupancy of the building," Mark says. While Tom continued to direct the construction company, Mark created Redmond Commercial Development Corporation (RCDC). Initially the corporation developed commercial and retail space, while Redmond Construction built for RCDC and other clients as well. Working together, the two companies complemented one another.

Long before design/build became a popular delivery method, Mark and Tom recognized the need and benefit of providing additional in-house services. To that end they added a full-time architectural staff to dispense design expertise to their growing list of clients. The business was becoming steadily stronger and by 1999, after many years of service, Tom Redmond was ready to retire—leaving Mark to acquire 100 percent ownership of the company. To reflect the firm's emphasis of more diverse service offering that went beyond just construction, the name was changed from Redmond Construction Company to The Redmond Company (TRC).

Today, TRC offers the core services of consulting, design, and construction. "When it comes to consulting, we start by listening,"

Mark Redmond says. "We let our client's business drive the real estate and facility process. Our consultants dig deep to understand the client's strategic plan, business model, and short and long term goals." In terms of design, it is much more than blueprints and graph paper at TRC. The design phase includes understanding the objectives of the organization for which they are working. They begin by asking questions such as: "What is this company's brand?" "What kind of merchandise or service are they selling?" "How can the facility best meet those needs?" Through an organized group of team leaders, architects, project managers, and superintendents, there is a strong emphasis on "idea to occupancy" delivery. This results in keeping the project moving forward quickly and very cost effectively, while maintaining a strong focus on the client's core short/long term goals.

When applied on a master scale, Redmond Commercial Development Corporation and The Redmond Company—as developer, designer, and builder—create a unique combination that brings value to the bottom line of each client, today and long into the future. With the core entities of RCDC and TRC, there are two adjunct entities that make up The Redmond Group. These are MRED Management, which delivers facility and property management services; and Structures of Significance (SOS), which is a design/build firm specializing in the mausoleum and funeral home markets.

Being the leader in each of these areas requires finding, developing, and utilizing strong talent. With that understanding in mind, Mark brought Rick Zarkos on board in 2000 as president of The Redmond Company. With a diverse construction, real estate, and management consulting background, Rick has further defined the vertical delivery of services to

Redmond developed and built this 222,000-square-foot shopping center in Menomonee Falls. It includes a Wal-Mart and a Pick 'n Save grocery store.

clients while sharpening their execution. Together, Mark and Rick added SOS to the Group and have expanded MRED into facility management for regional companies. TRC has expanded from a limited market focus to a firm that is very active in three sectors: commercial, retail, and financial. The core top talent of the Redmond Group is intact, and key additions in both RCDC and TRC have further strengthened its ability to be *The Idea to Occupancy Leader* (the firm's vision statement).

Structures of Significance is an example of progressive thinking. "This newest element is one on a list of ideas that we thought of when considering expansion," Mark Redmond says. "We were able to align ourselves with the premier pre-cast crypt supplier to produce a very valuable product. We're most excited about it."

Growth through talent and ability are clear values at Redmond. "You grow companies by growing people," Rick Zarkos says. "Each day, I wake up and ask myself, 'Is everybody growing?'" We are a company that

takes great pride in the service we provide to our customers," Redmond adds "The people of our company are the ones who give that service. Therefore, our most important asset is the people who make up our team." In support of his 60 employees, Redmond offers excellent benefits and stresses the importance of continual education and training.

This focus on people extends from internal communication to job-site safety. With projects completed in 27 states and an aggressive long-term strategic plan, The Redmond Group is dedicated to working closely with local municipalities and trade subcontractors. The firm does not employ its own masons, carpenters, or ironworkers, but prefers to utilize trade subcontractors. "Trade subcontractors are the most competitive and expert in their respective areas. A traditional general contractor cannot provide a customer with market-competitive pricing just using their own forces" says Zarkos. In addition to being cost effective, Redmond also believes this practice benefits the local communities where each project is located.

Mark Redmond's sense of caring for the community is not only limited to work, however. He is an active member in many civic and religious organizations, as well. One of Mark and his family's greatest joys was participating in a trip to Piura, Peru to hand out presents at Christmas time. A visiting priest, who was a native of Wisconsin, had come from Peru to speak at the church where Mark serves as president of the parish council. For $25 a month a parishioner could adopt a family from Peru; a donation which fed a family of four for a month. Mark and his family were thrilled not only to sign up for the project, but to travel to Peru and meet their adopted family as well.

Another activity which Mark Redmond enjoys is mentoring at Na-

The Sanchez family in Peru was "adopted" by the Redmonds. The family is seen here with Mark Redmond and his daughter on the left.

tivity Jesuit Middle School, a Latino, all-boys school that is committed to developing leaders. The president of the school was a high school classmate of Redmond's and introduced him to the program. Once mentors are assigned they follow the boys' progress through high school and college, serving as advisors and friends throughout their educational years. The school offers a rigorous all-day schedule from 8:00 a.m. through evening study halls. A six-week summer camp is part of the training as well. "Essentially this program keeps at-risk kids off the streets and equips them for leadership roles," Mark says. "It's a wonderful program."

The employees at Redmond give back to their local communities in a typically enthusiastic fashion. From holiday decorating for a Waukesha organization known as Hebron House to 34 employees participating in a recent Arthritis Foundation Run/Walk, Redmond team members deliver benefits through their projects and their own personal time.

Redmond is a preferred developer for Walgreens and has built over 125 Walgreens in a multi-state area.

Between community service and running an ever-growing company, Mark Redmond and his staff members are excited about what the future holds. Mark attributes the success of his organization to hiring the right people over the years and staying focused. His is a company that is not afraid of change, and he insists upon integrity in everything the firm does. "I feel quite protective of the Redmond name," he says. "We're proud of our reputation amongst our competitors, and proud of the leaders we produce." From its origin as a small, local, construction company that brought in $90,000 in 1976 to becoming a regional development, design, and construction powerhouse with $50 million of projects in place in 2003, The Redmond Group is poised for its next 25 years of outstanding growth and success as *The Idea to Occupancy Leader.*

*The picturesque Madison skyline features a spectacular view
of Lake Monona. Photo by Joe Demaio, courtesy,
Wisconsin Department of Tourism.*

RUEKERT/MIELKE

The chance association between a young assistant city engineer and an even younger college student was the basis for what has become the consulting engineering firm of Ruekert/Mielke. This two-man operation has evolved into a multidisciplinary firm of 150 employees, with eight different departments focusing on meeting the complex needs of municipal clients. The company now works on projects of such variety and technical sophistication that it is hard to imagine its humble beginnings.

John Mielke and Frank Ruekert started moonlighting in their homes at night designing subdivisions for the housing market, which was driven by returning World War II veterans. Mielke came home from a commission in the Army Corps of Engineers to join Ruekert, then an engineer with the City of Waukesha, Wisconsin. Ruekert/Mielke was formed on May 6, 1946, with the company located in a two-room, upstairs office at 203 North Grand Avenue in Waukesha. Lois Mielke and Mabel Ruekert, John and Frank's wives, did all of the clerical work in an office that included a hand-crank calculator and some used transits and levels.

In 1951, after five years of hard work and long hours, a building was

Ruekert/Mielke's headquarters, located in Waukesha, Wisconsin.

constructed at 420 Frederick Street to serve as professional office space. There was one conference room, one office for both principals, and one wall telephone used by all employees. By 1955 the partnership became a corporation, and the firm concentrated on community sewer and water systems and work for private developers. But, the population shift to the suburbs started to change the focus of the company's work. More and more municipal engineering projects replaced the work of private clients.

Ruekert/Mielke assisted many communities in their development, such as its involvement in the incorporations of the village of Menomonee Falls and the cities of Brookfield, New

Berlin, and Muskego. The firm also designed sewer and water systems for all of these communities, as well as the majority of municipal wells and water towers throughout Waukesha County. From developing the largest industrial park in Wisconsin for the city of New Berlin to designing the water system for Brookfield Square Shopping Mall, the firm gained a strong reputation for undertaking challenging projects.

As the firm began to grow, so did its expertise in many new areas. The Hartford Wastewater Treatment Facility pioneered the first use of microscreen tertiary treatment in Wisconsin. The resulting discharge was so clean that it was able to flow into a trout stream. In the village of Pewaukee, the firm was the first in the nation to use rotating biological contactors to treat the wastewater. Most recently, as part of a joint project, the company completed work on the $45 million Fox River Water Pollution Control Center.

As the firm continued to grow, a member of the new generation stepped up to the plate. William J. Mielke, now president and chief executive officer of the firm, started as a summer

A roundabout included in the village of Okauchee revitalization project.

survey crew helper in 1964 (before going on to receive his degree in civil engineering from the University of Wisconsin-Madison). He is both a registered professional engineer and a registered land surveyor, and has held both national and state offices in numerous professional engineering organizations. He has also served on various governors' task forces and is the vice chairman of the Wisconsin Land Council.

Through his leadership, the company has expanded its services to include Geographic Information Systems (GIS), a financial services department, supervisory control and data acquisition design, landscape architecture services, and a planning division. The firm has also established a new division called Aquifer Science and Technology (AST) that specializes in groundwater studies and investigations nationwide. The firm's knowledge and experience in these areas has resulted in ground breaking, award winning projects throughout southeastern Wisconsin.

The Racine Intergovernmental Agreement is one such example. When leaders from eastern Racine County came together on April 25, 2002 to sign a landmark intergovernmental agreement, history was made. In one of the most comprehensive intermunicipal agreements ever negotiated in the state of Wisconsin, the city of Racine and six villages and towns set the framework for how the area will develop over the next 50 years. The agreement included provisions for the sharing of costs for a major wastewater treatment facility expansion and upgrade, a variety of cultural amenities, and one of the first voluntary property tax revenue sharing plans in the country. Ruekert/Mielke designed the revenue sharing plan and developed a financial formula for its implementation that has never before been used in the United States. The visionary thinking and

Aerial view of the Fox River Water Pollution Control Center.

dogged determination on the part of Ruekert/Mielke, which acted as a negotiator, and the firm's team of financial analysts, engineers, and other professional staff produced an innovation in public works funding and intergovernmental relations that could serve as a model for the rest of the nation.

The firm's fingerprint on southeastern Wisconsin continues with the recent completion of sewer systems for Okauchee Lake, Upper and Lower Nashotah Lakes, Upper and Lower Nemahbin Lakes, and Silver Lake. Major award winning downtown revitalization projects have been completed for the villages of Palmyra and Okauchee. Extensive involve-

Mission style architecture characterizes the city of Brookfield's Well Number 30.

ment in Tax Incremental Financing (TIF) districts for several communities and the resultant economic impact will generate over $2 billion dollars of new tax base.

The firm is currently managing the largest TIF development in Wisconsin, located at the Pabst Farms in the city of Oconomowoc. This 1,500-acre project will include a 250-acre technology and research park, commercial, business, residential, and institutional development. It will result in 2,000 new residential units and include one of the first "Lifestyle Center" commercial developments in the state of Wisconsin.

Ruekert/Mielke's staff takes great pride in knowing that virtually every community in southeastern Wisconsin has one of their projects as part of its infrastructure. Employees live in all of these communities and pledge their ongoing commitment to provide sound solutions to problems. The firm's greatest achievements are tied to the philosophy that engineering excellence and service to clients, is its most important product.

SAINT JOSEPH'S HOSPITAL

Saint Joseph's Hospital has a history as rich in sacrifice as its modern day accomplishments are wealthy in technology. From its beginning, the Sisters of the Sorrowful Mother founded their healthcare ministry on their faith in God and His call to them to heal others. That ministry has expanded far beyond the dreams of the first Sisters who came to Marshfield more than 114 years ago. From a rented home with six patient beds, Saint Joseph's Hospital has grown into a teaching hospital with more than 500 beds and is one of the largest rural referral centers in the United States. Serving Wisconsin and the Upper Peninsula of Michigan, Saint Joseph's Hospital now admits more than 19,000 patients annually, and has more than 2,500 employees.

Though located in a rural community, Saint Joseph's Hospital was one of the first in the nation to offer Leksell Gamma Knife™ Model C radio surgery, a revolutionary, non-invasive treatment for patients with brain tumors and other neurologic diseases; and Intraoperative MRI, allowing neurosurgeons to take MRI scans in a standard operating room, providing near real-time images during all stages of the actual surgery.

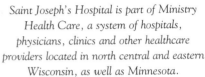

Saint Joseph's Hospital is part of Ministry Health Care, a system of hospitals, physicians, clinics and other healthcare providers located in north central and eastern Wisconsin, as well as Minnesota.

For two years running, the hospital has been named one of the top cardiovascular teaching hospitals in the country. It is verified by the American College of Surgeons as a Level II Trauma Center and is home base for the Spirit of Marshfield helicopter and ground medical transportation service.

But while the hospital may have outgrown the original Sisters' image of the future, it still embraces the values they held. Hospital employees continue to follow the Sisters' four core values of service, vision, presence, and justice. Their mission is to improve the health of all people, especially the poor.

It was the essence of that mission that led Amalia Streitel, a young nun and founder of the Sisters of the Sorrowful Mother, to leave her native Germany in the late 1800s. In 1890 Amalia (now known as Mother Mary Frances) and five other Sisters from

her order answered a call from Father Paul Geyer. The priest, who also was pastor of St. John's Catholic Church in Marshfield, wanted the Sisters to establish a hospital in the small, lumber community. Optimistically, because of her trust and love for St. Joseph, patron saint of carpenters and buildings, she named the yet-to-be-built hospital in his name.

Unfortunately when they arrived on December 9, 1890, they found the promised hospital building was not yet finished. The Sisters, undaunted, moved into a rented house that they scrubbed down and set up for six patients. They had little money, but had faith in their purpose and a belief that the new hospital would be completed. Finally, on February 2, 1891, the Sisters moved into their new 3,200-square-foot Saint Joseph's Hospital.

The building, however, was nothing more than a shell. The basement, where the Sisters would live for the next 17 years, had no flooring or heat. In the winter the washbasins would freeze overnight. In summer, hoards of mosquitoes would enter through windows. Screens were a luxury afforded only to windows of patient rooms. The Sisters had to resort to housekeeping and home nursing in

The first addition to Saint Joseph's Hospital which included six patient rooms and a chapel (at right) was built in 1901, just to the east of the original structure.

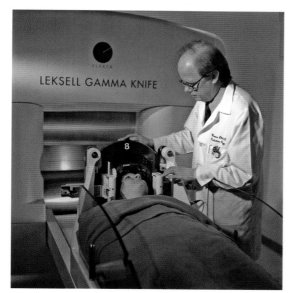

The Gamma Knife is a non-invasive treatment for patients with deep brain tumors and abnormal blood vessels in the brain.

exchange for food or 25 cents a day in wages.

Help came in early 1891 when Father Joseph Joch, an Austrian priest, was appointed as extraordinary confessor to the Sisters at Saint Joseph's Hospital. He had an idea to sell "ticket insurance" to the lumberjacks in the area. Tickets of $5 and $10 guaranteed free hospital care and medications to the holder for a year. In 1892 Father Joch's own illness required he undergo a special treatment in Germany called the Kneipp Water Cure, which involved the frequent use of pure water both externally and internally. Patients drank herbal teas and ate whole grains. They were wrapped in wet sheets and given hot and cold baths. Upon his healthy return to Marshfield, Father Joch suggested that the cure be used at Saint Joseph's Hospital. He obtained a state license and trained the Sisters in the practices.

By the summer of 1893 patients were coming from as far away as Minnesota, Illinois, and Nebraska for treatment. Their numbers grew from four patients in 1892 to 122 in 1893. The income from the water cure was enough to pay off the mortgage, finish and furnish the basement, buy additional land, and begin hospitals in Oshkosh, Rhinelander, and Tomahawk.

In 1895 Dr. Karl W. Doege, a colleague of Monsignor Joch's, proposed that the Sisters discontinue the water cure and, with his assistance, they re-established a more conventional hospital. Dr. Doege had studied abroad and learned the most advanced surgical techniques of that time. He was convinced that a well-equipped hospital with specialized technology and 24-hour nursing care were key to a successful modern-day hospital. The plan was consistent with the Sisters' original mission and a clear course was set for the future.

Confidence in Saint Joseph's Hospital grew. As patient numbers increased, so did the number of new Sisters and other medical staff. The hospital underwent its first expansion in 1901 with the addition of a chapel and six more patient rooms. In keeping with Dr. Doege's plan, the Sisters were determined to keep the hospital current in the latest medical technology, and committed to educating their growing staff about how to ensure quality care.

In 1909 a new wing was added. This four-story addition included an operating room, surgical dressing rooms, additional patient rooms, and the hospital's first elevator. By 1918 another wing costing $152,000 was added, featuring a laundry room, laboratory, operating rooms, powerhouse, and classrooms. Expansions were made possible from donations by both individuals and local organizations.

In 1916 Dr. Doege and five other physicians established Marshfield Clinic, one of the earliest group practices in the country. The relationship between the hospital and clinic facilitated the growth of both, resulting in a medical complex that provided exceptional care for its unique, rural location.

From early on, the Sisters were committed to nursing education. In 1922 a three-story brick home was built for students who were enrolled in Saint Joseph's Hospital School of Nursing. It was expanded in 1941. Although the school was discontinued in 1988, the hospital continues its commitment to education by partnering with the University of Wisconsin-Eau Claire in a four-year, satellite-nursing program.

Throughout the 1920s and 1930s, the hospital's mission remained focused on serving the growing and changing needs of the community. Separate departments were established for pediatrics, urology, cardiology, cancer, maternity, and eye/ear/nose and throat. The hospital provided general surgery, radium therapy, hydro and photoelectric therapy, oxygen therapy, and EKG services. However, without the frugality and hard work of the Sisters,

Nursing students in Marshfield monitor classes via satellite from the university.

advances at Saint Joseph's Hospital would have been impossible. There were no payroll expenses for the Sisters, as they took no salary. They regularly worked 12 to 15 hour days, six and seven days a week, with rarely a vacation. They raised their own food, for themselves and for patients. Even the needles were sharpened and reused; nothing went to waste. Because of the Sisters' thriftiness, the hospital was able to survive the Great Depression and continued to accept the increasing numbers of poor and homeless who came to its door.

In the early 1940s Saint Joseph's Hospital became short staffed, as many of its nurses and doctors joined the military efforts of World War II. Wartime building restrictions limited any new growth. Once the war ended, however, a $1.5 million addition provided 100 more beds, seven op-

Saint Joseph's Hospital offers many varied opportunities for healthcare professionals. One area of nursing specialties is the Neonatal Intensive Care Unit, which provides high-tech and high-touch care for pre-term newborns and ill neonates.

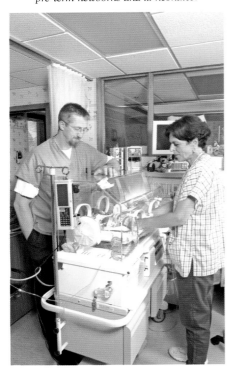

The Hope Lodge serves as a "home away from home" for those undergoing outpatient cancer treatment.

erating rooms, and additional space for overcrowded departments. Advances derived from wartime, medical treatments brought forth the first generation of antibiotics and the beginnings of new technology. The hospital responded accordingly by establishing schools for medical and radiology technicians.

Construction continued as well. Another major expansion came in 1964 when two five-story additions were built, at a cost of $5.5 million, adding 107 beds and areas for a variety of other functions. The hospital's largest addition, a $28 million eight-story tower, was completed in 1978. In the 1990s, projects included a new parking deck, and a $25 million, three-story addition for the emergency department, outpatient surgery, respiratory care, coronary care services, and support departments. The pediatrics and pediatric intensive care units were remodeled, and a new employee child care center was also built.

Changes also were happening in hospital management. A growing number of services, as well as more employees, eventually required a more complex administration. The Sisters themselves formed the Sisters of the Sorrowful Mother-Ministry Corporation in 1984 to ensure ad-

ministrative changes would not alter their values and mission. This corporation was renamed Ministry Health Care in 1997 and has grown today into a values-based, healthcare delivery network of aligned hospitals, clinics, long-term care facilities, home health agencies, dialysis centers, and many other programs in Wisconsin and Minnesota.

Despite the hospital's impressive growth and numerous technological advances, it remains faithful to the mission and values of its founding Sisters. Its healthcare professionals are known not only for their expertise and quality care, but for their compassionate care. Like the Sisters of old, the hospital and its employees give generously to help the poor and needy through gifts of time, expertise, and financial aid. Its mission remains to "further the healing ministry of Jesus Christ by continually improving the health and well being of all people, especially the poor, in the communities we serve." That mission will continue to guide Saint Joseph's Hospital through whatever the future holds.

Visitors to the popular Flake Out Fest enjoy a sleighride during a wintery day in Wisconsin Dells. The festival features snow sculpting, a snowman-making contest, Eskimo Pie eating contest, tricycle races, ice carving, kite flying, hot air balloons, ice skating, sleigh rides, and cross-country skiing. Courtesy, Wisconsin Department of Tourism

ST. PAUL ELDER SERVICES

In 1943 a group of local citizens in Kaukauna, Wisconsin approached the Franciscan Sisters of Christian Charity to ask if they would care for an elderly resident who could no longer care for herself. Edith Grignon was the last surviving member of her family and there was no one who could look after her. Her home, the Grignon Mansion, was one of the town's most impressive houses (today it is a historical landmark). The Sisters accepted Mrs. Grignon into their home, and that was the start of what would become known as the St. Paul Home for the Aged. It was named in appreciation of the generosity of Bishop Paul Rhode, the head of the Green Bay Diocese. Mrs. Grignon entered the home on September 13, 1943, a date that is considered the official beginning of St. Paul Elder Services (SPES).

A group of five citizens had agreed to pay for her stay with the Sisters. Soon, other elderly women from the community also moved into St. Paul's. To accommodate the new guests the Sisters moved up to the attic floor and created an 18-bed area on the second floor.

The original St. Paul Home, itself a local landmark, was first owned by Oscar Thilmany, the founder of Thilmany Pulp and Paper. The house was built in the Fox River Valley as his family residence and later sold to the Wertheimer family, whose wish was that the mansion would some-

Sister Ambrosette Pflueger, former St. Paul administrator, was the driving force behind the upgrade and expansion of the Home in the 1960s.

day "accomplish a maximum of usefulness and happiness." They also wanted the home to remain "in a state of good repair to thus continue the dignified and useful history of the family homestead." To fulfill that wish, Robert Wertheimer deeded the home to the Diocese of Green Bay in 1939 and that same year Bishop Rhode officially transferred the deed to the Franciscan Sisters.

The federal and state codes for nursing homes were significantly tightened in 1960. An order was received from the state that non-ambulatory people had to be housed in fire-resistant structures, a standard that the St. Paul Home did not meet. Sister Ambrosette Pflueger, the home's administrator, decided to find a way to bring the property up to code.

She had previously incorporated St. Paul Home and shortly thereafter formed a lay advisory board. She then began a capital fund drive. A gift of $48,000 jump-started the campaign and by 1963 enough funding had been raised to begin construction on a new fire-resistant wing, replacing the original ballroom which had served as the chapel. On September 1, 1964 residents moved into the

54-bed addition. In no time there was a waiting list for admittance, at one point totaling 250 hopeful residents.

In the 1980s recommendations were made by the Wisconsin Department of Health and Social Services for the upgrading and expansion of the home to better meet the needs of the residents. The Sisters responded by renovating the second floor of the Wertheimer Mansion to house eight ambulatory senior citizens. The renovated building became known as St. Paul Manor. In turn, St. Paul Home purchased the Neil McCarty residence next door to the mansion, which became the convent for the Sisters who staffed the home.

On April 29, 1988 construction began on a 129-bed facility at a new site adjacent to the Kaukauna Community Hospital. The cornerstone was laid on the Feast of the Conversion of St. Paul on January 25, 1989, and the building officially opened in July.

While the new nursing home was under construction, a study had been underway to determine the feasibil-

Today St. Paul Elder Services provides a full range of therapy services to the residents of the retirement community.

A Franciscan Sister visits with a resident during the early days at the St. Paul Home.

ity of renovating the original St. Paul Home as a manor for assisted-living residents. The renovation also took place in 1989, and by the following September the new St. Paul Manor opened its doors to 26 residents.

With these new improvements, St. Paul Home and St. Paul Manor quickly acquired a reputation for the high quality of care they provided for the elderly citizens of the Fox River Valley. This reputation was enhanced even further when in April 1997 St. Paul Home joined Wellspring, an alliance of 11 nonprofit nursing homes whose common purpose was to improve the quality of care provided to residents in long-term facilities throughout the nation.

In 1998 St. Paul Home acquired the Kaukauna Community Hospital. The old facility was razed and construction began on a $4.5 million elder campus, which included an 18-bed Alzheimer's unit, 34 assisted-living apartments, a therapy facility, and a community center.

SPES has grown exponentially in all aspects of its operations. In the past eight years it has added 118,605 square feet of new construction to the south campus, which includes St. Paul Home and St. Paul Villa. Its workforce has also grown from 145 to 277 associates. Besides the physical growth of the campus, new services have been added to meet the increased demands of older adults. Today, SPES provides housing and skilled nursing services to 246 seniors, as well as a range of outreach services to individuals in their own homes.

Throughout the growth of the organization, the value of dignity has remained constant and is a driving force behind everything St. Paul Elder Services does. It is the organization's belief that in bringing the healing ministry of Jesus to our elders, it is respecting the dignity of each individual. For more than 60 years the Franciscan Sisters of Christian

Charity have ensured that St. Paul Elder Services is known far and wide for the compassionate care that is provided throughout the campus, and in the homes of those to whom SPES offers outreach services.

As new programs are developed, the intent of each is to address an identified need. In some cases the service may be provided in collaboration with another organization or agency; however, the values and philosophy of St. Paul Elder Services is integrated throughout all of its endeavors.

As a continuing care retirement community, St. Paul Elder Services has grown to be a premier provider of services for senior adults in the Fox River Valley of Wisconsin. It has thereby ensured that the vision of

St. Paul Villa was added to the continuum of senior housing in 2000 and expanded in 2003.

the Franciscan Sisters of Christian Charity will remain vital and alive for many years to come.

Since its beginning in 1943, St. Paul Elder Services has strived to reflect the ministry of Jesus, enabling the elderly citizens of its community to maintain quality health and a full life. Its core values have always emphasized compassion, hospitality, the stewardship of services, and the dignity of all persons.

Residents of St. Paul Manor enjoy a leisurely lifestyle in a gracious, peaceful setting.

CG SCHMIDT, INCORPORATED

CG Schmidt, Incorporated has built its reputation on the integrity of three generations and 85 years of dedication to the growth of Milwaukee and its surrounding community. It is a construction company whose main objective is not just to build buildings, but to uphold the missions of the people who will occupy them. Whether it is a utilitarian hospital structure or an intricate creative design such as the Milwaukee Art Museum addition, CG Schmidt embarks upon each project with reverence for the building's purpose.

"Building a better community through leadership and innovation" is the company's mission statement. A bold commitment CG Schmidt has upheld since the company's humble beginnings. Perhaps the reason for such dedication originates in the character of the company's founder, Charles G. Schmidt.

The story began in 1907 when 19-year-old Charles Schmidt arrived in the U.S. from his homeland of Rosendaal, Holland. After working at a meat packing plant in Kansas City, the young man decided to relocate to Milwaukee where he was employed as a maintenance worker for a local brewing company. His willingness to

Charles G. Schmidt, president from 1929–1950.

Charles Schmidt, founder.

work and learn went beyond his maintenance duties and soon Charles became adept in the crafts of masonry and carpentry. These were trades integral to the construction industry. By 1920 Charles Schmidt had enough experience and courage to set out on his own. He launched Charles Schmidt and Sons with a dedication to exceptional craftsmanship and personalized service.

Although Charles' skills and desire were firmly in place, his revenue was not. "He had a truck, a wheel barrel, and a shovel when he started his busi-

ness," quips Richard Schmidt, chairman of the board and CEO of CG Schmidt, Inc. Charles' only employees were his two sons, but his tenacity paid off and the company grew slowly but steadily.

In 1929 Charles G. Schmidt took the helm and the number of employees grew from two to 12. In 1941 Charles Jr. decided to incorporate and the name of the company officially changed to CG Schmidt, Incorporated. He transitioned the business from simply pouring basements and driveways to constructing major building projects. He faithfully remained with the corporation until his death at the age of 78.

Today the corporation is run by Richard Schmidt, Charles G.'s son and grandson of the founder. His leadership style is direct, as he guarantees exceptional craftsmanship in fulfilling the requirements of each building design. However, his main objective is to insure his clients' total satisfaction. "We build great buildings and we make great friends," proclaims Richard Schmidt, a man dedicated to his clients. The company develops a partnership with each client by which they work together

Milwaukee Art Museum, Calatrava addition.

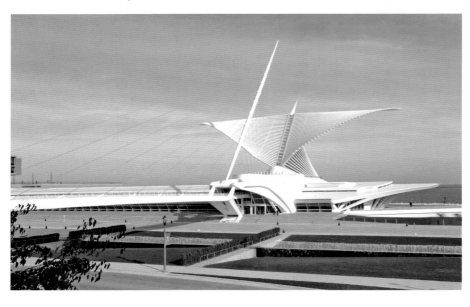

discussing options for design and approach for a particular project. CG Schmidt then puts the appropriate design and construction team together to complete the job. The result is a unique design for each satisfied customer. Clients are pleased with this strategy as evidenced by a 70 percent annual repeat business rate. The most frequent repeat customer has been using the expertise of the company for over 50 years.

The longevity of client relationships is not only due to the consistent quality of work provided by CG Schmidt, but also to the company's reputation and integrity. For instance, the firm was made aware of a job completed over 35 years ago where structural flaws were only now becoming evident. Without hesitation, Richard Schmidt sent a structural engineer to investigate the problem. The situation was rectified in a timely manor at considerable cost to CG Schmidt. "Our reputation is worth much more," responded Richard Schmidt when asked about the project. "Integrity above all else" is a standard by which he operates his business and personal life.

This honorable quality spills over into Richard's community involvement. He is dedicated to multiple organizations, and loans his time and energy to them. He is a committee member for the FBI Citizens Agency, The Hunger Task Force, The Milwaukee Downtown Kiwanis, and the Curative Rehabilitation Center Fund. He is also the Milwaukee Zoology Society Steering Committee Chairman. Upon Richard Schmidt's approval, CG Schmidt donated roughly $107,000 to various organizations in 2003 alone.

Community involvement is encouraged from the top and extends to company employees as well. There is an annual CG Schmidt Community Service Award given to the employee who has shown the

Richard L. Schmidt, chairman and CEO.

most dedication to a particular organization. Winners of this award not only receive $500, but CG Schmidt also donates an additional $500 to the organization of the winner's choice. Employees are proud of their community involvement and the standard for integrity on the job. *Milwaukee Magazine* named CG Schmidt one of the "Best Places to Work" in 2003.

CG Schmidt's employees are no longer mere tradesmen; they are university graduates and civil engineers. As the company's professional staff has become more sophisticated, so have its projects. One job that the

---

Waukesha Memorial Hospital's northwest addition.

company is most proud of is the Milwaukee Art Museum addition. The company vied for the job in conjunction with a nationally-known construction company. When the larger company failed to produce what was requested, CG Schmidt was asked to continue the job on its own. The company did so, and embarked upon new technological challenges which resulted in innovative construction solutions. Those new methodologies have been incorporated into the company's knowledge base and have raised the bar for all future projects.

When Richard Schmidt took over the company in 1980, there were about 60 employees working for the firm. Now the company employs about 100 in-house staff and close to 250 in the field and on construction sites. Although the family-owned business employs several family members, it recognizes the value and expertise of others. Under Richard Schmidt's guidance, the company's vision and operations are lead by president and board member Steve Chamberlin (who succeeded Geoff Knudson, now vice-chairman of the board).

Richard Schmidt has a fresh approach to running his business which has earned CG Schmidt the distinguished position of being one of the premier general contractors and construction managers in southeastern Wisconsin. Projects range in value from $100,000 to an impressive $100 million. However, the company is first and foremost a family-run business dedicated to the specific needs of its clients. It is a philosophy that goes beyond company policy and enriches Milwaukee and the surrounding areas.

SENSIENT TECHNOLOGIES CORPORATION

In one form or another, Sensient Technologies has been a part of the Wisconsin landscape since 1882. From its early beginnings as a small distillery, the company has evolved into a leading global manufacturer and marketer of colors, flavors, and fragrances. Sensient employs advanced technologies at facilities around the world to develop food and beverage systems, cosmetic and pharmaceutical ingredient systems, inkjet and specialty inks, and display imaging chemicals. The company's customers include major international manufacturers representing some of the world's best-known brands.

Originally named Meadow Springs Distillery, the company was founded by three German businessmen: Leopold Wirth, Gustav Niemeier, and Henry Koch, Jr. The men set up shop at the corner of the Menomonee River Valley, on the outskirts of Milwaukee. The endeavor was underwritten by Adolph C. Zinn, one of the city's most prominent businessmen and owner of the highly successful Milwaukee Malt House.

Sensient was founded in 1882 as Meadow Springs Distillery in Milwaukee, Wisconsin.

However, Wirth was the driving force behind the fledgling distillery. Eventually, two more generations of his family would become integrally involved in the direction and growth of the business.

In the late 1800s the company reorganized, changing its name to the National Distilling Company. It was then under the direction of August Grau, who acted as president of the corporation from 1887 until 1922. At that time the company set out to broaden its base, and began selling its

surplus distilled spirits to companies beyond the Wisconsin area. The firm also moved its corporate offices from the outskirts of the city into the central business district of Milwaukee.

In 1919 the business faced a huge challenge as Prohibition threatened an end to its existence. Most distilleries went out of business, but by then National Distilling had created a business selling yeast—a by-product of their distilling process. John Wiedring, who was in charge of the company's laboratory, went to the Berlin Institute of Fermentation to study the yeast making process. He returned with an idea that would save the business: an aeration process for making yeast that the company introduced that same year.

The company cut and packaged the product under the name "Red Star Yeast," and a new direction of growth took place. Yeast turned out to be a boon for the company. It began to be touted as a health food and from the 1920s on, people flocked to their local stores to buy the Red Star product. Accordingly, the company's

Workers in 1912 inside the Meadow Springs Distillery, a forerunner of Sensient.

name was changed from National Distilling to Red Star Compressed Yeast Company. By 1921 the company had 50 branches around the Midwest and eastern U.S.

After the end of 14 years of Prohibition, Red Star had a brief run at distilling spirits again, but it was its yeast manufacturing that kept the company thriving. The business ceased the distilling of spirits in 1937—and added vinegar to its offerings.

In the '60s Red Star moved out of its single product line and became a highly-diversified food company. In 1961 the first non-yeast acquisitions were made with the purchase of Universal Foods Company of Chi-

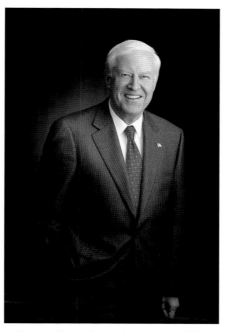

Sensient Technologies chairman and CEO Kenneth P. Manning.

company's 100th anniversary in 1987, it had extended into five major marketing areas: cheese, beverage, frozen foods, fermentation, and import and specialty products which included product flavoring and coloring.

The corporation hired a new group vice president in 1987, Kenneth P. Manning, who had previously been with the W.R. Grace Company in New York. Manning quickly became a dynamic force for change within the company. He realized that the

business needed to reinvent itself to prosper in an increasingly competitive environment. The firm had become a mature business of commodity products with little opportunity for growth. Manning's vision was to move the company toward the anticipated needs of the twenty-first century, and Universal Foods began to sell its commodity business and acquire new higher potential businesses. In 1990 the company's cheese business was sold, which was followed by the sale of its frozen foods dealings in 1994.

Manning was named chief executive officer of Universal Foods in 1996, and began aggressively steering the business in a new direction. Manning devised a matrix upon which the company plotted its future growth. The central elements of that blueprint were building upon the firm's strengths and knowledge in the areas of color and flavor, and the strategic acquisition of companies to complement its new direction. To that end, Universal Foods accelerated its expansion by developing, manufacturing, and supplying colors to the cosmetic, pharmaceutical, inkjet ink, and digital imaging industries.

The global headquarters for Sensient's Flavors and Fragrances Group is located in Indianapolis, Indiana.

Flavors and fragrances are manufactured at Sensient's state-of-the-art production facilities.

cago, which manufactured food products for the institutional trade. The company then changed its name in 1962 to the Universal Foods Corporation, to emphasize the planned growth in operations.

In 1977 Universal Foods went public, listing its stock on the New York Stock Exchange. The corporation expanded exponentially from a net worth of $8 million dollars in 1960 to $400 million by 1980. By the

One of Manning's first acquisitions was the purchase of a cosmetic color manufacturer based in France. Originally purchased for $10 million dollars, today it is responsible for $50 million in sales. Manning, who personally negotiated all the company's acquisitions, also saw the symbiotic relationship between its French acquisition and another company in Spain which created fragrances. Another major purchase was a German company known for its cutting-edge imaging technology. The business had great technological expertise in photographic and organic chemicals for light-emitting diodes. Today, its technology for fourth generation flat screens is considered to be on the leading edge of this burgeoning field. Manning has always been certain to carefully weigh each acquisition to ensure they complement the company's goals. Since 1997 the corporation has acquired 20 companies, turning Manning's vision into solid reality.

In 2000 Universal Foods changed its corporate name to reflect the company's exciting new direction, and the Sensient Technologies Corporation was born. The name is a reflection of the company's mission, which is "to enhance sensory experiences through specialized ingredients, delivered through proprietary technologies." In 2001 Sensient sold Red Star Yeast, which had been a division of the company since 1887, as part of its strategy to divest itself of unprofitable commodity businesses. When the yeast business was sold, yeast was selling for the same price it had during the Depression.

Sensient Technologies Corporation is comprised of three groups: the Flavors and Fragrances Group, the Color Group and the Asia Pacific Group. The Flavors and Fragrances Group develops and manufactures flavor systems for the food and beverage industry, and fragrances for the

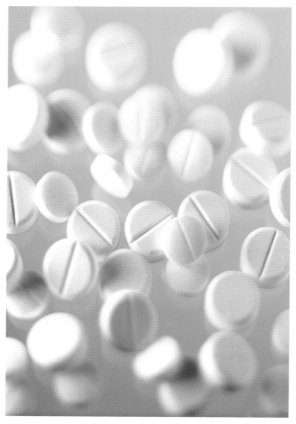

Sensient's natural colors and coatings are ideal for pharmaceuticals.

personal and home care markets. The Color Group manufactures and markets synthetic and natural food colors; formulations for cosmetics; color systems for pharmaceuticals and technical colors for industrial applications and digital imaging, including inkjet inks and display imaging.

In the cosmetics industry, Sensient has developed strong ties with the leading cosmetics companies. It is considered the world's leading supplier of both natural and synthetic colors and fragrances. Along with the many advanced color techniques and proprietary pigments produced by the company, Sensient has created a proprietary process that has resulted in the elimination of "color bleeding."

The fragrance unit of Sensient Technologies is a leading producer of aroma chemicals and essential oils.

Sensient also offers its clientele a vast array of technically-innovative hues and tints for its products, as well as a myriad of color solutions for products such as lipsticks, eye make-up, lotions, and creams. In yet another area, Sensient manufactures and supplies ingredients for home care, fabric care, and personal care products.

"Performance chemicals," considered an area of major strength and innovation for the company, reflects Sensient's expertise in specialized chemistry related to analog and digital printing. Sensient offers finished inks, pigments, and component dyes through a full spectrum of products and capabilities for use in digital imaging. Some of these key digital applications include desktop inkjet

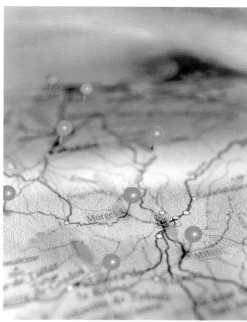

*Sensient's unique formulations
add value to
consumer products worldwide.*

printing for business and personal use; the rapidly expanding area of wide-format printing for both graphic and commercial applications; and photographic printing. The company also produces the chemicals used in organic light-emitting diodes—

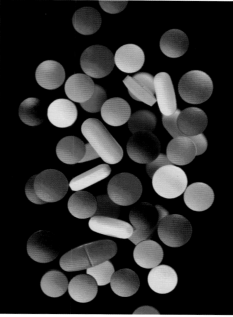

*Sensient is ranked second in
natural colors and coatings for the
pharmaceuticals market.*

fourth-generation technology used in flat panel display units.

In pharmaceuticals, Sensient develops coating systems. This includes colors that can be utilized by companies for their drug products, including generic and over-the counter remedies. By emphasizing solutions to product development challenges for its customers—with value-added technologies and ingredient systems—Sensient builds on current technologies to create new products that can be quickly commercialized.

Sensient's strategic plan includes the building of a corporate culture that draws upon the strengths of regions throughout the world. The company has operations in 77 locations, in 30 countries on six continents. Sensient's Asia Pacific Group, located in Singapore, is the umbrella for the company's colors, flavors, and fragrance activities in the region. The company also maintains manufacturing operations in China, Japan, the Philippines, and Austra-

lia. As of 2003 Sensient employed 3,700 people worldwide, of which more than 50 percent were foreign nationals. Revenues per employee for 2003 were $266,000, up from $168,000 in 1996—a testament to the company's growing productivity.

As part of Sensient's outreach to the community, the company formed the Sensient Technologies Foundation. It contributes more than $500,000 annually to support charitable projects like hospitals and shelters, educational programs at colleges and universities, civic projects, and cultural and arts organizations throughout the United States.

Sensient's transformation was accomplished under the leadership of innovative thinking with an eye to the future. This philosophy has transformed a domestic, commodity-based company into one that accurately anticipates the global needs of a 21st century world and provides high-performance, technology-driven products.

*Sensient Cosmetic Technologies
develops colors that are custom-designed
for specialty cosmetic applications.*

SILVER LAKE COLLEGE

To get to know Silver Lake College, you must look deeper than the serenity of its campus environment. You must see beyond the brick and glass. For Silver Lake College has a commitment to the God-given gifts of knowledge and wisdom. So if you really want to know Silver Lake College, you must look into the hearts of students, faculty, and alumni. This is where mind, body, and soul harmonize in a celebration of human growth. This is where Silver Lake College truly comes to life.

Silver Lake College has experienced several evolutionary changes since the Franciscan Sisters of Christian Charity established its forerunner institution in 1885 on the shores of Silver Lake. Its purpose then was to prepare young women who entered the religious community for the apostolic work of teaching in schools and other institutions served under the auspices of Holy Family Convent.

By the turn of the century, 44 elementary schools in Wisconsin, Illinois, Ohio, Missouri, and Nebraska were staffed with teachers who had graduated from the two-year normal school. A decade later, 250 Sisters were sent to 53 schools throughout the Archdiocese of Milwaukee and the dioceses of Green Bay, LaCrosse, and Superior in Wisconsin; the dio-

Master's degree recipient Natalie Terrien Rein speaks on behalf of her class at the school's commencement ceremony.

ceses of Grand Rapids and Marquette in Michigan; and the dioceses of Columbus, Ohio and Omaha, Nebraska.

With the advancement of quality education in the country, there were demands for teaching beyond normal school requirements. In a progressive move, Sisters were sent to other teachers' colleges and universities. And, as the number of Sisters grew, it became feasible for those with newly-earned, advanced degrees to return to Manitowoc County and the convent at Silver Lake. There they formed the core of a new, emerging, educational enterprise. In 1935 Holy Family College was established with a charter granted by the state of Wisconsin to conduct a full, four-year, baccalaureate program of study.

The Sisters then expanded their educational mission to include high schools. Degreed graduates, more than two-thirds of whom were directly involved with education, staffed more than 100 elementary and high schools, conservatories of music and art, and nursing schools by 1946.

Though lay women had attended the college by special arrangement with the Holy Family Hospital School of Nurs-

An aerial view of the Silver Lake College campus.

ing in Manitowoc, 1957 would see women admitted on a regular basis. During this time, the college had again expanded its teacher education programs with more discipline-specific fields of study.

In the latter half of the 1950s a capital campaign was launched for a new college building, which would provide educational opportunities for a broader spectrum of the public. Through the positive response of area businesses and individuals, a significant sum for that era—over $1 million—was contributed toward the construction of a new building. The structure would be built on a 36-acre tract adjacent to the Motherhouse (convent), and the new college opened in 1960.

This modern, well-designed, complex included four multi-level wings in the form of a cross. Inside was an expansive library, the only college library facility within a 40-mile radius; numerous classrooms and lecture halls; science laboratories; art and music studios; administrative offices; a special education clinic; a cafeteria; and faculty residences. An inspiring chapel, walled by stained-glass windows and depicting several of the first academic majors offered at the school, continues to be a central gathering space for the entire college community, visitors, and guests—even to this day. It is there that not only liturgical celebrations are shared, but a host of other public and academic community activities are offered.

By the end of the decade the college admitted its first male students. In 1969, with a student body representing all socioeconomic groups in the region, the school officially became known as Silver Lake College (SLC)—a name chosen to better reflect the diversity of its student body and constituents.

During the late 1970s and early 1980s, as spiraling inflation and high unemployment plagued the entire country and lakeshore region, Silver Lake College responded by expanding major programs of study for traditional and non-traditional students alike. The institution also methodically secured substantially more financial assistance for students. By doing so, the college helped the area and its residents weather the economic downturn. While recording steady enrollment gains, Silver Lake College also reinforced its partnering efforts and on-going value to eastern Wisconsin and beyond.

Business and computer science programs became important compo-

Dr. Steve Vanden Avond
confers with two undergraduates.

nents in the college's diversification. Beginning in the mid-'80s the college also offered degree-completion programs and professional development coursework at various Wisconsin locations for businesspeople, educators, and those who were already in the workforce. The era of the "adult learner" served to provide the next level of enrollment growth for the institution and created greater name recognition for SLC outside of its traditional service area. With more than two dozen undergraduate majors and three graduate-level programs (education, management and organizational behavior, and music-Kodaly emphasis), several hundred Wisconsin employers offer tuition assistance to their employees, in order to access Silver Lake College programs of study.

These positive outcomes could not be achieved without exceptional faculty, dedicated staff, and forward looking administrators; many of whom serve in leadership and support roles in all sectors of the local community. The college has also developed specialized, pre-collegiate experiences for area youth, as well as a Lifelong Learning Program for senior citizens, thus serving local learners of all ages. As another demonstration of its commitment to the lakeshore community, the sponsoring congregation of Franciscan Sisters of Christian Charity, along with Silver Lake College, have completely renovated the century old St. Joseph Parish and adjoining school that is located west of Holy Family Convent on the college cam-

Sr. Michaela Melko, Ph.D. works with today's professional educator.

pus. The new Generose Enrichment Center, opened in 2003 and named for the first college president (Mother M. Generose Cahill), incorporates a unique blend of architectural history with state-of-the-art technology. Together, it creates an aesthetically pleasing environment. A spacious, upper conference hall complements six individual seminar rooms, a social hall/serving kitchen, and ample parking. The center is large enough to accommodate the needs of the college community and other schools, area businesses, and civic organizations that need space for meetings, workshops, or other project-centered activities.

Silver Lake College clearly preserves the religious traditions and high educational standards of the original Holy Family Convent Normal School and Holy Family College. At the same time, it has invested in its growing service area to the point where its statewide economic impact is calculated at more than $150 million each year. With its exemplary religious, educational, and economic contributions, Silver Lake College stands as a testament to the vision of its founderesses and benefactors, as well as a dynamic resource for students and the community at large.

SISTERS OF ST. FRANCIS OF ASSISI

When most people think of a religious congregation of women they envision nuns cloistered in a convent, wearing the traditional habit, and spending most of their days in quiet solitude and prayer. The modern-day Sisters of St. Francis of Assisi, however, bear little resemblance to this customary notion.

The nearly 350 women who make up the religious congregation headquartered in Milwaukee, Wisconsin are devoted to a life of service that takes them beyond the walls of the convent and into the world outside. Of course prayer and contemplation are still a part of their lives, but their ministries take them directly into the community. And it's their good deeds and their commitment to creating a better world for the people in their community and around the globe that really sets them apart.

Whether it's teaching children and adults with special needs, helping the poor, or protesting for peace, these women are making a difference

Graduates line up to receive their diplomas at one of the three St. Coletta schools. Since 1904 the Sisters of St. Francis of Assisi have helped people with disabilities achieve their full potential. St. Coletta schools are located in Wisconsin, Illinois, and Massachusetts.

For over 100 years the Sisters of St. Francis of Assisi prepared children at Milwaukee's St. John's School for the Deaf to meet the challenges of a hearing world.

every day. Unlike their cloistered sisters from the past, the Sisters of St. Francis of Assisi are free to choose their areas of ministry based on their own individual interests and skills. They put their talents to use as graphic designers, teachers, university professors, psychologists, midwives, pharmacists, interpreters, administrators, musicians, and artists. There's even an acupuncturist and a plant pathologist.

This new way of religious life took root in 1967 when Vatican II opened up a world of possibilities for women in religion. Personal responsibility in decision-making replaced "blind obedience" in the congregation and cloistered living was discouraged in favor of building ties within the community. Sisters moved out of the convent and began living together in small groups or apartments, and most of them traded in their habits for street clothes. These days the only identifying object they are required to wear is a gold ring with an insignia.

Essentially Vatican II took the sisters out of the cloister and placed

them squarely into the world. This more closely mirrored the life of their patron St. Francis who preached among the people. Born in 1182 to a wealthy family, St. Francis chose to relinquish all material possessions and dedicate himself to caring for the lepers who were outcasts in his day, serving the poor, promoting peace, and showing respect and reverence for all of God's creation. Since St. Francis' time, hundreds of groups of women and men throughout the world have claimed the ideals of Francis as their inspiration and guide. So it was with the Sisters of St. Francis of Assisi.

Their story began in 1849 when the first archbishop of Milwaukee invited a group of lay Franciscans living in the small rural village of Ettenbeuren, Bavaria to come to Wisconsin to serve as missionaries. Six women and five men accepted the offer and made the voyage to

America. After arriving, the men built the convent and then served at the seminary, but the women's dreams of becoming teachers were put on hold. Instead, the women were asked to provide domestic services in the seminary, including housekeeping, cooking, laundering, mending, gardening, even milking cows.

It wasn't until the 1870s that the archbishop granted the sisters' repeated requests to become teachers. In a short time the congregation began to accept teaching assignments in rural schools. By the turn of the century, they were enrolling in institutions of higher learning, preparing for teaching at all levels. In 1904 the Sisters of St. Francis opened St. Coletta's, a school for mentally-challenged children and adults in Jefferson, Wisconsin. Since that time the congregation has educated thousands of students with special needs. The Sisters also worked actively with children at St. John's School for the Deaf in Milwaukee, which closed in 1983, for more than 100 years.

Following Vatican II the congregation increased its activities beyond teaching. In 1971 U.S. Bishops handed down a mandate to all Catholics to work for justice and peace. To that end, the Sisters of St. Francis of

St. Francis Convent (located at 3221 South Lake Drive in St. Francis, a suburb of Milwaukee) was built in the late 1800s. Today it serves as headquarters for the congregation of the Sisters of St. Francis of Assisi.

Assisi worked as agents of long-term social change. They protested the build-up of nuclear arms. They marched in Selma, Alabama. They boycotted lettuce and grapes. They even got involved in providing better working and living conditions for farm workers. They also fund programs to promote social justice, from digging wells in Haitian villages to teaching African and Hispanic women how to build solar ovens.

The congregation's involvement in social justice and peace reflects the way St. Francis himself sought to bring about peace. Like Francis, the sisters are nonviolent and preach by example. Above all, they educate themselves and others to be politically aware, socially active citizens, who work together to create a more just world society.

As the Sisters of St. Francis of Assisi ventured into their new active role in society following Vatican II, they opened up their ministries to lay people (men and women who have not taken vows). Previously, only sisters were involved in operating and maintaining their various concerns. That meant the sisters did everything from acting as janitors and gardeners to holding positions as school principals and teachers.

Now there are more lay people than sisters involved in their organizations, which include 11 corporate ministries throughout the country and in Taiwan. In Milwaukee the congregation sponsors a retirement community, a day care center for adults and children, a center for nonprofit organizations, and Cardinal Stritch University. Lay people currently hold positions as CEOs, presidents, and administrative workers. Sisters hold leadership positions running diocesan offices, parish ministries, housing developments, clinics, day care, and other corporate structures. Sisters serve on the boards of directors of their corporate ministries and offer their Franciscan presence and heritage to the decision-making process.

Throughout its history the religious congregation has been in a continuous state of evolution. Although the lives they lead have changed dramatically since their foundresses first arrived in the mid-1800s, the Sisters of St. Francis of Assisi still feel firmly grounded to the past. By the same token, they are dedicated to meeting the needs of a changing world. Most importantly, they are confident that they will continue to find ways to make the world a better place.

Peace rallies are just one way the Sisters of St. Francis of Assisi work to create a better world.

A. O. SMITH CORPORATION

Milwaukee-based A. O. Smith Corporation has enjoyed a number of firsts in its rich, 130-year history:

♦ *The company perfected the first mass-produced automobile frame in 1906.*

♦ *Its research resulted in major improvements in arc welding, helping make welding the preferred method of joining steel.*

♦ *In 1921 one of the world's first examples of automation was unveiled, an automobile frame assembly line that could produce 10,000 frames daily while requiring just 181 employees.*

♦ *It helped create the natural gas industry in the United States by introducing an economical method of producing large-diameter line pipe.*

♦ *In 1936 it patented the process for glass lining the tank of a residential water heater, helping make hot water an affordable convenience for American homeowners.*

Much of the credit for these achievements goes to the vision and uncompromising values of the Smith family. Charles Jeremiah (C.J.) Smith, who founded the business in 1874, his son Arthur Oliver (A. O.

A. O. Smith was one of the first U.S. manufacturers to construct a stand-alone research operation. Its engineers worked in a wide range of fields including metallurgy, ceramics, mechanical engineering, and welding technology.

In addition to designing new motors for applications such as central air conditioners and swimming pool pumps, A. O. Smith developed new process technologies to meet customer demands for quality and on-time delivery.

Smith), and his grandson, Lloyd Raymond (L. R.) Smith believed in the power of technology. They inspired their employees to constantly search for "a better way" through the use of engineering and innovation. They also believed in conducting business with honesty and integrity, practices that remain in place today.

C. J. Smith, an immigrant from England trained in metalworking, started the business on Milwaukee's

north side as a maker of "hardware specialties." The company was soon making parts for baby carriages, shoemaking equipment, and machine tools for the rapidly growing Milwaukee industrial base. The first breakthrough came in the early 1890s, when the company fabricated a tubular steel front fork for bicycles. C. J. Smith followed that success with bicycle frames, sprockets, and other parts, and by 1895, the company was the largest bicycle component manufacturer in North America.

The following year, A. O. Smith joined the business. Another resourceful engineer, he became interested in the fledgling automobile industry and began to experiment with car frames. At the time, frames were made of heavy, expensive, structural steel. Using the company's experience in metalworking, he developed a frame made of lightweight and relatively inexpensive sheet steel in 1899. Orders began to come in from manufacturers such as Peerless, Locomobile, and Cadillac. In 1906 Henry Ford approached A. O. Smith

A. O. Smith was North America's leading supplier of bicycle parts in the 1890s. The company manufactured bicycle frames, front forks, sprockets, and other components.

about producing frames for his new Model N, expected to be the world's first mass-produced car. The order was unprecedented at the time—build 10,000 frames in four months (at a time when the company was making 10 frames per day). Undaunted, A. O. Smith and his engineers modified their tooling, presses, and production processes and met the deadline. By 1910 A. O. Smith Company was North America's leading manufacturer of automobile frames.

L. R. Smith, entrepreneurial, inventive, and driven, took over the business in 1913 upon his father, Arthur's, death. Under his leadership and commitment to research and engineering, the company expanded in a number of different industries. Seizing the opportunity to increase the size and output of the automotive business, L. R. Smith and his engineers set out to build an automated frame assembly plant that required few employees to operate. After six years of development, what became known as the "Mechanical Marvel" went into production in Milwaukee in 1921. The sheer magnitude of the automatic frame plant was unprecedented for its time. The facility consisted of four manufacturing lines laid out to form a rectangle with 552 separate operations performed on a 10-second cycle. The plant was capable of producing up to 10,000 automobile frames a day with just 181 employees and operated virtually non-stop for 37 years. A. O. Smith Corporation remained in the automotive business until 1997.

L. R. Smith did not limit his visionary interests to the automotive industry. During World War I, A. O. Smith engineers perfected a new method of electric arc welding. The company used that technology in the 1920s to introduce new welded products, such as pressure vessels that were used in oil refining. It also developed a method to fabricate 40-foot

"Glass That Bends with the Steel."
In the 1920s, A. O. Smith researchers
developed a method of fusing
a microscopically thin layer of glass
to steel to provide for corrosion resistance.
The company later used this technology
to develop the process
to glass line a water heater tank.

lengths of large-diameter welded steel line pipe for oil and gas transmission. At that time, the entire production of large-diameter pipe in the U. S. was one-and-a-half miles per year. The oil industry responded favorably to the superior performance of the A. O. Smith product, realizing it could use the economical high-pressure line pipe to transport natural gas from the oil field to population centers all over the country. By 1929 A. O. Smith had produced 2,500 miles of pipe and had orders for another 1,600 miles. It remained in the business for nearly 45 years.

With a staff of 500 engineers, the company conducted research in a number of areas, including corrosion-resistant coatings to protect steel. In the late 1920s researchers developed a process to fuse a microscopically thin layer of glass to steel at temperatures of 1,600 degrees Fahrenheit. The first uses were beer kegs and large-volume beer tanks, but the most

noteworthy development was a process to glass line residential water heater tanks. The process, patented in 1936, made hot water affordable for virtually any home, and A. O. Smith began mass production of water heaters following World War II. In 1948 the company began manufacturing commercial water heating equipment. Today, A. O. Smith is one of the two largest manufacturers of water heaters in North America with plants in the United States, Mexico, Canada, the Netherlands, and China.

In 1940 the company acquired a small manufacturer of electric motors to support its line pipe business. The firm expanded its motor business through growth and acquisition, eventually consolidating operations in Tipp City, a suburb of Dayton, Ohio. Throughout the 1950s and 1960s the motor business created new designs for a wide range of residential, commercial, and industrial applications. Thanks to four strategic acquisitions since 1997, A. O. Smith is one of the three largest motor manufacturers in North America today with operations in the United States, Mexico, Ireland, England, Hungary, and China.

Although A. O. Smith Corporation has changed dramatically over the last 130 years, a number of important characteristic remain the same. The company still calls Milwaukee its "hometown." The business and its employees remain committed to customer service, quality products, and engineering excellence. And the Smith family remains actively involved in the company, with two members of the fifth generation serving on the board of directors and two others working in senior management. Throughout its history A. O. Smith has lived up to its values as well as exemplifying its early slogan: "Through Research A Better Way."

SPACESAVER CORPORATION

When Theodore W. Batterman acquired the insolvent Staller Cabinet Company in rural Fort Atkinson, Wisconsin in 1972, the operation, housed in a barn that covered 8,000 square feet and employed seven people including the owners, was renamed Spacesaver Corporation. Today the company employs more than 350 people at three sites, which total 300,000 square feet. All of the company's facilities are now located within the city of Fort Atkinson itself.

At the time Batterman's goal was to use the engineering and management skills that he acquired when he was corporate vice-president of Warner Electric Brake & Clutch Company in Beloit, to develop an independent engineering, marketing, and manufacturing business. He wanted the firm's products to have a proprietary nature, and he sought to establish a unique marketing approach.

The idea was high-density mobile storage, particularly motorized mobile storage. The Staller Cabinet Company, which was inspired by a wooden carriage that was imported into the U.S. from Sweden, had developed a

Theodore W. Batterman, retired president and CEO of Spacesaver Corporation.

metal carriage system that was patented in 1972. The original mobile products were essentially wheeled carriages that were sold as accessories to shelving. Batterman saw high-density mobile storage as a product, in its own right, that could be specified by engineers and architects for new as well as existing construction. It would be installed and serviced by local contractors.

However, not everyone shared Batterman's vision that the corpo-

ration he wanted to buy had the potential to realize his goals. When he first applied for a loan to purchase the company, his application was denied. Batterman went back and requested that the bank president allow him to make a presentation to the loan committee in person to persuade them to approve his loan. He was successful in his quest, and the committee approved his application.

With the founding of Spacesaver, Batterman launched not only a company, but also an entire industry. Today there are more than 20 firms competing in the high-density, mobile storage industry, which totals over $200 million in sales and is growing at a rate of more than 5 percent annually. By far the largest in the field, Spacesaver has installed more than 85,000 high-density mobile storage systems, more than the rest of the industry combined.

Batterman's success is attributed largely to his highly-innovative leadership/marketing concept. He developed a unique distribution network of entrepreneurial local sales, installation, and service companies that operate as a single organization called The Spacesaver Group. Unlike "one-size-fits-all" commodities, the concept was to design and market high-density mobile storage products as complete systems that were engineered to meet the specialized storage needs of a wide variety of industries. The Spacesaver Group would add the finishing details and special touches that were required by each individual customer to tailor the Spacesaver system to their workplace.

Together, Spacesaver and The Spacesaver Group pioneered a whole new approach to the storage products industry and quietly revolutionized the way many hospitals, libraries, law-enforcement, government and military facilities, offices, and warehouses now store their materials. It resulted in billions of dollars in

The barn that originally housed the fledgling Spacesaver Corporation.

facility cost savings for businesses, industries, institutions, and government organizations.

Spacesaver systems range in size from very small, five feet long or less for private offices, to several hundred feet for industrial applications. Load capacities range from less than a few hundred pounds to more than 250 tons. Spacesaver focuses its sales efforts around five core markets: healthcare; museums; business; libraries and education; and government and justice—and the architects and designers who serve those industries.

What spacesaver offers these diverse customers is a product that saves on the increasingly expensive cost of space, particularly whatever is required for the storage of files and materials. By eliminating the need for multiple aisles, Spacesaver systems can store over 100 percent more in the same space as conventional storage units—or free up half the space for other activities.

A novelty in the 1960s and '70s, high-density mobile storage became a necessity in the '80s and '90s. In May 1988, the company announced its entry into the steel shelving business with the completion of a state-of-the-art automated metal-fabrication facility for 4-post steel shelving. In July 1998 the company was acquired by Krueger International, Inc. (KI) in Green Bay, and Batterman retired in January 1999.

Spacesaver continues to operate as a stand-alone division and has maintained its distribution channel separate from KI. Its product offering has expanded significantly since the acquisition. In October 1999

Spacesaver became the first mobile storage systems manufacturer in the United States to achieve ISO 9001 certification. Although a milestone for the company, it is only one step in Spacesaver's pursuit of excellence through continuous improvement.

What really sets Spacesaver apart, however, is the innovative character of its organization with its nationwide network of area contractors (The Spacesaver Group). There are 47 of these companies in the U.S.; 13 in Canada; and other representatives throughout Mexico, parts of South America, Europe, the Middle East, and Asia. They provide storage expertise and solutions, while handling sales, installation, and service. That allows Spacesaver corporate to concentrate on product development, manufacturing, and marketing operations. The combined financial strength of the large corporation with the entrepreneurial flexibility of the small businesses has been a successful recipe for Spacesaver and customers alike.

The largest Spacesaver mobile storage systems are found in the edu-

Spacesaver spearheaded the growth of a whole new industry—high-density mobile storage. Pictured here is one of Spacesaver's powered high-density mobile systems. By eliminating the need for multiple aisles, Spacesaver systems can store over 100 percent more than conventional storage in the same space—or free up half the space for other activities.

cational and government markets, such as the University of Illinois' library addition with 55 miles of shelving and the Veterans Administration Records Processing Center in St. Louis with 107 miles of mobile files. The world's largest mobile storage system is at the National Archives Building, Archives II, in College Park, Maryland, where two million cubic feet of mobile storage capacity is compacted into an area of 691,572 square feet.

Today Spacesaver is not only the world's leading manufacturer of high-density mobile storage systems, but a total storage solutions provider that offers stationary and rotary storage products as well.

E. C. STYBERG ENGINEERING

A strong dedication to excellence and a willingness to take on whatever is necessary to serve its customers characterizes E. C. Styberg Engineering Company, Inc. An unshakeable desire to meet and exceed the obligations and responsibilities that are required to be a supplier of quality engineering solutions, drives much of the firm's practices. The company strives to maintain its established client relationships, basing them on mutual trust and respect. This is today, as it was more than 75 years ago when the firm was initially established. Engineering practices have changed unimaginably since those days, but Styberg's commitment to improving its unique capabilities remains firm. The operating philosophies and practices that have always served the Racine, Wisconsin firm speak well for its continued growth and success in the future.

E. C. Styberg, Sr. emigrated to the U.S. from Sweden with his parents at the age of 20. The family settled in Racine, as their relatives had before

In 1927 the company's original building was a converted garage on Winslow Street in Racine.

E.C. Styberg, Sr. founded the company in 1927.

them. Styberg worked for 17 years in various local industries before striking out on his own in 1927.

His tool and die shop, located in a two-car garage behind his house on Winslow Street, did a brisk trade from the beginning. Styberg hired several toolmakers, and the business quickly outgrew the garage. Styberg then bought lots on DeKoven and Kearney Avenues, erecting a red brick factory to house the growing business. He and his eight toolmakers settled into the

new factory just months before the stock market crash of 1929.

With the start of the Great Depression, business came to a standstill. Styberg expanded his firm's reach, soliciting business throughout the Milwaukee and Chicago areas. By 1933, with business again going well, Styberg began to diversify. In addition to the jobbing tool and die work, he began fabricating production parts on his punch presses. Early customers for Styberg's production parts included Johnson Wax Company, a Racine firm, and Schwinn Bicycle Company, headquartered in Chicago.

During World War II Styberg Engineering produced precision components for several types of military products, including dies for cartridge shells, bearing and cooler parts for aircraft engines, valves for ships and submarines, and electromechanical assemblies for radar units. Increased production led to a need for more space, and Styberg purchased an additional building on Junction Avenue. In 1950 the firm consolidated its facilities, moving to the former Wright Rubber Company plant building on Goold Street in Racine.

Throughout the decades, Styberg Engineering continued to exceed customers' expectations, using established relationships of mutual respect as a basis for business transactions. The company kept pace with industrial advances following World War II, manufacturing precision components for military and civilian jet engines. To this day, the Wisconsin firm remains an important manufacturer of these parts made from specially alloyed steel, requiring a variety of precise fabricating processes. Automatic transmissions for motor trucks and off-highway vehicles represent a second, rapidly expanding market, moving Styberg into the production of clutch plates and housings, Belleville disc springs, brake and clutch discs, and connecting drums.

In 1968 E. C. Styberg, Jr. was elected company president. He still maintains that title in the now privately-held company, with his wife, Bernice, serving as secretary. E. C. Styberg, Sr. remained chairman of the board until his death in 1974. Over the years his company, which started out as a jobbing shop, has grown into a contract manufacturer which supplies a variety of complex solutions to customers' design challenges. The 150,000 square-foot Goold Street location now houses 150 employees, all of whom take their responsibilities to the firm's clients very seriously.

The company's practice of implementing its unique capabilities continued during the 1960s, with the development of a line of patented hydraulic mechanical clutches. As opposed to becoming a commodity supplier, Styberg Engineering continued to employ its strategy of developing niche markets in which to excel. Process simplification, designing with simpler and fewer operations to affect cost reductions, also drove much of Styberg's response to customer requests.

Today, customers still avail themselves of E. C. Styberg's design expertise in the production of heavy gauge, complex components. Styberg reviews customers' designs and presents ideas aimed toward greater efficiency and reduced costs. These design solutions incorporate the use of fewer materials and manufacturing operations, sometimes reducing a multi-piece unit into a single unit of production. Styberg's knowledge of materials and manufacturing capabilities, honed by over 75 years experience in the industry, also allows the company to assess clients' designs in terms of increasing component strength. Styberg engineers review component dimensions with an eye toward providing time and cost savings to customers. The innovative approach often results in a reduction

E.C. Styberg, Jr., president of the firm since 1968.

in the requisite number of steps in the manufacturing process. A reduced cost to clients is one of the many benefits of process simplification.

Design solutions requiring less machining, tooling costs, and capital equipment are strongly in line with E. C. Styberg's commitment to providing its customers with the most

cost-effective design solutions. Styberg engineers work with both existing and proposed client designs, providing novel approaches to facilitate increased efficiency and overall cost reduction. The company's unusually complete line of machining operations accommodates a wide range of client requests, with complex design challenges offering the most dramatic solutions in terms of competitive pricing. Skilled personnel employ numerous capability and process control procedures and ensure the quality that clients have come to expect from an established firm of this caliber.

E. C. Styberg Engineering moves forward with confidence into the twenty-first century, approaching growth as it always has—with tolerance for risk and an enduring capacity to succeed. The long-established firm plans and prepares for the transition into the future by allowing sound and sensible priorities to determine financial stability. Above all, Styberg will maintain its emphasis on trust with its clients, an approach that has guided the firm for three-quarters of a century.

Current E.C. Styberg Engineering office and plant, located on Goold Street in Racine.

TILLMANN LANDSCAPE NURSERY, INC.

Ernst W. Tillmann, founder of Tillmann Landscape Nursery, Inc. of Green Bay, learned his craft from one of the best in the business. In the early days of his career in Chicago, Tillmann worked with Jens Jensen—the Danish landscape architect, renowned for his innovative approach to residential and commercial landscaping.

"It was certainly a lucky day when he met Jensen," Tillmann's widow, Otti, noted in an interview recorded after her husband's death. The couple met in Chicago in the 1920s, both of them having emigrated from Germany in 1918. Ernst came from a "big farm," Otti from Bad Hamburg, near Frankfurt. They married in Chicago in 1929 and Tillmann continued to work in the city with his mentor, until Jensen's retirement in 1938. The company's landscaping projects at that time included dozens of estates along Chicago's North Shore, such as the Florsheims and other Midwestern manufacturers. Otti recalled her husband's work with the Henry Ford

Left to right: Ron, Jeff, and Steve Tillmann in front of the Garden Shop and Landscaping Center.

family, which included planting an apple tree and building an adjacent porch where Mrs. Ford could sit under the tree. Tillmann also helped landscape the World's Fair held in Chicago in 1933–1934, a venue that drew 48 million visitors.

In 1938 Tillmann went to work for the state of Illinois, spending two years helping to design and construct the Illinois State Park on the Illinois River in Marseilles. The park, built with the help of Civilian Conservation Corps members, stands today as a 500-acre haven for songbirds, waterfowl, and other wildlife. Taking Jensen's suggestion, Tillmann moved

to Green Bay in 1940 to start his own landscaping business. He started out, as Otti notes, "with a shovel and a wheelbarrow."

The couple purchased a 40-acre farm just north of Green Bay Settlement, Wisconsin, using all of their savings for the purchase. The nursery's first seedlings were from Naperville Nurseries in Illinois, and most were of the native variety. When World War II began, Tillmann joined many area men in the war effort and worked as a welder at the Sturgeon Bay Shipyard. A small dairy farm helped support the family during wartime.

In the early years, before the days of large commercial landscaping accounts, Tillmann worked on residences in the Green Bay area. When assistants were needed, he hired from the local farming community for the going rate of 25 to 40 cents an hour. Otti tended and sold nursery stock every spring, answered the phone, and did the bookkeeping in the firm's early days. Tillmann built his business using Jensen's techniques, including the natural rock ledges and stone terracing that were hallmarks of the Danish landscaper's work.

Ernst Tillmann heeling in seedlings brought to Green Bay by car in the spring of 1940.

Tillmann Landscape Nursery's corporate offices, retail garden center, and greenhouse.

Ernst and Otti's sons, Ronald and Albert, both worked for the business, and started out by hoeing in the nursery. Eventually, a horse took over the cultivating chores and then, in Ron's words, "an old, heavy, Ford tractor." Both sons joined the firm full-time after completing their schooling and military duties. They continued their father's use of native perennials, shrubs, and trees—including rose bushes tough enough to survive the harsh Midwestern winters. After Ernst's death in 1966, his sons took over the business. They divided the duties, with Al in charge of landscaping and Ron working the nursery and garden center. The brothers also started a retail garden center. They incorporated the business as Tillmann Landscape Nursery, Inc. in 1967.

Tillmann Landscape Nursery continued to grow steadily. The brothers purchased 120 acres in Outagamie County for use as a sod farm, and retained the original acreage to grow the large shade trees for which Tillmann Landscape Nursery had become known. In 1977 highway development caused the firm to relocate to its present site at 2735 E. University Avenue, on the northeast side of Green Bay. This site now houses a retail garden shop and landscape center.

The firm's growth into commercial landscaping brought expansion, and eventually diversification. When Al retired in the mid-'80s, Ron Tillmann divided company operations into "stand-alone" businesses, all under the umbrella of Tillmann Landscape Nursery, Inc. Separate divisions were established to streamline management responsibilities, better understand profit centers, and enhance accounting practices. Management duties were clarified and divided, with each division identified as an individual profit center.

Tillmann's strategies worked admirably and his company became "vertically integrated," growing its own sod, propagating nursery stock, designing and installing landscaping, operating a retail garden center, and offering lawn and landscaping maintenance services. A greenhouse was added for winter sales, which included Christmas trees, gifts, and ornaments.

The company began to operate as four divisions under one umbrella. The firm included Tillmann Exteriors, for landscape design and installation; Tillmann Wholesale Growers, which included a field and container nursery and sod farm; Tillmann Garden Shop and Landscape Center; and Tillmann Care, a new lawn and maintenance center. Three landscape architects and one full-time accountant were added to the payroll.

Less dependence on other growers led not only to greater autonomy, but better quality control. "When you can dig the tree and plant it, you have a much lower mortality rate," notes Ron Tillmann, proving that indigenous plant use carries commercial benefits as well. Successful completion of landscaping projects led to maintenance contracts, including the business parks that now represent a large part of the company's clientele. This repeat business allowed Tillmann to showcase its considerable talents.

Today, 250 of the nursery's working acres are devoted to the growing of larger trees which are shipped to markets in Wisconsin, Minnesota, Iowa, Illinois, and Michigan. Container growing areas house softwood cuttings for flowering shrubs. Most of these cuttings are then grown in two or three-gallon containers until ready for sale at a height of two to three feet. Landscaping, a major part of the business since its founding, is giving way somewhat to wholesale growing operations—the area of Tillmann Landscape Nurseries that enjoys the fastest growth. Many local landscapers purchase Tillmann plants for area jobs. The company also delivers its nursery stock to garden centers and landscape contractors throughout Wisconsin and Michigan's Upper Peninsula.

Ron Tillmann retired from the business in 1996, but still keeps a

hand in the nursery trade by growing Christmas trees for seasonal sale. He and his wife Judy enjoyed a remarkable trip to the Florida Keys in 1998, piloting their boat through Lake Michigan, various rivers, and on through the Gulf of Mexico to St. Petersburg. Their return trip the following spring took them up the East Coast, then along the Hudson River to the Erie Canal and on into Canada. Ron Tillmann called the trip "the experience of a lifetime."

While head of Tillmann Landscape Nursery, Ron noted that the basis of the firm's reputation rested on honesty, determination, perseverance, and integrity. This was the case in the company's dealings with both its customers and employees. His sons Jeff and Steve, who now operate the nursery, share this philosophy. Jeff notes that the company's continued success rests on the provision of quality goods and services to its customers. Steve points to Tillmann's employees as a major contributor to the firm's continued success.

Jeff Tillmann with his son, Landon.

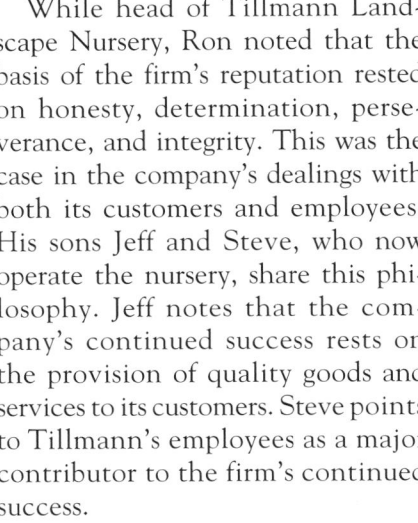

Jeff Tillmann and his nursery crew planting small shade trees for future use.

Steve and Jeff Tillmann learned the trade as their father did, "from the bottom to the top," as their mother Judy says. She describes Jeff's lifelong love of plants, noting that while growing up he once tended over 90 varieties of house plants—and all of them flourished. His green thumb served him well at Michigan State University, where he received a degree in horticulture. Jeff now serves as head of Tillmann's wholesale growing services, which among many other things includes propagating thousands of flowering shrubs and perennials. Steve's mom remembers him as "always outside" when he was growing up, planting and digging in the woods by their home. Steve, who studied landscape architecture at Ohio State University, now manages landscape construction and maintenance for Tillmann, coordinating the efforts of construction crews and three landscape architects. Both Steve and Jeff have sons of their own. Their mother predicts that "there will probably be a fourth generation coming up" at Tillmann Landscape Nurseries.

In the 1990s the city of Green Bay honored Tillmann Landscape Nurseries with various awards, including a Continuing Beautification Award from the mayor's office, noting the firm's "work to improve the beauty of the city and its contributions to Green Bay's desirability and quality of life." Or, as a company slogan puts it, for helping to "put the green in Green Bay."

A visitor to a traditional pumpkin farm peruses
the aisles for the perfect jack-o-lantern.
Courtesy, Wisconsin Department of Tourism

WISCONSIN HOUSING
& ECONOMIC DEVELOPMENT AUTHORITY

Wisconsin Housing & Economic Development Authority (WHEDA) boasts a pretty substantial promise to the low and moderate income citizens of Wisconsin—to make their dreams come true. For more than three decades, the people at WHEDA have been successful in satisfying that promise. They started out in the business of helping individuals rent or own their first homes. They later expanded into a full economic development organization and began helping individuals start and own their own businesses. This, in turn, strengthened communities and positively impacted Wisconsin as a whole.

The idea began back in 1971 when Governor Patrick Lucey proposed a state housing authority to the state legislature. In 1972 the legislature created WHFA, the Wisconsin Housing Finance Authority to aid lower and middle-income families in rent-

Louise Dotter welcomes Noelle Delaine, the WHEDA underwriter, who helped mortgage her Spring Green bungalow. Dotter is one of many customers who have used the Internet to coordinate a WHEDA mortgage.

ing and owning homes. Just two years later, the Authority issued its first bond offering and raised $27 million for multi-family and single-family loans. In 1975 WHFA became one of the first state housing finance agencies to have newly-constructed units in occupancy.

By the end of the 1970s, WHFA had committed nearly $200 million to various housing programs and had financed more than 12,000 housing units. The Housing Authority was operating efficiently and in 1979 it

was able to present a check for $250,000 to Governor Lee Dryfus, repaying in full the initial seed money appropriated to the state.

In the early 1980s, the Authority's vision was growing and new ideas on how to better serve its expanding client base were being generated quickly. A necessary advancement was computerizing the WHFA's data processing and record keeping methods. This helped organize loan techniques and clients' accounts to better process each loan case. The Authority pursued new programs to aid lower income homebuyers and received $75 million in additional bonding authority for single-family housing rehabilitation loans. Moreover, the Authority saw the advantage of specialization in particular client groups. In 1982 it financed rental development for visually-handicapped people.

Specialization continued. The Authority recognized loan needs not only for unique client groups,

Nestled in a downtown Milwaukee neighborhood, Roots Restaurant is a popular gathering spot for local residents. With the help of WHEDA's business loan guarantee, this once vacant and decaying building has become a viable business that is spurring new economic development in the area.

but for business owners as well. This type of financing posed more risk to the agency. A regrouping of the existing Housing Authority was necessary.

In 1983 Governor Anthony Earl succeeded in getting the legislature to restructure WHFA into the Wisconsin Housing and Economic Development Authority (WHEDA). The Authority's vision encompassed economic development and broadened to include not only financing for housing, but loan guarantees for small businesses and agriculture. A WHEDA loan guarantee is a pledge of support on a bank loan. In conjunction with a network of commercial lenders throughout the state, WHEDA will guarantee a portion of a loan made to a local lender. A loan guarantee provides assurance to the lender and, in turn, makes financing available to small business owners that otherwise may not be available.

New businesses generated more jobs within communities, extending financial growth and fulfilling more dreams. This was, and still is, all part of WHEDA's economic development mission. By extending help to individuals, whole communities are impacted which greatly improves Wisconsin's overall economic health.

The year of 1992 marked 20 years of success for the Authority. Employees of WHEDA celebrated by doing what they do best—building dreams. The Authority joined Habitat for Humanity and built homes for families in Milwaukee and Portage.

Although new emphasis had been given to small business loan guarantees in the mid-'80s, the Authority continued its initial effort of getting families into homes. In 1994 WHEDA ranked seventh as the nation's most active state housing agency. In 1997 alone, the Authority made nearly 4,000 single-family home loans totaling $228 million. Agribusiness loans and bonds reached $27 million, and small business

The interior courtyard of Garton Toy Factory is an example of adaptive reuse of a vacant structure. Located along the riverfront in downtown Sheyboygan, the former toy factory now provides multi-family housing for area residents. This development was financed with affordable housing tax credits from WHEDA.

The Historic Fifth Ward Lofts is a classic example of breathing new life into an old, tired, yet structurally sound, factory. Nestled in between elevated railroad trestles, this structure now provides 98 apartment units just south of downtown Milwaukee. The $12 million renovation of Historic Fifth Ward Lofts was financed with WHEDA affordable housing tax credits and state and federal historic tax credits.

loans rounded out to $6 million. The century came to a close with WHEDA extending grants to provide temporary housing for victims of the Sheboygan flood and the Door County tornado.

In 2002 WHEDA celebrated its third decade of progress. Governor Jim Doyle had this to say about the Authority's contributions through the years. "The Wisconsin Housing and Economic Development Authority has improved our state visibly and economically. Through its finance programs the Authority has created thousands of affordable new apartments and tens of thousands of first-time homeowners across Wisconsin. WHEDA financing also has preserved or created many hundreds of jobs in the small business and agricultural sector."

Dreams continue to come true in the new century as individuals seek financing for homes and businesses. Inventive programs such as the Lindsay Heights Project show new initiative by WHEDA employees to help clients reach their goals. One of the Authority's community relations officers took special notice of the hundreds of vacant lots in Milwaukee's central city neighborhoods and realized the potential for new low-income housing. These lots provided an ideal opportunity for lower

income families to build and own their own homes. The Authority formed a partnership with the city of Milwaukee and created home ownership opportunities for up to 100 new residents in several central city neighborhoods.

Results were very positive for these communities. Crime fell a dramatic 24 percent from 1998 levels. New residents not only took ownership of their homes, they also took pride in their new neighborhoods. This program has become a remarkable standout. WHEDA now offers guided tours of the well-groomed areas of which they are rightfully proud. Officials from Washington have taken notice of the Lindsay Heights success story and hold the project up as a model for its own inner-city housing endeavors.

More importantly is Joy Moore's success story. Joy is now a home owner in Lindsay Heights. This single mom with three children never believed she would be able to afford a home of

Francisco and Betsy Angulo with their children Elsa, Alexandra, and Talia in front of their Delavan home. They and five other families helped build six homes in the subdivision, including theirs, through a federal rural development program sponsored locally by the Southeast Wisconsin Housing Corporation. WHEDA provided homebuyer education for the initiative.

With WHEDA financing, Joy Moore was able to purchase a new home to raise her family. This factory-built, yet charming home located in Milwaukee is part of Lindsay Heights—an award-winning partnership between WHEDA and the City of Milwaukee to create homeownership opportunities.

her own. When asked what she thought of her new neighborhood, Moore replied, "No problems, I just love my house." Moore's next-door neighbor, Pat Fitten, chimed in that she loved sitting outside on her porch on warm summer nights. "This feels like home," she says.

Among the several new initiatives WHEDA has introduced on the economic development front is the Neighborhood Business Revitalization Guarantee (NBRG), a $12 million set-aside aimed at small businesses in key urban areas. Developments tend to be very visible and very strategic.

One recent such deal is Roots Restaurant and Cellar, a high-class restaurant of very compelling architecture. It's located at the edge of Brewer's Hill, a newly restored residential area just north of Milwaukee's downtown and not far from the Schlitz Park office complex. Along a street that not long ago consisted of littered lots and vacant buildings, Roots already is receiving rave reviews. But it's not just for the food. It's for what the establishment has done to help transform its neighborhood into an even more desirable place to live and visit. Roots is helping inspire additional residential and business development nearby.

The concept for Roots would be trendy even in places like Beverly Hills or Manhattan. The farmer and chef co-owners grow some of their own raw vegetables and get meat and other products from nearby sources in Wisconsin. The young entrepreneurs have carved out a following within the neighborhood and across southeastern Wisconsin. The NBRG made sure they could secure an otherwise risky loan from a private lender, and Roots' already considerable clientele has now certified WHEDA's judgment by making the restaurant and its tavern a lively place of their own.

Kyle Fagerland is another prime candidate for success. The 32-year-old entrepreneur who studied at Stout, used to design and build dairy barns and buildings for farmers. He then decided he had some farming ideas of his own and started his own business. Fagerland Farms specializes in raising milk heifers for dairy products. The farm manages about 1,300 cows at a time and houses them in large, customized barns of Fagerland's own design. His methods are unique and set him apart from other dairy farmers. Fagerland explains, "Most dairymen want to maximize their productive land base for milking. They don't have the room or the resources to raise heifers properly." Thanks to WHEDA CROP and FARM guarantees, Fagerland has both.

CROP (Credit Relief Outreach Program) is a loan guarantee program designed for Wisconsin farmers. The program helps them obtain agricultural production loans, up to $30,000, through partner lenders. Farm Asset Reinvestment Management (FARM), provides guarantees for agricultural expansion and modernization loans. Both WHEDA programs have helped make Fagerland's dream a reality.

The amount of dollars and loans represented by WHEDA pose the question of client delinquency. Astonishingly, the delinquency rate for clients represented by the Authority is one of the lowest in the financial industry. This is primarily due to the thorough educational process clients complete before becoming homeowners. WHEDA not only educates its clients on credit responsibilities; it also walks them through the steps of getting a mortgage. "Knowledge is power;" explains Antonio Riley, executive director for WHEDA. "If we help them to understand how to make smart choices, they can stay in their homes. That is part of our mission." There are prepayment fees and hidden costs with some mortgage companies. WHEDA employees make it part of the loan package to educate clients, thus empowering them to make the right decisions. When individual clients are successful, they contribute positively to the neighborhoods and their communities.

WHEDA takes a holistic approach to economic development. Through outreach, its community relations officers assess factors such as employment, housing, education, healthcare, natural environment, etc. The officers take these aspects into consideration when generating new ways to aid a community. They realize that each situation is as different as a fingerprint. The plans and products made available to a community are specifically-designed for that client-based

Previously, Kyle Fagerland designed and constructed structures for farms, until he decided to build a farm for himself. Now Fagerland Farms specializes in raising heifers for area dairy farmers. Fagerland has been actively growing his operation, thanks to WHEDA CROP and FARM guarantees that have covered the operation's new barns and other upgrades.

need. This is where creativity from WHEDA employees comes into play.

All WHEDA employees are encouraged to suggest ideas on how to better serve clients. They are trained to be creative and come up with innovative ways to get people into homes. "Anyone who has an idea can bring that forward to any manager or director and say, 'Hey, I think this would be a good way to help people get into homes,'" Riley says. Whether the employee is a receptionist or loan officer, his or her suggestion will be considered with the potential of having it implemented. The Lindsay Heights Project is an example of an employee idea coming to fruition.

Another employee-generated idea is the "Homes for Our Heroes" Project. This recent endeavor offered a 30-year, fixed mortgage to first-time

homebuyers who work as private and public school teachers, firefighters, or police officers. "They are in critical community jobs yet earn less than the county median income in the counties where they reside," says Riley. "That is why everyone at WHEDA has been especially pleased to help these individuals become first-time homebuyers."

From the executive director to the receptionist, all Authority staff is proud to be part of WHEDA's mission. "If you ask anyone around here what it is we do, they will tell you 'We help people get into homes' or 'We help people finance their businesses,'" says Riley proudly. Employees are aware of their employer's goal. They work together as a team to attain it.

In 2003 WHEDA had a record year for single-family lending. The Authority did more than $360 million to that sector. That's the equivalent to lending almost $1 million a day, seven days a week, for the entire year. In multi-family home lending, the Authority did $176 million. In the area of economic development it did almost $20 million in agricultural and small business loan guarantees. That influx of funds into various communities created 1,430 jobs just within the last year. All totaled, WHEDA had a $1.3 billion impact on the state of Wisconsin.

Those figures are beyond impressive from an economic perspective. But when Antonio Riley is asked what WHEDA is most proud of, he answers, "At the end of the day, I know we've helped someone achieve his or her dream."

A TIMELINE OF WISCONSIN HISTORY

12,000 BC

An 1,800 square-mile lake drained in only three days after an earthen dam burst. The torrential power of this event re-routed the Wisconsin River and carved out the Dells. The glacial lake's bottom emerged to form what is now Wisconsin's Sand Counties.

7,000-5,000 B.C

A mastodon skeleton, killed by Paleo-Indians using fluted spears, was left behind on the bank of a stream near modern-day Boaz in Richland County.

300 B.C to 1600 AD

The Effigy Mound builders, living mostly in southern Wisconsin yet as far north as Green Bay, constructed ceremonial and burial mounds primarily near rivers and lakes. These distinctive mounds included the forms of buffalo, turtles, beaver, deer, bears, cranes, eagles, hawks, lizards, and long-tailed panthers.

1608

French explorer Samuel de Champlain began fur trading with the Huron and Ottawa Indian tribes.

In the summer of 1837 Mrs. E.E. Bailey painted Peck Cabin *in Madison. It was the town's first house, replete with a covered wagon and neighboring teepee. Courtesy, Wisconsin Historical Society (WHi 3804)*

1634

French explorer Jean Nicolet was sent to find the "People of the Water" who could show him the water route to China. Nicolet packed a robe of damask silk and traveled by canoe to the shores of Red Banks in present-day Green Bay. As the first known European to arrive in Wisconsin, Nicolet was greeted by the Winnebago Indians (now known as Ho-Chunk).

1654

The first French fur traders in Wisconsin, Pierre-Esprit Radisson and Medart Chouart Des Groseilliers, wintered among the Potawatomi Indians near Green Bay.

1658

Radisson and Groseilliers wintered with the Chippewa (now known as Ojibwe) at Lac Courte Oreilles in northern Wisconsin.

1661

Arriving a year earlier to save Indian souls, Catholic missionary Rene Menard disappeared while canoeing down the Wisconsin River.

Catholic missionary Claude Allouez founded a new mission at La Pointe on the southwest shore of Chequamegon Bay.

1666

The French fur trade reaches Wisconsin, near Green Bay, and fur trader Nicolas Perrot brought metal utensils, weapons, and textiles to the area.

1669

Father Rene Menard wintered in the Green Bay area to minister to several tribes, but returned to Sault St. Marie the following spring.

1670

Catholic Jesuit missionary Claude Dablon described Green Bay as "an earthly paradise in beauty" despite contending with the Fox River's white rapids.

1671

Jesuit missionaries, including Father Allouez and fur trader Nicolas Perrot who acted as interpreter, gathered together Indian tribes in Sault St. Marie for an important announcement. The French Jesuits solemnly declared that all Northwest lands, including Wisconsin, now belonged to the French Sun King, Louis XIV.

1672

Father Allouez returned to Wisconsin with Louis Andre to begin the St. Francois Xavier Mission for the Menominee and Potawatomi, near present-day De Pere. They also founded the St. Marc Mission for the Fox Indians (now known as Mesquakie) and St. Jacques for the Mascouten.

1673

French explorers Louis Joliet and Father Jacques Marquette canoed Wisconsin's rivers to discover the Mississippi River for Europeans. They were the first explorers to map this diagonal water route from Green Bay to Prairie du Chien and the Mississippi. They canoed the Mississippi as far south as the Arkansas River, convinced the river led to the Gulf of Mexico. Their return voyage brought them to Chicago and Lake Michigan.

1678

Daniel Greysolon Sieur du Lhut (Duluth) began exploring Lake Superior's western edge and hunted with Sioux Indians on Wisconsin soil.

1679

The French King Louis XIV sent explorer Robert Calvelier de La Salle to monopolize the western fur trade. La Salle arrived in Green Bay on the first European boat to sail the Great Lakes, the Griffon. La Salle sent the boat back to New France filled with fur pelts, while he switched to easier travel by canoe and explored present-day Illinois via the St. Joseph and Kankakee rivers.

1680

Daniel Greysolon Sieur du Lhut (Duluth) discovered, for Europeans, the connection between Lake Superior and the Mississippi River by way of the Brule and St. Croix rivers.

1689

Yet again, Nicolas Perrot ceremoniously proclaimed King Louis XIV as ruler of the Indian people and landed at Lake Pepin's Fort St. Antoine.

1690

Nicolas Perrot discovered Indian lead mines in Wisconsin and Iowa, although continued fighting between the Sioux and Wisconsin tribes increasingly made the Wisconsin River unsafe for French traders.

1693

The French built their first fort on Madeline Island.

1701–38

The Fox Indian Wars slowed the spread of French fur trading.

1717

The French built a fort at Green Bay, most likely on the site of Fort Howard.

1732

The French post at Green Bay was rebuilt as the Fox Indian Wars continued.

1755–1763

In the early French and Indian wars, French-Ottawa, mixed-blood, fur trader Charles Langlade led Wisconsin Indians to defeat British General Braddock.

1761

The French Fort at Green Bay became British.

1763

The Treaty of Paris made Wisconsin part of British colonial territory.

1764

Charles de Langlade managed his father's fur trading post as he settled in Green Bay as Wisconsin's first official resident, a European-Indian.

1774

The Quebec Act made Wisconsin part of the British Province of Quebec.

1776

Wisconsin Indians, worried about American encroachment of their lands, fought on the side of the British in the Revolutionary War.

1781

French settlement began in Prairie du Chien.

1783

French trader Michel Cadotte established trade with the Chippewa on the Chippewa River.

Under the Northwest Ordinance, Wisconsin became a territory of the new United States.

1785

Julien Dubuque visited Prairie du Chien and explored the lead mines of Wisconsin and Iowa.

1787

Wisconsin became part of the

In 1836 the new territory's legislature used Wisconsin's first capitol in Belmont for only 46 days. Madison was quickly declared the permanent capitol largely due to the persuasive charm and bribery of Judge James Doty. By 1917 the first capitol was used as a barn, until it was purchased and restored as a landmark. Courtesy, Wisconsin Historical Society (WHi 10476)

Northwest Territories under the Ordinance of 1787.

1795

Fur trader Jacques Vieau built trading posts at Kewaunee, Manitowoc, Sheboygan, and made his headquarters at the Indian village of Milwaukee.

1797

The Spanish in St. Louis incited Sauk and Fox Indians against British traders in Prairie du Chien while a Sioux and Chippewa war waged on in northern Wisconsin.

1800

Wisconsin became part of Indiana Territory.

A Spanish gunboat patroled the Mississippi River as far north as Prairie du Chien in defense of British insurgents.

1804
A U.S. treaty with the Sauk and Fox ended Indian title to the lead mining region.

A French clerk for the North West Fur Company built a fort and trading post at Lac du Flambeau in northern Wisconsin.

1809
Wisconsin became part of Illinois Territory.

1812
Wisconsin territory may have been U.S. in title, but it remained Indian and British in population and commerce. Wisconsin Indians and the French joined the British in the War of 1812 against the U.S. government.

1814
The British captured Prairie du Chien's Fort Shelby and changed its name to Fort McKay.

1815
The War of 1812 ended and the British left Fort McKay

German artist Otto Becker painted an alluring ad for Milwaukee's 1882 Mardi Gras celebration. Railroad stations sold tickets and offered half-price fares to visitors. Courtesy, Wisconsin Historical Society (WHi 1865)

1816
Prairie du Chien's British Fort McKay closed and was rebuilt as the American Fort Crawford.

Construction of Fort Howard began in Green Bay.

John Jacob Astor extended his American Fur Trade Company into Wisconsin, while the U.S. government established fur trade factories at both Prairie du Chien and Green Bay.

1817
Green Bay opened the first school in Wisconsin.

1818
Wisconsin became part of Michigan Territory.

Solomon Juneau bought fur trading post in Milwaukee, on the east bank of the Milwaukee River, from his father-in-law Jacques Vieau.

Willard Keyes opened a school in Prairie du Chien.

1820
Lewis Cass, governor of Michigan Territory, explored the region that included Wisconsin. He hired young New York attorney James Duane Doty to be secretary of the expedition.

1822
New York forced Indian tribes to move to Wisconsin. Many Indians traveled on the first steamer to navigate the upper lakes, the Walk-in-the-Water.

Lead mining attracted an influx of European, Welsh, and Cornish settlers into southwestern Wisconsin.

1823
President Monroe appointed James Duane Doty as judge, to bring law to Wisconsin lands. Doty made Green Bay his home and purchasing land along the Fox River and present-day Fond du Lac.

1825
Wisconsin Indian tribes convened a grand counsel at Prairie du Chien to sign a "Peace and Friendship Treaty," which was actually the first step in identifying tribal territories before the U.S. government embarked upon Indian land cession.

1827
Tensions between white settlers and Winnebago Indians erupted into the killing of two white settlers, and became known as the Winnebago Indian War. Chief Red Bird surrendered to bring peace but died in a U.S. prison at Prairie du Chien.

1829
Indian tribes of southern Wisconsin were forced to sign U.S. treaties ceding their claim to land.

Thousands of miners settled in the lead-rich region.

The U.S. Army completed Fort Winnebago at the Fox and Wisconsin rivers portage.

1830
The forests surrounding the Wisconsin River created the region's first lumber boom.

1832
In response to land cessions and forced removal of Indian tribes, Black Hawk rebelled and tried to return to his original homeland. From Iowa he crossed the Mississippi River and led 1,000 of his starving Sauk and Fox back to Illinois. The U.S. Army pursued him. The Black Hawk War culminated in the U.S. Army's refusal to recognize his surrender attempts on the Wisconsin River. Instead, the army massacred over 850 women, children, and unarmed men at the mouth of the Bad Axe River where it emptied into the Mississippi.

1833
U.S. land treaties with Winnebago, Potawatomi, Menominee, and Chippewa tribes cleared southern Wisconsin for white settlement.

Wisconsin's first newspaper, the *Green Bay Intelligencer*, was established.

After the Black Hawk War, the U.S. Congress hired James Duane Doty to map and survey the Military Road. Tired of traveling by canoe, Doty had laid out a road that ran from Green Bay to Fond du Lac (where Doty owned land) and passed about ten miles north of the Four Lakes (now Madison) and west to the Blue Mound of southern Wisconsin.

1835

Byron Kilbourn claimed land on the west bank of the Milwaukee River and north of the Menominee River and called it Kilbourntown. He refused to merge with Solomon Juneau's Juneautown.

The first steamboat arrived in Milwaukee with settlers.

The first bank in Wisconsin opened in Green Bay.

1836

Wisconsin became part of Wisconsin Territory extending into Minnesota, Iowa, and much of North and South Dakota. About 50 percent of its 11,683 European and American residents lived in the lead mining district of southwestern Wisconsin.

James Doty and a partner purchased 1,000 acres in Four Lakes. They staked out a few streets and name it "City of Madison," after former president James Madison who had died earlier in the summer.

Indian fighter Henry Dodge was appointed territorial governor by President Andrew Jackson.

Judge James Doty stopped in Four Lakes where he planned to lobby for Madison as the permanent capital. He and Green Bay's newspaper editor envisioned and mapped a town square in the center of Four Lake's isthmus.

Doty brought the map to Belmont, along with a full stock of buffalo robes and real estate plans, to sell Madison town lots to interested legislators—including the son of Governor Dodge.

1837

Kilbourntown merged with Juneautown to form Milwaukee County.

Madison was officially surveyed and construction of the first capitol began. The Panic of May 1837 forced the failure of all territorial banks due to the unscrupulous practices of wildcat banking.

Sioux and Chippewa ceded their land claims to northern Wisconsin in U.S. treaties.

1838

The territorial legislature met in Madison.

The Milwaukee and Rock River Canal Company are chartered.

1840

The Wisconsin River lumber boom spread to the forest areas of the Green Bay, Wolf, Black, and St. Croix River districts during the coming decade.

Three Welsh immigrants started Milwaukee's first brewery at Huron (later Clybourn) Street.

1841

U.S. President John Tyler appointed James D. Doty as territorial governor.

1842

The last of the U.S. treaties with Chippewa cleared land titles in Wisconsin. Wisconsin Indian tribes now had only a few reserves that belonged to them, but in exchange they had legal promises from the U.S. government that retained their rights to off-reservation hunting and fishing.

German brewmeister Jacob Best started the Empire Brewery in Milwaukee.

1845

Swiss immigrants began settlement in New Glarus.

1846

Although not yet a state, historians planned ahead by starting the State Historical Society of Wisconsin, which was chartered in 1853.

1847

The federal census reported Wisconsin's population at 210,546.

The U.S. government began attempts to remove the Winnebago tribe to Minnesota, however, they would eventually return to their original homelands in Wisconsin.

1848

Wisconsin became the 30th state on May 29, 1848.

The state's new public university was incorporated in Madison.

Wisconsin's first telegram was received in Milwaukee.

1849

John Muir's family immigrated from Scotland to Wisconsin when he was 11 years old. Muir attended the University of Wisconsin from 1860 to 1863, but didn't graduate. Instead, as founder of the Sierra Club, John Muir, became known as the father of the national park system.

Wisconsin's first free, tax-supported, school began in Kenosha.

August Krug started a Milwaukee brewery that later became Schlitz.

1850

Fifty percent of Wisconsin's population of 305,000 were Yankees from New York or New England.

New York's Erie Canal provided Wisconsin with a water outlet to the Atlantic Ocean.

The Wisconsin Institute for Education of the Blind began in Janesville.

The Compromise of 1850 admitted California into the union in exchange for the adoption of the Fugitive Slave Law of 1850. This allowed Southern slave owners to recapture their runaway slaves. Wisconsin residents protested in meetings throughout the state since slavery now legally reached into Wisconsin.

1851
The first railroad train traveled from Milwaukee to Waukesha.

Wisconsin's first state fair was held at Janesville.

1852
A school for deaf children was opened in Delavan.

Waupun began prison construction.

1853
Wisconsin became the third state to abolish capital punishment.

1854
In Ripon, protests over the extension of slavery into the north incited the formation of a new political party, later named the U.S. Republican party.

The University of Wisconsin graduated its first class—two men.

Wisconsin became the first state to give funding to its historical society.

Fugitive slave Joshua Glover was arrested in Racine at a card game with two other black men. An angry mob broke into the Milwaukee jail where Glover was imprisoned and freed the ex-slave. Glover eventually escaped to Canada. The Wisconsin Supreme Court later declared the Fugitive Slave Law of 1850 unconstitutional.

1855
Frederick Miller arrived in Milwaukee with $10,000 in gold and the knowledge of how to make German beer.

Wisconsin's tourist industry began as soon as visitors could travel by rail or steamboat. Along the glacial-borne bluffs of the Wisconsin River, generations of Winnebago ceremonial dancers and singers shared their culture in special performances. Courtesy, Wisconsin Historical Society (WHi 7825)

1856
Margarethe Meyer Schurz opened the first kindergarten in the United States in Watertown.

1857
The Milwaukee & Mississippi Railroad was completed to Prairie du Chien, and its first train began running the following year.

1859
Abraham Lincoln spoke at the state fair in Milwaukee.

1860
The Chippewa River Valley began supplying large-scale commercial lumber.

Waterpower, which primarily supported lumber and flour mills, was still the dominant form of industrial energy—although larger companies were beginning to use steam power.

The federal census reported a Wisconsin population of 775,881.

1861
The Civil War began. By war's end, 96,000 Wisconsin soldiers had served and 12,216 had been killed.

1862
Madison's Camp Randall received about 700 Confederate prisoners.

1864
Chester Hazen, a New Yorker, built Wisconsin's first cheese factory at Ladoga, between Waupun and Oshkosh. This began a new market for dairy cows, since even the smallest cheese factory required 200 cows.

1866
The Morrill Land Grant College Act reorganized the University of Wisconsin's Agricultural College by giving public lands to state universities that emphasized agriculture, mechanics, and engineering.

1867
Children's author Laura Ingalls Wilder was born in Pepin. At age 65 she published the first book of her homesteading family, *Little House in the Big Woods*.

*Wagons hauled the beer
that made Potosi famous,
before delivery trucks replaced
horse-drawn wagons.
This was the case especially in rural
and often roadless Wisconsin in the early
twentieth century. Courtesy, Wisconsin
Historical Society (WHi 1957)*

Architect Frank Lloyd Wright was born in Richland Center.

1869

A logjam on the Chippewa River backed up for 15 miles. Logs piled-up 30 feet high in places.

1870

The federal census reported a Wisconsin population of just over 1 million people.

1871

More than 1,000 were killed in the Peshtigo fire that swept through the six timber-rich, drought-plagued, counties of northeastern Wisconsin. Another terrible fire that razed Chicago opened new markets for Milwaukee beer makers, since water and beer were suddenly scarce.

1872

Henry Dempster Hoard and other dairymen organized the Wisconsin Dairyman's Association in Watertown. Hoard persuaded the state's railroads to carry Wisconsin dairy products in the new refrigerated train cars. In addition to silage and the cheese factory, Wisconsin began its dairy revolution in both the national and international marketplaces.

The U. S. Congress forced the removal of Winnebago Indians from their lands in southern Wisconsin. However, many returned.

1873

After years of experimenting, Christopher Latham Sholes perfected the first typewriter and sold the rights for $12,000 to the E. Remington Company.

1875

Congress amended the General Homestead Act of 1862 to allow Winnebago Indians to return to their original homelands in Wisconsin. However, it established them as homesteaders—without a reservation.

The free high school law was passed.

Women were now eligible for election to school boards.

Fire destroyed nearly all of Oshkosh on April 28.

1877

John T. Appleby patented the knotter for twine binders to improve crop farming.

1878

Wisconsin sponsored the first automobile race from Green Bay to Madison. Alexander Gallagher of Oshkosh was awarded $10,000 for winning—by averaging six miles per hour.

1881

Dean William A. Henry of the UW School of Agriculture received legislative funding to build an experimental silo on the UW's farm. Dean Henry began campaigning for silage as the new scientific feeding system.

1882

Appleton established the nation's first hydroelectric plant, which operated a paper mill on the Fox River. The company was also the first to power electric light bulbs in the private mansion of the mill's owner, Henry Rogers.

1883

The University of Wisconsin established the nation's first agricultural experiment station.

1886

Five people died in Milwaukee during strikes that supported an 8-hour work day.

Appleton began its first electric street railway.

1889

Wisconsin passed the controversial Bennett Law that required English to be spoken in the classroom instead of German.

Celebration of Arbor Day begins in Wisconsin.

Captain Frederick Pabst, who married the daughter of brewer Philip Best, renamed Wisconsin's largest brewery after himself.

1890

The federal census reported a population in Wisconsin of 1,686,880.

UW Professor Stephen M. Babcock invented a quick and accurate butter-fat milk test for farmers that ensured the integrity of Wisconsin milk.

The Fox River Valley had 27 paper companies that used mostly wood pulp instead of rags and straw.

1891

The Bennett Law was repealed after bitter opposition from German immigrants.

1892

Wisconsin was one of the first states to use the tuberculin test to detect tuberculosis in cattle.

1898

Wisconsin sent 5,460 soldiers to the Spanish-American War and 134 were killed.

Schlitz won the legal right to use its slogan "the beer that made Milwaukee famous."

1900

The federal census reported a Wisconsin population of 2 million people, an increase of 25 percent since 1890.

In 1900 maypole dancers at the University of Wisconsin's (UW) Bascom Hill could gaze at the capitol about a mile away. Courtesy, Wisconsin Historical Society (WHi 3159)

Wisconsin established the first state park near St. Croix Falls.

1901

Robert M. "Fighting Bob" La Follette, was inaugurated as governor.

1904

Governor La Follette ushered in the Primary Election Law which established the direct election of law makers, as opposed to election by delegates at party conventions or the caucus system. In addition, Wisconsin originated the open primary system which allowed voters to select the political party of their choice during secret ballot. In contrast, all other states used the closed primary system which stipulated that voters declare their political party before they cast their vote.

An early morning fire destroyed the state capitol.

Wisconsin athlete George C. Poage became the first black to compete in the Olympics and won bronze medals in the 200 and 400 meter hurdles in St. Louis.

1905

Wisconsin's Railroad Commission was created to regulate railroads rates, and later utilities, and became a model for other states.

Wisconsin passed its first automobile license law.

1907

Construction of the current capitol began.

Wisconsin created the State Park Board to develop a park system and preserve Wisconsin's scenic beauty.

Milwaukee elected the first Socialist representative, Victor Berger, to the U.S. Congress.

1909

Charles Warner of Beloit invented the first speedometer for automobiles.

1910

Ole Evinrude invented the first outboard gasoline engine for boats in Milwaukee.

Milwaukee elected Socialist mayor, Emil Seidel.

1911

Wisconsin was the first state to establish a modern income tax law.

Wisconsin legislators established some of the first protections in the country that gave rights to Wisconsin residents in the workplace.

Wisconsin launched its state highway program.
1913
Wisconsin was the first state to establish a successful prisoner parole program, known as the Huber Law, for county jail prisoners who were allowed to hold day jobs to support their families.
1914
The radio station 9XM began at the University of Wisconsin. It was later renamed WHA, and is now the oldest radio station in the nation.

Wisconsin was the first state to establish statewide building codes that covered both public buildings and places of employment.
1915
Wisconsin was the first to establish an accredited herd program that certified whether cattle were free from bovine tuberculosis.
1917
Wisconsin sent 120,000 soldiers to World War I, 3,932 of whom died.

The state capitol was completed at a cost of $7.2 million.
1918
Wisconsin was the first state to number its highways (roads running north and south were given odd numbers, and those that ran east and west were given even numbers.
1919
The Eighteenth Amendment, prohibition, was ratified.

Wisconsin was the first state to introduce the agricultural standardization of grading fruits, vegetables, hay, honey, cheese, poultry, and eggs.
1920
The Nineteenth Amendment, women's suffrage, was ratified and Wis-

Wisconsin became the first state to deliver its ratification of the Nineteenth Amendment to Washington D.C. The Wisconsin Woman Suffrage Association led by its president, Mrs. Henry Youmans, was part of Wisconsin's progressive movement. Courtesy, Wisconsin Historical Society (WHi 1927)

consin was the first state to deliver ratification to Washington D.C.

Residents of northern Wisconsin abandoned farming as the best use for cutover lands and gradually built an economy on reforestation and tourism.
1921
Wisconsin was the first state to enact comprehensive certification for public librarians.

Wisconsin author Edna Feber received the Pulitzer Prize for her novel, *Miss Lulu Bett.*
1922
Wisconsin author Hamlin Garland received the Pulitzer Prize for his novel, *A Daughter of the Middle Border.*
1924
Robert La Follette ran for president as the Progressive party candidate.
1925
Wisconsin was the first state that required medical doctors to complete

training in the basic sciences of anatomy, physiology, pathology, and diagnosis.

Wisconsin author Zona Gale received the Pulitzer Prize for her play, *So Big.*
1928
Wisconsin author Thornton Wilder received the Pulitzer Prize for his novel, *The Bridge of San Luis Rey.*
1929
Wisconsin repealed all laws for state enforcement of prohibition.

Professor Harry Steenbock produced Vitamin D in food through irradiation and ultraviolet light.
1932
Wisconsin was the first state to provide unemployment compensation, which gave unemployed workers monetary support.
1933
Wisconsin voted to repeal the Eighteenth Amendment, prohibition.

Wisconsin was the first state to prohibit the use of race or national origin in the hiring criteria for teachers.

UW's pioneering historian Frederick Jackson Turner was awarded the Pulitzer Prize in history.

The Coon Creek Watershed project in Vernon County was the nation's first large-scale demonstration of soil and water conservation.
1935
The first automatic clothes dryer was invented by the Hamilton Company of Two Rivers.
1938
Wisconsin author Thornton Wilder receives the Pulitzer Prize for his play, *Our Town.*
1941
World War II began and Wisconsin sent 375,000 soldiers, with 7,980 casualties.
1942
Wisconsin author Thornton Wilder

received the Pulitzer Prize for his play, *The Skin of Our Teeth.*

1945
Wisconsin was the first state to enact aid for disabled persons.

1950
The Korean War began and Wisconsin sent 132,000 soldiers, with 800 casualties.

U.S. Army Corporal Mitchell Red Cloud Jr., a Winnebago, was posthumously awarded the Congressional Medal of Honor. He was the first member of a Wisconsin Indian Nation to receive this honor.

The town of Baraboo established the Circus World Museum and its extensive collection of restored, hand-painted, circus wagons.

1951
Wisconsin was the first state to teach conservation and preservation of plant and animal species, and also acquire and manage natural areas for scientific research.

1954
The U.S. Congress passed the Menominee Termination Act that abolished tribal status to the Menominee Nation—with disastrous results in employment, forestry, and education.

1958
UW geneticist Professor Joshua Lederberg won the Nobel Prize in medicine for his discoveries in genetic recombination and the organization of the genetic material of bacteria.

1962
Wisconsin was the first state to require the installation of seat belts in all cars.

1964
The Vietnam War began and Wisconsin sent 165,400 soldiers. More than 1,000 were killed by the war's end in 1975.

1965
Wisconsin was the first state to prohibit hiring discrimination on the basis of disability.

A 1950 harvest of cranberries. In 2003 Wisconsin was the leading producer of its native berry with over 56 percent of the nation's total. Courtesy, Wisconsin Historical Society (WHi 1874)

1966
Wisconsin was the first state to establish a bikeway that crossed an entire state

1967
University of Wisconsin student protests against the Vietnam War turned into a riot with injuries.

The Green Bay Packers won the first Super Bowl over Kansas City.

1968
The Green Bay Packers won the second Super Bowl over Oakland.

1969
The Interstate Highway system was completed in Wisconsin.

1970
One graduate student was killed when anti-war protesters set off a bomb at the University of Wisconsin.

Wisconsin was the first state to ban DDT, a poisonous pesticide that is toxic to bald eagles, fish, and mammals.

Menominee activists began lobbying the U.S. Congress to repeal the Menominee Termination Act.

1973
Bingo was permitted under a state constitutional amendment.

Congress repealed the 1954 Menominee Termination Act and restored tribal status to the Menominee Nation.

The Wisconsin Rustic Roads Program was established as the only statewide program in the nation to identify and preserve scenic, rural roads.

The International Crane Foundation was founded in Baraboo to protect the 15 species of cranes around the world, 11 are vulnerable to extinction.

1974
Kathryn Morrison was the first woman elected to Wisconsin's state senate.

1975
UW-Madison scientist Dr. Howard Temin shared the Nobel Prize in physiology-medicine for his discoveries regarding the interaction between tumor viruses and the genetic material of cells.

1976
Shirley Abrahamson was appointed as the first woman justice to the Wisconsin Supreme Court.

1977
Georgia O'Keefe, a Sun Prairie native and nationally-known artist, received the Presidential Medal of Freedom.

1979
Shirley Abrahamson was the first woman justice elected to the Wisconsin Supreme Court.

1980
Madison speed skater Eric Heiden won five gold medals at the Olympics.

1982
State unemployment hit the highest level since the Great Depression.

Stroh Brewing Company bought Joseph Schlitz and closed the Milwaukee brewery.

Wisconsin was the first state to prohibit housing and employment discrimination on the basis of sexual orientation.

1983
The Wisconsin Department of Natural Resources estimated that commercial fishermen illegally caught 1 million pounds of fish, chiefly trout, from Lake Michigan each year.

1984
Wisconsin's state park system grew to 60 with the vast majority on lakes, streams, and rivers.

A tornado killed nine and razed the town of Barneveld.

Ojibwe (formerly Chippewa) tribes asserted treaty rights with off-reservation fishing amid public controversy in northern Wisconsin.

1985
An air crash in Milwaukee killed 31 people.

1986
Legal drinking age was raised from 19 to 21.

1987
Alan Bond takes over G. Heileman Brewing Company of La Crosse.

1988
The driest summer on record since the 1930s.

The first state lottery began.

1988
The Chrysler Corporation closed the nation's oldest car plant in Kenosha.

1990
The Gulf War began and Wisconsin sent 1,400 National Guards and Reserve soldiers, with 11 casualties.

Wisconsin's comprehensive state recycling program was the first to use a broad-based business tax to fund mandatory recycling efforts.

1991
The first Indian gaming compact was signed in Wisconsin after the U.S. Congress passed the Indian Gaming Regulatory Act in 1988.

1993
California passed Wisconsin in milk production.

1995
Elk are reintroduced in Wisconsin.

A heat wave killed 172 people.

1996
The welfare reform program Wisconsin Works—known as W-2—required recipients to work or receive job training in return for benefits.

Pabst Brewing closed its 152-year-old brewery in Milwaukee.

1997
The Green Bay Packers won Super Bowl XXXI over the New England Patriots.

1998
Tammy Baldwin was the first Wisconsin woman elected to the U.S. Congress.

2001
On September 11 Army Lt. Colonel Dennis M. Johnson, of Port Edwards, died in the terrorist attack at the U. S. Pentagon.

Tommy Thompson ended a record 14 years as governor and began his new post as U.S. Secretary of Health and Human Services.

Margaret Farrow was the first woman appointed as lieutenant governor.

Chronic Wasting Disease was discovered in the state's deer herd.

Milwaukee Brewers' Miller Baseball Park opened.

2002
Barbara Lawton was the first woman elected as lieutenant governor.

Peggy Lautenschlager was the first woman elected as state attorney general.

"America's Dairyland" was number one in cheese production and productivity of dairy plants, however, it trailed California in milk and butter production. Wisconsin agriculture retained its national lead in corn for silage, and cranberries and snap peas for processing.

2003
Wisconsin spent $14.7 million combating Chronic Wasting Disease in Wisconsin's deer population.

Panelists on the Wisconsin Economic Summit IV recommended that Wisconsin invest not only in emerging high-technology companies, but also in Wisconsin's traditional industries.

2004
The Department of Workforce Development reported that Wisconsin lost 80,000 manufacturing jobs since 2001, with many jobs going to China and Mexico.

Governor Jim Doyle declares 2004 "The Year of Wisconsin Forestry" to celebrate 100 years of forest management, including sustainable forest management and the successful recovery of Wisconsin's forests which now cover 16 million acres.

BIBLIOGRAPHY

Alexander, J.H.H. "A Short Industrial History of Wisconsin." *The State of Wisconsin Blue Book*. Madison: Wisconsin Legislative Reference Bureau, 1929.

Bowman, Francis. *Why Wisconsin*. Madison: F.F. Bowman, 1948.

Clark, James I. *Chronicles of Wisconsin*. Madison: State Historical Society of Wisconsin, 1955.

Current, Richard N. *Wisconsin: A Bicentennial History*. New York: W.W. Norton & Co., 1977.

_____. *The History of Wisconsin, Vol. 2: The Civil War Era, 1848-1873*. Edited by William Fletcher Thompson. Madison: State Historical Society of Wisconsin, 1976.

Glad, Paul W. *Progressive Century, The American Nation in Its Second Hundred Years*. Lexington, Mass.: D.C. Heath and Company, 1975.

Nesbit, Robert C. *Wisconsin: A History*. Madison: State Historical Society of Wisconsin, 1973.

_____. *The History of Wisconsin, Vol. 3: Urbanization and Industrialization, 1873-1893*. Edited by William Fletcher Thompson. Madison: State Historical Society of Wisconsin, 1985.

Paul, Justus F., and Paul, Barbara Dotts, eds. *The Badger State, A Documentary History of Wisconsin*. Grand Rapids, Mich.: William B. Erdmans Publishing Company, 1979.

Smith, Alice E. *The History of Wisconsin, Vol. 1: From Exploration to Statehood*. Edited by William Fletcher Thompson. Madison: State Historical Society of Wisconsin, 1985.

Still, Bayrd. *Milwaukee: The History of a City*. Madison: State Historical Society of Wisconsin, 1965.

CHAPTER ONE

Black, Robert F. "The Physical Geography of Wisconsin." *The State of Wisconsin Blue Book*. Madison: Legislative Reference Bureau, 1964.

Clark, James I. "Wisconsin: Land of Frenchmen, Indians and the Beaver." *Chronicles of Wisconsin*. Madison: State Historical Society of Wisconsin, 1955.

Gilman, Rhoda R. "The Fur Trade." *Wisconsin Magazine of History*. 58 (Autumn, 1974): 3-18.

Hodge, William H. "The Indians of Wisconsin." *The State of Wisconsin Blue Book*. Madison: Legislative Reference Bureau, 1975.

Kellogg, Louise P. *Early Narrative of the Northwest, 1634-1699*. New York: Charles Scribner's Sons, 1917.

_____.*The French Regime in Wisconsin and the Northwest*. New York: Cooper Square Publishers, Inc., 1968.

Ritzenthaler, Robert, and Ritzenthaler, Pat. *The Woodland Indians of the Western*

Great Lakes. Garden City, New York: American Museum of Natural History, 1970.

_____. *Prehistoric Indians of Wisconsin*. Revised by Lynne G. Goldstein. Milwaukee: Milwaukee Public Museum, 1985.

Schultz, Gwen. *Wisconsin's Foundations, A Review of the State's Geology and Its Influence on Geography and Human Activity*. Madison: Kendall/Hunt Publishing Company, 1986.

Snow, Dean. *The Archeology of North America, American Indians and Their Origins*. London: Thames and Hudson, 1976.

U.S. Geological Survey and Wisconsin Geological and Natural History Survey for the Committee on Interior and Insular Affairs, U.S. Senate. *Mineral and Water Resources of Wisconsin*. Washington, D.C.: U.S. Government Printing Office, 1976.

CHAPTER TWO

Andersen, Theodore A. *A Century of Banking in Wisconsin*. Madison: State Historical Society of Wisconsin, 1954.

Blanchard, W.O. *The Geography of Southwestern Wisconsin*. Wisconsin Geological and Natural History Survey. No. 65, 1924.

Clark, James I. "The Wisconsin Lead Region." *Chronicles of Wisconsin*. Madison: State Historical Society of Wisconsin, 1955.

Current, Richard N. *Wisconsin: A Bicentennial History*. New York: W.W. Norton & Co., 1977.

Gilman, Rhoda R. "The Fur Trade." *Wisconsin Magazine of History*. 58 (Autumn 1974): 3-18.

Kuehnl, George J. *The Wisconsin Business Corporation*. Madison: The University of Wisconsin Press, 1959.

Lurie, Nancy Oestreich. *Wisconsin Indians*. Madison: The State Historical Society of Wisconsin, 1980.

Miller, David Harry, and Savage, Jr., William W., eds. *The Character and Influence of the Indian Trade in Wisconsin: A Study of the Trading Post as an Institution*. Norman, Okla.: University of Oklahoma, 1977.

Mollenhoff, David V. *Madison: A History of the Formative Years*. Dubuque: Kendall/ Hunt Publishers, 1982.

Nesbit, Robert C. *Wisconsin: A History*. Madison: State Historical Society of Wisconsin, 1973.

Nichols, Roger L. "The Black Hawk War in Retrospect." *Wisconsin Magazine of History*. 65 (Summer 1982): 239-246.

Smith, Alice E. *The History of Wisconsin, Vol. 1: From Exploration to Statehood*. Madison: State Historical Society of Wisconsin, 1985.

Still, Bayrd. *Milwaukee: The History of a City*. Madison: State Historical Society of Wisconsin, 1965.

Turner, Frederick Jackson. *The Frontier in American History*. New York: Henry Holt and Co., 1920.

CHAPTER THREE

Alexander, J.H.H. "A Short Industrial History of Wisconsin." *The State of Wisconsin Blue Book*. Madison: Wisconsin Legislative Reference Bureau, 1929.

Andersen, Theodore A. *A Century of Banking in Wisconsin*. Madison: State Historical Society of Wisconsin, 1954.

Balasubramanian, D. "Wisconsin's Foreign Trade in the Civil War Era." *Wisconsin Magazine of History*. 46 (Summer 1963): 257-262.

Clark, James I. "Wisconsin Grows to Statehood, Immigration and Internal Improvement." *Chronicles of Wisconsin*. Madison: State Historical Society of Wisconsin, 1955.

_____. "Farm Machinery in Wisconsin." *Chronicles of Wisconsin*. Madison: State Historical Society of Wisconsin, 1955.

_____. "The Wisconsin Pineries, Logging on the Chippewa." *Chronicles of Wisconsin*. Madison: State Historical Society of Wisconsin, 1955.

Current, Richard N. *The History of Wisconsin, Vol. 2, The Civil War Era, 1848-1873*. Edited by William Fletcher Thompson. Madison: State Historical Society of Wisconsin, 1976.

Fries, Robert F. *Empire in Pine: The Story of Lumbering in Wisconsin, 1830-1900*. Madison: State Historical Society of Wisconsin, 1951.

Merk, Frederick. *Economic History of Wisconsin During the Civil War Decade*. Madison: The Society, 1916.

Nesbit, Robert C. *Wisconsin, A History*. Madison: State Historical Society of Wisconsin, 1973.

Raney, William F. "The Building of Wisconsin's Railroads." *Wisconsin Magazine of History*. 19 (1935-1936): 387-404.

Rice, Herbert W. "Early Rivalry Among Wisconsin Cities for Railroads." *Wisconsin Magazine of History*. 35 (Autumn 1951): 1-15.

Smith, Alice Walker. *The History of Wisconsin, Vol. 1: Settlement and Statehood*. Edited by William Fletcher Thompson. Madison: State Historical Society of Wisconsin, 1985.

Smith, Guy-Harold. "The Settlement and the Distribution of the Population in Wisconsin." *Transactions of the Wisconsin Academy of Sciences, Arts and Letters*. 24 (1929): 53-107.

Walsh, Margaret. *The Manufacturing Frontier: Pioneer Industry in Antebellum Wisconsin, 1830-1860*. Madison: State

Historical Society of Wisconsin, 1972.

CHAPTER FOUR

Alexander, J.H.H. "A Short Industrial History of Wisconsin." *The State of Wisconsin Blue Book.* Madison: Legislative Reference Bureau, 1929.

Archdeacon, Thomas J. *Becoming American: An Ethnic History.* New York: MacMillan, 1983.

Baron, Stanley. *Brewed in America, A History of Beer and Ale in the United States.* New York: Arno Press, 1972.

Cochran, Thomas C. *The Pabst Brewing Company, The History of an American Business.* New York: New York University Press, 1948.

Downard, William L. *Dictionary of the History of the American Brewing and Distilling Industries.* Westport, Conn.: Greenwood Press, 1980.

Holubetz, Sylvia Hall. *European Immigrants.* Madison: State Historical Society of Wisconsin, 1984.

Korman, Gerd. *Industrialization, Immigrants and Americanizers: The View from Milwaukee 1866-1921.* Madison: State Historical Society of Wisconsin, 1967.

Lawrence, Lee E. "The Wisconsin Ice Trade." *Wisconsin Magazine of History.* 48 (Summer 1965): 257-267.

McDonald, Sister M.J. *History of the Irish in Wisconsin.* Washington, D.C.: Catholic University of America Press, 1954.

Merk, Frederick. *Economic History of Wisconsin During the Civil War Decade.* Madison: The Society, 1916.

Nesbit, Robert C. *Wisconsin, A History.* Madison: State Historical Society of Wisconsin, 1973.

———.*The History of Wisconsin, Vol. 3: Urbanization and Industrialization, 1873-1893.* Edited by William Fletcher Thompson. Madison: State Historical Society of Wisconsin, 1985.

Paul, Barbara, and Paul, Justus, eds. *The Badger State, A Documentary History of Wisconsin.* Grand Rapids, Mich.: William B. Erdmans Publishing Company, 1979.

Rippley, La Vern J. *The Immigrant Experience in Wisconsin.* Boston: Twayne Publishers, 1985.

Schafer, Joseph. *A History of Agriculture in Wisconsin.* Madison: State Historical Society of Wisconsin, 1922.

Schefft, Charles E. "The Tanning Industry in Wisconsin: A History of Its Frontier Origins and its Development." Master's thesis, University of Wisconsin, 1938.

Scott, Franklin D. *The Peopling of America: Perspectives on Immigration.* Pamphlet No. 241. Washington, D.C.: American Historical Association, 1963.

Walsh, Margaret. "Industrial Opportunity on the Urban Frontier: 'Rags to Riches' and Milwaukee Clothing Manufacturers, 1840-1880." *Wisconsin Magazine of History* 57 (Spring 1974): 175-194.

Zeitlin, Richard H. *Germans in Wisconsin.* Madison: State Historical Society of Wisconsin, 1977.

CHAPTER FIVE

Alexander, J.H.H. "A Short Industrial History of Wisconsin." *The State of Wisconsin Blue Book.* Madison: Legislative Reference Bureau, 1929.

Anderson, W.J., and Bleyer, Julius, eds. *Milwaukee's Great Industries: A Compilation of Facts Concerning Milwaukee's Commercial and Manufacturing Enterprises, Its Trade and Commerce, and the Advantage It Offers to Manufacturers Seeking Desirable Locations for New or Established Industries.* Milwaukee: The Association for the Advancement of Milwaukee, 1892.

Baldwin, William. "Historical Geography of the Brewing Industry." Ph.D. dissertation (microforms), University of Illinois, 1966.

Bowman, Francis. *Why Wisconsin.* Madison: F.F. Bowman, 1948.

Branch, Maurice L. "The Paper Industry in Lake States Region, 1834-1947." Ph.D. dissertation, University of Wisconsin, 1954.

Clark, James I. "The Wisconsin Pineries, Logging on the Chippewa." *Chronicles of Wisconsin.* Madison: State Historical Society of Wisconsin, 1955.

Cochran, Thomas C. *Pabst Brewing Company: History of an American Business.* New York: New York University Press, 1948.

Current, Richard N. *Pine Logs and Politics: A Life of Philetus Sawyer.* Madison: State Historical Society of Wisconsin, 1950.

———. *Wisconsin, A Bicentennial History.* New York: W.W. Norton & Co., 1977.

Davies, Ayres. "Wisconsin, Incubator of the American Circus." *Wisconsin Magazine of History.* 25 (March 1942): 283-296.

Fries, Robert F. *Empire in Pine: The Story of Lumbering in Wisconsin 1830-1900.* Madison: State Historical Society of Wisconsin, 1951.

Garland, Hamlin. *A Son of the Middle Road.* Edited by Henry M. Christman. New York: Macmillan, 1961.

Hilton, Robert T. "Men of Metal: A History of the Foundry Industry in Wisconsin." Master's thesis, University of Wisconsin, 1952.

Kaysen, James P. *The Railroads of Wisconsin, 1827-1937.* Boston: The Railway and Locomotive Historical Society, 1937.

McDonald, Forest. *Let There Be Light: The Electric Utility Industry in Wisconsin, 1881-1955.* Madison: American History Research Center, 1957.

Nesbit, Robert C. "Making a Living in Wisconsin," *Wisconsin Magazine of History.* 69 (Summer 1986): 251-283.

Peterson, Walter F. *An Industrial Heritage: Allis-Chalmers Corporation.* Milwaukee: Milwaukee County Historical Society, 1978.

Raney, William F. "The Building of Wisconsin Railroads." *Wisconsin Magazine of History.* 19 (June 1936): 387-404.

Rath, Sara. *Pioneer Photographer, Wisconsin's H.H. Bennett.* Madison: Tamarack Press, 1979.

Stark, William F. *Ghost Towns of Wisconsin.* Sheboygan, Wisc.: Zimmerman Press, 1977.

Still, Bayrd. *Milwaukee, The History of a City.* Madison: State Historical Society of Wisconsin, 1949.

CHAPTER SIX

Carstensen, Vernon Rosco. *Farms or Forests: Land Policy for Northern Wisconsin, 1850-1932.* Madison: University of Wisconsin College of Agriculture Press, 1958.

Clark, James I. "Farm Machinery in Wisconsin." *Chronicles of Wisconsin.* Madison: State Historical Society of Wisconsin, 1955.

———. "Wisconsin Agriculture: The Rise of the Dairy Cow." *Chronicles of Wisconsin.* Madison: State Historical Society of Wisconsin, 1955.

———. "Cutover Problems, Colonization, Depression, Reforestation." *Chronicles of Wisconsin.* Madison: State Historical Society of Wisconsin, 1955.

———. "Farming the Cutover, The Settlement of Northern Wisconsin." *Chronicles of Wisconsin.* Madison: State Historical Society of Wisconsin, 1955.

Current, Richard N. *Wisconsin, A Bicentennial History.* New York: W.W. Norton & Co., 1977.

Ebling, Walter H. "A Century of Agriculture in Wisconsin." *The State of Wisconsin Blue Book.* Madison: Wisconsin Legislative Reference Library, 1940.

Kane, Lucille. "Settling the Wisconsin Cutovers." *Wisconsin Magazine of History.* 40 (Winter 1956-1957): 91-98.

Lampard, Eric E. *The Rise of the Dairy Industry in Wisconsin: A Study in Agricultural Changes, 1820-1920.* Madison: State Historical Society of Wisconsin, 1963.

Osman, Loren. *W.D. Hoard, A Man for His Times.* Fort Atkinson, Wisc.: W.D. Hoard & Sons, 1985.

Schafer, Joseph. *A History of Agriculture in Wisconsin.* Madison: State Historical Society of Wisconsin, 1922.

CHAPTER SEVEN

Acrea, Kenneth. "The Wisconsin Reform Coalition, 1892-1900: La Follette's Rise to Power." *Wisconsin Magazine of History*. 52 (Winter 1968-1969): 132-157.

Asher, Robert. "The 1911 Wisconsin Workmen's Compensation Law: A Study in Conservative Labor Reform." *Wisconsin Magazine of History*. 57 (Winter 1973-1974): 123-140.

Brownlee, Jr., W. Elliot. "Income Taxation and the Political Economy of Wisconsin, 1890-1930." *Wisconsin Magazine of History*. 59 (Summer 1976): 299-324.

Campbell, Ballard. "The Good Roads Movements in Wisconsin, 1890-1911." *Wisconsin Magazine of History*. 43 (Summer 1966): 273-293.

Carstensen, Vernon. "The Origin and Early Development of the Wisconsin Idea." *Wisconsin Magazine of History*. 39 (Spring 1956): 181-188.

Clark, James 1. "The Wisconsin Labor Story." *Chronicles of Wisconsin*. Madison: The State Historical Society of Wisconsin, 1955.

_____. "Farm Machinery in Wisconsin." *Chronicles of Wisconsin*. Madison: The State Historical Society of Wisconsin, 1955.

Clark, Victor S. *History of Manufactures in the United States, 1860-1914*. Washington, D.C.: Carnegie Institute of Washington, 1928.

Cooper, Jr., John Milton. "Robert M. La Follette: Political Prophet." *Wisconsin Magazine of History*. 69 (Winter 1985-1986): 91-105.

Crabb, Richard. *Birth of a Giant: The Men and Incidents that Gave America the Motorcar*. Philadelphia: Chilton Book Company, 1969.

Epstein, Ralph C. *The Automobile Industry, Its Economic and Commercial Development*. New York: Arno Press, 1972.

Glad, Paul W. *Progressive Century, The American Nation in Its Second Hundred Years*. Lexington, Mass.: D.C. Heath and Company, 1975.

Gurda, John. *The Quiet Company: A Modern History of Northwestern Mutual Life*. Milwaukee: The Northwestern Mutual Life Insurance Company, 1983.

Hoeveler, Jr., J. David. "The University and the Social Gospel: The Intellectual Origins of the 'Wisconsin Idea.'" *Wisconsin Magazine of History*. 59 (Summer 1976): 282-298.

Holbrook, Stewart H. *Machines of Plenty*. New York: Macmillan, 1955.

Korman, Gerd. *Industrialization, Immigrants and Americanizers, The View from Milwaukee, 1866-1921*. Madison: The State Historical Society of Wisconsin, 1967.

Nesbit, Robert. *The History of Wisconsin, Vol. 3: Urbanization and Industrial-*

ization, 1873-1893. Edited by William Fletcher Thompson. Madison: State Historical Society of Wisconsin, 1985.

Ozanne, Robert. *The Labor Movement of Wisconsin*. Madison: State Historical Society of Wisconsin, 1984.

Peterson, Walter F. *An Industrial Heritage: Allis-Chalmers Corporation*. Milwaukee: Milwaukee County Historical Society, 1978.

Rae, John B. *The American Automobile Industry*. Boston: G.K. Hall & Company, 1984.

Rock, James M. "A Growth Industry: The Wisconsin Aluminum Cookware Industry, 1893-1920." *Wisconsin Magazine of History*. 55 (Winter 1971-1972): 86-99.

Stevens, John D. "Suppression of Expression in Wisconsin During World War I." Ph.D. dissertation, University of Wisconsin, 1967.

Stone, Fanny S. *History of Racine County, Vol. 1*. Chicago: S.J. Clarke Publishing Co., 1916.

"Wisconsin Played a Pioneer Role in Development of Automobiles." *Wisconsin Then and Now*. 21 (March 1975): 4-6.

CHAPTER EIGHT

Blake, Peter. *The Master Builders*. New York: Alfred A. Knopf, 1960.

Christensen, Chris L. "The Future of Agriculture in Wisconsin." *The State of Wisconsin Blue Book*. Madison: Legislative Reference Bureau, 1937.

Danbom, David B. "The Professors and the Plowmen in American History Today." *Wisconsin Magazine of History*. 69 (Winter 1985-1986): 106-128.

Fried, Orrin A. "Wisconsin Manufacturing Since 1929." *The State of Wisconsin Blue Book*. Madison: Legislative Reference Bureau, 1933.

Glad, Paul W. "When John Barleycorn Went into Hiding in Wisconsin." *Wisconsin Magazine of History*. 68 (Winter 1984-1985): 119-136.

Goldberg, Robert. "The Ku Klux Klan in Madison, 1922-1927." *Wisconsin Magazine of History*. 58 (Autumn 1974): 31-44.

Lurie, Nancy Oestreich. *Wisconsin Indians*. Madison: State Historical Society of Wisconsin, 1980.

Marshall, Douglas G. *Wisconsin's Population, Changes and Prospects*. Madison: Wisconsin Agricultural Experiment Station, 1959.

Nesbit, Robert. *The History of Wisconsin, Vol. 3, Urbanization and Industrialization, 1873-1893*. Madison: State Historical Society of Wisconsin, 1985.

Ozanne, Robert. *The Labor Movement in Wisconsin*. Madison: State Historical Society of Wisconsin, 1984.

CHAPTER NINE

Corporation for Enterprise Development. "Taken for Granted: How Grant Thornton's Business Climate Index Leads States Astray." Washington, D.C.: Corporation for Enterprise Development, November 1986.

_____. "Making the Grade: The Development Report Card for the States." Washington, D.C.: Corporation for Enterprise Development, March 1987.

Eisinger, Peter. "Business Location Factors." *Task Force Report to Wisconsin Strategic Development Commission*. State of Wisconsin, 1985.

Krikelas, Andrew, and Mondschean, Thomas. "An Economic Analysis of Wisconsin Regions." Madison: Wisconsin Department of Development; 1987.

Krueger, Lillian. "Waukesha, the Saratoga of the West." *Wisconsin Magazine of History*. 24 (June 1941): 394-424.

McKay, Tom, and Kmetz, Deborah E., eds. *Agricultural Diversity in Wisconsin*. Madison: State Historical Society of Wisconsin, 1987.

Malin, Steven R. "Service Sector Growth and Regional Economies: New Concerns and Opportunities." *Regional Economies and Markets*. 1 (Spring 1987): 1-7.

Myers, Dowell. "Our Best Weapon." *Corporate Report Wisconsin*. 2 (February 1987): 22-24.

Rath, Sara. *Pioneer Photographer, Wisconsin's H.H. Bennett*. Madison: Tamarack Press, 1979.

Strang, William A. *Wisconsin's Economy in 1990: Our History, Our Present, Our Future*. Madison: University of Wisconsin-Madison, 1982.

Wisconsin Agricultural Statistics Service. *1986 Wisconsin Agricultural Statistics*. Madison: Wisconsin Department of Agriculture, 1986.

Wisconsin Strategic Development Commission. *The Final Report*. State of Wisconsin, 1985. (See also Task Force Reports at the Legislative Reference Bureau.)

CHAPTER TEN

Bioscience Wisconsin 2004, annual report, Milwaukee: Wisconsin Association for Biomedical Research & Education, 2004.

Dresser, Laurel and Rogers, Joel. *The State of Working Wisconsin: Update 2003*. Madison: University of Wisconsin-Madison Center on Wisconsin Strategy (COWS), (August 31, 2003).

Drucker, Peter. *The Age of Discontinuity*. New York: Harper Collins, 1969.

Florida, Richard. *The Rise of the Creative Class and How It's Transforming Work, Leisure, Community and Everyday Life*. New York: Basic Books, 2002.

"Highlights of History in Wisconsin," *The State of Wisconsin Blue Book 2003-2004.* Madison: State of Wisconsin Legislative Reference Bureau, 2003, pp. 611-795.

Jesse, Eward V. "Rethinking Dairyland: Background for Decision About Wisconsin's Dairy Industry," Madison: Cooperative Extension, University of Wisconsin-Madison. (June 2002).

Loew, Patty. *Indian Nations of Wisconsin: Histories of Endurance and Renewal.* Madison: Wisconsin Historical Society Press, 2001.

Loohauis, Jackie. "Wisdom in the Woods: Ojibwe Village Retraces a Vibrant Past." *Milwaukee Journal Sentinel,* (September 3, 2003).

Lurie, Nancy Oestreich. *Wisconsin Indians.* Madison: Wisconsin Historical Society Press, 2002.

Mason, W. Dale. *Indian Gaming: Tribal Sovereignty and American Politics.* Norman, Oklahoma: University of Oklahoma Press, 2000.

Nesper, Larry. *The Walleye War: The Struggle for Ojibwe Spearfishing and Treaty Rights.* Lincoln: University of Nebraska Press, 2002.

Seely, Ron. "State Tribes' Influence Has Broadened over Years." *Wisconsin State Journal,* November 2, 2003, B-4.

Still, Tom. "Traveling the IQ Corridor: Upper Midwest Technology Future is Bright," Inside Wisconsin, *Business Beat.* Madison: Chamber of Commerce, Sept. 14, 2003.

_____. "Conferences Underscore Wisconsin's Role in the Health Technology Revolution," Inside Wisconsin, *Business Beat.* Madison: Chamber of Commerce, Oct. 21, 2003.

_____. "From Rustbelt to Techtown: Milwaukee is Building a New Image– And a New Economic Reality," Inside Wisconsin, *Business Beat.* Madison: Chamber of Commerce, Dec. 14, 2003.

"The Evolution of Legalized Gambling in Wisconsin," Madison: State of Wisconsin Legislative Reference Bureau, Research Bulletin 00-1, May 2000.

VanDer Puy, Nick. "A History of News Holes." www.FightingBob.com (March 30, 2004).

Vision 2020: A Model Wisconsin Economy. Madison: Wisconsin Technology Council, 2003.

TIMELINE

Bogue, Margaret. "Exploring Wisconsin's Waterways." *Wisconsin Blue Book 1989-1990*: 101-297. State of Wisconsin Legislative Reference Bureau, Madison, 1989.

Brown, Jennifer S.H. and Vibert, Elizabeth. *Reading Beyond Words: Contexts for Native History.* (Toronto, Canada: Broadview Press), pages 193-211.

"Highlights of History in Wisconsin." *Wisconsin Blue Book 1985-1986*: 713-721. State of Wisconsin Legislative Reference Bureau, Madison, 1985.

"Highlights of History in Wisconsin." *Wisconsin Blue Book 2003-2004*: 684-698. State of Wisconsin Legislative Reference Bureau, Madison, 2003.

Loew, Patty. *Indian Nations of Wisconsin: Histories of Endurance and Renewal.* Madison: Wisconsin Historical Society Press, 2001.

Lurie, Nancy Oestreich. *Wisconsin Indians.* Madison: Wisconsin Historical Society Press, 2002.

"Outline of Wisconsin History." *Wisconsin Blue Book 1925*: 61-93. State of Wisconsin Legislative Reference Bureau, Madison, 1925.

Risjord, Norman K. *Wisconsin Indians.* Madison: Wisconsin Historical Society Press, 2002.

Schenck, Theresa (2003). "William W. Warren's History of the Ojibwe People: Tradition, History, and Context."

"Some Landmarks in Wisconsin History," *Wisconsin Blue Book 1958*: 213-223. State of Wisconsin Legislative Reference Bureau, Madison, 1958

"Ten Evens that Shaped Wisconsin's History." *Wisconsin Blue Book 1999-2000*: 101-147. State of Wisconsin Legislative Reference Bureau, Madison, 1999.

"Wisconsin at 150 Years," *Wisconsin Blue Book 1997-1998*: 24-32. State of Wisconsin Legislative Reference Bureau, Madison, 1997.

WEBSITES OF INTEREST:

Biotechnology Ethics: www.bioethics.gov/bookshelf

Great Lakes Fish and Wildlife Commission: www.glifwc.org

Lac du Flambeau's Cultural Village: www.waswagoning.com

Native American Tourism of Wisconsin: www.natow.org

Stem Cells: www.news.wisc.edu/packages/stemcells/3327.html

Wisconsin Biotechnology & Medical Devices Association: www.wisconsinbiotech.org

Wisconsin Technology Council: www.wisconsintechnologycouncil.com

INDEX